Directory of International Periodicals and Newsletters on the Built Environment

Directory of International Periodicals and Newsletters on the Built Environment

Frances C. Gretes

VNR **VAN NOSTRAND REINHOLD COMPANY**
New York

Printed in the United States of America
Designed by Rose Delia Vasquez

Published by Van Nostrand Reinhold Company Inc.
115 Fifth Avenue
New York, New York 10003

Van Nostrand Reinhold Company Limited
Molly Millars Lane
Wokingham, Berkshire RG11 2PY, England

Van Nostrand Reinhold
480 La Trobe Street
Melbourne, Victoria 3000, Australia

Macmillan of Canada
Division of Gage Publishing Limited
164 Commander Boulevard
Agincourt, Ontario M1S 3C7, Canada

16 15 14 13 12 11 10 9 8 7 6 5 4 3 2 1

Library of Congress Cataloging-in-Publication Data

Gretes, Frances C.
  Directory of international periodicals & newsletters on the built
environment.

  Includes indexes.
    1. Architecture—Periodicals—Directories.
2. Building—Periodicals—Directories. I. Title.
II. Title: Directory of international periodicals and newsletters.
NA1.G7 1986   016.72   85-17904
ISBN 0-442-23003-6

Contents

Acknowledgments

A directory of this scope would not have been possible without the cooperation of the more than 1,000 publishers who responded to their questionnaires and generously sent samples of their periodicals and newsletters. I am greatly indebted to them for their participation in this international project.

Since some publishers were not able to send sample issues for review, I had to spend many hours at libraries borrowing and examining current issues. For their hospitality and generous assistance, I particularly wish to thank Mr. Bill O'Malley, reference librarian at Avery Architectural Library, Columbia University; Stephanie Byrnes and Sally Hanford, librarians at the headquarters library of the American Institute of Architects; and the staff of the Engineering Societies Library.

Opinions on the selection, quality, and usefulness of various building and design publications were necessary ingredients for the success of this directory. For their advice on the publications of specific countries, I wish to thank:

Steen Andersen, architect at Palle Leif Hansen (Denmark); Mr. Orestis Doumanis, publisher-editor of *Architecture in Greece* (Greece); Emanuella Recchi, architect (Italy); Marco Lanata, architect (Italy); Emanuel Kakavelakis, designer (Greece, Italy, U.S.); Jack Serabian, architect at Skidmore, Owings & Merrill (Saudi Arabia); Anne Hartmere, architectural librarian, The Architects Collaborative.

Introduction

This directory was prepared primarily to assist professionals who are involved in the planning, design, construction, and preservation of the built environment to locate international serially published sources of information relevant to their specific interests.

Architects, engineers, interior designers, contractors, preservationists, landscape architects, planners, real estate professionals, and building product and equipment manufacturers rely heavily on very current information to perform their activities. They also are showing a great interest in sharing resources that cross international boundaries. Professionals want to read and exchange ideas from other countries as well as open new markets. All subscribe extensively to periodicals and newsletters to acquire information.

In the past few years, however, the world has witnessed a tremendous outpouring of new periodicals and newsletters dealing with the built environment that has made the process of identifying and locating relevant subscriptions difficult and expensive. These publications emanate from architecture schools, architectural associations, government agencies, private consultants, and nonprofit organizations, as well as large publishing companies.

The overwhelming number of titles seems to indicate a growing public interest in architecture and planning and an enormous increase in published research in the field of building design and related disciplines. For these reasons there was a need for a directory such as this one, which would guide a specialized audience through the maze of international publications.

Although many outstanding general periodical directories such as *Ulrich's International Periodical Directory* exist, until now, there were none that specialized in the subject of buildings from an interdisciplinary point of view or which included editorial notes and detailed indexes.

I embarked on this project in early 1984 by collecting relevant titles from several standard published directories and indexes, architectural and engineering library serials lists, magazine stands, publishers' advertisements, and colleagues overseas. Questionnaires were sent to approximately 1,500 publishers along with requests for sample issues. Most of the publishers responded. When sample issues of a title were not sent, I examined a year's worth of issues at local libraries. Opinions on the quality and usefulness of many of the foreign titles were obtained from professionals overseas and incorporated into the editorial descriptions. Titles were matched against periodical indexes to determine where they are indexed.

The criteria for the selection of titles were:

1. The publication had to include a substantial number of articles on the built environment or the building profession.
2. In the case of foreign periodicals, either English summaries or illustrations had to be included.
3. Titles had to be currently published.
4. Sufficient bibliographic data (i.e., publisher's address) had to be available by the time of the directory's publication.

A year's worth of research resulted in a selection of 1,199 titles from 53 countries. This total is by no means a complete listing of all titles in the field but is the most comprehensive in print as of this date and the only international classified directory with editorial comments.

This directory will be useful to a wide international audience, including architects, interior designers, landscape architects, contractors, planners, preservationists, building product and equipment dealers and manufacturers; universities, colleges, and public libraries; corporate executives, facility planners, advertising agencies, public relations firms; freelance writers; publishers.

Among the possible uses are:

1. Acquisition tool for librarians responsible for building a periodical collection.
2. Quick guide to sources for contractors, suppliers, manufacturers, and retailers.
3. Guide for advertisers and public relations professionals to identify markets for publicity in this industry more easily.
4. Guide for researchers to identify where a periodical is indexed.
5. Guide for writers, designers, and photographers to identify publications and editors that might be interested in publishing their work.
6. Acquisition tool for magazine store purchasing agents.
7. Source for periodical publishers to learn about their competitors.

Compiling data for this directory and communicating with an international community has been a satisfying experience. I hope that this directory will be useful in developing stronger ties among people who have mutual interests in the built environment.

User's Guide

Arrangement

Entries for periodicals are arranged alphabetically under fourteen major subject categories. Abbreviations in titles are listed before full-word titles. The full description of each title appears under the primary subject heading only. If a periodical falls under more than one subject category, the title appears again with a number referring the user to the main entry. Also included are indexes by title, detailed subject, and country of origin.

Description of Entry

Each entry includes the following information, as available:

main entry number	editor's telephone number	annual or special issues
periodical title	publisher's telex number	contents features
country of origin	number of issues per year	where it is microfilmed
former title	subscription cost	editorial description
editorial address	date of first publication	International Standard
subscription address	circulation	Serial Number
name of editor	where it is indexed	

Notes on Entry Descriptions

Entries are based, in most cases, on information supplied by publishers. Titles of publications are listed as they appear on the cover. Costs are given for U.S. subscriptions only. The brief editorial descriptions were sometimes based on information from the publishers but in most cases were written after a review of the most current issues. Descriptions briefly list the subjects covered, the style, format, scope, and type of readership.

General Abbreviations and Symbols

A	annual
abstr.	abstracts
adv.	advertising
Bi-a	every two years
Bi-m	every two months

Bi-w	every two weeks
bibl.	bibliographies
bk. rev.	book reviews
circ.	circulation
cum. ind.	cumulative index
D	daily
dwgs.	drawings
Ed. Bd.	editorial board
Irreg.	irregular
M	monthly
Q	quarterly
S-a	twice annually
sub.	subscription
3/mo.	three times per month
3/yr.	three times per year
W	weekly
+	no response from publisher
*	based on publisher's description, issues not reviewed

Country Codes

AG	Argentina	GE	Germany, East	NR	Nigeria
AT	Australia	GR	Greece	NZ	New Zealand
AU	Austria	GW	Germany, West	PH	Philippines
BA	Bahrain	HK	Hong Kong	PL	Poland
BE	Belgium	HU	Hungary	PO	Portugal
BL	Brazil	IE	Ireland	RH	Zimbabwe
BU	Bulgaria	II	India	RM	Rumania
CC	China, Mainland	IO	Indonesia	SA	South Africa
CH	China, Nationalist	IS	Israel	SI	Singapore
CK	Colombia	IT	Italy	SP	Spain
CL	Chile	JA	Japan	SU	Saudi Arabia
CN	Canada	KE	Kenya	SW	Sweden
CS	Czechoslovakia	KO	Korea, South	SZ	Switzerland
CY	Cyprus	LU	Luxembourg	UK	United Kingdom
DK	Denmark	MM	Malta	UR	USSR
DR	Dominican Republic	MX	Mexico	US	United States
FI	Finland	NE	Netherlands	YU	Yugoslavia
FR	France	NO	Norway		

Money Symbols

Aus. $	dollars	Australia
Can. $	dollars	Canada
Cr.	cruzeiros	Brazil
DM.	marks	West Germany
$	dollars	various
Dr.	drachmas	Greece
F.	francs	France
fl.	florins	Netherlands
Fmk.	marks	Finland
Fr.	francs	Belgium, Switzerland
Kcs.	koruny	Czechoslovakia
Kr.	kroner	Scandinavian countries

L.	lire	Italy
M.	marks	East Germany
N.Z.$	dollars	New Zealand
£	pounds	United Kingdom
Ptas.	pesetas	Spain
R.	rands	South Africa
Rs.	rupees	India
Rub.	rubles	U.S.S.R.
S.	schillings	Austria
S$	dollars	Singapore
Yen	yen	Japan

Abstracting and Indexing Services

A.P.I.	Architectural Periodicals Index
Amer: H&L	America: History & Life
App. Mech. Rev.	Applied Mechanics Review
App. Sci. Tech. Ind.	Applied Science & Technology Index
Arch. Ind.	Architectural Index
Art Bib.	Art Bibliographies Modern
Art Ind.	Art Index
Avery	Avery Index to Architectural Periodicals
B.P.I.	Business Periodicals Index
Br. Hum. Ind.	British Humanities Index
CJPI	Criminal Justice Periodical Index
C.P.I.	Canadian Periodical Index
Ceram. Abstr.	Ceramic Abstracts
Chem. Abstr.	Chemical Abstracts
Comp. Lit. Ind.	Computer Literature Index
Compendex	Compendex
Comput. Data.	Computer Database
Data Process. Dig.	Data Processing Digest
ERIC	ERIC Clearinghouse
Educ. Ind.	Education Index
Ekist. Ind.	Ekistic Index
Energy Ind.	Energy Index
Eng. Ind.	Engineering Index
Excerp. Med.	Excerpta Medica
Hist. Abst.	Historical Abstracts
Hosp. Lit. Ind.	Hospital Literature Index
INSPEC	INSPEC
Ind. Med.	Index Medicus
Leg. Per.	Index to Legal Periodicals
Lib. Lit.	Library Literature
Mag. Ind.	Magazine Index
Mgt. Contents	Management Contents
Mid East File	Mid-East File
Newsnet	Newsnet
P.A.I.S.	Public Affairs Information Service
Poll. Abstr.	Pollution Abstracts
Predicasts	Predicasts
Psychol. Abstr.	Psychological Abstracts
R.G.	Readers Guide to Periodical Literature

R.I.L.A.	R.I.L.A. (International Repertory of the Literature of Art)
S.S.C.I.	Social Sciences Citation Index
Sci. Abstr.	Science Abstracts

Micropublishers

ABI	ABI/Inform
ACI	American Concrete Institute
BLH	Bell & Howell
BTI	British Technology Index
MIM	Microforms International Marketing Co.
MML	Micromedia, Ltd.
UMI	University Microfilms

Architecture

General

0001 A & S   (UK)

(Formerly: *Architect and Surveyor*)
Incorporated Association of Architects & Surveyors, Jubilee House, Billing Brook Rd., Weston Favell, Northampton, England. Ed. Adrian Prest. Bi-m; 1928. *Indexed*: A.P.I. *Notes*: adv., bk. rev., dwgs. (0308-4930) +

0002 A & U/ARCHITECTURE AND   (JA)
       URBANISM
A&U Publishing Co., Ltd., 30-8 Yushima 2-Chome, Bunkyo-Ku, Tokyo 113, Japan. Japan Architect Co., Ltd., 31-2 Yushima 2-chome, Bunkyo-Ku, Tokyo 113, Japan. Ed. Toshio Nakamura. Tel. (03) 816-2935. M; Yen 25,000; 1971; circ. 25,000. *Indexed*: A.P.I., Art Ind., Avery, April issue (in Japanese). *Notes*: adv., bk. rev., plans, photos (B&W, color).

An international review of current architecture. Usually each issue devotes broad coverage to several projects of a particular firm. Monthly columns on interior spaces and landscapes. This publication is noted for its high-quality photographs and use of many plans and elevations. Text in Japanese and English.

0003 A PLUS   (BE)
Regie Publicitaire S.P.R.L., 4 rue Fin, B-1080 Brussels, Belgium. Bi-m. *Indexed*: A.P.I. +

0004 AA FILES: ANNALS OF THE   (UK)
       ARCHITECTURAL
       ASSOCIATION SCHOOL OF
       ARCHITECTURE
(Formerly: *AA Quarterly*)
Architectural Association, 34-36 Bedford Square, London WC1B 3ES, England. Ed. Mary Wall. Tel. (01) 636-0974. 3/yr.; $50; 1982; circ. 3,000. *Indexed*: A.P.I., Art Ind., Avery. *Notes*: bibl., bk. rev., dwgs., photos (B&W, color), plans.

These annals are the major publications of a unique institution that has long been considered London's center of architectural activity. The articles are written by lecturers at the school and cover architectural history, theory, and contemporary work, and international themes. Of scholarly quality. (0261-6823)

0005 AIT/ARCHITEKTUR INNEN   (GW)
       ARCHITEKTUR
       TECHNISCHER AUSBAU
(Formerly: *Architektur und Wohnwelt*)
Verlagsanstalt Alexander Koch GmbH, Fasanenweg 18, 7022 Leinfelden-Echterdingen, W. Germany. Ed. Liselotte Drabarczyk. Tel. 0711/ 7989-280. Telex 7255609. 8/yr.; DM.104; 1890; circ. 10,000. *Indexed*: A.P.I., Avery. *Annual Issues*: Spring, Fall—Office Buildings. *Notes*: adv., bk. rev., dwgs., photos (B&W, color), plans.

A major professional design publication aimed at architects and interior designers of all building types. Each article is well illustrated with plans, details, and exterior and interior views. Equal attention is given to design and technical aspects. Covers German architecture almost exclusively. Text in German. (0173-8046)

0006   AMC (ARCHITECTURE,   (FR) MOUVEMENT, CONTINUITE)
(Formerly: *Architecture, Mouvement, Continuite*)
17 rue d'Uzes, 75002 Paris, France. Ed. Marc Vigier. Tel. (1) 296-15-50. Telex U Presse 680876 F. Q; F. 345; 1967; circ. 5,000. *Indexed*: A.P.I., Avery. *Notes*: adv., bk. rev., bibl., photos (B&W, color).
Current and historic architecture worldwide is reviewed. Text is brief but informative. Extensive use of plans and photographs. Interviews and details on construction add to its usefulness. Text in French; notes in English. (0336-1675)

0007   ARQ ARCHITECTURE/   (CN) QUEBEC
1463 Prefontaine, Montreal, Quebec H1W 2N6, Canada. Ed. Pierre Boyer Mercier. Tel. (514) 523-6832. Bi-m; 1981; circ. 2,716. *Notes*: adv., photos (B&W), plans.
A general review of architecture in Quebec. Text in English and French.

0008   A.T. ARKITEKTTIDNINGEN   (SW)
Norrlandsgatan 18, S-111, 43 Stockholm, Sweden. Ed. Eva Paulsson. Tel. (08) 240230. 16/yr.; Kr. 195; 1970; circ. 5,700. *Notes*: adv., bibl., bk. rev., calendars, dwgs., photos (B&W, color).
A slim journal of the National Association of Architects. Features articles on historical and contemporary Swedish architecture, competitions, architectural education, planning, and other topics of interest to the practicing professional. Text in Swedish. (0004-2005)

0009   A.U.C.A. (ARQUITECTURA,   (CL) URBANISMO, CONSTRUCCION Y ARTE)
Ediciones AUCA, Monsenor Miller 15, Santiago, Chile. Ed. Raul Farru. Tel. 2235113. 3/yr.; $33; 1965; circ. 3,500. *Indexed*: Avery. *Notes*: adv., bk. rev., calendars, dwgs., photos (B&W, color).
An international review of architecture, planning, construction, and the arts with relevance to Chilean development. Text in Spanish. (0567-428X)

0217   ACROSS ARCHITECTURE

0010   AFFICHE D' ALSACE ET DE   (FR) LORRAIN—MONITEUR DES SOUMISSIONS ET DES VENTES, DE BOIS DE L'EST
20 rue des Charpentiers, B.P. 238/R6, 67006 Strasbourg, Cedex, France. Ed. Willard Pierre. Tel. (88) 351281. Telex ISTRADA 880383F. Bi-w; F.204; 1929; circ. 12,000. *Indexed*: Avery. (0001-9666) *

0783   AKTUELLES BAUEN

0011   ALBENAA   (SU)
P.O. Box 522, Riyadh, Saudi Arabia. Ed. Ibrahim Abdallah Aba al Khil. Tel. 4642556. Telex 200494 BENAASJ. $150; circ. 30,000. *Indexed*: A.P.I. *Notes*: adv., dwgs., photos (B&W, color).
Saudi Arabia's major architectural periodical features new and proposed projects designed by Saudi and foreign architects in Saudi Arabia. The articles are well illustrated with clearly readable drawings and colorful renderings. Descriptions of the architectural firms are included with descriptions of the projects. All building types are reviewed. Worldwide circulation. Text in Arabic and English.

0012   APPROACH   (JA)
Takenaka Komuten Co., Ltd., 21-1, 8 chome, Ginza, Chuo-ku Tokyo 104, Japan. Ed. Shunichi Hirao. Tel. 06-252-1201. Telex 06-266-0012. Q; free to qualified subscribers; 1964; circ. 1,100. *Notes*: calendars, dwgs., photos (B&W, color), plans.
A promotional publication of a major design/building company in Japan. Each issue presents recent work of the firm. Outstanding graphics. Text in Japanese; summaries in English. (0003-7117)

0013   ARCH PLUS   (GW)
Brabant Str. 45, 5100 Aachen. Klenkes, Druck and Verlag GmbH, Oranienstr. 9, 5100 Aachen, W. Germany. Ed. Nikolaus Kuhnert. Tel. (0241) 507338. 5/yr.; DM. 63.80; 1969; circ. 3,000. *Indexed*: A.P.I., Avery. *Notes*: adv., bibl., bk. rev., dwgs., photos (B&W), plans.
A critical review of current architecture, planning, and housing with emphasis on the social and economic aspects. Scope is international. Text in German. (0587-3452)

0014   ARCHIGRAM   (UK)
Archigram Group. 59 Aberdare Gardens, London NW6, England. Ed. Peter Cook. Irreg.; 1961; circ. 6,000. *Indexed*: A.P.I., Avery. *Notes*: adv., bk. rev.
  Format varies. (0066-6092)

0015   DE ARCHITECT   (NE)
Prinssessegracht 21, The Hague, Netherlands. Ed. C. Zwinkels. Tel. (070) 924311. Telex 33079. 11/yr.; fl.134.65; 1970; circ. 4,500. *Indexed*: A.P.I., Avery. *Notes*: adv., bibl., bk. rev., dwgs., photos (B&W, color).
  The leading Dutch architectural and planning periodical. Read by professionals and students. Reviews primarily current work in Europe but includes international projects. Text in Dutch. (0044-8621)

0016   ARCHITECT & BUILDER   (SA)
Laurie Wale (Pty) Ltd., Box 4591, Cape Town, South Africa. Ed. Laurie Wale. Tel. (021) 468029. M; R.40; 1951; circ. 2,500. *Indexed*: A.P.I., Avery. *Notes*: adv., bk. rev., dwgs., photos (B&W, color), plans.
  A review of modern architecture, construction, and building news primarily in South Africa. Includes monthly survey of design and architecture worldwide. (0003-8407)

0017   ARCHITECT (W.A.)   (AT)
  (Formerly: *Architect*)
Royal Australian Inst. of Architects, Western Australian Chapter, 22 Altona St., W. Perth 6005, Australia. Ed. Bernard Seeba. Tel. (09) 335-2958. Q; Aus. $3.50 ea.; 1939; circ. 1,000. *Indexed*: A.P.I., Art Ind. *Notes*: adv., bk. rev., dwgs., photos (B&W, color).
  General architecture review for the Australian architect. (0003-8407) *

0018   ARCHITECTES/   (FR)
        ARCHITECTURE
140 Av. Victor-Hugo, 75116 Paris, France. Ed. Charles Rambert. Tel. 553-5856. M; F. 180. *Indexed*: A.P.I. *Notes*: adv., bk. rev., dwgs., photos (B&W, color).
  A review of the Ile-de-France Council of the French Architectural Association. In addition to professional news of interest to French architects, each issue focuses on an interesting theme relating to a specific building type or building material, a geographic region, or a topic of current interest. Political and legislative issues are included. Scope of feature articles is international. (0006-6122)

0019   ARCHITECTS FORUM   (CN)
  (Formerly: Architectural Inst. of British Columbia Forum)
201-2425 Quebec St., Vancouver, BC V5T 4L6, Canada. Ed. K.C. Mooney. Irreg.; $23.60; 1980. *Notes*: adv., bk. rev., dwgs., photos (B&W, color).
  Covers architecture in western Canada. (0703-9085)

0020   ARCHITECTS' JOURNAL   (UK)
Architectural Press, Ltd., 9 Queen Anne's Gate, London SW1 H 9BY, England. Ed. Peter Carolin. Tel. (01) 222-4333. Telex 8953505. W; £36; 1894; circ. 20,000. *Indexed*: A.P.I., Avery, Br. Hum. Ind. *Annual Issues*: Jan.—Review of Information Sources. *Notes*: adv., bibl., bk. rev., calendars, dwgs., photos (B&W, color). *Micro*: UMI.
  The leading professional architectural journal in the U.K. In addition to articles on current projects and professional practice, it presents longer features on planning, landscape architecture, and construction. Attention given to building type studies, product reviews, and legal issues. (0003-8466)

0021   ARCHITECTS TRADE   (II)
        JOURNAL
Architects Publishing Corp. of India, 51 Sujata, Rani Sati Marg, Malad East, Bombay 400064, India. Ed. Santosh Kumar. Tel. 69442. Bi-m; Rs. 75 (3 years); 1960; circ. 2,000. *Notes*: adv., bibl., bk. rev., dwgs., photos (B&W, color).
  Straight text on professional and technical issues of interest to Indian architects. (0304-8594)

0022   ARCHITECTURAL DESIGN   (UK)
42 Leinster Gardens, London W2, England. Acrowshal Ltd., 7-8 Holland St., Kensington, London W8, England. Ed. Andreas Papadakis. Tel. 01-402-2141. Telex 896928 ACADEMG. M; $75; 1930; circ. 10,000. *Indexed*: A.P.I., Art Ind., Avery. *Notes*: adv., bk. rev., photos (B&W, color).
  An international periodical that presents critical interpretations of architectural history, theory, and practice. Includes extensive arts and design coverage, reviews, articles, and projects. Irregularly publishes special issues that focus on specific themes or architects. (0003-8504)

0023   ARCHITECTURAL JOURNAL/   (CC)
        JIANZHU XUEBAO
Gouji Shudian (China Publications Centre), Chegong Zhuang Xilu 21, P.O. Box 339, Beijing,

Peoples Republic of China. M. *Indexed*: A.P.I. *Notes*: dwgs., photos (B&W, color).

A publication of the Architectural Society in China and one of China's three main architectural journals. Articles focus on design and planning issues in China. The topics range from problems in building reconstruction and restoration to garden design. They occasionally appraise foreign work in China, compare with work by Chinese architects, and suggest ways to modernize China without disturbing the society or destroying the environment. Text in Chinese; table of contents and abstracts in English.

0024 ARCHITECTURAL   (UK)
      MONOGRAPHS
7 Holland St., London W8, England. Ed. Frank Russell. Tel. 01-4022141. Telex 896928 ACADEMG. Irreg.; $75; 1978; circ. 12,000. *Indexed*: A.P.I., Avery. *Notes*: bibl., dwgs., photos (B&W, color).

Issues cover the work of historical and contemporary architects. Each issue is illustrated and includes a complete list of buildings. Text in English; summaries in French, German, Spanish, and Italian. *

0025 ARCHITECTURAL   (US)
      PSYCHOLOGY
      NEWSLETTER
University of Utah, Building 403, Salt Lake City, UT 84112. Q; $2.50. +

0026 ARCHITECTURAL RECORD   (US)
1221 Ave. of the Americas, New York, NY 10020. P.O. Box 555, Hightstown, NJ 08520. Ed. Mildred F. Schmertz. Tel. (212) 512-2594. M (Bi-w in May, Sept.); $33; 1891; circ. 78,000. *Indexed*: A.P.I., App. Sci. Tech. Ind., Art Ind., Avery, Compendex, Eng. Ind., Mag. Ind., R. G., R.I.L.A., Dec. issue. *Annual Issues*: Mid-April—Record Houses; mid-Sept.—Record Interiors; Dec.—Product Reports. *Notes*: adv., dwgs., photos (B&W, color). *Micro*: UMI.

One of the leading American architectural periodicals. Features articles on noteworthy designs, primarily in the U.S. Each issue focuses on a particular building type. Also contains articles on office practice and issues of concern to the profession such as rehabilitation, energy, computer-aided design, and education. Includes extensive product reviews. Industry events, design awards programs, and competitions are well covered. (0003-858X)

0027 ARCHITECTURAL REVIEW   (UK)
Architectural Press, Ltd., 9 Queen Anne's Gate, Westminster, England. Ed. Peter Davey. Tel. (01) 222-4333. Telex 8953505. M; $85; 1897; circ. 16,000. *Indexed*: A.P.I., Arch. Ind., Art Ind., Avery, R.I.L.A., April & Oct. issues. *Notes*: adv., bk. rev., dwgs., photos (B&W, color). *Micro*: UMI.

This is one of the leading British architectural journals and one of the most popular abroad, providing international coverage of current and historic architecture and planning with an emphasis on British work. Column devoted to interior design. Well-written book reviews and detailed coverage of new products. (0003-861X)

0028 ARCHITECTURAL SCIENCE   (AT)
      REVIEW
University of Sydney, Dept. of Architectural Science, Sydney N.S.W. 2006, Australia. Ed. Prof. H.J. Cowan. Tel. 692-2686. Q; Aus.$30; 1958; circ. 568. *Indexed*: A.P.I., Eng. Ind., cum. ind. every 2 years, *Notes*: adv., bibl., bk. rev., dwgs., photos (B&W, color).

A technical review of architecture. (0003-8628) *

0029 ARCHITECTURAL   (UK)
      TECHNOLOGY
      (Formerly: *A.A.T. News*)
Society of Architectural and Associated Technicians, 397 City Road, London EC 1V 1NE, England. Ed. David A. Hernandez-Purnell. Tel. (01) 852-4997. Bi-m; £15; 1983; circ. 6,000. *Indexed*: A.P.I. *Notes*: adv., bk. rev., dwgs., photos (B&W).

Covers architecture, construction technology, building materials, techniques, and services. (0265-2110) *

0030 ARCHITECTURAL   (US)
      TECHNOLOGY
A.I.A. Service Corp., 1735 New York Ave., N.W., Washington, DC 20006. Ed. Mitchell Rouda. Tel. (202) 626-7590. Q; $36; 1983. *Indexed*: Avery. *Notes*: adv., bibl., bk. rev., dwgs., photos (B&W, color).

One of the leading U.S. professional journals for architects. Technical and design information primarily generated from A.I.A. research activities is presented. The purpose is to expand technical, practice, and design information available to the profession. The emphasis is on practical help rather than scholarship. (0740-6142)

0031   ARCHITECTURE: THE A.I.A.   (US)
       JOURNAL
(Formerly: *A.I.A. Journal*)
American Institute of Architects, 1735 New
York Ave., N.W., Washington, DC 20006. Ed.
Donald Canty. Tel. (202) 626-7478. M; $26 (free
to members); 1944; circ. 44,000. *Indexed*:
A.P.I., Arch. Ind., Art Ind., Avery. *Annual Issues*: March—Convention Issue (with report on
convention city); April—Resources Directory;
May—Awards Issue; Sept.—Review of Recent
World Architecture. *Notes*: adv., bk. rev., calendars, dwgs., photos (B&W, color). *Micro*:
UMI.

This major professional association publication keeps the practicing American architect up
to date on the latest design and technological
developments. It provides expansive coverage
of a specific theme such as a region, building
type, or issue. The news section presents briefs
on legislation, new projects, awards, and competitions. Lengthy book reviews. Also includes
notes on firms, programs, tours, and new products. Summaries in French and Spanish. (0746-0554)

0032   ARCHITECTURE &   (SZ)
       BEHAVIOR (ARCHITECTURE
       ET COMPORTEMENT)
DA-EPFL, P.O. Box 1024, 1001 Lausanne,
Switzerland. Georgi Publishing Co., Old Post
Rd., Brookfield, VT 05036. Ed. Kaj Noschis. Q;
$70; 1981; circ. 500. *Indexed*: A.P.I. *Notes*:
adv., bibl., bk. rev., dwgs., photos (B&W).

An international and interdisciplinary journal
devoted to research on man's relationship with
the built environment. It consists of original papers that span a wide range of disciplines, such
as psychology, sociology, history, economics,
and semantics as they relate to architecture. The
issue reviewed included some fascinating articles on the social-psychological features of domestic architecture, a topic that receives little
attention in psychological research. Text in English or French; table of contents and summaries in both languages. (0379-8585)

0033   ARCHITECTURE &   (II)
       BUILDING INDUSTRY
87-88 New Market, Begam Bridge, Meerut,
Uttar Pradesh, India. Balvir Singh. M; $7; 1969.
Notes: adv., bibl., bk. rev., dwgs. (0003-8652) +

0034   ARCHITECTURE &   (GW)
       COMPETITIONS
(Formerly: *Architektur und Wettbewerbe*)
Karl Kraemer Verlag, P.O. Box 800650, 7000
Stuttgart 80, W. Germany. Ed. Karl Kraemer.
Tel. (0711) 610700. Q; DM. 94; 1939; circ. 5,000.
Indexed: A.P.I. *Notes*: adv., bibl., bk. rev.,
dwgs., photos (B&W).

An outstanding collection of competition designs arranged by building type. Projects plus
contributions on theory are selected from many
countries, principally from West Germany, and
reflect the most current design trends. Documentation is compiled by architects, for architects, planners, and architecture schools.
Includes landscape design. The subject arrangement of the designs and the comprehensive bibliography at the end of each subject area help to
make this an extremely useful publication. Text
in German and English.

0035   ARCHITECTURE & SOCIETY/   (BU)
       ARKHITEKTURA I
       OBSHTESVO
International Editorial Council, 16 Gourko St.,
P.O. Box 1345, Sofia, Bulgaria. Hemus, 6
Rouski Blvd., 1000 Sofia, Bulgaria. Tel. 87-20-
93. S-a; $12; 1983. *Notes*: dwgs., photos
(B&W).

Major new projects from the Soviet bloc are
examined in detail. Town planning, housing,
public buildings, and theory are given special
coverage. Well illustrated. Text in English and
Russian; summaries in French and Spanish.
(0205-065X)

0036   ARCHITECTURE   (AT)
       AUSTRALIA
(Formerly: *Architecture in Australia*)
Royal Australian Inst. of Architects, Strand
Publishing Pty., Ltd., G.P.O. Box 1185, Brisbane, Qld 4001, Australia. Ed. Tom Heath. Tel.
(07) 31-2171. Telex AA42523. Bi-m; Aus.$40;
1904; circ. 9,200. *Indexed*: A.P.I., Avery.
Notes: adv., bk. rev., dwgs., photos (B&W,
color).

AA is the official journal of the Royal Australian Institute of Architects and is the most important architectural periodical in Australia. It
covers all aspects of the profession and is of
primary interest to the practicing architect in
Australia, as well as to those interested in current design work there.

0037   ARCHITECTURE CANADA   (CN)
Royal Architectural Inst. of Canada, 160 Eglinton Ave. East, Toronto, 12 Ontario, Canada. M; 1924. *Micro*: UMI. +

0038   ARCHITECTURE CONCEPT   (CN)
Sentinel Business Publications, 6420 Victoria Ave., #8, Montreal, Quebec H3W 2S7, Canada. Ed. Marcel Dufresne. Tel. (514) 731-3523. Bi-m; $20; 1945; circ. 4,172. *Indexed*: A.P.I., Avery. *Notes*: adv., bibl., bk. rev., calendars, dwgs., photos (B&W, color).
   Articles cover the design and construction of residential and commercial buildings in Quebec. Text in French.

**0039   ARCHITECTURE CULTURE/   (JA)
         KENCHIKU BUNKA**
Shokokusha Publishing Co., Ltd., 25 Sakamachi, Shinjuku-ku, Tokyo 160, Japan. Hiroyoshi Tajiri. Q; 1947. *Indexed*: Avery. (0003-8490) +

**0040   ARCHITECTURE   (FR)
         D'AUJOURD'HUI**
Group Expansion, 67 Ave. de Wagram, 75017 Paris, France. Ed. Marc Emery. Tel. 763-12-11. Telex 650242 EXPANSN. Bi-m; $80; 1929; circ. 27,000. *Indexed*: A.P.I., Art Ind., Avery, Feb. issue (in French). *Notes*: adv., bk. rev., photos (B&W, color), plans.
   A well-illustrated international review of current architecture. Each issue includes briefs on new projects, features focusing on a particular theme, a section on notable projects, and design product reviews. Text in French; summaries in English. (0003-8695)

**0041   ARCHITECTURE EAST   (UK)
         MIDLANDS**
Royal Inst. of British Architects, East Midlands Region. Midland Design & Building Center, 202 Derby Rd., Nottingham NG7 1NQ, England. Bi-m; 1965. *Indexed*: A.P.I. +

**0042   ARCHITECTURE FROM   (DK)
         SCANDINAVIA**
World Pictures, Martinsvej 8, DK-1926 Copenhagen, Denmark. (U.S. Sub.) World Pictures, P.O. Box 305, Racine, WI 53401. Ed. Kirsten Bjerregaard. Tel. (01) 370044. Irreg.; $12; 1974. *Notes:* dwgs., photos (B&W, color).
   Pictorial guide to Scandinavian architecture in Scandinavia and abroad. Includes interior and exterior architecture. Detailed text accompanies the extensive color photographs. Text in English, French, German, and one of the Scandinavian languages (different each issue).

0043   ARCHITECTURE IN GREECE   (GR)
5 Kleomenous St., GR-10675 Athens, Greece. P.O. Box 3545, GR-102-10 Athens, Greece. Publisher-Ed. Orestis B. Doumanis. Tel. 721-3916. A; $25; 1967; circ. 5,000. *Indexed*: A.P.I., Avery, Vol. 11, Vol. 16. *Notes*: adv., bk. rev., dwgs., photos (B&W, color-[cover]).
   This leading architectural journal in Greece presents ideas and projects influencing and shaping the human environment in Greece as well as major international trends and developments. The editor's aim is to promote an interdisciplinary collaboration in the study and design of the man-made environment. Articles cover architecture, regional and town planning, architectural competitions, and student projects. It is an important journal because Greek architects generally receive little coverage in the architectural press. Text in Greek; summaries in English. (0066-6262)

0044   ARCHITECTURE S.A.   (SA)
Institute of South African Architects, Box 704, Cape Town 8000, South Africa. Ed. George Warman. Tel. (021) 24-5320. Bi-m; R. 20; 1915; circ. 3,000. *Indexed*: A.P.I. *Notes*: adv., bibl., bk. rev., calendars, dwgs., photos (B&W).
   A review of current South African architecture.

**0045   ARCHITECTURE WEST   (UK)
         MIDLANDS**
Royal Inst. of British Architects, West Midlands Region. c/o James Hook, 32 Laburnum Ave., Kenilworth CV8 2DR, England. Q; 1976. *Indexed*: A.P.I. (0308-6747) +

0046   ARCHITECTURES   (US)
496 La Guardia Place, New York, NY 10012. Eastview Editions, 1185 Morris Ave., Union, NJ 07083. Ed. Andrew McNair. Tel. (212) 226-1861. Q; $24; 1985. *Notes*: adv., dwgs., photos (B&W).
   A tabloid on contemporary art and architecture.

0047   DER ARCHITEKT   (GW)
Forum-Verlag GmbH, Postfach 700-262, D-7000 Stuttgart 70, W. Germany. Ed. Ingeborg Flagge. Tel. 0711-764025. Telex 7255849 FORUD. M; DM. 84; 1951; circ. 6,000. *Indexed*: A.P.I. *Notes*: adv., bibl., bk. rev., dwgs., photos (B&W).
   A general review of architecture. Text in German. (0003-875X)

0048 ARCHITEKTUR AKTUELL   (AU)
Fachjournal Verlagsgesellschaft mbH, Max-ingstr. 28a, A-1130, Vienna, Austria. Ed. Oskar Schmid. Tel. 829298. Bi-m; S. 350; 1976; circ. 5,000. *Notes*: adv., bibl., bk. rev., dwgs., photos (B&W, color).
Covers architecture and design. Text in German. (0570-6602)

0049 ARCHITEKTUR DER DDR   (GE)
VEB Verlag fuer Bauwesen, Franzoesischer Str. 13/14, 1080 Berlin, E. Germany. Ed. Gerhard Krenz. Tel. 2-04-10. M; 1951; circ. 10,000. *Indexed*: A.P.I., Avery, R.I.L.A. *Notes*: adv., bk. rev., bibl., dwgs., photos (B&W).
Devoted to architecture, building, planning, and housing in Germany. Contains detailed analyses of the reconstruction of various cities and historic structures as well as the entire design and construction processes of new housing projects and industrial complexes. Many drawings and photographs. The best source for learning about architectural projects, processes, and firms in East Germany. Summaries in English, German, French, and Russian. (8323-3413)

0050 ARCHITEKTUR UND BAU   (AU)
Dynamis Werbe und Verlagsgesellschaft. Heine-str. 3, A-1020 Vienna, Austria. Ed. H. Parton. S-a. +

0051 ARCHITEKTUR UND   (GW)
    WOHNEN
Jahreszeiten-Verlag GmbH. Possmoorweg 1, 2000 Hamburg 39, W. Germany. S-a; 1958. +

0052 ARCHITEKTURA   (PL)
ul.Krolewska 27, pok.235, 00-060 Warsaw, Poland. Ed. Andrzej Glinski. Tel. 27-66-17. Bi-m; $33; 1947; circ. 15,000. *Indexed*: A.P.I., Avery. *Notes*: adv., bibl., bk. rev., dwgs., photos (B&W).
The major journal of the Polish Association of Architects. Covers architecture in Poland and current work abroad. Text in Polish and English. (0003-8814)

0053 ARCHITEKTURA A   (CS)
    URBANIZMUS/
    ARCHITECTURE UND
    URBANISM
Veda, Publishing House of the Slovak Academy of Sciences. Klemensova 19, 814 30 Bratislava, Czechoslovakia. John Benjamins B.V. Amstedijk 44, Amsterdam (2) Netherlands. Ed. E. Hruska. Q; 1967. (0044-8680) +

0054 ARCHITEKTURA CSR   (CS)
Union of Czech Architects, Letenska 5, 118 45 Prague 1, Czechoslovakia. Ed. Jan Novotny. Tel. 539742. 10/yr.; $92.40; 1938; circ. 6,000. *Indexed*: A.P.I., Avery, Jan. issue. *Notes*: adv., bibl., bk. rev., calendars, dwgs., photos (B&W).
Text in Czech; summaries in English, French, German, and Russian. (0300-5305) *

0055 ARCHITETTO   (IT)
Consiglio Nazionale Architetti, via Nazionale 69, 00184 Rome, Italy. Ed. Gianni Boeri. Tel. 465504. M; free; circ. 35,000. *Indexed*: A.P.I. *Notes*: adv., bibl., bk. rev., calendars, dwgs., photos (B&W).
An association publication. Text in Italian.

0056 L'ARCHITETTURA—   (IT)
    CRONACHE E STORIA
Via Nomentana 150, 00162 Rome, Italy. Gruppo Editoriale Fabbri, via Mecenate 91, 20138 Milan, Italy. Ed. Bruno Zevi. Tel. (06) 8320684. 11/yr.; L.105,000. *Indexed*: A.P.I., Art Ind., Avery, Dec. issue. *Notes*: adv., dwgs., photos (B&W, color).
One of the finest international architectural journals. Well illustrated with informative text that describes projects in a historical context and relates them to trends occurring worldwide. Most of the projects featured are in Italy, but work in other countries also appears. Each issue also includes a section on technology. This journal is recommended for all architectural collections. Text in Italian; summaries in English, French, German, and Spanish.

0197 ARCHIVES
    D'ARCHITECTURE
    MODERNE

0057 ARCUS   (GW)
Institut fur Internationale Architektur Documentation GmbH, Franz Joseph Strasse 9, 8000 Munich 40, W. Germany. Ed. Dr. J. Martina Schneider. Tel. (089) 39-14-83. Bi-m; DM. 54; 1983; circ. 4,000. *Indexed*: A.P.I. *Notes*: adv., bibl., bk. rev., calendars, dwgs., photos (B&W).
Technical articles on architecture, engineering, physics, chemistry, biology, and ecology. All the articles relate to a theme such as new building material composition, strength, design, and application. Text in German and English. (0724-2034)

0543   AREA

0058 ARHITECTURA   **(RM)**
Univnea Arhitectilor din Republica Socialista
Rumania, Str. Academiei Nr. 18-20, Bucharest,
Rumania. Ilexim, Str. 13 Decembrie Nr. 3, P.O.
Box 136-137, Bucharest, Rumania. Ed. Stefan
Rader Ionescu. Bi-m; $60; 1906; circ. 5,000. *In-
dexed*: A.P.I. *Notes*: photos (B&W).

A review of traditional and contemporary Rumanian architecture. Extensive use of plans and
details; working drawings are not reproduced
well but are still useful. The square format aids
in viewing the many drawings. Text in Rumanian; summaries in English, French, and Russian. (0300-5356)

0059 ARHITEKTURA   **(YU)**
(Formerly: *Arhitektura-Urbanizam*)
Savez Arhitekdta Hrvatske, Trg Republike 3/I,
41000 Zagreb, Yugoslavia. Ed. Maijan Hrzic.
Tel. (041) 274-796. Q; $35; 1947; circ. 2,500. *In-
dexed*: A.P.I. *Notes*: adv., bk. rev., dwgs., photos (B&W, color).

Architecture and town planning review. Text
in Croatian; summaries in English and Russian.
(0350-3666)*

0060 ARKHITEKTURA   **(BU)**
Suiuzna Arkhitektite v Gourko Str. 16, P.O.
Box 1345, Sofia 1080, Bulgaria. Hemus 6 Rouski
Blvd., Sofia 1000, Bulgaria. Ed. Zdravko Gen-
chev. Tel. 8720-93. 10/yr.; $33; 1953; circ. 4,500.
Indexed: A.P.I. *Notes*: adv., dwgs., photos
(B&W, color).

Publication of the Union of the Architects of
Bulgaria. Presents an overview of current Bulgarian architecture with an emphasis on housing
and urban planning. Text in Bulgarian; summaries in English, German, French, and Russian.
(0324-1254)

0061 ARKHITEKTURA SSR   **(UR)**
Ul. Shcheseva 3, Moscow K-1 USSR. Ed. Al-
exandr Kudriavtsev. M; Rub.13.20; 1933; circ.
26,000. *Indexed*: A.P.I. *Notes*: dwgs., photos
(B&W, color).

Theoretical, technical, and practical review of
contemporary and historical architecture in the
Soviet Union. Includes profiles of architects and
some rural and urban planning projects. Text in
Russian; table of contents in English, French,
and German; summaries in English. (0004-1939)

0062 ARKITEKTEN   **(DK)**
Federation of Danish Architects, Nyhaven 43,
DK-1051, Copenhagen K, Denmark. Ed. Poul
Erik Skriver. Tel. (01) 13 6200. Telex GIRO 9-
00-31-34. 23/yr. (Bi-w except July); Kr. 500;
1898; circ. 7,100. *Indexed*: A.P.I. *Notes*: bibl.,
dwgs., photos (B&W). *Micro*: UMI.

Official journal of the Federation of Danish
Architects. Articles on professional subjects,
projects competitions, etc. Text in Danish.
(0004-198X)

0063 ARKITEKTNYTT   **(NO)**
Norwegian Architects' League, Josefinesgt 34,
Oslo 3, Norway. Dag Rognlien. 20/yr.; 1951.
(0004-1998) +

0064 ARKITEKTUR   **(SW)**
National Assn. of Swedish Architects, Arkitek-
turfoerlag AB, Box 1742, 111 87 Stockholm,
Sweden. Ed. Eva Ericksson. Tel. 08-23-31-05.
10/yr.; Kr. 265; 1901; circ. 6,000. *Indexed*:
A.P.I., Avery. *Notes*: adv., bk. rev., dwgs.,
photos (B&W, color).

The major review of Swedish architecture.
Thoroughly details all major building types and
includes editorials and features on themes of
current interest such as architectural education.
Text in Swedish; summary in English. (0004-
2021)

0065 ARKITEKTUR DK   **(DK)**
(Formerly: *Arkitektur*)
Arkitektens Forlag, Nyhavn 43, DK-1051, Co-
penhagen K, Denmark. Ed. Kim Dirckinch-
Holmfeld. Tel. (01) 13 6200. Telex GIRO 9-00-
31-34. 8/yr.; Kr. 47; 1957; circ. 4,000. *Indexed*:
A.P.I., Avery. *Notes*: adv., dwgs., photos
(B&W, color).

Review of current Scandinavian architecture.
Covers all building types. Text in English, German, and Danish; English and Danish captions.
(0004-2013)

0066 ARKKITEHTI/FINNISH   **(FI)**
       ARCHITECTURAL REVIEW
Finnish Association of Architects, Etelaesplan-
acli 22A, 00130 Helsinki 13, Finland. Ed. Norri
Marya-Riitta. Tel. 90-640-801. 8/yr.; 1903; circ.
3,614. *Indexed*: A.P.I., Avery. *Notes*: adv.,
photos (B&W, color).

A well-illustrated review of contemporary and
traditional Finnish architecture. Emphasis is on
residential design. Includes interior views.
(0004-2129)

**0067 ARKKITEHTIUUTISET/   (FI)
ARKITEKTNYTT**
Finnish Association of Architects, Etelaesplan-acli 22A, 00130 Helsinki 13, Finland. Ed. Markku Junnonaho. 20/yr.; 1948. (0044-8915) +

**0068 ARKKITEHTUURIKILPAILUJA/ (FI)
ARCHITECTURAL
COMPETITIONS IN FINLAND**
A well-illustrated bimonthly insert in magazine format that is published with *Arkkitehti*.

0069 ARQUITECTURA   (PO)
Lisbon, Portugal. 1959. *Indexed*: A.P.I., Avery. +

0070 ARQUITECTURA   (SP)
Colegio Oficial de Arquitectos de Madrid, Barquillo 12, 28004 Madrid, Spain. Tel. 2325499. Bi-m; $40; 1918; circ. 8,000. *Indexed*: A.P.I., Avery. *Annual Issues*: Nov./Dec. issue. *Notes*: adv., bk. rev., dwgs., photos (B&W, color).
Features the most outstanding projects by Spanish architects. Includes historical structures. Articles are well illustrated with photographs and drawings. Text in Spanish. (0004-2706)

0071 ARQUITECTURAS BIS   (SP)
Lauria 130 404F, 08037 Barcelona, Spain. Tel. (93) 2070299. Q; $45; 1974; circ. 3,000. *Indexed*: A.P.I. *Notes*: adv., bk. rev., dwgs., photos (B&W).
Journal of architecture and urban design. Text in Spanish. *

0072 ARTS AND ARCHITECTURE   (US)
Schindler House, 835 N. Kings Rd., Los Angeles, CA 90069. 1147 S. Hope St., Los Angeles, CA 90015. Ed. Barbara Goldstein. Tel. (213) 651-3112. Q; $21; 1982; circ. 10,000. *Indexed*: A.P.I., Arch. Ind., Art Ind. *Notes*: adv., bk. rev., dwgs., photos (B&W, color). *Micro*: UMI.
An innovative publication that focuses on the relationship between architecture and the other arts. Well-known architects frequently contribute. Each issue explores a particular theme and tries to cover art, architecture, landscape design, and applied arts in the western U.S. Includes product reviews. (0730-9481)

0073 ARUP JOURNAL   (UK)
Ove Arup Partnership, 13 Fitzroy St., London WIP 6BQ, England. Q; 1966. *Indexed*: A.P.I., Avery. *Notes*: bibl., bk. rev., dwgs., photos (B&W).

The international projects of the world-renowned Arup Partnership are presented in detail from planning phase through completion. Design and construction problems are discussed, including notes on the research.

**0074 ASIAN ARCHITECTURE &   (HK)
BUILDER**
Thomson Press Hong Kong Ltd., 1930-5 Tai Sang Commercial Bldg., 24-34 Hennessey Rd., Hong Kong. Julia Fung. M; 1972. +

0075 ATRIUM   (MM)
17/4 Valletta Buildings, South Street, Valletta, Malta. Ed. Dennis De Lucca. Tel. 620806. Telex 1814 Medesco MW. S-a; £M4; 1981; circ. 2,700. *Indexed*: A.P.I. *Notes*: adv., bk. rev., calendars, dwgs., photos (B&W, color).
Architectural/engineering review for the Mediterranean, North African, and Middle East regions. The editorial goal is to foster a close architectural relationship among these countries. *

0076 BAUFORUM   (AU)
Nikolsdorfer Gasse 7-11, 1051 Vienna, Austria. Ed. Peter Hauer. Tel. 55-55-85. Bi-m; S. 396; 1967. *Indexed*: A.P.I., Avery. *Notes*: adv., bk. rev., dwgs., photos (B&W).
A journal of current Austrian architecture. Occasionally includes articles on earlier periods. Emphasis is on design rather than professional or technical issues. Text in German.

0077 BAUMEISTER   (GW)
Verlag Georg D.W. Callway, Streitfeld Str. 35, Postfach 800409, 8000 Munich 80, W. Germany. Ed. Dr. Paulhans Peters. Tel. 089/433096. Telex 5216752. M; DM. 99.60; 1903; circ. 16,000. *Indexed*: A.P.I., Avery. *Notes*: adv., bibl., bk. rev., dwgs., photos (B&W, color).
A highly esteemed international periodical that covers a wide range of architectural and planning projects in a selective, critical way. The emphasis is on presenting work of high quality rather than just the current achievements and trends. All building types, from the public to the vernacular, are examined in a way that encourages critical evaluation from readers. The issue reviewed presented the topic of atrium design in detail. Projects are extensively illustrated with views depicting all phases from models and renderings to completion. Text in German; summaries in English. (0005-674X)

0078 BAUTEN DER KULTUR   (GE)
Henschelverlag Kunst und Gesellschaft, Oranienburger St. 67-68, 104 Berlin, E. Germany. S-a; 1978. *Indexed*: A.P.I. +

0079 BAUWELT   (GW)
Bertelsmann Fachzeitschiften GmbH, Schlüter Str. 42/IV, 1000 Berlin, West Germany. Ed. Ulrich Conrads. Tel. 030/8812045. W; DM. 273.60; 1910; circ. 12,500. *Indexed*: A.P.I., Avery, Compendex, Eng. Ind. *Notes*: adv., bibl., bk. rev., dwgs., photos (B&W). *Annual Issues*: March, June, Sept., Dec.—City Planning.

An architectural periodical with thematic issues that focus on building technique, design, and planning. One of the major journals that molds international architectural opinion. Text in German. (0005-6855)

0080 BINARIO   (PO)
Praca de Londres 10, Lisbon 1, Portugal. Jose Luis Quintino. M; $20; 1958. *Indexed*: June, Dec. issues. *Notes*: adv., bibl., bk. rev., dwgs. (0006-2804) +

0081 BLUEPRINT   (UK)
Burston House, Burston Rd., Putney, London, SW12 6AR, England. Ed. Deyan Sudjic. Tel. 01-785-2738. M; £18.80; 1984. *Notes*: adv., dwgs., photos (B&W).

A lively magazine of design, architecture, and style similar to New York's *Metropolis* in format. Contains interesting reviews and features on the contemporary English design scene. Criticisms are often controversial. Enlightens as well as entertains.

0082 BLUEPRINTS   (US)
National Building Museum, 440 G St., N.W., Washington, DC 20001. Ed. Joyce Elliott. Tel. (202) 272-2565. Q; $15; 1981; circ. 10,000. *Indexed*: A.P.I., Avery. *Notes*: bk. rev., dwgs., photos (B&W).

Short illustrated articles cover activities of the Building Museum as well as current and historic U.S. projects. Includes notes on new publications, films, exhibits, archives, and tours. (0742-0552)

0906 BOUW

0083 BUILDING   (UK)
Building Services Publications, Ltd., Builder House, 1-3 Pemberton Row, London EC4P 4H2, England. Ed. Graham Rimmer. Tel. (01) 353-2300. Telex BUILDA G 25212. W; £65; 1842; circ. 21,000. *Indexed*: A.P.I., Avery,

Semiannually. *Notes*: adv., bk. rev., dwgs., photos (B&W, color). *Micro*: UMI.

About fifty pages of editorial news, features, and product reviews for British architects and builders. Includes professional, technical, legal, and economic news related to the construction industry. Along with *Architects Journal*, this is the most widely read and best source of up-to-date construction information in Great Britain. (0007-3318)

0084 BUILDING DESIGN   (UK)
Morgan-Grampion Construction Press Ltd., 30 Calderwood St., London SE18 6QH, England. Ed. Martin Pawley. W; $65; 1970. *Indexed*: A.P.I. *Notes*: adv., bk. rev., dwgs.

A newspaper that comments on new British buildings and presents brief technical notes. (0007-3423) +

0085 BUILDING DESIGN &   (US)
       CONSTRUCTION
Cahners Publishing Co., 475 Park Ave. South, New York, NY 10016. Ed. Philip G. Schreiner. Tel. (212) 686-0555. M; $35; 1958; circ. 63,500. *Annual Issues*: March-May—Glass Reconstruction/Retrofit/Renovation; June—Life Safety; July—Top 300 Design/Construction Giants; November—Emerging Technology; December—300 Owner Giants. *Notes*: adv., dwgs., photos (B&W, color).

Presents current information on the building industry, including news briefs and in-depth features on new projects; innovative building techniques, trends, or materials; industry leaders and legislation. Equal coverage is given to design, technology, and management. Each feature article includes details on design and costs. (0007-3407)

0086 BUILDINGS DESIGN   (US)
       JOURNAL
Communications Channels, Inc., 6255 Barfield Rd., Atlanta, GA 30328. Ed. Ray Pelosi. Tel. (404) 256-9800. M; $39; 1982; circ. 53,000. *Indexed*: Avery. *Notes*: adv., calendars, photos (B&W, color). *Micro*: UMI.

This high-quality newspaper features new projects utilizing the most current techniques in design and construction. A variety of building types are included. Monthly columns report on firms and new projects. Topics such as energy and telecommunications are frequently covered in depth. National in scope. Readers include architects, contractors, developers, and facility planners.

0220 BUILT

0087 BYGGEKUNST   (NO)
Norwegian Architects' League, Josefinesgt. 34,
Oslo 3, Norway. Ed. Ulf Gronvold. Tel. 60-22-
90. 8/yr.; Kr. 300; 1919; circ. 5,000. *Indexed*:
A.P.I., Avery. *Notes*: adv., bk. rev., dwgs.,
photos (B&W, color).
  The major profesional architectural journal
for Norway. Examines professional topics and
reviews projects by Norwegian architects. Text
in Norwegian; summaries in English. (0007-
7518)

0088 CADERNOS BRASILIEROS   (BL)
        DE ARQUITETURA
Projeto Editores Associados Ltda., Rua Cinder-
ela 62, CEP 01455, Sao Paulo, Brazil. Ed. Adail
Rodriguez. 3/yr.; 1972. +

0089 CANADIAN ARCHITECT   (CN)
Southam Communications, Ltd., 1450 Don
Mills Rd., Don Mills, Ontario M3B 2X7, Canada. Ed. Robert Gretton. Tel. (416) 445-6641.
M; Can. $30 (US$ 56); 1956. *Indexed*: A.P.I.,
Art Ind., Avery, C.P.I. *Annual Issues*: Decem-
ber—Design Awards. *Notes*: adv., bk. rev.,
dwgs., photos (B&W, color).
  The goal of the editors is to serve Canadian
architectural professionals by informing them of
innovative trends in building design, methods,
and technology, including materials and products, business techniques, and new events that
will affect them as professionals. (0008-2872)

0090 CARRE BLEU   (FR)
Feuille Int'l d'Arch, 33 Rue des Francs-Bour-
geois, 75004 Paris, France. Ed. Andre Schim-
merling. Tel. 1-2715265. Q; F. 150; 1958; circ.
1,000. *Notes*: adv., dwgs., photos (B&W).
  A review of contemporary architecture and
planning. Text in French; summaries in English.
(0008-6878)

0091 CASABELLA   (IT)
Gruppo Editoriale Electa, S.p.A., via Goldoni
1, 20129 Milan, Italy. Ed. Vittorro Gregotti. Tel.
02/704023. M; $80; 1928; circ. 30,000. *Indexed*:
A.P.I., Art Ind., R.I.L.A. *Notes*: bk. rev.,
dwgs., photos (B&W, color).
  A major international architectural review
with an emphasis on European projects. In-
depth coverage of competitions. Text in Italian;
summaries and captions in English. (0008-7181)

0092 CENTER, A JOURNAL FOR   (US)
        ARCHITECTURE IN
        AMERICA
Southwest Center for the Study of American Architecture, Univ. of Texas, Austin, TX 78712.
A; $15.75; 1984. *Indexed*: Avery.
  Analyzes architectural topics with emphasis
on social and environmental aspects of American architecture in the South and West. +

0093 CERCHA   (SP)
Consejo Superior de Colegios Oficiales de Apa-
rejadores y Arquitectos Tecnicos. Avda. Gener-
alisimo 73, Madrid 16, Spain. Q; $12; 1968. +

0094 CESKOSLOVENSKY   (CS)
        ARCHITEKT
Svaz Architektu, CSR, Letenska 5, 118 45
Prague 1, Czechoslovakia. Ed. Jan Novotny.
Tel. 539768. Bi-w; $36.10; 1955; circ. 6,000. *In-
dexed*: Feb. issue. *Notes*: adv., calendar, dwgs.,
photos (B&W, color).
  Professional architectural journal. Text in
Czech. (0009-0697)*

0095 CHICAGO ARCHITECTURAL   (US)
        JOURNAL
Chicago Architectural Club, Suite 1600, 80 East
Jackson Blvd., Chicago, IL 60604. Rizzoli International, 712 Fifth Ave., New York, NY 10019.
A; $15; 1981. *Indexed*: Avery. *Notes*: dwgs.,
photos (B&W).
  A catalog of the work of members of the Chicago Architectural Club, but not limited to midwestern projects.

0765 CIMAISE: ART ET
      ARCHITECTURE ACTUELS

0250 CITE: AN ARCHITECTURE
      AND DESIGN REVIEW OF
      HOUSTON

0096 CITTA E CAMPAGNA   (IT)
via Concordia 20, 00183 Rome, Italy. Mario
Ciranna. M. +

0097 CONSTRUCTION MODERNE   (FR)
Societe d'Edition et de Publicite Techniques et
Artistiques, 47 rue des Renaudes, 75017 Paris,
France. Bi-m; $10 (free to qualified subscribers);
1884. *Indexed*: A.P.I. *Notes*: adv., bibl., bk.
rev., dwgs. (0010-6852) +

0098 CONTROSPAZIO/   (IT)
      COUNTERSPACE
Edizioni Dedalo S.p.A., P.O. Box 362, 70100
Bari, Italy. Tel. 371555. Q; L.45,000; 1969; circ.
16,000. *Notes*: adv., bk. rev., dwgs., photos
(B&W, color).
    Text in Italian. *

0099 COSTRUIRE PER ABITARE   (IT)
Editrice Abitare Segesta S.p.A., Corso Monforte 15, 20122 Milan, Italy. G.P.E. Stampa
S.p.A., V. Fontana 18, 20122 Milan, Italy. Ed.
Leonardo Fiori. Tel. (02) 704251. Telex 315302
ABITI. M; L.42,900; 1982; circ. 25,000. *Indexed*: Dec. issue. *Notes*: adv., bk. rev., dwgs.,
photos (B&W, color).
    One of the leading building design periodicals
in Italy, with wide readership among architects,
contractors, engineers, public officials, and students. Each issue is divided into three sections
dealing with a general architectural topic, product information, and cultural themes. Scope is
international. Text in Italian.

0100 COVJEK I PROSTOR   (YU)
Savez Arhitekata Hrvatske, Trg Republike 3/I,
4100 Zagreb, Yugoslavia. Ed. Branko Siladin.
Tel. (041) 274-741. M; $35; 1953; circ. 3,000.
Indexed: A.P.I. *Notes*: adv., bk. rev., dwgs.,
photos (B&W).
    A journal of architecture, planning, historic
preservation, and interior design. Text in Serbo-
Croatian; English summaries. (0011-0728) *

0101 DBZ/DEUTSCHE   (GW)
      BAUZEITSCHRIFT
Bertelsmann-Fachverlag, Carl Bertelsmann Str.
270, Postfach 5555, 4830 Guetersloh, W. Germany. Ed. S. Linke. Tel. (05241) 80-2111. Telex
933646. M; DM. 144; 1953; circ. 18,500. *Indexed*: A.P.I., Avery, Excerp. Med. *Notes*:
adv., bibl., bk. rev., dwgs., photos (B&W,
color).
    An architectural journal that covers all impor-
tant building projects planned or newly completed in Germany and other countries.
Emphasis is on technical aspects of construction. Each issue examines many projects and
includes many plans. Text in German; occasional summaries in English. (0001-4782) *

0102 DESIGN AND ART IN   (GR)
      GREECE
    (Formerly: *Design in Greece*)
P.O. Box 3545, GR 102-10, Athens, Greece. Ed.
Orestis B. Doumanis. Tel. (01) 721-3916. A; $25;
1970; circ. 5,000. *Indexed*: A.P.I., vol. 12.
Notes: adv., bk. rev., dwgs., photos (B&W).
    A presentation of major international trends
and developments that influence the human environment in Greece. Covers themes in architecture, interior furnishings, art, industrial and
graphic design. The editor's aim is "to promote
the collaboration between architecture and the
visual and applied arts." Along with its compan-
ion publication, *Architecture in Greece*, this periodical presents the finest in Greek design. Text
in Greek; summaries in English. (0074-1191)

0103 DESIGN QUARTERLY   (US)
Walker Art Center, Vineland Place, Minneapolis, MN 55403. M.I.T. Press, Journals Dept., 28
Carlton St., Cambridge, MA 02142. Ed. Mildred
S. Friedman. Tel. (612) 375-7686. Q; $15
(indiv.); $30 (inst.); 1946; circ. 9,200. *Indexed*:
A.P.I., Art Bib., Art Ind., Avery, Mag. Ind.
Notes: adv., dwgs., photos (B&W, color).
Micro: UMI.
    Edited by the Walker Art Center, Minneapo-
lis, this quarterly is devoted to presenting landmark issues in contemporary architecture and
design. Each issue covers a single topic with
imagination and flair. It is well known for its
outstanding graphic design. (0011-9415)

0104 DETAIL   (CN)
Dept. of Architecture, 230 College St., Toronto,
Ont. M5S 1A1, Canada. Ed. Paul Sandori. 8/yr.;
$72; 1984. *Notes*: dwgs., photos (B&W).
    Provides detail drawings and selected specifi-
cations of various types of Canadian buildings.
Each issue is devoted to one building. Includes
photographs of the completed structure.

0105 DETAIL   (GW)
Verlag Architektur und Baudetail GmbH, Franz
Joseph Str. 9, 8000 Munich 40, W. Germany.
Institut fur Internationale Architektur—Doku-
mentation, Vertriebs Service, Luitpoldstr. 4,
D-8500, Nuremberg, W. Germany. Ed. Hans
Baessler. Bi-m; DM. 58; 1960; circ. 14,000. *Indexed*: A.P.I., Avery. *Notes*: adv., bk. rev.,
dwgs., photos (B&W, color).
    Presents detail drawings and explanations of
all building types and materials. International
projects are covered. Text in German. (0011-
9571)

0106 DETAIL/DITERU   (JA)
Shokokusha Publishing Co., Inc., 25 Sakamachi, Shinjuku-ku Tokyo 160, Japan. Ed. Tai-

shiro Yamamoto. Q; $15; 1964. *Notes*: adv., dwgs.

Text in Japanese. (0012-4133) +

0107 DEUTSCHE BAUZEITUNG (GW)
Deutsche Verlagsanstalt GmbH, Neckarstr. 121, Postfach 209, 7000 Stuttgart 1, W. Germany. Ed. Karl Wilhelm Schmitt. Tel. (0711) 2631-295. M; DM.100.80; 1867; circ. 34,500. *Indexed*: A.P.I., Avery, Excerp. Med. *Notes*: adv., bk. rev., calendars, dwgs., photos (B&W, color).

A thorough analytical review of German architecture and construction. Theoretical as well as technical themes are dealt with. Occasionally the theme of the issue will cover the architecture of another country. Includes product reviews and notes on new projects. Text in German; summaries in English. (0721-1902)

0108 DEUTSCHES (GW)
ARCHITEKTENBLATT
Forum-Verlag GmbH, Postfach 700262, D-7000 Stuttgart 70, W. Germany. Ed. Gerhard Schoeberl. Tel. 0711-764025. Telex 7255849 forud. M; DM. 60; 1968; circ. 61,000. *Indexed*: Avery. *Notes*: adv., bibl., bk. rev., calendars, dwgs., photos (B&W).

An official publication of architecture and construction in Hessen, Rheinland-Pfalz, and Saarland. Provides extensive coverage of all building types as well as technical data. Text in German. (0012-1215)

0571 DOMUS

0109 DUTCH ART AND (NE)
ARCHITECTURE TODAY
Bureau Beeldende Kunst Buitenland, Box 2242, 1000 CE Amsterdam, Netherlands. Tel. (020) 26-61-41. Telex 16078 START. S-a; fl.25; 1977; circ. 1,700. *Indexed*: Avery, R.I.L.A. *Notes*: adv., calendars, dwgs., photos (B&W).

A review of contemporary Dutch art and architecture. Editors and contributing authors are freelance critics, art historians, professors, and curators. It is intended for a non-Dutch reading public. Financed by the Ministry for Cultural Affairs, *DA and AT* is the medium for presenting Dutch art and architecture abroad. It represents official recognition of significant new developments in the visual arts.

0110 EDILDOMANI (IT)
Via Roma 28, 22053 Lecco, Italy. Ed. Luigi Bonanomi. M. +

0111 EDILIZIA POPOLARE (IT)
Quadrato della Concordia 9, 00144 Rome, Italy. Ed. Luciano Zerbinati. Tel. (06) 592-5693. Bi-m; L.40,000; 1954; circ. 3,500. *Indexed*: A.P.I. *Notes*: adv., bibl., bk. rev., dwgs., photos (B&W, color).

An international review that examines in detail technical and aesthetic aspects of architecture and town planning. Topics include restoration, energy conservation, housing, etc. Plans are extensively used in articles and are well reproduced. Emphasis is on Italian projects. Text in Italian. (0422-5619)

0201 EUPALINO

0112 FACILITIES PLANNING (US)
NEWS
115 Orinda Way, Orinda, CA 94563. Ed. Steven Westfall. Tel. (415) 254-1744. Bi-m; $40; 1982; circ. 17,000. *Notes*: adv., bk. rev., calendars, dwgs., photos (B&W).

A newspaper that covers projects, expansions, or renovations in the planning, design, or construction phases. Emphasis is on healthcare and high-tech facilities. Economic trends and technological innovations are given special attention. Articles are written primarily for facility planners and managers, but they are also of interest to architects and interior designers. Contacts for further information on projects are usually included in each article.

0113 AL-FAISAL ARCHITECTURE (SU)
AND PLANNING JOURNAL
Editor-in-Chief, College of Architecture and Planning, King Faisal University, P.O. Box 2397, Damman 31451, Saudi Arabia. Ed. Ghazi Sahal Al-Otaibi. Tel. 8578206. Telex 670020 Faisal SJ. Bi-a; 1981. *Indexed*: Avery. *Notes*: dwgs., photos (B&W, color).

Saudi Arabia's concern for the preservation of its rich architectural tradition and interest in innovative planning and design techniques are expressed in this journal. The professors and students who contribute papers are working toward producing a high-quality environment. Theoretical articles, case studies, and features discuss design, planning, construction, and preservation of buildings and cities throughout the Middle East but primarily in Saudi Arabia.

0114 FORUM (NE)
Vereniging Architectura et Amicitia, Waterlooplein 211, 1011 PB, Amsterdam, Netherlands. Tel. 020-220188. Q; fl.54; circ. 3,300. *Indexed*:

A.P.I., Avery. *Notes*: adv., bibl., bk. rev., calendars, dwgs., photos (B&W, color).

A Dutch- and English-language journal containing contemplative articles written by and about architects. (0015-8372)

0115   FRAMES/PORTE & FINESTRE   (IT)
Faenza Editrice, via Firenze 276, 48018 Faenza, Italy. Ed. Franco Rossi. Tel. (0546) 43120. Telex 550410. Bi-m; L. 55,000; 1983. *Notes*: adv., bk. rev., dwgs., photos (B&W, color).

A glossy, abundantly illustrated magazine devoted to frames and frame elements in building —an area of increasing importance in design and building. Examines technological and aesthetic aspects. Articles on energy conservation, maintenance, security, and design appear. Includes sections on new products and specific applications by international designers. Well-written and informative text in Italian and English.

**0116   GA (GLOBAL   (JA)
   ARCHITECTURE) DETAIL**
A.D.A. Edita, 3-12-14 Sendagaya, Shibuya-ku, Tokyo, Japan. Irreg. *Indexed*: Avery. *Notes*: dwgs., photos (B&W).

Presents working detail drawings of the same buildings that appear in comparative volumes of the Global Architecture series.

**0117   GA (GLOBAL   (JA)
   ARCHITECTURE)
   DOCUMENT**
A.D.A. Edita Tokyo Co., Ltd., 3-12-14 Sendagaya, Shibuya-ku, Tokyo, Japan. Ed. Yukio Futagawa. Tel. 03-403-1581. Q; Yen 2,900. *Indexed*: A.P.I., Art Ind., Avery. *Notes*: dwgs., photos (B&W, color).

Documents the latest architectural developments and significant works from all over the world. Abundant high-quality photographs illustrate the critical essays written by prominent architecture critics and historians.

0118   GLOBAL ARCHITECTURE   (JA)
A.D.A. Edita Tokyo Co., Ltd., 3-12-14 Sendagaya, Shibuya-ku, Tokyo, Japan. Irreg.; 1977. *Notes*: dwgs., photos (B&W, color).

An outstanding softcover series of monographs on architects from around the world. Each issue focuses on one or two buildings. Known for its fine photographs. Text in Japanese and English.

0119   GRAN BAZAAR   (IT)
Edizioni S.Y.D.S. Italia S.r.l., viale Stelvio 57, 20100 Milan, Italy. Agenzia Italiana di Esportazione, via Gadames 89, 20151 Milano, Italy. Ed. Giuseppe Della Schiava. Tel. 6886118. Telex 325244 Bazaar I. Bi-m; $50; 1978; circ. 44,000. *Notes*: adv., photos (B&W, color).

A refined intellectual magazine devoted to architecture, design, furnishings, and decoration.

**0120   GREAT LAKES   (US)
   ARCHITECTURE &
   ENGINEERING**
E.B. Stapleford, Inc., 13320 Enterprise Ave., Cleveland, OH 44135. Bi-m; 1954; circ. 5,500. +

0121   HINTERLAND   (IT)
Via Revere 7, 20123 Milan, Italy. Agenzia Italiana di Esportazione, via Gadames 89, 20151 Milan, Italy. Tel. 4695222. Telex 315367 AIMI-1. Q. *Indexed*: A.P.I.

A magazine that offers a global vision of contemporary architectural and town planning themes. It publishes special feature issues on current research work and developments in various building types as well as on their implications for their architectural contexts. *

0122   INDIAN ARCHITECT   (II)
A 15 Pamposh Enclave, New Delhi 11048, India. Ed. D.N. Dhar. M; 1959; $12. *Indexed*: A.P.I., Avery. *Notes*: adv., bk. rev., photos (B&W).

A technical magazine covering topics of interest to architects, planners, and engineers. Emphasis is on work in India but includes case studies from abroad. Text in English. (0019-4409)

**0123   INDIAN INSTITUTE OF   (II)
   ARCHITECTS JOURNAL**
Architects Publishing Corp. of India, 51 Sujata, Quarry Rd. Crossing, Malad East 97, Bombay 400097, India. Ed. Uttam C. Jaim. Tel. 69442. Q; Rs.100 (3 yrs.); 1937; circ. 3,500. *Indexed*: A.P.I. *Notes*: adv., bibl., bk. rev., calendars, dwgs., photos (B&W, color).

Official publication of the professional architects association of India. Issues present profiles of particular firms, new building research, or essays on contemporary problems of Indian architecture. (0019-4913)

**0124   INDUSTRIA DELLE   (IT)
   COSTRUZIONI**
Edilstampa, via Guattani 20, 00161 Rome, Italy. Ed. Giuseppe Nannerini. Tel. 8488325. Telex 613439 ANCE 1. M; L.120,000; 1967; circ.

9,000. *Indexed*: A.P.I. *Notes*: adv., bk. rev., dwgs., photos (B&W, color).

A major architectural review that presents international work. Articles include summaries of programs of each project and emphasize technical aspects of the construction. Text in Italian and English; summaries in French, German, and Spanish.

**0125   INGENIERIA   (CK)
         ARQUITECTURA
         CONSTRUCCION**
Sociedad Colombiana de Arquitectos, Seccional de Antioquia, Calle 49-B, no. 63-21, Piso 4, Apartado Aereo 1197, Medellin, Colombia. Q; 1968. (0020-1014) +

**0126   ISLAMIC ART AND   (US)
         ARCHITECTURE**
17042 Devonshire St. #209, Northridge, CA 91325. Undena Publications, P.O. Box 97, Malibu, CA 90265. Ed. A. Daneshvari. Tel. (818) 366-1744. Irreg.; 1981; circ. 520. *Indexed*: Avery. *Notes*: dwgs., photos (B&W).

A series of essays on Islamic art and architecture. (0742-1125)

0127   JAPAN ARCHITECT   (JA)
Japan Architect Co., Ltd., 31-2 Yushima, 2 chome, Bunkyo-ku, Tokyo 113, Japan. Ed. Takeshi Ishido. Tel. 03-811-7101. 11/yr.; $81; 1956; circ. 15,000. *Indexed*: A.P.I., Art Ind., Avery, June & Nov./Dec. issues. *Notes*: adv., bk. rev., dwgs., photos (B&W, color).

One of the major architectural periodicals in Japan. There is equal emphasis on contemporary and traditional Japanese architecture. Richly illustrated. Contains news of the current projects underway by internationally active Japanese architects. Also includes historical analyses and critiques. English edition now available. (0448-8512)

**0214   JOURNAL OF
         ARCHITECTURAL AND
         PLANNING RESEARCH**

**0256   JOURNAL OF DESIGN AND
         CONSTRUCTION**

**0128   KENCHIKU TECHO/   (JA)
         ARCHITECT**
Kinryudo Co., Ltd., 2-3 Higashi Veno, 5 chome, Taito-ku, Tokyo 11, Japan. Ed. Shigeru Kikuchi. M; 1957. +

0129   DIE KUNST   (GW)
(Formerly: *Die Kunst und das Schoene Heim*)
Verlag Karl Thiemig, Pilgersheimer Str. 38, 8000 Munich 90, W. Germany. Ed. Antonie Modes. Tel. 089-6248233. Telex 05-23-981. M; DM. 120; 1885; circ. 9,900. *Indexed*: Avery, Jan. issue. *Notes*: adv., bibl., bk. rev., calendars, dwgs., photos (B&W, color).

Gives equal coverage to fine art, graphics, architecture, and interior design. Richly illustrated. Text in German; summaries in English. (0023-5423)

**0130   KWARTALNIK   (PL)
         ARCHITEKTURY I
         URBANISTYKI**
Plac Inwalidow 10, pok. 116, 01-552 Warsaw, Poland. Ed. Wojceich Kalinowski. Q; $25; 1956; circ. 817. *Indexed*: Avery, cum. every 5 years. *Notes*: dwgs., photos (B&W).

Theory and history of architecture and planning, primarily in Poland. Text in Polish and in English. (0023-5865)

0865   LANDSCAPE

0131   LATENT IMAGES   (US)
Dirsmith Group, Inc., 318 Maple Ave., Highland Park, IL 60035. Ed. Suzanne Dirsmith. Tel. (312) 433-3616. Q; 1981; circ. 6,000. *Notes*: dwgs., photos (B&W, color).

Covers architecture, landscape design, interior design, and engineering (according to the editor). *

**0132   LENINGRADSKAYA   (UR)
         PANORAMA**
(Formerly: *Stroitel 'stvo i Arkhitektura Leningrada*)
Gorodskoi Sovet Deputov Trudyashchikhsya, Lenizdat Fontanka 59, Leningrad USSR. Ed. A.I. Knyazev. M; $16.20; 1939; circ. 6,000. *Indexed*: A.P.I. (0039-2413) +

0816   LIVABILITY DIGEST

0257   LIVABLE CITY

0133   LIVING ARCHITECTURE   (DK)
Vestergade 8-B-1456K, Copenhagen, Denmark. (U.S. sub.) c/o Architectural Record, 1221 Ave. of the Americas, New York, NY 10020. Ed. Per Nagel. Tel. 451-13-7613. S-a; $15; 1983. *Indexed*: Avery. *Notes*: adv., dwgs., photos (B&W, color).

High-quality full-color photography, drawings, and English text illustrate the best of traditional and contemporary Scandinavian architecture, design, and craftsmanship. (0108-4135)

0134 LOTUS INTERNATIONAL (IT)
Gruppo Editoriale Electa S.p.A., via Goldoni 1, 20129 Milan, Italy. (U.S. sub.) Rizzoli Publications, Inc., 712 Fifth Ave., New York, NY 10019. Ed. Pier Luigi Nicolin. Tel. (02) 704023. Q; 1963. *Indexed*: A.P.I., Art Ind., Avery. *Notes*: dwgs., photos (B&W, color).
A review of contemporary architecture. Each issue focuses on key themes and analyzes them from an international point of view. Text in Italian and English.

0135 MAGYAR EPITOMUVESZET (HU)
Dienes Laszlo Utca 2, 1088 Budapest, Hungary. Kultura, Box 149, H-1389, Budapest, Hungary. Ed. Dr. Alkos Moravanszky. Tel. 336-532. Bi-m; $34; 1907; circ. 6,000. *Indexed*: A.P.I., Avery. *Notes*: adv., bibl., bk. rev., dwgs., photos (B&W, color).
Problems of architectural design are examined from a cultural and artistic point of view. Emphasis on Hungary and Central Europe. Text in Hungarian; summaries in English, Russian, French, and German. (0025-0082)

0774 MARG: A MAGAZINE OF THE ARTS

0136 MIMAR: ARCHITECTURE IN (SI)
DEVELOPMENT
Concept Media, Ltd., 19 Tanglin Rd., #06-52, Singapore 1024. (U.S. sub.) MIT Press Journals, 28 Carlton St., Cambridge, MA 02142. Ed. Hasan-Uddin Khan. Tel. 7340910. Telex Mimar RS50943. Q; $36 (indiv.); $56 (inst.); 1981. *Indexed*: A.P.I., Art Ind., Avery. *Notes*: adv., bibl., bk. rev., dwgs., photos (B&W, color).
Mimar ("master builder" in Arabic, Turkish, Farsi, and Urdu) is a beautifully illustrated design magazine covering contemporary architecture in the developing world. Each issue focuses primarily on a particular theme, region, or project. In addition to promoting an appreciation and knowledge of indigenous design and craftsmanship, this journal comments on how new technologies from industrialized countries can be adapted. Emphasis is on the Islamic world. It is oriented toward architects, planners, preservationists, designers, and anyone interested in the developing world. Back issues are available. (0129-8372)

0137 MODERN BUILDING (AT)
ARCHITECTURE AND
ENGINEERING IN
AUSTRALIA
J. Carroll & Co., P.O. Box 36, Drummoyne NSW 2047, Australia. Bi-m; 1967. +

0138 MODULO (BL)
rua Professor Alfredo Gomes 28, Botafogo 22251, Rio de Janeiro, Brazil. Tel. (021) 246-8216. Cr.$12; 1955. *Indexed*: Avery.
Review of architecture and the visual arts in Brazil. Text in Portuguese.

0139 MONTREAL SOCIETY OF (CN)
ARCHITECTS COMMUNIQUE
Montreal Society of Architects, 1825 Dorchester Blvd. W., Montreal, Quebec, Canada. +

0140 MUR VIVANT (FR)
Art et Maitrise Publicite, 9 rue de Trevise, 75009 Paris, France. Ed. R. Javin. Tel. 770-50-01. Q; F. 400; 1966; circ. 5,000. *Indexed*: A.P.I. *Notes*: adv., dwgs., photos (B&W, color).
Text in French. *

0141 NATO MAGAZINE (UK)
Architectural Assn., 36 Bedford Square, London WC1, England. A; £3; 1983. *Indexed*: Avery. *Notes*: adv., photos (B&W).
NATO (Narrative Architecture Today) departs from the mainstream of architectural publishing. The editor says, "Its pursuance of current lifestyle as the sustaining parallel to the design of cities forms the basis of its spirit of optimism." Large format with bold graphics. (0265-6663)

0142 NEUF (BE)
Socorema, Rue du Merlo 84, A, B-1180, Brussels, Belgium. Ed. J. Laffineur. Bi-m; Fr.930; 1965. *Indexed*: A.P.I., Avery. *Notes*: adv., bk. rev., bibl., dwgs. +

0143 NEW ZEALAND ARCHITECT (NZ)
New Zealand Inst. of Architects, P.O. Box 19-082, Te Aro, Wellington S.W., New Zealand. Associated Group Media, Ltd., Private Bag, New Market, Aukland, New Zealand. Ed. Gerald Melling. Tel. (04) 843-174. Bi-m; N.Z.$20; 1913; circ. 1,600. *Indexed*: A.P.I. *Notes*: adv., bibl., bk. rev., calendars, dwgs., photos (B&W, color).
A professional journal for architects that describes current architecture in New Zealand and reports briefly on major international work.

Also includes short articles on practice and education. (0110-425x)

**0144 NOVA SCOTIA   (CN)
       ASSOCIATION OF
       ARCHITECTS**
Nova Scotia Assn. of Architects, 6009 Quinpool Rd., Halifax, B3J 1Y9, Canada. M; membership. +

0145 NUESTRA ARQUITECTURA   (AG)
Editorial Contempora s.r.l., Sarmiento 643, Piso 5, 1382 Buenos Aires, Argentina. Ed. Norberto Mario Muzio. Bi-m; $54; 1929. *Indexed*: A.P.I., Avery. (0029-5701) +

0146 NUOVA CITTA   (IT)
Fondazione Giovanni Michelucci, via B. Angelico 15, 50014 Fresole-Firenze, Italy. Opus Libri S.r.l., via della Torretta 16, 50137 Firenze, Italy. Ed. Giovanni Michelucci. Tel. 597149. S-a; L.18,000; 1983.
   Covers architecture and planning. Text in Italian. *

0147 OP CIT   (IT)
Edizioni il Centro, via Vincenzo Padula 2, Naples 80123, Italy. Ed. Renato de Fusco. 3/yr.; L.11,000; 1964; circ. 1,000. *Indexed*: A.P.I. *Notes*: bibl., bk. rev.
   A journal of architecture, design, and art. Text in Italian. (0030-3305) *

**0148 ORDRE DES ARCHITECTES   (CN)
       DU QUEBEC. BULLETIN**
Order of the Architects of Quebec, 1825 W. Blvd. Dorchester, Montreal, Quebec H3H 1R4, Canada. Ed. J.P. Pelletier. Tel. (514) 937-6168. M; Can.$24; 1966. (0316-9200) +

0823 OUT OF JERUSALEM

0149 PARAMETRO   (IT)
Faenza Editrice S.p.A., Casella Postale 68, via Firenze 276, 48018 Faenza, Italy. Ed. Giorgio Trebbi. Tel. 582112. 10/yr.; L.70,000; 1970. *Indexed*: A.P.I., Avery. *Notes*: dwgs., photos (B&W).
   An architectural and planning review. Text in English and Italian; summaries in English, French, German, and Spanish. (0031-1731)

**0150 PERIODICA   (HU)
       POLYTECHNICA.
       ARCHITECTURE**
Technical University, Budapest 1521, Hungary. Kultura Foreign Trade Co., 1389 POB149, Budapest, Hungary. Ed. I. Szabadvary. Tel. 665-011. Telex 225931 MUEGY. Q; $8; 1956. *Notes*: bk. rev., dwgs., photos (B&W).
   Text in English and German. (0324-590x) *

**0151 PHILIPPINE ARCHITECTURE   (PH)
       & BUILDING JOURNAL**
Constantino F. Agbayani, 404 Garcia Bldg., Rizal Ave., Manila, Philippines. Q; 1960. +

**0152 PHILIPPINE   (PH)
       ARCHITECTURE,
       ENGINEERING &
       CONSTRUCTION RECORD**
Paencor, Inc., 154 Araneta Ave., P.O. Box 1295, Quezon City, Philippines. Ed. Placido Urbanes. M; 1953. (0031-7470) +

0153 PLAN   (IE)
Irish Trade and Technical Publications, Ltd., 5-7 Main St., Blackrock, Dublin, Ireland. Ed. Neil Steedman. Tel. (01) 885001. Telex 92258. M; £18; 1969; circ. 3,200. *Indexed*: A.P.I. *Annual Issues*: April—Review of Irish Architecture. *Notes*: adv., bibl., bk. rev., calendars, dwgs., photos (B&W, color).
   The architectural magazine for all Ireland. It reaches an audience of architects, planners, interior designers, estimators, engineers, lighting and acoustical consultants, contractors, and specifiers. In addition to covering new projects, much attention is given to reviewing new products and building techniques.

**0154 PLAN: MAANDBLAD VOOR   (NE)
       ONTWERP ON OMGEVING**
Postbus 19607, 1000 G P Amsterdam, Netherlands. Ed. H.J. Bakker. Tel. 020-228111. M; fl.194; 1970; circ. 3,500. *Indexed*: A.P.I. *Notes*: adv., bk. rev., calendars, dwgs., photos (B&W, color).
   The major journal for design and environment in the Netherlands. It is international in scope and interdisciplinary, focusing on problems in the built environment rather than on isolated topics. It has a reputation of being trend-setting. The readership consists primarily of architects in practice as well as those in academia, professional planners, and government officials in planning and building. Text in Dutch; table of contents and summaries in Dutch, English, and French. (0006-8357)

0155 PLANEN UND BAUEN   (SZ)
A.N.A.G., P.O. Box 132, Winzlerstr. 112, CH-8049, Switzerland. Ed. Landolt Armin. Tel. (01) 56-30-80. Telex 822669 Anag. M; Fr.104; 1968;

circ. 6,000. *Notes*: adv., dwgs., photos (B&W, color).

Aimed at a wide audience of architects, engineers, and builders. Covers new construction and renovation of all building types. Text in German. *

0830 PLANNING AND BUILDING DEVELOPMENTS

0156 POLA   (IO)
Departemen Arsitekter Institut, Teknologi Bandung, Jalan Ganesha 10, Bandung, Indonesia. Ed. Agus Basuki. Bi-m; 1975. +

0157 PORTICO   (UK)
Institute of Registered Architects, Faculty of Architects and Surveyors, 15 St. Mary St., Chippenham, Wilts. SN15 3JN, England. Ed. Tom Morris. Q; £10; 1929. *Indexed*: A.P.I. *Micro*: UMI. (0032-4914) +

0158 PROA   (CK)
Carlos Martinez, Calle 40, no. 19-52, Bogota, Colombia. Ed. Lorenzo Fonseca. Tel. 2456447. M; $40; 1946; circ. 6,000. *Indexed*: A.P.I. *Notes*: adv., bibl., bk. rev., dwgs., photos (B&W, color).

The leading architectural review for Colombia. Text in Spanish. (0032-9150) *

0159 PROCESS: ARCHITECTURE   (JA)
Process Publishing Co., Ltd., 3-1-3 Koishikawa, Bunkyo ku, Tokyo, Japan. Ed. Katsuhiko Ichinowatari. Tel. (03) 816-1695-1696. Irreg. *Indexed*: A.P.I., Avery. *Notes*: dwgs., photos (B&W, color). *Micro*: UMI.

Each issue is devoted to a specific architectural theme such as a building type, region, or style. Recent issues emphasize Japanese architecture. Text in Japanese and English. (0386-037x)

0160 PROFIL   (FR)
Editions G.M. Perrin, 108 Ave. Ledru Rollin, 75011 Paris, France. Bi-m; F.185; 1974. +

0161 PROGRESSIVE   (US)
         ARCHITECTURE
Reinhold Publishing Co., Inc., 600 Summer St., P.O. Box 1361, Stamford, CT 06904. P.O. Box 95759, Cleveland, OH 44101. Ed. John Morris Dixon. Tel. (203) 348-7531. M; $25; 1920; circ. 72,000. *Indexed*: A.P.I., Arch. Ind., Art Ind., Avery, Eng. Ind., R.I.L.A. *Annual Issues*: Jan. —Awards; April—Energy; Sept.—Interior Design; Nov.—Preservation. *Notes*: adv., bibl.,

bk. rev., calendars, dwgs., photos (B&W, color). *Micro*: UMI.

One of the leading American architectural periodicals. Includes critiques of important new work; monthly reports on new products, techniques, and technologies; timely columns on law, specification writing, books; coverage of key trade shows; articles on historical achievements that currently influence professional thinking. There is basically a balance between articles on design and technical issues, with a slight leaning toward techniques rather than aesthetics. Many of the articles are written by practicing architects. Readership includes architects, interior designers, engineers, contractors, specifiers, government agencies, and building owners/managers. (0033-0752)

0162 QUADERNS   (SP)
         D'ARQUITECTURA I
         URBANISME
Colegio Oficial de Arquitectos de Catalunya, Plaza Nova 5, Barcelona 2, Spain. Libreria Internacional, Corsega 491, Barcelona 25, Spain. Ed. Josep Lluis Mateo. Tel. 3-1-301-5000. Telex 50873 ARQCE. Q; Ptas. 4500; 1931; circ. 6,000. *Indexed*: A.P.I. *Notes*: adv., bibl., dwgs., photos (B&W, color).

A critical review of Spanish architecture in relation to international contemporary trends. Text in Catalan, Spanish, and English.

0163 R.I.A.I. BULLETIN   (IE)
Royal Inst. of the Architects of Ireland, Clavis Press, 33 Priory Dr., Stillorgan Co., Dublin, Ireland. Ed. J. Owen Lewis. Bi-m. +

0164 R.I.B.A. JOURNAL   (UK)
R.I.B.A. Publications, Ltd., 66 Portland Place, London W1N 4AD, England. Ed. Peter Murray. Tel. 5805533. M; £30; 1893; circ. 27,000. *Indexed*: A.P.I., Art Ind., Avery, R.I.L.A. *Notes*: adv., bibl., bk. rev., calendars, dwgs., photos (B&W, color). *Micro:* UMI.

Presents a wide range of Institute and professional news as well as technical notes and product information not generally picked up by other British publications. Interior design supplement distributed every two months. (0035-8932) *

0990 RAKENNUSTAITO

0165 RASSEGNA: ARCHITETTURA   (IT)
         E URBANISTICA
Edizioni Kappa, Piazza Borghese 6, 00186 Rome, Italy. Ed. Federico Gorio. Tel. (06)

461045. Q; $65. *Indexed*: A.P.I. *Notes*: dwgs., photos (B&W).

A scholarly publication that discusses current and proposed projects and their relation to the environment. Prepared under the auspices of the University of Rome. Scope is international. Text in Italian. (0021-2458)

0166   RECHERCHE ET   (FR)
       ARCHITECTURE
Avenue du Recteur Poincare, 75782 Paris Cedex 16, France. Ed. Marie Therese Mathieu. Tel. (1) 5244302. Q; F.220; 1970; circ. 11,500. *Indexed*: A.P.I., Avery. *Notes*: dwgs., photos (B&W).

This quarterly review presents contemporary French architecture in its most innovative form. Includes all building types, but many articles are devoted to housing. Emphasis is on the use of new materials or innovative applications for traditional materials. Includes detailed illustrations. Text in French. (0373-4285)

0167   REVUE FORMES   (LU)
       NOUVELLES
20 rue des Trevires, Luxembourg, Luxembourg. Ed. J.A. Schmit. 1952. +

0168   S.I.A.J.   (SI)
Singapore Institute of Architects, Publications Board, Block 23, Outram Park #2-393, Singapore 0316, Singapore. Tel. 2203456. Telex RS22652 SINARC. Bi-m; S$47; 1966; circ. 1,000. *Indexed*: A.P.I., Avery. *Notes*: adv., photos (B&W, color).

Official journal of the Singapore Institute of Architects. Includes news of practicing architects and students. (0049-0520)

0834   S.P.A. JOURNAL

1169   SCHWEIZER INGENIEUR
       UND ARCHITEKT

0169   SCHWEIZER JOURNAL   (SZ)
Hans Frey, Kreuzstr. 11, 8712 Staefa, Switzerland. M; Fr.96; 1957. (0036-7370) +

0170   SECTION A   (CN)
Editions Section A, Inc., P.O. Box 909, La Cite, Montreal, Quebec H2W 2P5, Canada. Ed. Odile Henault. Tel. (416) 279-9009. Bi-m; $25; 1983. *Notes*: adv., bk. rev., calendars, dwgs., photos (B&W, color).

Architecture, planning, landscape design, and historic preservation (primarily in Canada) are presented in a lively style. Some issues are thematic. Articles are well illustrated and topics are covered in depth. Text in French and English. (0715-9781)

0171   SINTEZA   (YU)
Zveza Drustev Arhitekor Slovenije, Erjaveeva Cesta 15-1, 6100 Ljubljana, Yugoslavia. Q; $40; 1964. *Indexed*: A.P.I. (0049-0601) +

0172   SITES   (US)
446 W. 20th St., New York, NY 10011. Ed. Dennis Dollens. Tel. (212) 924-0642. Q; $12; 1979; circ. 1,000. *Notes*: bk. rev., dwgs., photos (B&W).

A literary magazine on buildings, places, and monuments.

0173   SOCIETY FOR THE STUDY   (CN)
       OF ARCHITECTURE IN
       CANADA. BULLETIN
Don Lovell, Ed., 109 Eagle Cr., Nahaimo, BC, V9S 2ST, Canada. Box 2935, Station D, Ottawa, Ont. K1P 5WP, Canada. Q; $20 (indiv.); $30 (inst.); 1976; circ. 300. *Indexed*: Avery. *Notes*: adv., bibl., bk. rev., dwgs., photos (B&W).

Examines Canadian architecture and the historical and cultural influences that shape it. Also discusses contemporary issues affecting buildings, towns, and the countryside. Pro'' 'es members with information on research in progress, current books, employment opportunities, and activities across the country regarding the built environment. Acts as a forum for members to exchange information and present regional viewpoints. Subscribers include practicing architects, architectural historians, conservationists, planners, geographers, librarians, and archivists. Newsletter format. Text in French and English. (0228-0074)

0174   SOUTH AFRICAN   (SA)
       ARCHITECTURAL RECORD
Inst. of South African Architects, Sheila Baille & Assoc., 75 Howard House, Loveday St., Johannesburg, South Africa. M; 1915. +

0175   SOUTH AUSTRALIAN INST.   (AT)
       OF ARCHITECTS' MONTHLY
       BULLETIN
Royal Australian Inst. of Architects (S.A. chapter), Commercial Publications of S.A. Pty. Ltd., 86 Franklin St., Adelaide 5000, Australia. Ed. R.L. Noble. M; 1945. (0038-2922) +

0176   SPACE/KONGGAN   (KO)
Space Group of Korea, 219 Wonso-dong, Chongroku, Seoul 110, S. Korea. Ed. Swoo Geun. M; 1966. +

0177   SPACE DESIGN   (JA)
Kajima Inst. Publishing Co., Ltd., 5-13 Akasaka 6-chome, Minato-ku, Tokyo 107, Japan. Ed. Kobun Ito. Tel. (03) 589-2928. M; Yen 30,000; 1965; circ. 35,000. *Indexed*: A.P.I., Avery, Dec. issue (in Japanese). *Annual Issues*: Dec.—Review of Major Japanese Work. *Notes*: adv., bk. rev., dwgs., photos (B&W, color).

An international review of current and historic architecture and design, with emphasis on the work of Japanese designers. In addition to the main feature, each issue includes a critical essay, a photographic essay of an outstanding historical site, a lengthy book review, and notes on a specific theme compiled from foreign architectural magazines. Text in Japanese; table of contents and summaries in English.

0206   SPAZIO E SOCIETA/SPACE AND SOCIETY

0178   STADT   (GW)
Jessenstrasse 1, D-2000 Hamburg 50, W. Germany. Kurfurstendamm 188-189, D-1000 Berlin 15, W. Germany. Ed. Manfred Burchardt. Tel. (040) 380-17-820. Q; DM. 52; 1954. *Indexed*: Avery. *Notes*: adv., bk. rev., dwgs., photos (B&W, color).

An outstanding international review of the design of urban centers with an emphasis on the redevelopment of German cities. The city is discussed in a historical, geographical, and social context. New projects are described in depth, with many photographs of models, plans, renderings, construction, and completed buildings. Highly recommended for planners and architects in practice, research, or teaching. Text in German. (0722-8352)

0179   SUMMA   (AG)
Ediciones Summa, Peru 718 PB, 1068 Buenos Aires, Argentina. Ed. Lala Mendez Mosquera. Tel. 362-5801. M; $159; 1963; circ. 10,000. *Indexed*: A.P.I. *Notes*: adv., bibl., dwgs., photos (B&W).

A survey of the current architecture of Latin America but primarily of Argentina. Includes some news of professional practice and the construction industry. Text in Spanish. (0325-4615)

0180   T.A.   (SP)
Miguel Duran-Loriga, Francisco Suarez 16, Madrid 16, Spain. M; 1958. +

0181   TECHNIQUES ET ARCHITECTURE   (FR)
380 F. Societe des Editions Regirex-France, 62 rue Ampere, 75017 Paris, France. Ed. Max Blumenthal. Tel. 267-43-13. Bi-m; 1942; circ. 14,323. *Indexed*: A.P.I., Avery, Dec./Jan. issue. *Notes*: adv., bk. rev., dwgs., photos (B&W, color).

Publication is international in scope but the emphasis is on the work of French designers and engineers. Each issue gives in-depth coverage of a specific topic such as office design or architecture in developing countries. News briefs on general building topics are included. Text in French; summaries in English and Spanish. (0373-0719)

0182   THIRTIES SOCIETY JOURNAL   (UK)
3 Park Square W., London NW1, England. Ed. Dr. Gavin Stamp. A; £6; 1980; circ. 1,000. *Indexed*: A.P.I. *Notes*: adv., dwgs., photos (B&W, color).

Scholarly illustrated articles on British architecture and design after 1914. +

0183   TRACE: A CANADIAN REVIEW OF ARCHITECTURE   (CN)
Suite 330, 144 Front St. W., Toronto, Ont. M5J 2L7, Canada. Q; 1981. *Indexed*: Avery. +

0207   TRANSACTIONS

0184   TRANSACTIONS OF THE ARCHITECTURAL INSTITUTE OF JAPAN   (JA)
Architectural Inst. of Japan, 26-20 5-chome Shiba, Minato-ku, Tokyo, Japan. *Notes*: dwgs., photos (B&W).

Technical and design coverage of Japanese architecture. Text in Japanese; contents page and summaries in English. (0387-1185)

0185   U.I.A.—INTERNATIONAL ARCHITECT   (UK)
(Formerly: *International Architect*)
International Architect Publishing Co., Box 85, 36 Bedford Sq., London W1B 3EH, England. Ed. Haig Beck. Tel. (01) 986-5849. Bi-m; $48; 1979; circ. 6,000. *Indexed*: A.P.I., Avery. *Notes*: bk. rev., dwgs., photos (B&W, color).

An international review of architectural projects, theory, practice, and criticism. Certain issues are devoted to the architecture of a particular country or architect. One of the most highly regarded architectural journals.

0186   ULSTER ARCHITECT   (UK)
12 Mount Charles, Belfast BT7 IN2, N. Ireland. Ed. Anne Davey Orr. Tel. (0232) 247427. 10/yr.; £10; circ. 3,200. *Notes*: adv., bibl., bk. rev., calendars, dwgs., photos (B&W, color).
Journal of architecture and building in Northern Ireland. Emphasis is on practical, professional, and technical information rather than design. Extensive coverage of products and techniques. News of new projects, legislation, and conferences.

0853   URBIS

0187   VISION   (HK)
Vision Press, Ltd., 41F Block A5, Hay Wah Bldg., 71-85 Hennessy Rd., Hong Kong. Ed. Julia Fong. Tel. 5-202-733. M; $75; 1983. *Notes*: adv., dwgs., photos (B&W, color).
A glossy, well-illustrated magazine covering architecture, planning, and design in Hong Kong. Management and legal topics as well as world architectural news briefs are included.

0188   WERK/ARCHITHESE   (SZ)
Federation Suisse des Architects Independents, Zollikofer AG, Fuerstenlandstr. 122, CH-9001 St. Gallen, Switzerland. 10/yr.; 1977. *Indexed*: A.P.I., Art Ind., Avery. +

0189   WERK, BAUEN UND   (SZ)
        WOHNEN
(Formerly: *Bauen und Wohnen*)
Verlag Bauen + Wohnen GmbH, Vogelsangstr. 48, Postfach 8033, Zurich, Switzerland. Zollikofer AG, Furstenlandstr. 122, 9001 St. Gallen, Switzerland. Tel. 362-95-66. M; Fr.125; 1933; circ. 16,000. *Indexed*: A.P.I., Art Ind. *Notes*: adv., bibl., bk. rev., calendars, dwgs., photos (B&W, color).
Text in German; summaries in English and French. *

0190   WERK UND ZEIT   (GW)
Lyckallee 10, 1 Berlin 19, W. Germany. Deutscher Werkbund E.V., Alexandraweg 26, 6100 Darmstadt, W. Germany. Ed. Gina Koehler. Tel. 06151-46434. Q; DM. 36; 1977; circ. 3,500. *Notes*: adv., bibl., bk. rev., calendars, dwgs., photos (B&W).

Each issue critically analyzes a theme related to architecture, design, town and country planning, or aesthetics. Concerned with social issues in architecture. Text in German. (0049-7150)

0191   WOMEN IN DESIGN   (US)
        INTERNATIONAL
P.O. Box 984, Ross, CA 94957. Tel. (415) 457-8596. Q. +

0192   WONEN-TABK   (NE)
Leidsestraat 5, 1017 NS Amsterdam, Netherlands. Libresso b.v., Postbus 23, 7400 GA Deuenter, Netherlands. Ed. Hans van Dijk. Tel. 010-234188. Bi-w; fl.162.25; 1973; circ. 6,500. *Indexed*: A.P.I., Avery. *Notes*: adv., bibl., bk. rev., dwgs., photos (B&W, color).
A journal devoted to architecture, urbanism, and the visual arts in many countries. Articles appear on theory, history, planning, social housing, and landscape architecture. The editorial emphasis is on design. Of interest to academic and practicing professionals. Text in Dutch. (0165-3504)

0193   WORLD ARCHITECTURE   (CC)
Quingha University, Main Bldg. 8th fl., Beijing, China. Ed. Lu Zengbiao. Tel. 282451-2923. M. *Notes*: adv., dwgs., photos (B&W, color).
Each issue reports on architectural and design trends worldwide. Well illustrated with many photographs and clearly readable drawings. Articles trace the origins and development of architecture in various countries and examine a wide range of building types by the most noted architects in each country. Text in Chinese; summaries and titles in English.

0194   YORKSHIRE ARCHITECT   (UK)
Paull & Goode Publishing Ltd., 4-6 Lombard St., Newcastle-upon-Tyne, England. Bi-m; 1968. *Indexed*: A.P.I. (0044-0582) +

0195   Z.E.D./ZIMBABWE   (RH)
        ENVIRONMENT AND
        DESIGN
Box 3592, Harare, Zimbabwe. Ed. Bd. S-a. *Notes*: adv., bk. rev., dwgs., photos (B&W).
The official journal of the Institute of Architects of Zimbabwe and the Zimbabwe Institute of Regional and Urban Planners. Covers problems of practice, issues in design education, and current projects in Zimbabwe. Includes profiles of design offices in each issue.

0780   ZYGOS

Theory and Criticism

0004   AA FILES: ANNALS OF THE
       ARCHITECTURAL
       ASSOCIATION SCHOOL OF
       ARCHITECTURE

0196   ABACUS   (FI)
Museum of Finnish Architecture, Helsinki, Finland. A. *Indexed*: Avery. *Notes*: dwgs.; photos (B&W).
   A yearbook of architectural articles on various critical and historical themes, sometimes based on lectures. The only critical and historical review of Finnish architecture. Text in English and Finnish. (0357-7465)

0217   ACROSS ARCHITECTURE

0197   ARCHIVES   (BE)
       D'ARCHITECTURE
       MODERNE
M. Culot, 6 rue Paul Spaak, 1050 Brussels, Belgium. 14 rue Defacqz, 1050 Brussels, Belgium. Ed. M. Culot. Tel. 537-87-45. A; Fr. 1,600; 1958. *Indexed*: A.P.I., Avery. *Notes*: adv., bk. rev., dwgs., photos (B&W, color).
   Among the most respected critical journals in architecture. The Archives, an organization dedicated to the conservation of architectural documents, presents the work of prominent former and current architects from the western world. Each issue is devoted to a specific theme such as rationalism or public spaces. Leon Krier is among the distinguished contributors. Text in French or English.

0007   ARQ ARCHITECTURE/
       QUEBEC

0223   CRIT

0198   DAIDALOS: BERLIN   (GW)
       ARCHITECTURAL JOURNAL
Bertelsmann Fachzeitschriften GmbH, Schluterstrasse 42, D1000 Berlin 15, W. Germany. Ed. Anna Teut. Tel. (030) 8812045. Q; $70; 1981. *Indexed*: A.P.I., R.I.L.A. *Notes*: adv., dwgs., photos (B&W, color).
   An architectural critical journal that concentrates on sociological and historical themes. Text in German and English. (0721-4235)

0199   DESIGN BOOK REVIEW   (US)
1418 Spring Way, Berkeley, CA 94708. Ed. Bd. Q; $15 (indiv.); $18 (inst.); $22 (abroad); 1983. *Indexed*: Spring issue. *Notes*: adv., photos (B&W).
   In-depth criticisms of current design literature are written by professors, practicing architects, historians, and other qualified reviewers. Reviews are arranged according to themes such as history, contemporary design, regional and vernacular architecture, interior design and the decorative arts, landscape design, cities, and the profession. Only English-language books are reviewed, but the scope is international. All articles are signed and have full bibliographic documentation. (0737-5344)

0200   DESIGN STUDIES   (UK)
Box 63, Westbury House, Bury St., Guilford Surrey GU2 5BH, England. Butterworth Scientific Ltd., Oakfield House, Perry Mount Rd., Haywards Heath, Sussex RH16 3DH, England. Ed. Joanna Wexler. Tel. (0483) 31261. Q; $164; 1979. *Indexed*: A.P.I., Avery. *Notes*: adv., bk. rev., photos (B&W).
   This scholarly journal published in cooperation with the Design Research Society provides a forum for developing a common understanding of design. Design is discussed in relation to buildings, plans, furniture, and engineering applications. Covers such topics as design theory and design teamwork. Encourages interdisciplinary discussions. (0142-694x)

0201   EUPALINO   (IT)
Via Gregoriana 25, Rome, Italy. L'Erma di Bretschneider, via Cassiodoro 19, 00193 Rome, Italy. Ed. Paolo Portoghesi. Q; L. 100,000; 1984; circ. 7,000. *Indexed*: Avery. *Notes*: adv., dwgs., photos (B&W, color).
   One of the most readable and attractive critical journals in print. This new quarterly presents a series of dialogues on topics in architecture and the design of cities. Distinctive for its large format with tinted lithographs. Text in Italian, English, and French.

0224   FIFTH COLUMN

0226   HARVARD ARCHITECTURE
       REVIEW

0134   LOTUS INTERNATIONAL

0202   MODULUS   (US)
University of Virginia, School of Architecture, Charlottesville, VA 22903. A; $14; 1965. *In-*

dexed: Avery. *Notes*: dwgs., photos (B&W, color).

A journal of original discussion, design, and analysis. Although published by students, contributors include professors and practicing professionals. (0191-4022)

0203 9H   (UK)
3 Mall Studios, Tasker Rd., London NW3 2YS, England. Ed. Wilfried Wang. Bi-a; £8.50 (indiv.); £17 (inst.); 1980. *Notes*: adv., bibl., bk. rev., dwgs., photos (B&W).

An architectural magazine that publishes translations, criticisms, and projects from around the world. (0144-7726) +

0204 PARACHUTE   (CN)
4060 Blvd. St.-Laurent, Bureau 501, Montreal, Quebec H2W 1Y9, Canada. Bernard De Boer, Inc., 113 E. Centre St., Nutley, NJ 07110. Ed. Chantal Pontbriand. Q; $36; 1977. *Indexed*: Art Bib. *Notes*: adv., bibl., bk. rev., dwgs., photos (B&W).

Essays and criticism of contemporary art and architecture. Text in French and English. (0318-7020)

**0233 PERSPECTA; YALE
       ARCHITECTURAL JOURNAL**

0826 PLACES

0235 PRECIS

0205 PRINCETON JOURNAL   (US)
School of Architecture, Princeton University, Princeton, NJ 08544. Princeton Architectural Press, 40 Witherspoon St., Princeton, NJ 08540. Tel. (609) 924-7911. A; $15; 1983. *Indexed*: Avery. *Notes*: dwgs., photos (B&W, color).

Thematic studies in architecture. The first volume presented essays on the contemporary association of ritual and architecture. The second volume was devoted to landscape design. (0741-1774)

0237 REFLECTIONS

0206 SPAZIO E SOCIETA/SPACE   (IT)
       AND SOCIETY
Via Mascheroni 18, 20145 Milan, Italy. (U.S. sub.) MIT Press Journals, 28 Carlton St., Cambridge, MA 02142. Ed. Giancarlo de Carlo. Tel. (02) 435582. Q; $35 (indiv.); $56 (inst.); 1976; circ. 3,500. *Indexed*: Avery. *Notes*: adv., bk. rev., dwgs., photos (B&W, color).

International journal of architecture and environmental design. Its editorial policy is "to include projects and buildings in continuity with theoretical studies, commentary, conjecture and documentation. The goal is to generate processes rather than to confine itself to the display of objects." Readership includes anyone with an interest in the built environment and the relationship between space and society. Text in Italian and English. (0392-4947)

0207 TRANSACTIONS   (UK)
R.I.B.A. Magazines, Ltd., 66 Portland Place, London W1N 4AD, England. Ed. Peter Murray. S-a; 1982. *Indexed*: A.P.I., Avery. *Notes*: dwgs., photos (B&W, color).

Presents a series of popular and intellectual lectures given at the Royal Institute of British Architects. Topics range from aesthetics to practical professional issues. Contains the accessions list of the British Architectural Library. (0263-2152)

0208 TRANSITION: DISCOURSE   (AT)
       ON ARCHITECTURE
22 Alma Rd., St. Kilda, Victoria 3182, Australia. P.O. Box 179, Collingwood, Victoria 3066, Australia. Ed. Ian McDougall. Tel. (03) 534-5922. Q; $23. *Indexed*: A.P.I., Avery. *Notes*: bk. rev., dwgs., photos (B&W).

An international critical publication that contains interviews, essays, letters, and reviews on architecture. Utilizes innovative graphics. (0157-7344)

0209 TRANSPARENT   (AU)
Guenther Feurstein, Wiedner Haupstr. 40, A-1040 Vienna, Austria. Ed. Guenther Fuerstein. Tel. 57-73-07. Bi-m; $25; 1970; circ. 1,000. *Indexed*: Avery. *Notes*: adv., bk. rev., dwgs., photos (B&W).

Essays on theories, critiques of exhibitions, and competitions. Scope is international. Text in German. (0041-1302)

**0242 TULANE ARCHITECTURAL
       VIEW**

**0185 U.I.A.—INTERNATIONAL
       ARCHITECT**

0210 UMRISS   (AU)
Institut fur Informationsentwicklung, Grunagergasse 1, A-1010 Vienna, Austria. Ed. Peter Noever. Tel. (0222) 532207. S.600; 1983. *Notes*: adv., bk. rev., photos (B&W).

Conveys opinions of students and professors in Viennese schools of architecture and reports on architectural developments in the Third World. Includes interviews. Text in German; summaries in English.

0244 VIA

Research

0909 BUILDING AND ENVIRONMENT

0327 CONSTRUCTION MANAGEMENT AND ECONOMICS

0211 DESIGN METHODS AND   (US) THEORIES
(Formerly: *DMG Newsletter*)
Donald P. Grant, Box 5, San Luis Obispo, CA 93406. Ed. Donald P. Grant. Q; $24; 1966; circ. 1,000. *Indexed*: A.P.I., 4th-quarter issue. *Notes*: adv., bibl., bk. rev., calendars, dwgs.

Articles on the education and communication of design methodology and applied design methods. Presents original research and bibliographies. (0147-1147)

0212 E.A.R./EDINBURGH   (UK) ARCHITECTURAL RESEARCH
University of Edinburgh, Dept. of Architecture, 20 Chambers St., Edinburgh EH1 1JZ, Scotland. Tel. 031-667-1011. Telex 727442. A; £2; 1973; circ. 250. *Indexed*: A.P.I., Avery. *Notes*: dwgs., photos (B&W).

Consists primarily of working papers on research in progress by staff and architecture students of the university. (0140-5039)

0213 ENVIRONMENT AND   (US) BEHAVIOR
Dept. of Psychology, University of Arizona, Tucson, AZ 85721. Sage Publications, 275 South Beverly Dr., Beverly Hills, CA 90212. Ed. Robert Bechtel. Tel. (602) 621-7430. Bi-m; $28; 1969. *Indexed*: Avery, Psychol. Abstr. *Notes*: adv., bibl., bk. rev., calendars, dwgs., photos (B&W). *Micro*: UMI.

Presents interdisciplinary studies on the behavioral response to the environment. Studies include: theoretical work, methodological papers, reports on research related to evaluation of environments designed to accomplish specific objectives, and attitudinal research. (0013-9165)

0214 JOURNAL OF   (US) ARCHITECTURAL AND PLANNING RESEARCH
(Formerly: *Journal of Architectural Research*)
Inst. of Urban Studies, P.O. Box 19588, Univ. of Texas, Arlington, TX 76019. Elsevier Science Publishing Co., 52 Vanderbilt Ave., New York, NY 10017. Ed. Andrew Seidel. Q; $40 (indiv.); $65 (inst.); 1984. *Indexed*: A.P.I., Avery, P.A.I.S. *Notes*: adv., bk. rev., dwgs., photos (B&W).

A new journal that provides interdisciplinary coverage of architectural and urban planning research and design. Original papers present findings and report innovative practices in such fields as architectural technology, environmental behavior, design programming, energy, site planning, topology, and computer applications. This unique publication links theoretical and practical information for both researchers and practicing professionals. (0738-0895)

0215 JOURNAL OF   (UK) ENVIRONMENTAL PSYCHOLOGY
University of Surrey, Guildford, Surrey GU2 5HX, England. Academic Press, Inc., 24-28 Oval Rd., London NW1 7DX, England. Ed. David V. Canter. Tel. 0483-71281. Q; $86; 1981. *Indexed*: A.P.I. *Notes*: bibl., bk. rev., dwgs., photos (B&W).

A multidisciplinary research journal that analyzes the transactions and interrelationships between people and their sociophysical surroundings. Emphasis is on sociological aspects of the environment. Includes in-depth book reviews. (0272-4944)

Student Publications and Architectural Education

0216 ACSA NEWS   (US)
Assn. of Collegiate Schools of Architecture, Inc., 1735 New York Ave., N.W., Washington, DC 20006. Ed. Ellen K. Showen. Tel. (202) 785-2324. 7/yr.; free to members; 1969; circ. 3,800. *Notes*: adv., bk. rev., dwgs., photos (B&W). *Micro*: UMI.

A newsletter for individuals involved with architectural education. Contains news briefs on people, exhibitions, seminars, and curricula. Includes calls for papers and announcements of faculty openings. (0149-2446)

0217 ACROSS ARCHITECTURE (UK)
Architectural Assn. School of Architecture, 36 Bedford Sq., London WC1, England. Ed. Dimitri Vannas. Tel. (01) 636-0974. Irreg.; £2.50 ea.; 1984. *Notes*: dwgs., photos (B&W).

This lively new publication produced entirely by the students of the Architectural Association serves as a platform for presenting the work of students from many schools and related disciplines. Its purpose is to stimulate creativity and encourage dialogue among students, teachers, and practicing architects. It does not reflect the opinions of the AA but rather attempts to challenge them by presenting "rough sketches, partial schemes and ideas in the raw."

0218 ARCHIMAGE (US)
University of Wisconsin, School of Architecture, P.O. Box 413, Milwaukee, WI 53201. Tel. (414) 963-4014. Bi-m; $3.60; 1982; circ. 100. *Indexed*: Avery. *Notes*: adv., bibl., bk. rev., calendars, dwgs., photos (B&W).

Architectural topics discussed by students and faculty.

**0219 ARCHITECTURE AND (US)
         PLANNING**
Graduate School of Architecture and Planning, UCLA, 405 Hilgard, Los Angeles, CA 90024. Ed. Chuck Halloran. Tel. (213) 206-0696. S-a. *Indexed*: Avery. *Notes*: dwgs., photos (B&W).

Presents the projects and activities of the schools, professors, alumni, and current students.

0220 BUILT (US)
Modern Guise, Graduate School of Architecture, Univ. of California, Los Angeles, CA 90024. Ed. David Rapp. Tel. (213) 825-3457. A; $2.50 ea.; 1978; circ. 400. *Indexed*: Avery. *Notes*: bk. rev., dwgs., photos (B&W).

Exploration of current architectural issues and historical analysis. (0731-6402) *

**0221 CENTRAL PAPERS ON (US)
         ARCHITECTURE**
University of Cincinnati, School of Design, Cincinnati, OH. 1980. *Indexed*: Avery. +

**0250 CITE: AN ARCHITECTURE
         AND DESIGN REVIEW OF
         HOUSTON**

**0222 CORNELL JOURNAL OF (US)
         ARCHITECTURE**
Dept. of Architecture, Cornell University, Ithaca, NY 14853. Rizzoli Publications, 712 Fifth Ave., New York, NY 10019. A; $20; 1981. *Notes*: dwgs., photos (B&W).

Focuses on the past and present work of students at Cornell.

0223 CRIT (US)
(Formerly: *Telesis*)
American Inst. of Architects., Assn. of Student Chapters, 1735 New York Ave., NW, Washington, DC 20006. Ed. Laura Todd. Tel. (202) 626-7472. S-a; $6; 1976; circ. 13,000. *Indexed*: A.P.I., Avery. *Notes*: adv., bibl., bk. rev., dwgs., photos (B&W, color).

Includes news and essays on current issues in architecture and architectural education in the U.S. Articles by students. (0277-6863)

0224 FIFTH COLUMN (CN)
Royal Architectural Inst. of Canada, Canadian Students of Architecture, 3480 University St., Ste. 13, Montreal, Que. H3A 2A7, Canada. Tel. (514) 392-5409. Q; Can.$15; 1980; circ. 1,000. *Indexed*: A.P.I., Avery. *Notes*: adv., bk. rev., dwgs., photos (B&W).

One of the most interesting critical journals examined. Challenging issues from Canadian universities are presented. Covers theory, history, and criticism. Text in English and French. (0229-7094)

0225 GSD NEWS (US)
Harvard University, Graduate School of Design, Gund Hall, 48 Quincy St., Cambridge, MA 02138. Ed. Yvonne Chabrier. 5/yr.; free; 1973; circ. 10,500. *Indexed*: Avery. *Notes*: adv., bk. rev., dwgs., photos (B&W).

News of current students, faculty, and alumni. (0193-6107)

**0226 HARVARD ARCHITECTURE (US)
         REVIEW**
Harvard University, Gund Hall, 48 Quincy St., #301, Cambridge, MA 02138. Journals Dept., M.I.T. Press, 28 Carlton St., Cambridge, MA 02142. Tel. (617) 495-2591. A; $30 (indiv.); $40 (inst.); 1980. *Indexed*: A.P.I., Art Ind., Avery. *Notes*: bk. rev., dwgs., photos (B&W, color).

Scholarly articles focus on one specific theme per issue. Scope is international. Includes detailed documentation of selected new projects. (0194-3650)

**0227 JOURNAL OF (US)
         ARCHITECTURAL
         EDUCATION**
Assn. of Collegiate Schools of Architecture, Inc., 1735 New York Ave., N.W., Washington,

DC 20006. Ed. Peter C. Papademetriou. Tel. (202) 785-2324. Q; $30; 1947; circ. 4,000. *Indexed*: A.P.I., Arch. Ind., Art Ind., Avery. *Notes*: bk. rev., dwgs., photos (B&W). *Micro*: UMI.

This journal presents articles on design education and student projects in the U.S. and Canada. (0149-2993)

0228   JOURNAL OF   (US)
ENVIRONMENTAL
EDUCATION
Heldref Publications, 4000 Albemarle St., NW, Washington, DC 20016. Ed. Susan Fauls. Tel. (202) 362-6445. Q; $35; 1969; circ. 995. *Indexed*: Avery. *Notes*: adv., bibl. *Micro*: BLH, UMI.

A journal that assists communicators and educators in motivating people of all ages to play a more responsible role in shaping their habitats. Includes case studies, research reports, and reports dealing with behavior patterns, values, attitudes, public policy, and philosophy of environmental education. Edited for teachers on all levels as well as for education specialists in museums, zoos, parks, camps, etc. and specialists in adult and nontraditional education programs. Text in English; summaries in French and Spanish. (0095-8964)

0229   MASS   (US)
Albuquerque School of Architecture and Planning, University of New Mexico, Albuquerque, NM 87106. Q; 1983. *Indexed*: Avery. +

0202   MODULUS

0230   MONTANA STATE   (US)
ARCHITECTURAL REVIEW
School of Architecture, Montana State University, Bozeman, MT 59715. Ed. Christian Bergum. Tel. (406) 994-4670. A; $3; 1982; circ. 1,000. *Notes*: dwgs., photos (B&W).

A student publication that reflects current design and design theory. Article submissions are reviewed mid-February each year. (0741-6849) *

0231   NORTH CAROLINA STATE   (US)
UNIVERSITY: THE STUDENT
PUBLICATION OF THE
SCHOOL OF DESIGN
North Carolina State University, Raleigh, NC 27650. Tel. (919) 737-2200. *Indexed*: A.P.I., Avery. +

0232   NOTRE DAME   (US)
ARCHITECTURE REVIEW
University of Notre Dame, School of Architecture, Notre Dame, IN 46556. Ed. Robert Amico. (219) 239-6137. Irreg.; $3 per issue; 1982; circ. 2,000. *Indexed*: Avery.

A publication of student projects selected from design studies. It is intended as a reference tool as well as documentation of the architectural program.

0233   PERSPECTA; YALE   (US)
ARCHITECTURAL JOURNAL
P.O. Box 2121, Yale Station, New Haven, CT 06520. Journals Dept., M.I.T. Press, 28 Carlton St., Cambridge, MA 02142. Tel. (203) 436-2131. A; $30 (indiv.); $40 (inst.); 1963. *Indexed*: A.P.I., Art Ind., Avery. *Notes*: dwgs., photos (B&W).

The oldest and most prestigious of the collegiate journals. Contains criticism, analysis, and theory of historic and modern themes. (0079-0958)

0234   POLITECHNICO DI TORINO   (IT)
Politechnico di Torino, Instituto de Scienza dei Sistemi Architettonici e Territoriali della Facolta de Architettura Studi e Ricerche. Giardini Editori e Stampatori, via Santa Bibbiana 28, 56100 Pisa, Italy. 3/yr. +

0235   PRECIS   (US)
Columbia University, Graduate School of Architecture and Planning, New York, NY 10027. A; $12; 1979. *Notes*: dwgs.

A summary of student and faculty work from the previous academic year. Projects primarily reflect the character of the school but sometimes present diverse opinions centering around a theme.

0205   PRINCETON JOURNAL

0236   RE:CAP   (US)
College of Architecture and Planning, Ball State University, Muncie, IN 47306. Tel. (317) 285-5859. 3/yr.; free; 1970; circ. 3,500. *Notes*: calendars, dwgs., photos (B&W).

Articles include profiles of students, alumni, and faculty; new research, study programs in architecture, landscape architecture, urban studies, and planning.

0237   REFLECTIONS   (US)
University of Illinois at Urbana-Champaign, School of Architecture, 608 E. Loredo Taft Dr.,

Champaign, IL 61820. Ed. Michael J. Andreja-sich. Tel. (217) 333-1992. A; $18; 1983; circ. 1,100. *Indexed*: Avery. *Notes*: bk. rev., dwgs., photos (B&W).

A substantial journal of theory and criticism primarily representing works produced by the School of Architecture faculty. Its purpose is to stimulate intellectual exchange among students, faculty, and the public. Essays give space to thoughts on architecture's relation to other disciplines. (0739-9448)

0238   SEMESTER REVIEW   (US)
Clemson Architectural Foundation, Clemson, SC 29631. 1983. *Indexed*: Avery. (0009-871x) +

0239   SEQUENCE   (US)
University of North Carolina, College of Architecture, Charlotte, NC 28223. +

0240   THRESHOLD   (US)
University of Illinois at Chicago, School of Architecture, Chicago, IL 60680. Rizzoli Books, 712 Fifth Ave., New York, NY. A; 1982. *Indexed*: Avery. +

0241   TRIGLYPH   (US)
College of Architecture and Environmental Design, Arizona State University, Tempe, AZ 85281. Ed. Marcus Whiffen. Tel. (602) 965-7171. S-a; $15; 1984; circ. 1,000. *Indexed*: Avery. *Notes*: bk. rev., dwgs., photos (B&W, color).

A journal of architecture, planning, and industrial and interior design with emphasis on the southwestern U.S. *

0242   TULANE ARCHITECTURAL   (US)
         VIEW
School of Architecture, Tulane University, New Orleans, LA 70118. Irreg. *Indexed*: Avery. *Notes*: bibl., dwgs., photos (B&W).

Contains essays and criticisms on architecture and urban design. Papers are contributed by professors and students from a wide range of fields, including physics, philosophy, and political science as well as architecture.

0243   UNIVERSITY OF   (US)
         TENNESSEE JOURNAL OF
         ARCHITECTURE
(Formerly: *Portfolio*)
University of Tennessee, School of Architecture, Knoxville, TN 37996. Tel. (615) 974-5276. A; $10; 1982. *Indexed*: Avery. *Notes*: adv., bibl., bk. rev., dwgs., photos (B&W, color).

An intellectual journal that discusses and debates current architectural issues relating to

buildings, urban design, planning, and theory. Edited by students. +

0244   VIA   (US)
University of Pennsylvania, Dept. of Architecture, Graduate School of Fine Arts, Philadelphia, PA 19104. M.I.T. Press, 28 Carlton St., Cambridge, MA 02142. Tel. (215) 898-5728. A; $30 (indiv.); $40 (inst.); 1975. *Indexed*: A.P.I., Avery. *Notes*: bibl., dwgs., photos (B&W).

Critical journal of high quality edited by graduate students. Thematic content varies from year to year. (0506-8346)

Regional Architecture and Building Publications

0245   ALABAMA BUILDER   (US)
P.O. Box 17361, Louisville, KY 40217. Home Builders Assn. of Alabama, Box 827, Montgomery, Alabama 36102. Ed. Bob Lanham. Tel. (502) 636-3593. M; 1958. *Notes*: adv. +

0246   AVENUE MAGAZINE   (US)
145 E. 57th St., New York, NY 10022. Ed. Michael Schnayerson. Tel. (212) 758-9517. M; $50. *Notes*: adv., photos (B&W).

A glossy magazine devoted to news of interest to people living on the luxurious Upper East Side of Manhattan, particularly Park Avenue. Although it consists primarily of advertising, there is an interesting monthly section of photos and an article on the historic homes of the district. Early photos are shown, with notes on the original owners and architects. In addition, there are frequent features on interiors of apartments or offices of local executives or celebrities. (0279-1226)

0247   BUILDING INDUSTRY   (US)
         DIGEST OF HAWAII
Trade Publishing Co., 287 Mokauea St., Honolulu, HI 96819. Ed. John Black. Tel. (808) 848-0711. M; $25; 1954; circ. 3,000. *Notes*: adv., photos (B&W, color).

A building magazine that serves all segments of the design, construction, and development professions in Hawaii. Features discuss construction disputes, computers, safety, etc. Regular columns on financing, local politics, and work "on the boards."

0248   CALIFORNIA BUILDER   (US)
Fellom Publications, 693 Mission St., Penthouse, San Francisco, CA 94105. Ed. Thor Nyman. Tel. (415) 781-1431. Bi-m; $12; 1959; circ. 8,000. *Notes*: adv., photos (B&W). *Annual*

Issues: May or June—Pacific Coast Builders Convention Issue.

Presents industry news of local interest to builders and contractors engaged in the construction of single homes, multifamily housing, light and commercial buildings, shopping centers, and motels. *

**0249 CALIFORNIA BUILDER AND (US)
ENGINEER**
California Builder and Engineer, Inc., Box 10070, 4110 Transport, Palo Alto, CA 94303. Ed. Cole N. Danehower. Bi-m; $15; 1893. *Notes*: adv., bk. rev., dwgs. (0045-3900) +

**0250 CITE: AN ARCHITECTURE (US)
AND DESIGN REVIEW OF
HOUSTON**
Rice Design Alliance, William Marsh Rice University, P.O. Box 1892, Houston, TX 77251. Ed. John Kaliski. Tel. (713) 524-6297. Q; $8; 1982; circ. 11,500. *Notes*: adv., bibl., bk. rev., dwgs., photos (B&W).

A refreshing quarterly that contains news reports and illustrated features on new buildings and urban development in Houston and Harris County. In addition, there are regular extensive reviews of books, exhibitions, and lectures on design-related topics. Focus is on current issues. Articles are written by professors, practicing architects, and freelance writers. Of interest to architects and the general Houston public in addition to the local academic architectural community.

**0251 CONNECTICUT (US)
CONSTRUCTION**
P.O. Box 9768, Wethersfield, CT 06109. Ed. David Benford. Tel. (203) 529-3246. Bi-m; $18; 1962; circ. 4,500. *Annual Issues*: March/April— State and Highway Equipment. *Notes*: adv., bibl., bk. rev., calendars, dwgs., photos (B&W, color).

Articles are of interest to everyone involved in public and private construction in Connecticut and Southern New England. *

0252 DESIGN ACTION (US)
Architectural Arts of Washington, DC, Pension Bldg., National Bldg. Museum, Room 122, 440 G St., N.W., Washington, DC 20001. Ed. Richard Etlin. Tel. (202) 737-8582. Bi-m; $12. *Notes*: bk. rev., dwgs., photos (B&W).

Signed, illustrated articles discuss architecture and design in the Mid-Atlantic states but primarily in Washington, D.C. Proposed, newly constructed, and historic projects are reviewed,

including feature articles on architects of the region. A good source for information on federal buildings. (0734-4538)

0253 FLORIDA BUILDER (US)
Peninsula Publishing Co., 3300 Henderson Blvd., Ste. 105, Tampa, FL 33609. Ed. Joan Antoine. Tel. (813) 870-2445. M; $9 (US only); 1946; circ. 9,000. *Annual Issues*: Feb.—Annual Products Directory. *Notes*: adv., bibl., bk. rev., calendars, dwgs., photos (B&W, color).

Covers residential and commercial structures in Florida. Articles cover technological developments, construction reports, financial news, new products, and trends. (0015-3923) *

**0254 FLORIDA CONSTRUCTION (US)
INDUSTRY**
I.M. Marketing Group, P.O. Drawer 520, Orlando, FL 32751. Ed. Gustav Berle. Tel. (305) 671-6457. Bi-m; $6 (US); $12 (abroad); 1945; circ. 12,000. *Notes*: adv., bk. rev., calendars, dwgs., photos (B&W).

Florida building business news. Reports permits, new products, and building activities. (0192-3501) *

0255 INLAND ARCHITECT (US)
Inland Architect Press, Box 10394, Chicago, IL 60610. Ed. Cynthia C. Davidson-Powers. Tel. (312) 321-0583. Bi-m; $15; 1957; circ. 6,000. *Indexed*: A.P.I., Avery. *Notes*: adv., bk. rev., calendars, dwgs., photos (B&W, color). *Micro*: UMI.

A magazine covering all aspects of architecture in the Midwest or by midwesterners. Lengthy features discuss specific projects in various cities. Also included are notes on Midwestern architects and a column on historic topics. (0020-1472)

**0256 JOURNAL OF DESIGN AND (US)
CONSTRUCTION**
Midwest Advertising Service, 3501 Skyline Dr., Des Moines, IA 50310. Ed. Kirk von Blunk. Tel. (515) 277-1881. Bi-m; $15; 1983; circ. 6,500. *Indexed*: March/April issue. *Notes*: adv., bibl., bk. rev., calendars, dwgs., photos (B&W, color).

Thematic issues on midwestern architecture, building products, and building techniques, primarily in Iowa. In addition to case studies that analyze the use or installation of a product, there are articles on professional practice. The issue examined covered exterior finishes, including glass-fiber reinforced concrete and brick-tile veneer. Intended for a midwestern professional audience but includes articles of general interest.

0257   LIVABLE CITY   (US)
Municipal Art Society, 457 Madison Ave., New York, NY 10022. Ed. Virginia Dajani. Q; with membership only; 1974. *Notes*: dwgs., photos (B&W).

Covers all aspects of New York City's environment, including architecture, planning, interior design, landscape, historic preservation, and public art. *

0258   METROPOLIS   (US)
177 E. 87th St., New York, NY 10028. Ed. Sharon Lee Ryder. Tel. (212) 722-5050. 10/yr.; $20; 1981; circ. 8,500. *Indexed*: Avery. *Notes*: adv., bk. rev., calendars, dwgs., photos (B&W, color).

An architecture and design magazine of New York. Lively up-to-date coverage is given to buildings, landscape design, furniture, graphics, and general design issues. Articles attempt to relate the arts to the needs of the consumer and to social and political attitudes. Thoughtful reviews and professional critical essays are featured in each issue. Includes an extensive calendar of local design events and exhibits. (0279-4977)

**0259   NEW ENGLAND ARCHITECT   (US)
         AND BUILDER
         ILLUSTRATED**
Norbrook Publishing Co., 601 Washington St., Norwood, MA 02062. M; 1958. +

0260   NEW ENGLAND   (US)
         CONSTRUCTION
27 Muzzey St., Box 49, Lexington, MA 02173. Ed. H.S. Swartz. Tel. (617) 862-2355. Bi-m; $25; 1936. (0028-470x) +

**0261   NEW YORK CONSTRUCTION   (US)
         NEWS**
300 Madison Ave., New York, NY 10017. Ed. Harry S. Ferguson. (212) 697-7655. W; $18; 1953; circ. 2,900. *Notes*: adv., dwgs., photos (B&W).

An eight-page newspaper offering news on people in the construction field and on new projects in the New York-New Jersey area. Most projects reported are at the ground-breaking stage, but some are proposed or newly completed. (0028-7164)

0262   NORTHWEST   (US)
         ARCHITECTURE
303 Harvard E., Ste. 101, P.O. Box 12099, Seattle, WA 98102-0099. Ed. Joan Whinihan. Tel. (206) 322-5120. Q; 1976; circ. 2,800. *Notes*: adv., dwgs., photos (B&W, color). *

0263   UPDATE   (US)
Architectural Design Center, P.O. Box 205; Largo, FL 34294. Ed. Jack Klein. Tel. (813) 535-0541. M; free to members; 1984. *Notes*: adv., bk. rev., calendars, dwgs., photos (B&W, color).

A new publication on the Florida construction industry. Includes student submissions and current information from schools of architecture in Florida. Important source for updates on local building codes. Of interest to builders, architects, designers, and building officials working in Florida.

Chapter Publications of U.S. Architectural Associations

**0264   A.I.A. COLORADO FIELD   (US)
         REPORT**
Colorado Society of Architects/AIA, 1459 Pennsylvania St., Carriage House, Denver, CO 80203. Ed. Richard Lightle. Tel. (303) 831-6183. Bi-m; free to members; $12 to others; 1980; circ. 1,700. *Notes*: calendars, dwgs., photos (B&W).

Newsletter format.

0265   A.I.A. MEMO   (US)
American Inst. of Architects, 1735 New York Ave., NW, Washington, DC 20006. Ed. Peter McCall. Tel. (202) 626-7465. M; $5. *Indexed*: A.P.I., Avery. *Notes*: calendars, photos (B&W).

A national newsletter providing news briefs of interest to association members and other architects. Covers topics such as legislation, industry surveys, conference and research activities, and announcements of awards, competitions, and new publications. Articles usually include the name of an A.I.A. contact person for further information. (0001-1487)

0266   A.I.A. REPORTS   (US)
Illinois Council/AIA, 802 Lincoln Tower, 520 South 2nd St., Springfield, IL 62701. Ed. Shirley Norvell. Tel. (217) 522-2309.

Newsletter of statewide interest.

0267   ASO NEWS JOURNAL   (US)
Architects Society of Ohio AIA, 37 West Broad Street, Ste. 301, Columbus, OH 43215. M. +

0268 ALABAMA ARCHITECT (US)
Alabama Council of the AIA, P.O. Box 237, Montgomery, AL 36101. A; free to members; 1965; circ. 1,600. *Notes*: adv., calendars, dwgs., photos (B&W, color).

A review of work completed in the state and in the state's architecture schools. Includes a membership directory.

0269 ARCHITECTURE CALIFORNIA (US)
California Council/AIA, 1303 J St., Ste. 200, Sacramento, CA 95814. Ed. Janice Fillip. Tel. (916) 448-9082. Bi-m; $24 (US); $56 (abroad); 1979; circ. 85,000. *Annual Issues*: May/June—Monterey Design Conference; Sept./Oct.—CCAIA Convention. *Notes*: adv., bk. rev., calendars, dwgs., photos (B&W, color).

Reports on state chapter matters but also includes general articles on design in California and notes on practice, legislation, and competitions. (0738-1131)

0270 ARCHITECTURE MINNESOTA (US)
Craftsman Press, Inc., 314 Clifton Ave., Minneapolis, MN 55403. Ed. Linda Mack. Tel. (612) 874-8771. Bi-m; $12; 1975; circ. 5,500. *Indexed*: Avery, Dec. issue. *Annual Issues*: May—Minnesota Architects Directory. *Notes*: adv., bk. rev., calendars, dwgs., photos (B&W, color).

An interesting publication with state design news and articles of interest to the practicing professional. Well illustrated with features on historical and current projects in Minnesota. (0149-9106)

0271 ARCHITECTURE NEW JERSEY (US)
New Jersey Society of Architects, 1000 Rt. 9, Woodbridge, NJ 07095. Ed. Helen Schneider. Tel. (201) 636-5680. Q; $6; 1967; circ. 4,000. *Indexed*: Avery.

Advances an awareness of the visual environment through the presentation of current projects in New Jersey. Distributed to leaders in commerce, industry, banking, education, religion, and government as well as to architects. (0003-8733)

0272 CSA/AIA NEWS (US)
Connecticut Society of Architects, 85 Willow St., New Haven, CT 06511. Ed. Lois Flesche. Tel. (203) 488-3585. Bi-m; free; 1960; circ. 1,200. *Notes*: adv., calendars, dwgs., photos (B&W). *

0273 COLUMN (US)
Arizona Society of Architects/AIA, 3738 16th St., Ste. F, Phoenix, AZ 85016. Ed. Eleanor Smith. Tel. (602) 279-0032. M; 1975; circ. 1,000. *Notes*: photos (B&W). *

0274 COLUMN (US)
New York State Assn. of Architects/AIA, 235 Lark St., Albany, NY 12210. Ed. Barbara J. Rodriguez. Tel. (518) 449-3334. Bi-m; 1972; circ. 3,100. *Notes*: adv., photos (B&W).

Newsletter format. Particularly good for disseminating information on legislation of interest to New York architects.

0275 CONTACT (US)
Florida Assn./AIA, P.O. Box 10388, Tallahassee, FL 32302. Ed. Craig Crosby. Tel. (904) 222-7590. Bi-m; free to members; circ. 1,800. *Notes*: calendars, dwgs., photos (B&W).

Newsletter format.

0276 EAGLE (US)
Alabama Council of Architects/AIA, P.O. Box 237, Montgomery, AL 36101. Ed. John McDonald. Bi-m; 1970; circ. 1,600. *Notes*: calendars, dwgs., photos (B&W).

Newsletter format.

0277 FLORIDA ARCHITECT (US)
Florida Assn./AIA, P.O. Box 10388, Tallahassee, FL 32302. Ed. Diane Greer. Tel. (904) 222-7590. Bi-m; $12; 1954; circ. 6,500. *Notes*: adv., bk. rev., photos (B&W, color).

A glossy magazine that includes the work of Florida architects, landscape architects, interior designers, and planners. Well-illustrated features. (0015-3907)

0278 HAWAII ARCHITECT (US)
319B No. Cane St., Wahiawa, HI 96789. Hawaii Society of Architects/AIA, 233 Merchant St., Ste. 200, Honolulu, HI 96813. Ed. Karen St. John. Tel. (808) 621-8200. M; $18; 1969; circ. 2,500. *Annual Issues*: Dec.—Yearbook. *Notes*: adv., photos (B&W, color).

Reports on local projects, student exhibits, and design awards as well as professional developments.

0279 IOWA ARCHITECT (US)
Iowa Chapter/AIA, 512 Walnut St., Des Moines, IA 50309. Ed. Kirk von Blunk. Tel. (515) 244-7502. Bi-m; $12; 1958; circ. 5,600. *Indexed*: March/April issue. *Annual Issues*: March/April—Membership Directory. *Notes*:

adv., bk. rev., calendars, dwgs., photos (B&W, color).

A glossy review of Iowa architecture. (0021-1206)

0280 KSA REVIEW   (US)
Kentucky Society of Architects/AIA, P.O. Box 22238, Lexington, KY 40522. Q. +

0281 L.A. ARCHITECT   (US)
Los Angeles Chapter/AIA, 8687 Melrose Ave., Ste. M-72, Los Angeles, CA 90069. Ed. Barbara Goldstein. Tel. (213) 749-6982. 11/yr.; $18; 1975; circ. 2,700. *Indexed*: A.P.I., Avery. *Annual Issues*: Jan.—LA/AIA Election Results; Nov.—LA/AIA Design Awards. *Notes*: adv., bk. rev., calendars, dwgs., photos (B&W).

Newsletter format. In addition to chapter news and notes, there are reviews of specific projects.

0282 MCA NEWSLETTER   (US)
Missouri Council of Architects/AIA, 204A East High St., Jefferson City, MO 65101. Ed. Randall Endecott. Tel. (913) 649-9200. 3/yr.; 1975; circ. 1,200. *Notes*: photos (B&W). *

0283 M S A MONTHLY BULLETIN   (US)
Michigan Society of Architects, Michigan Architectural Foundation, 553 E. Jefferson, Detroit, MI 48226. Ed. Rae Dumke. Tel. (313) 965-4100. M; free with membership; 1926; circ. 1,600. *Notes*: adv., bk. rev., calendars, dwgs., photos (B&W).

Newsletter format. (0024-8363)

0284 MISSISSIPPI ARCHITECT   (US)
Mississippi Chapter/AIA, 814 N. President, Jackson, MS 39202. Ed. Robert Ivy. Tel. (601) 327-9558. Q; $4; 1969; circ. 2,000. *Notes*: adv., bk. rev., calendars, dwgs., photos (B&W, color).

0285 MISSOURI ARCHITECT   (US)
Missouri Council of Architects, Inc., 306 E. High St., P.O. Box 401, Jefferson City, MO 65101. Tel. (314) 635-8555. Q; membership; 1951. (0026-6477) +

0286 NCAIA   (US)
North Carolina Chapter/AIA, 115 W. Morgan St., Raleigh, NC 27601. Ed. Lillian Woo. Tel. (919) 833-6656.

Newsletter format.

0287 NEW MEXICO   (US)
        ARCHITECTURE
New Mexico Society of Architects/AIA, P.O. Box 1207, Santa Fe, NM 87504. Ed. John Conron. Tel. (505) 983-6948. Bi-m; $6; 1964. *Indexed*: 20-year cum. index Nov./Dec. 1983. *Notes*: adv., bk. rev., calendars, dwgs., photos (B&W, color).

This state chapter publication does an outstanding job of presenting current and historic architecture in New Mexico. (0545-3151)

0288 NEWS   (US)
Washington Chapter/AIA, 1777 Church St., NW, Washington, DC 20036. Irreg. +

0289 NEWSLETTER   (US)
Nebraska Society of Architects/AIA, 1910 S. 44th St., Ste. 100, Omaha, NB 68105. +

0290 NORTH CAROLINA   (US)
        ARCHITECT
Shaw Communications, 212 S. Tryon St., Ste. 1450, Charlotte, NC 28281. Ed. Whitney G. Shaw. Tel. (704) 372-9794. Bi-m; $12; 1954; circ. 3,100. *Indexed*: Avery, 20-year cum. index. *Notes*: adv., bk. rev., calendars, dwgs., photos (B&W, color).

Well-illustrated magazine with news, designs, and award winners of North Carolina architecture. (0029-2427)

0291 NORTHWEST   (US)
        ARCHITECTURE
Washington Council/AIA, McCleary Mansion, Ste. 6, 111 21st Ave., SW, Olympia, WA 98501. Bi-m; $20; 1978. +

0292 OC/AIA ADVISOR   (US)
Oklahoma Chapter/AIA, 405 N.W. 15th St., Oklahoma City, OK 73103. +

0293 OCULUS   (US)
New York Chapter/AIA, 457 Madison Ave., New York, NY 10022. Ed. C. Ray Smith. Tel. (212) 838-9670. M; $25; circ. 2,200. *Indexed*: Avery. *Notes*: adv., calendars, dwgs., photos (B&W).

Newsletter format.

0294 P S A NEWS   (US)
Pennsylvania Society of Architects/AIA, P.O. Box N, Harrisburg, PA 17108. Q; members only.

Newsletter format. *

0295   QUAPAW QUARTER (US)
CHRONICLE
Quapaw Quarter Assn., Box 1104, Little Rock, AR 72203. Ed. Starr Mitchell. Bi-m; $20; 1974. +

0296   R.I.A.I.A. NEWSLETTER (US)
Rhode Island Chapter/AIA, 150 Pine St., Providence, RI 02903. Bi-m. +

0297   RESOURCE (US)
Kansas Society of Architects/AIA, 724 Kansas Ave., Topeka, KS 66603. M. +

0298   SCAIA NEWSLETTER (US)
South Carolina Chapter/AIA, 1522 Richland St., Columbia, SC 29201. Irreg. +

0299   SAN FRANCISCO BAY (US)
ARCHITECTS REVIEW
San Francisco Chapter/AIA, 790 Market St., 3rd fl., San Francisco, CA 94102. Ed. Michael Stanton. Tel. (415) 398-3760. Q; $15; 1977; circ. 2,800. *Indexed*: Avery. *Notes*: adv., bk. rev., calendars, dwgs., photos (B&W). *

0300   TENNESSEE ARCHITECT (US)
Tennessee Society of Architects/AIA, 223 1/2 6th Ave., N. Nashville, TN 37219. Ed. Connie Wallace. Tel. (615) 256-2311. Q; $10; 1979; circ. 3,500. *Notes*: adv., bk. rev., calendars, dwgs., photos (B&W, color).
Presents an overview of architectural innovation and design in Tennessee as well as profiles on architects and news on related subjects. *

0301   TEXAS ARCHITECT (US)
Texas Society of Architects, 1400 Norwood Tower, Austin, TX 78701. Ed. Larry Paul Fuller. Tel. (512) 478-7386. Bi-m; $18; 1950;

circ. 8,000. *Indexed*: Avery. *Annual Issues*: Nov./Dec.—Honor Awards. *Notes*: adv., bk. rev., dwgs., photos (B&W, color).
Broad coverage of architecture and interior design in Texas. Notes on firms and proposed projects as well as features on historic properties are included. (0040-4179)

0302   TEXAS SOCIETY OF (US)
ARCHITECTS NEWSLETTER
Texas Society of Architects/AIA, 1400 Norwood Tower, Austin, TX 78701. Ed. David Brooks. Tel. (512) 478-7386. 10/yr.; free to members; circ. 4,700.

0303   UTAH ARCHITECT (US)
Utah Society of Architects/AIA, 555 E. South Temple, Salt Lake City, UT 84102. Q; $12; 1960. *Indexed*: Avery. +

0304   VIRGINIA RECORD (US)
Virginia Publishers Wing, Inc., 301 E. Franklin St., Drawer 2Y, Richmond, VA 23205. Ed. Joe Young. Tel. (804) 644-6717. Bi-m; $10; 1878; circ. 4,500. *Indexed*: A.P.I. *Annual Issues*: Jan./Feb.—Directory of Virginia Officials. *Notes*: adv., bk. rev., calendars, dwgs., photos (B&W, color).
Detailed coverage is given to projects by Virginia architects. Includes articles on economic development, revitalization, and general construction in Virginia. (0042-6768)

0305   WISCONSIN ARCHITECT (US)
Wisconsin Society of Architects/AIA, 321 S. Hamilton St., Madison, WI 53703. Ed. Eric Englund. Tel. (608) 257-8477. M; $30; 1932; circ. 2,000. *Annual Issues*: Feb.—Resource Issue; July—Awards Issue. *Notes*: adv., dwgs., photos (B&W, color). *

2

Office Practice

General

0020   ARCHITECTS' JOURNAL

0026   ARCHITECTURAL RECORD

0306   CONTRACTOR PROFIT NEWS   (US)
114 Beaufort Ave., Needham, MA 02192. Practice Management Association, Ltd., 126 Harvard St., Brookline, MA 02146. Ed. Richard Garaffo. Tel. (617) 731-1913. M; $84; 1983.

Management newsletter for the construction industry that presents basic information on how to improve profits. Each issue deals with such topics as marketing, leasing, scheduling, budgeting, personnel, liability, and computers. (0741-4617) *

0307   GUIDELINES LETTER   (US)
(Formerly: *Guidelines Architectural Letter*)
Box 456, Orinda, CA 94563. Ed. Fred A. Stitt. Tel. (415) 254-0639. M; $56; 1972; circ. 3,000. *Micro*: UMI.

A four-page newsletter that presents hints on new practical techniques for the design professions. Includes notes on new office equipment, management guidelines, and new resources.

**0308   PROFESSIONAL SERVICES   (US)
          MANAGEMENT JOURNAL**
126 Harvard St., Brookline, MA 02146. MRH Assoc., Inc., Box 11316, Newington, CT 06111. Ed. Frank Stasiowski. Tel. (203) 666-9487. M; $72; 1974. *Indexed*: Aug. issue.

A six-page newsletter that presents advice and guidelines on many aspects of office practice. Frequent articles on marketing as well as topics of interest to project managers. (0732-2119)

Computers

0309   A/E SYSTEMS REPORT   (US)
P.O. Box 11316, Newington, CT 06111. Ed. George S. Borkovich. Tel. (203) 666-9487. M; $72. *Indexed*: Avery, 5-year cum. in June 1983. *Notes*: calendars, photos (B&W).

Newsletter format. Articles cover automation and reprographics for architects and engineers. Includes news on hardware, software, applications, new publications, seminars, surveys, directories of vendors and systems consultants. (0732-7951)

**0310   A-E-C AUTOMATION   (US)
          NEWSLETTER**
7209 Wisteria Way, Carlsbad, CA 92008. Ed. E. Forrest. Tel. (714) 438-1595. M; $97; 1977; circ. 4,100. *Notes*: bk. rev.

Reports and describes developments in automation for architects, engineers, and contractors. Articles include discussions of computer-aided engineering, computer-aided design and drafting, and computer-output microfilm, photography, reprographics, and technical publishing. (0277-1659)

0311   ASN QUARTERLY   (US)
Architects' Software Network, 1610 Washington Plaza, Reston, VA 22090. Ed. Dana K. Smith. Q; $20 (free to architects); 1984. *Notes*: adv., photos (B&W).

This sixteen-page tabloid includes notes on computer applications and new software for architects, by architects. It is primarily a software exchange publication. +

**0312   ANDERSON REPORT   (US)
        NEWSLETTER ON
        COMPUTER GRAPHICS**
4525 E. Industrial, #4L, Simi Valley, CA 93063. Ed. B.J. Anderson. Tel. (805) 581-1184. M; $125; 1978; circ. 2,000.

In-depth coverage of systems, companies, and people involved in CAD/CAM, business graphics, and architectural graphics. Each issue includes an "Inside Report" on a major computer graphics vendor. (0197-7040)*

**0313   CCAN/CONSTRUCTION   (US)
        COMPUTER APPLICATIONS
        NEWSLETTER**
Construction Industry Press, 1105-F Spring St., Silver Spring, MD 20910. Ed. Roberta Wiener. Tel. (301) 589-4884. M; $97 (US); $117 (abroad); 1982. *Indexed*: Newsnet. *Notes*: bk. rev., dwgs.

Contractors, construction managers, architects, and engineers will find this a useful newsletter. In addition to reviews on hardware and software, it includes articles on the use of computers in accounting, scheduling, project management, estimating, surveying, graphics, and site engineering. (0277-0407)

0314   C.E.P.A. NEWSLETTER   (US)
Society for Computer Applications in Engineering, Planning and Architecture, Inc., 15713 Crabb Branch Way, Rockville, MD 20855. Ed. Patricia Johnson. Tel. (301) 926-7070. Q; $30 (US); $40 (abroad); 1966; circ. 1,000. *Notes*: adv., bk. rev.

Includes society news and special technical feature articles on computer applications in A/E firms as reported by members. Also includes abstracts of articles in other publications. *

0315   CASE ONE   (US)
Engineering and Architectural Systems International, Inc., 2030 Union St., Suite 380, San Francisco, CA 94123. Ed. L. Louis Chu. Tel. (415) 563-9335. Telex 910-372-2196. Bi-m; $30; 1984; circ. 500. *Indexed*: Jan. issue. *Notes*: adv., bibl., bk. rev., calendars, dwgs., photos (B&W), plans.

A newsletter on computer applications for engineers, contractors, and architects. Its aim is to assist readers in increasing productivity by using computers effectively. It offers tips on automating the office, new uses for the computer, market trends, and new products. (0743-1732)

0316   COMPUTER-AIDED DESIGN   (UK)
IPC Science and Technology Press, Ltd., Box 63, Weatbury House, Bury St., Guildford, Surrey GU2 5BH, England. (U.S. sub.) 537 Madison Ave., Ste. 1217, New York, NY 10022. Ed. J. Wexler. Tel. (0483) 31261. Bi-m; $230; 1968; circ. 2,000. *Indexed*: A.P.I., Comput. Data., Eng. Ind., INSPEC. *Notes*: adv., bibl., bk. rev., dwgs., photos (B&W, color).

Technical articles on CAD including applications in architecture, building, and engineering. (0010-4485)

**0317   COMPUTER GRAPHICS   (US)
        NEWS**
8401 Arlington Blvd., Suite 601, Fairfax, VA 22031. c/o Scherago Assoc., Subscription Dept., 1515 Broadway, New York, NY 10109-0163. Ed. Robert A. Cramblitt. Tel. (212) 730-1050. Bi-m; $12 (free to qualified personnel); 1981; circ. 25,000. *Indexed*: Comput. Data. *Notes*: adv., photos (B&W, color).

A tabloid that presents articles on new developments in computer technology and new products and announcements of exhibits and seminars. Includes articles on problems in management in automated offices, new uses for computer graphics, and new publications. (0276-1440)

**0318   COMPUTER GRAPHICS   (US)
        WORLD**
(Formerly: *Computer Graphics*)
1714 Stockton St., San Francisco, CA 94133. Ed. Randall L. Stickrod. Tel. (415) 398-7151. M; $30; 1978; circ. 5,000. *Indexed*: Comput. Data., Dec. issue. *Notes*: adv., bk. rev., calendars, photos (B&W, color).

Articles and news of interest to users of computer graphics technology. Of increasing interest to architects and engineers. (0271-4159)

**0319   COMPUTERS AND   (US)
        STRUCTURES**
Pergamon Press, Headington Hill Hall, Oxford OX3 OBW, England. (U.S. Sub.) Pergamon Press, Fairview Park, Elmsford, NY 10523. Ed. Harold Liebowitz. Tel. (914) 592-7700. M; $250; 1971; circ. 1,500. *Indexed*: App. Mech. Rev., Compendex, Comput. Data., Eng. Ind. *Micro*: MIM, UMI.

Presents technical papers on the applications of computers in problems related to hydrospace, aerospace, and terrestrial structures. Particular attention is given to practical engineering aspects of structural analysis and design. (0045-7949)

0320   COMPUTERS FOR DESIGN   (US)
         AND CONSTRUCTION
Metadata Publishing Co., 310 E. 44th St., Suite 1124, New York, NY 10017. Ed. Joseph A. MacDonald. Tel. (212) 687-3836. Bi-m; $48; 1982; circ. 25,000. *Indexed*: Compendex, Comput. Data., Eng. Ind. *Annual Issues*: Aug.—Buyers' Guide; Dec.—Handbook. *Notes*: adv., bk. rev., calendars, dwgs., photos (B&W, color).

Designed to help professionals in the design/construction fields to select hardware and software and to establish office computer systems. Emphasis is on improving efficiency and profitability. A major computer periodical for architects. (0734-5402) *

0321   DESIGN GRAPHICS WORLD   (US)
         (Formerly: *Drafting and Repro Digest*)
Communication Channels, Inc., 6255 Barfield Rd., Atlanta, GA 30328. Ed. Michael Booth. Tel. (404) 256-9800. Telex 4611075. M; $18; 1977; circ. 36,003. *Indexed*: Jan. issue. *Notes*: adv., bk. rev., dwgs., photos (B&W, color).

Articles on CADD, CAD/CAM, reprographics, micrographics. Primarily of interest to architects, engineers, designers, and other individuals involved in reprographics and information handling systems. (0745-8754)

0322   ECAN/ENGINEERING   (US)
         COMPUTER APPLICATIONS
         NEWSLETTER
5 Denver Tech Center, P.O. Box 3109, Englewood, CO 80155-3109. Ed. Kenton Johnson. Tel. (303) 797-3603. M; $96; 1979; circ. 600. *Notes*: bk. rev., calendars.

For engineers with or without computer experience. Monthly analyses of hardware and software. Tutorials. (0740-414X) *

0323   IEEE COMPUTER GRAPHICS   (US)
         AND APPLICATIONS
IEEE Computer Society, 10662 Los Vaqueros Circle, Los Alamitos, CA 90720. 445 Hoes Lane, Piscataway, NJ 08854. Ed. Michael J. Wozny. Tel. (714) 821-8380. M; $20; 1981; circ. 15,800. *Indexed*: Comput. Data., Nov. issue. *Notes*: adv., bibl., bk. rev., calendars, dwgs., photos (B&W, color).

Technical articles on hardware, software, and various applications for computer graphics. (0272-1716)

0342   PLAN & PRINT

0324   S. KLEIN NEWSLETTER ON   (US)
         COMPUTER GRAPHICS
730 Boston Post Rd., P.O. Box 392, Sudbury, MA 01776. Ed. Stanley Klein. Tel. (617) 443-4671. Bi-w; $165; 1979.

Reports on developments in CAD/CAM, CADD, business graphics, image processing, mapping, etc. Issues focus on a product, company, technology, market, or business development. Editorial board is composed of accomplished computer graphics pioneers. (0731-9207) *

0325   TODAY'S S.C.I.P. (SMALL   (US)
         COMPUTERS IN PRACTICE)
EMA Management Assoc., Inc., 1145 Gaskins Rd., Richmond, VA 23233. Ed. C. Page Highfill. Tel. (804) 740-8332. M; $95; 1984.

An eight-page newsletter written by practicing professionals experienced in using computers in their A/E firms. Each issue presents practical applications of the computer in design, communications, and database management. The "Pipeline" column presents a monthly exchange of ideas, applications, and software. Micros and CADD systems are discussed. *

0326   WORKSTATION ALERT   (US)
         (Formerly: *CAD/CAM Alert*)
Reservoir Executive Park, 824 Boylston St., Chestnut Hill, MA 02167. P.O. Box 404, Newton, MA 02161. Ed. Bd. Tel. (617) 232-8080. M; $167 (US); $232 (abroad); 1984.

A newsletter that briefs engineers on uses of personal computers and new developments in CAD. Includes an "exchange" for used equipment. Highlights new products and companies. (0738-5722) *

Project Management

0327   CONSTRUCTION   (UK)
         MANAGEMENT AND
         ECONOMICS
Dept. of Construction Management, Univ. of Reading, Whiteknights, Reading RG6 2BU, England. Associated Book Publisher (UK), Ltd., Subscr. Dept., North Way, Andover, Hampshire SP10 5BE, England. Ed. John Bennett. Tel. 0734-875123. 3/yr.; $85; 1983. *Indexed*: Every third issue. *Notes*: adv., bibl., bk. rev., dwgs., photos (B&W).

A new international journal devoted to research in management economics in the building industry. Management is defined as construction and project management of new work, management of existing facilities, and management of construction and design firms. The economic aspects cover accounting, feasibility studies, estimating, cost control, and the relationship of the industry to the national and international economy. This is a unique journal that includes original papers, case studies, and reports on issues of interest to practitioners, researchers, and building owners worldwide. (0144-6193)

0334   GUIDELINES FOR
       IMPROVING PRACTICE:
       ARCHITECTS AND
       ENGINEERS PROFESSIONAL
       LIABILITY

0307   GUIDELINES LETTER

0328   INTERNATIONAL JOURNAL   (UK)
       OF PROJECT MANAGEMENT
Butterworth Scientific, Ltd., Box 63, Westbury House, Bury St., Guildford, Surrey GU2 5BH, England. Quadrant Subscription Services, Ltd., Oakfield House, Perrymount Road, Haywards Heath, W. Sussex RH16 3DH, England. Ed. G. Waller. Q; £60 ($120); 1983. *Notes*: bk. rev. (0263-7863) +

0308   PROFESSIONAL SERVICES
       MANAGEMENT JOURNAL

0329   PROFESSIONAL SERVICES   (US)
       QUARTERLY
Professional Services Management Assn., P.O. Box 15466, Santa Ana, CA 92705. +

0330   PROJECT MANAGEMENT   (US)
       QUARTERLY
Project Management Institute, P.O. Box 43, Drexel Hill, PA 19026. Tel. (215) 622-1796. Q; 1978. (0147-5363) +

Professional Liability

0331   A/E LEGAL NEWSLETTER   (US)
Office of Professional Liability Research, Victor O. Schinnerer & Co., Inc., 5028 Wisconsin Ave., N.W., Washington, DC 20016. Ed. Arthur T. Kornblut. Tel. (202) 966-5205. M; $175; 1973; circ. 450. *Indexed*: Jan. issue. *Notes*: bk. rev.
Newsletter published in cooperation with the American Institute of Architects for the purpose of keeping architects, engineers, and attorneys serving those professionals up-to-date on liability issues. Includes summaries and opinions of cases involving statute of limitations, arbitration, contracts, negligence, and design defects. Good current coverage of A/E liability is provided, but the weak subject index limits its usefulness for searching past cases. (0090-2411)

0332   CONSTRUCTION LAW   (CN)
       LETTER
Univ. of Toronto, Dept. of Architecture, 230 College St., Toronto, Ont. M5S 1A1, Canada. Bi-m; $38; 1983.
Summaries of selected decisions regarding construction disputes across Canada. +

0333   CONSTRUCTION   (US)
       LITIGATION REPORTER
Litigation Research Group, P.O. Box 77903, San Francisco, CA 94107. M; $180. *Indexed*: Semiannual issues.
Looseleaf service covering recent decisions of national significance. Each issue includes subject and jurisdiction index.

0334   GUIDELINES FOR   (US)
       IMPROVING PRACTICE:
       ARCHITECTS AND
       ENGINEERS PROFESSIONAL
       LIABILITY
Victor O. Schinnerer & Co., Inc., 5028 Wisconsin Ave., N.W., Washington, DC 20016. Ed. Paul L. Genecki. Tel. (202) 966-5205. Bi-m; $60; 1971; circ. 9,200. *Indexed*: cumulates from April 1971 every Dec.
Newsletters on professional liability are sent according to topics; type of structure, phase of professional service, special studies, general information, insurance, and legal highlights. (0091-8245)

0335   LEGAL BRIEFS   (US)
1221 Ave. of the Americas, New York, NY 10020. Ed. Victoria Craven. Tel. (212) 512-3213. Bi-w; $147; 1975; circ. 650.
A four-page newsletter that reports significant legal cases involving construction. Cites sources for acquiring copies of the full decisions on cases reported. Digests are written in layman's language with the goal of alerting readers to possible legal dangers. In addition, the newsletter reports on significant industry news and regulatory items. Subscribers also receive special reports from time to time. (0730-952X)

Marketing

0336   A/E MARKETING JOURNAL   (US)
   (Formerly: *Coxe Letter*)
2351 Powell St., Ste. 500A, San Francisco, CA
94133. MRH Assoc., Inc., Box 11316, Newington, CT 06111. Ed. Margaret Spaulding. Tel.
(415) 788-4395. M; $96; 1974; circ. 2,000.

A marketing intelligence newsletter that forecasts new markets, reports on successful promotion strategies, and offers the latest techniques in market research. Readership includes professional marketers in architectural and engineering firms.

0337   COMMUNICATOR'S   (US)
         ADVISOR
   (Formerly: *Presentation Advisor*)
Ernest Burden, 20 Waterside Plaza, New York,
NY 10010. Ed. Ernest Burden. Tel. (212) 889-
4672. Bi-m; $60; 1980. *Indexed*: Jan. issue. *Annual Issues*: May/June—Promotion Strategies
Conference; Sept./Oct.—SMPS Awards Program. *Notes*: bibl., bk. rev., calendars, dwgs.,
photos (B&W).

A useful newsletter that provides ideas on presentation techniques for architects, engineers, and planners. Articles offer strategies for interviews, ideas for more effective brochures, news, and case studies on the latest technology in photographic processes. Enables firms to learn what other firms are doing. Each issue informs as well as stimulates the imagination. Many of the major A/E firms subscribe.

0338   PROFESSIONAL   (US)
         MARKETING REPORT
Gerre Jones Assoc., Inc., P.O. Box 32387,
Washington, DC 20007. Ed. Gerre Jones. Tel.
(202) 333-2366. M; $85; 1976; circ. 1,000. *Notes*:
bk. rev.

A marketing newsletter for design professionals, marketing executives, and construction officials. Contains current, proven marketing ideas, tips, and techniques. Presents case histories of successful marketing programs. The notes on significant new publications are helpful references. (0160-0362)

0339   THE PROFIT CENTER   (US)
   (Formerly: *A/E Manager*)
Birnberg Assoc., 1905 N. Halsted St., Chicago,
IL 60614. Eds. Edward Birnberg, Rose Thomas.
Tel. (312) 664-2300. 11/yr.; $60; 1982; circ. 300.

Marketing newsletter for architectural and engineering firms. The information is timely and helpful but covers fewer topics in less detail than competing marketing newsletters.

0340   RESOURCE   (US)
Professional Development Resources, Inc.,
1000 Connecticut Ave., NW #9, Washington,
D.C. 20036. S-a; free. +

0341   SMPS NEWS   (US)
Society for Marketing Professional Services,
801 N. Fairfax St., Ste. 215, Alexandria, VA
22314. Ed. Deborah Molyneux. Tel. (703) 549-
6117. 11 yr.; $25 (with membership); 1978; circ.
3,100. *Notes*: bk. rev., calendars, photos
(B&W).

An association newsletter with useful articles and news of interest to marketing professionals in architecture, engineering, interior design, landscape architecture, planning, and construction management firms. Articles deal with topics such as international marketing, presentation, promotional materials, and marketing strategies. Includes a page of job opportunities. (0199-
3690)

Reprographics

0310   A-E-C AUTOMATION
         NEWSLETTER

0321   DESIGN GRAPHICS WORLD

0342   PLAN & PRINT   (US)
   (Formerly: *The International Blue Printer*)
International Reprographic Assn., 9931 Franklin Ave., P.O. Box 879, Franklin Park, IL 60131.
Ed. James Vebeck. Tel. (312) 671-5356. M; $15;
1928; circ. 22,000. *Annual Issues*: Aug.—Product Directory. *Notes*: adv., calendars, dwgs.,
photos (B&W, color). *Micro*: UMI.

Covers the latest equipment and methods of drawing reproduction, design/drafting, micrographics, Xerography, and computer-aided design. Useful to anyone responsible for managing or operating drafting rooms or commercial printing companies. (0032-0595) *

3

Building Types

Offices, Banks, Multiuse

0343   A.B.A. BANKING JOURNAL   (US)
(Formerly: *Banking*)
Simmons-Boardman Publishing Corp., 345 Hudson St., New York, NY 10014. P.O. Box 530, Bristol, CT 06010. Ed. Lyman B. Coddington. Tel. (212) 620-7215. Telex 425-421 SIMB-UI. M; $30; 1901; circ. 42,000. *Indexed*: B.P.I., P.A.I.S. *Notes*: adv., bk. rev., photos (color, B&W). *Micro*: UMI.

Primarily a professional journal on bank management but includes regular articles on space planning, renovation, adaptive reuse, and new construction of banks. Extensive coverage of new products, equipment, and systems. (0194-5947)

0344   BANK SYSTEMS AND   (US)
EQUIPMENT
Gralla Publications, 1515 Broadway, New York, NY 10036. Ed. Joan Prevete Hyman. Tel. (212) 869-1300. M; $16; 1964; circ. 22,000. *Indexed*: Data Process. Dig. *Annual Issues*: Jan.—Systems and Equipment Directory. *Notes*: adv., photos (B&W). *Micro*: UMI.

Broad coverage of construction, equipment, and physical operation of financial institutions. Articles focus on new computer systems, furnishings, security, and overall design. (0146-0900)

0345   CANADIAN OFFICE   (CN)
(Formerly: *Toronto Office*)
Whitsed Pub. Ltd., 55 Bloor St., W., Ste. 1201, Toronto, Ont. M4W 3M1, Canada. Ed. Bruce Glassford. Tel. (416) 967-6200. M; $20; 1970. *Notes*: adv., photos (B&W, color).

Articles focus on improving the office efficiency and environment. (0319-2148) +

0346   CORPORATE DESIGN &   (US)
REALTY
Cahners Publishing Co., 475 Park Ave. South, New York, NY 10016. 270 St. Paul St., Denver, CO 80206. Ed. Roger Yee. Tel. (212) 576-4162. Bi-m; $24; 1982; circ. 25,000. *Indexed*: Avery. *Annual Issues*: March/April—Top 100 Interior Design Giants. *Notes*: adv., bk. rev., photos (color, B&W).

Case studies illustrating newly designed corporate spaces are presented, aimed primarily at executives responsible for facility planning. They are also of great interest to architects and interior designers who design corporate spaces. Problems faced by management and the eventual solutions are examined in detail. Issues include regular business reports on site selection and office leasing activity. Each issue also includes a detailed project resources list and features on a new product or service related to facility operations. (0744-2750)

0347   FACILITIES DESIGN AND   (US)
MANAGEMENT
Gralla Publications, 1515 Broadway, New York, NY 10036. Ed. Anne Fallucchi. Tel. (212) 869-1300. 9/yr.; $30 (free to qualified subscribers); 1981; circ. 30,000. *Indexed*: Avery. *Annual Issues*: Feb./March—Directory of Manufacturing Companies, Assns., Mart Bldgs., Products and Services. *Notes*: adv., bk. rev., photos (color, B&W).

Published primarily for corporate executives, managers, and planners of office environments, this magazine is also useful to architects and interior designers. Well-detailed case histories of new projects are presented with discussions of the corporate philosophies of the facility planners involved. New products and real-estate trends are analyzed. (0279-4438)

0348 MANAGEMENT (US)
TECHNOLOGY
11 Commerce St., Norwalk, CT 06850. Ed. Paul B. Finney. Tel. (203) 852-1042. M; $18; 1983; circ. 30,000. Notes: adv., bk. rev., photos (color, B&W).

Presents technological solutions to problems encountered by organizations in integrating and utilizing information systems. Gives details of office systems of major companies. Contains announcements of new products. Good source for designers of offices as well as for corporate facility planners. (0736-5225)

0349 MOBILI PER UFFICIO (IT)
Viale Stelvio 21, 20159 Milan, Italy. Ed. Giuseppe Vallardi. Tel. (02) 6886723. A; $35.

Guide for purchasing office furniture, equipment, and accessories. Sources are primarily Italian. *

0350 MODERN OFFICE (US)
TECHNOLOGY
(Formerly: Modern Office Procedures)
Penton IPC, 1111 Chester Ave., Cleveland, OH 44114. Box 95795, Cleveland, OH 44101. Ed. Lura Romei. Tel. (216) 696-7000. M; $40; 1956; circ. 150,000. Indexed: Mgt. Contents. Annual Issues: Jan.—Buyer's Guide; June—Electronic Office Awards. Notes: adv., bk. rev., calendars, dwgs., photos (color, B&W). Micro: BLH, UMI.

Covers the latest technology and design of the office environment. Emphasis is on new equipment, management, and space planning. Useful to individuals responsible for selecting equipment as well as to architects and facility planners. (0746-3039)

0351 OFFICE (US)
Office Publications Inc., 1600 Summer St., Stamford, CT 06904. P.O. Box 1231, Stamford, CT 06904. Ed. William R. Schulhof. Tel. (203) 327-9670. M; $30; 1935; circ. 132,000. Indexed: B.P.I. Annual Issues: Jan.—Annual Forum (Reader's Product Survey); June—Office Design. Notes: adv., bk. rev., photos (B&W, color). Micro: UMI.

Reports on administration, systems, and equipment for the office. Short articles focus on monthly themes. Particularly useful are the frequent charts comparing manufacturers of various products such as copiers, microfilm reader/printers, and office computers. (0030-0128)

0352 OFFICE ADMINISTRATION (US)
AND AUTOMATION
Geyer-McAllister Publications, Inc., 51 Madison Ave., New York, NY 10010. Ed. William A. Olcott. Tel. (212) 689-4411. M; $20; 1940; circ. 65,000. Indexed: B.P.I., Comp. Lit. Ind., Dec. issue. Annual Issues: Jan.—Office Automation Award; May—Office of the Year; Dec.—Directory Issue. Micro: UMI.

Office managers and purchasing agents would find this magazine more valuable than architects or interior designers. Some articles appear on space planning and design, but the emphasis is on new products and management of automated systems. (0745-4325)

0353 OFFICE EQUIPMENT AND (CN)
METHODS
777 Bay St., Toronto, Ont. M5W 1A7, Canada. Ed. Arden Gayman. Tel. (416) 596-5920. 10/yr.; Can.$22; 1955. Annual Issues: Dec.—Buyer's Guide. Micro: UMI.

In-depth coverage of modern office systems. Emphasis on equipment selection, layout, and operations. Only Canadian products appear in the new products section. (0030-0179) +

0354 OFFICE EQUIPMENT NEWS (UK)
Business Publications, Ltd., Audit House, Field End Rd., Ruislip, Middlesex HA4 9LT, England. Ed. Rowland Morgan. Tel. (01) 868-4499. Telex 934171. M; £23; 1958; circ. 55,000. Notes: adv., bk. rev., photos (B&W, color).

Contains brief articles on office equipment and furnishings. Very similar in format and content to the American Today's Office. (0030-0187).

0355 OFFICE SYSTEMS (UK)
IPC Electrical-Electronics Press, Ltd., Quadrant House, Quadrant, Surrey SM2 5AS, England. +

0356 SKYLINES (US)
Building & Owners Management Assn. International, 1250 I St., NW, Ste. 200, Washington, DC 20005. Ed. Kathryn N. Hamilton. Tel. (202) 638-2929. M; $25; 1916; circ. 5,000. Indexed: B.P.I. Micro: BLH.

Newspaper that presents news of the office

building industry. Of interest primarily to building managers. Short articles on codes, legislation, industry events, leasing activities, security, and other facility planning and operating issues.

0357   TODAY'S OFFICE   (US)
(Formerly: *Office Product News*)
Hearst Business Communications, Inc., 645 Stewart Ave., Garden City, NY 11530. Ed. Eileen Feretic. Tel. (516) 222-2500. M; $30; 1982; circ. 160,000. *Indexed*: Jan. issue. *Notes*: adv., photos (color).
   Broad coverage of selection, implementation, and operation of the latest office systems. Technical and management issues are discussed. (0744-2815)

0358   UFFICIOSTILE   (IT)
Compagnia Pubblicazioni Internazionali, viale Stelvio 21, 20159 Milan, Italy. Ed. Mara Solari. Tel. (02) 6086655. M; circ. 200,000. *Notes*: adv., photos (B&W, color).
   Covers outstanding examples of office design worldwide. Includes articles on ergonomics, space planning, and new products. Text in English and Italian. (0503-0455)

Residential

0887   APARTMENT & BUILDING

0541   ARCHITECTURAL DIGEST

**0359   ARCHITECTURAL SERVICES   (UK)
           BOOK OF HOUSE PLANS**
45 Station Road, Redhill, Surrey, England. Ed. John Bailey. Tel. 68261. A. *Notes*: adv., dwgs., photos (B&W, color).
   A large volume of home designs. Each page includes exterior views, floor plans, room dimensions, and physical descriptions. Copies of sets of plans can be ordered from publisher. All homes are made of timber-framed components. Includes some financing news.

**0893   AUTOMATION IN HOUSING
           AND MANUFACTURED
           HOME DEALER**

**0606   BETTER HOMES AND
           GARDENS**

0476   BROWNSTONER

0360   BUILDER   (US)
(Formerly: *N.A.H.B. Builder*)
Hanley-Wood, Inc., National Housing Center, 15th & M Streets, NW, Washington, DC 20005. Ed. Frank Anton. Tel. (202) 822-0390. M; $20 (free with NAHB membership); 1947; circ. 175,000. *Indexed*: Arch. Ind. *Annual Issues*: Jan.—50 Favorite Products; May—Builder 100. *Notes*: adv., dwgs., photos (B&W, color). *Micro*: UMI.
   Official magazine of the National Association of Home Builders. Intended to help builders, architects, and other industry professionals keep up with the latest designs, housing products, and marketing strategies. A special project and new products are featured monthly. Includes some light commercial architecture. The "Outlook" column includes economic news, surveys of builder activities, and charts on housing statistics. Incorporates the former *Housing*. (0744-1193)

0248   CALIFORNIA BUILDER

0361   CASE AL MARE   (IT)
Di Baio Editore S.r.l., Via Settembrini 11, 20124 Milan, Italy. Ed. Guiseppe Maria Janghi-Lavarini. S-a; L.6,000; 1980. +

0362   CASE DI CAMPAGNA   (IT)
Di Baio Editore S.r.l., Via Settembrini 11, 20124 Milan, Italy. Ed. Guiseppe Maria Ganghi-Lauanni. S-a; L.6,000; 1979. +

0363   CASE DI MONTAGNA   (IT)
Di Baio Editore S.r.l., Via Settembrini 11, 20124 Milan, Italy. S-a; 1978. +

0364   COLONIAL HOMES   (US)
(Formerly: *House Beautiful's Colonial Homes*)
Hearst Magazines, 1700 Broadway, New York, NY 10029. Ed. Richard Beatty. Tel. (212) 903-5400. Bi-m; 1975. +

**0938   CONSTRUCTION REPORTS:
           HOUSING STARTS**

0365   COUNTRY LIFE   (UK)
IPC Magazines, Ltd., Rm. 2816, King's Reach Tower, Stamford St., London SE1 9LS, England. Oakfield House, 35 Perrymount Rd., Haywards Heath, W. Sussex RH16 3DH, England. Ed. Marcus Binney. Tel. (01) 261-7058. Telex 915748 MAGDIV G. W; $148; 1897; circ. 47,000. *Indexed*: A.P.I., Art Ind., Avery,

R.I.L.A. *Notes*: adv., bk. rev., calendars, dwgs., photos (B&W, color). *Micro*: UMI.

A review of the design, arts, gardens, and preservation of country estates. Some issues focus on the designs of a specific country. Beautiful coverage of antique furnishings. Presents descriptions of estates for sale. (0045-8856)

0613   DEMEURES ET CHATEAUX

0366   DISTINGUISHED HOME   (US)
          PLANS & PRODUCTS
Master Plan Service, 89 E. Jericho Turnpike, Mineola, NY 11501. Ed. Kenneth Miller. Q; $1.75; 1950. +

1015   DO IT YOURSELF

0948   EARTH SHELTER LIVING

0367   FINE HOMEBUILDING   (US)
Taunton Press, P.O. Box 355, Newtown, CT 06470. Ed. John Lively. Tel. (203) 426-8171. Bi-m; $16; $20 (abroad); 1981; circ. 180,000. *Indexed*: A.P.I., Avery. *Notes*: adv., bk. rev., calendars, dwgs., photos (B&W, color).

Well-illustrated magazine on fine custom home design and construction. Articles are written by experienced home builders who describe the process from design and construction or renovation through occupancy. Read by builders and the general public. (0273-1398)

0368   GA (GLOBAL   (JA)
          ARCHITECTURE) HOUSES
A.D.A. Edita Tokyo Co., Ltd., 3-12-14 Sendagaya, Shibuya-ku, Tokyo, Japan. Ed. Yukio Futagawa. Irreg.; $22.50 ea. *Indexed*: A.P.I., Avery. *Notes*: dwgs., photos (B&W, color).

Beautifully illustrated homes from around the world. Text in Japanese.

0369   GARLINGHOUSE HOME   (US)
          PLAN GUIDES
Garlinghouse Publishing Co., 320 S.W. 33rd St., Box 299, Topeka, KS 66601. Tel. (913) 267-2490. S-a; $7 (2 years); 1981; circ. 115,000. *Notes*: adv., dwgs.

Floor plans and descriptions of build-it-yourself homes. *

0370   HABITATION   (SZ)
Union Suisse pour l'Amelioration du Logement, Section Romande, Avenue de Tivoli 2, 1007 Lausanne, Switzerland. Ed. Pierre Etienne Monot. Tel. (021) 204141. 10/yr.; Fr. 42; 1928. *Indexed*: A.P.I. *Notes*: adv., photos (B&W).

A review of residential construction edited for architects. Text in French. (0017-6419)*

0615   HOME

0371   HOME AGAIN   (US)
P.O. Box 421, Village Station, 65 Bleeker St., New York, NY 10014. Ed. Kenneth Lelen. Tel. (212) 473-5583. Q; $29; 1983. *Notes*: adv., bk. rev., calendars, dwgs., photos (B&W).

A national magazine for professionals in the housing and community preservation fields. Feature articles written by professionals cover the techniques used to finance, develop, manage, and promote renovation projects. Each issue includes company profiles, product reviews, and notes on grants, workshops, and resources. Examines projects in selected regions, towns, and neighborhoods throughout the U.S. Offers opinions on rehabilitating historical structures, providing affordable housing, reducing energy consumption, and revitalizing commercial districts. (0739-3326) *

0958   HOME & BUILDING

0959   HOME BUILDER NEWS

1017   THE HOMEOWNER

0372   HOUSE AND BUNGALOW   (UK)
Architectural Service Planning Partnership Plan Magazines, Ltd., 45 Station Rd., Redhill, Surrey RH 1QH, England. Ed. John Bailey. Tel. (0737) 68261. A; £5; 1969; circ. 40,000. *Notes*: adv., dwgs., photos (B&W, color).

Magazine of English house plans used to promote the Architectural Services Books of house and bungalow plans. (0018-6392) *

0618   HOUSE AND GARDEN

0619   HOUSE AND GARDEN

0373   HOUSE BEAUTIFUL'S   (US)
          BUILDING MANUAL
Hearst Magazines, House Beautiful Special Publications, 1700 Broadway, New York, NY 10029. Ed. Gordon Firth. Tel. (212) 903-5051. S-a; $2.95 ea. (newsstand only); 1935; circ. 200,000. *Notes*: adv., bk. rev., dwgs., photos (B&W, color).

A consumer magazine that surveys fine residential designs that illustrate fundamental design principles. Aimed at families planning custom-built homes. Features economical building techniques, solutions to siting problems, ideas for kitchens and baths, and new building materials. Also features houses for which blueprints are available. Well illustrated and practical. (0018-6430)

0374   HOUSE BEAUTIFUL'S HOME   (US)
       REMODELING
1700 Broadway, 28th floor, New York, NY 10019. Ed. Gordon Firth. Tel. (212) 903-5051. Q; $2.95 (newsstand only); 1964; circ. 200,000. *Notes*: adv., bk. rev., dwgs., photos (B&W, color).
Edited for the general public, the articles range from do-it-yourself remodeling projects to major rehabilitation. Ideas are presented for kitchens, bathrooms, storage areas, decorating, and exterior improvements.

0375   HOUSE BEAUTIFUL'S   (US)
       HOUSES AND PLANS
1700 Broadway, 28th floor, New York, NY 10019. Ed. Gordon Firth. Tel. (212) 903-5051. A; $2.95 (newsstand only); 1957; circ. 175,000. *Notes*: adv., dwgs., photos (B&W, color).
A wide range of architect-designed homes is presented with notes on where to purchase sets of blueprints and specifications. Well illustrated with exterior renderings, floor plans, and detailed descriptions.

0376   HOUSE BUILDER AND   (UK)
       ESTATE DEVELOPER
Federated Employers Press, Ltd., 82 New Cavendish St., London W1M 8AD, England. Ed. Phillip Cooke. Tel. (01) 580-5588. Telex 265763. M; £26; 1974; circ. 20,000. *Indexed*: A.P.I. *Notes*: adv., dwgs., photos (B&W, color).
The official journal of the National Housebuilding Council, House Builders Federation, and New Homes Marketing Board. Covers the political, economic, and marketing aspects of the industry. Includes product news. Subscribers include every registered home builder in the UK. *

0377   LOG HOME &   (US)
       ALTERNATIVE HOUSING
       BUILDER
16 First Ave., Corry, PA 16407. Ed. Rick Martin. Tel. (814) 664-8624. Bi-m; $15. *Notes*: adv., photos (B&W, color).
Aimed at builder-dealers. Emphasis on industry news rather than the homeowner. Large product section. (2079-6368)

0378   LOG HOME GUIDE FOR   (CN)
       BUILDERS AND BUYERS
Muir Publishing Co., 1 Pacific, Gardenvale, Quebec H9X 1BO, Canada. Muir Publishing Co., P.O. Box 37, W. Rutland, VT 05777-0037. Ed. Doris Muir. Tel. (514) 457-2045. Q; $18; 1977. *Notes*: adv., bk. rev., photos (B&W, color).
A comprehensive magazine on log-cabin construction, products, techniques, and interior design including occasional features on log-cabin design in other countries. A good source for locating companies that sell plan books and kits. (0707-5006)

0379   MAISONS DE FRANCE   (FR)
Edinot, 21 rue Cassette, 75006 Paris, France. Ed. Jean Michel Reillier. M; $140; 1968. +

0590   MAISONS ET DECORS
       MEDITERRANEE

0380   MAISONS ET DECORS, SUD-   (FR)
       OUEST, MIDI PYRENEES
Compagnie Regionale de Publications Specialises, Section Sud-Ouest, Midi Pyrenees, 11 rue Cheverus, 3300 Bordeaux, France. Ed. Georges Alain Mahe. Bi-m; 1971. +

0970   MANUFACTURED HOUSING
       NEWSLETTER

0971   MANUFACTURED HOUSING
       REPORTER

0629   METROPOLITAN HOME

0381   MULTI-HOUSING NEWS   (US)
       (Formerly: *Apartment Construction News*)
Gralla Publications, 1515 Broadway, New York, NY 10036. Ed. Todd Zimmerman. Tel. (212) 869-1300. M; $20 (free to qualified subscribers); 1966; circ. 51,000. *Annual Issues*: March—Property Management Directory. *Notes*: adv., calendars, dwgs., photos (B&W).
A tabloid that presents ideas and news on the multihousing design, construction, and management industries. Articles focus on quality and profit. New products and government programs are reviewed. Apartments, condominiums, and townhouses are covered. (0146-0919)

0382   NEW SHELTER   (US)
Rodale Press, Inc., 33 E. Minor St., Emmaus, PA 18049. Ed. Robert Rodale. 9/yr.; $11; 1980; circ. 640,000. *Notes*: adv., photos (B&W). *Micro*: UMI.

Presents projects and plans of home construction with an emphasis on solar developments, energy, and useful home technologies. The products discussed have been tested and examined at in-house facilities. (0195-6582)

0383 101 HOME PLANS   (US)
Davis Publications, Inc., 229 Park Ave. S., New York, NY 10003. Q; 1968. +

0384 PROFESSIONAL BUILDER   (US)
AND APARTMENT
BUSINESS
Cahners Publishing Co., 475 Park Ave. South, New York, NY 10016. Ed. Roy L. Diez. Tel. (212) 686-0555. M; 1936; circ. 111,000. *Annual Issues:* Jan.—Builder of the Year; July—Housing Giants; Dec.—Consumer/Builder Survey. *Notes:* adv., photos (B&W, color).
Presents a wide range of topics of interest to the single and multifamily housing industries. Consideration is given to custom-designed homes, tract housing, prefabricated homes, and some light nonresidential projects. Contains ideas and news on construction techniques, new products, financing, market trends, and design. Includes a column on builders' plans for sale. Of interest to developers, builders, architects, engineers, and suppliers to the home industry. (0361-5326)

0985 PROFESSIONAL
REMODELING

0987 QUALIFIED REMODELER

0992 REMODELING
CONTRACTOR

0385 SELECT HOMES   (CN)
Builders Plus Enterprises, Ltd., 382 W. Broadway, Vancouver, BC B5Y 1R2, Canada. Ed. Ralph Westbrook. 5/yr.; Can.$11.95; 1976. (0713-8075) +

0386 SMALL HOME PLANS   (US)
Davis Publications, Inc., 380 Lexington Ave., New York, NY 10007. Ed. Gail Hayden. Tel. (212) 557-9100. Q; 1970. +

0634 SOUTHERN ACCENTS

0387 TOSHI-JUTAKU   (JA)
Kajima Inst. Publ. Co., 6-5-13 Akasaka, Minato-ku, Tokyo 107, Japan. Ed. Masahiro Yoshida. M; Yen 20,000. *Indexed:* Avery. *Notes:* adv., dwgs., photos (B&W, color).

A professional journal devoted to urban housing. Includes single-family dwellings as well as large-scale housing complexes. Primarily Japanese work is presented. Text in Japanese.

0880 TUTTOVILLE

0388 UNIQUE HOMES   (US)
Ziff-Davis Publishing, One Park Ave., New York, NY 10016. P.O. Box 2921, Boulder, CO 80322. Ed. Cathleen Johnson. Tel. (212) 725-7720. Bi-m; $24.97; circ. 75,000. *Notes:* adv., photos (B&W, color).
Distinguished U.S. residential properties that are available for sale are lavishly presented with photographs, dimensions, prices, and names of brokers. Primarily of interest to investors, it can also be useful to designers of luxury homes.

0636 VICTORIAN HOMES

0389 VILLE—GIARDINI   (IT)
via Trentacoste 7, 20134 Milan, Italy. Gruppo Editoriale Electa S.p.A., via Goldoni 1, 20129 Milan, Italy. Ed. Nani Prina. Tel. (02) 236931. Telex 313123 Tradex/Electa. M; L.30,000; 1957; circ. 70,000. *Indexed:* A.P.I., Avery. *Notes:* adv., dwgs., photos (color).
Offers a wide panorama of modern and traditional homes and how they relate to their landscapes. Richly illustrated. Emphasis is on single dwellings, particularly European villas and the gardens surrounding them. Also includes technical articles and interior layouts. (0042-6237)

0390 VIVIENDA/DWELLING   (AG)
Roberto Carmuega Pub., Lima 187, Piso 2, 1073 Buenos Aires, Argentina. Ed. Jorge Bottini. M; 1960. +

Hotels, Motels, and Restaurants

0391 CANADIAN HOTEL AND   (CN)
RESTAURANT
(Formerly: *Canadian Hotel & Restaurant Review*)
MacLean Hunter, Ltd., MacLean Hunter Bldg., 777 Bay Street, Toronto, Ont. M5W 1A7, Canada. Ed. Peter Brouwer. Tel. (416) 596-5782. M; Can.$20; 1923. *Annual Issues:* April, Oct.—Product Review; Nov.—Product Directory.
Features new products and systems in the Canadian lodging and restaurant industry. (0008-3801) +

1021 THE CONSULTANT

0392   FOODSERVICE &   (CN)
         HOSPITALITY
980 Yonge St., Suite 400, Toronto, Ont. CN
M4W, Canada. Ed. Michael McKean. Tel. (416)
923-8888. M; Can. $24; 1972; circ. 30,000. *Annual Issues*: June—Buyer's Guide; Sept.—Top
100 Firms; Nov.—Equipment Directory. *Notes*:
adv., bibl., calendars, dwgs., photos (B&W,
color).

Emphasis is on management issues and profiles of leaders in the lodging and hospitality industries. *

1034   FOODSERVICE EQUIPMENT
         SPECIALIST

0393   HOTEL & MOTEL   (US)
         MANAGEMENT
545 Fifth Ave., New York, NY 10017. One E.
First St., Duluth, MN 55802. Ed. Peter Romeo.
Tel. (212) 503-2949. M; $24; 1983; circ. 42,000.
Notes: adv., dwgs., photos (B&W, color).
Micro: UMI.

Emphasis is on industry news and management issues but also includes columns on hotel/
motel design and construction. (0018-6082) *

0394   HOTELS & RESTAURANTS   (US)
         INTERNATIONAL
(Formerly: *Service World International*)
P.O. Box 5080, Des Plaines, IL 60018. 270 St.
Paul St., Denver, CO 80206. Ed. Madelin M.
Schneider. Tel. (312) 635-8800. Telex 910 233
1658. 8/yr.; $25; 1966; circ. 18,207. *Annual Issues*: Jan.—Worldwide Buyer's Guide. *Notes*:
adv., photos (B&W, color).

Journal covers world chain operations, distribution, fast food, tourism, construction and design, and foodservice/catering. Scope is
international. (0744-3897)

0395   LODGING HOSPITALITY   (US)
Penton IPC, 1111 Chester Ave., Cleveland, OH
44114. P.O. Box 95759, Cleveland, OH 44101.
Ed. Edward Watkins. Tel. (216) 696-7000. M;
$40; 1949; circ. 44,000. *Annual Issues*: Jan.—
Technology; March—Products Data Guide;
April—Interior Design; Aug.—Top 400 Performers; Nov.—Design Awards; Dec.—Forecasts. *Notes*: adv., calendars, photos (B&W,
color). *Micro*: UMI.

Features and news on all aspects of the lodging industry, with emphasis on operation and
management. Articles cover financing, designing, building, and furnishing hotels as well as
staffing and productivity maintenance. (0148-
0766) *

0396   NATION'S RESTAURANT   (US)
         NEWS
Lebhar-Friedman Inc., 425 Park Ave., New
York, NY 10022. Ed. Charles Bernstein. Tel.
(212) 371-9400. Bi-w. *Annual Issues*: Dec.—
Company Profiles.

Focus is on business aspects of the restaurant
industry, but issues are also of interest because
of feature articles on design and new technology. (0028-0518)

0397   OPEN HOUSE   (AT)
Rank Publishing Co., P.O. Box 189, St. Leonards NSW 2065, Australia. Ed. Simon Kent.
Tel. 4382300. Telex AA21822SY371. *Indexed*:
A.P.I. *Annual Issues*: Jan.—Product Digest.
Notes: adv., calendars, photos (B&W, color).

The latest news on the foodservice and catering industries, with special application to Australia.*

0398   RESTAURANT AND HOTEL   (US)
         DESIGN
(Formerly: *Restaurant Design*)
Restaurant Business, Inc., 633 Third Ave., New
York, NY 10017. Ed. Barbara J. Knox. Tel.
(212) 986-4800. Bi-m; $24; 1979; circ. 40,000.
Notes: adv., bk. rev., calendars, dwgs., photos
(B&W, color). *Micro*: UMI.

National coverage of leading restaurant and
hotel design with attention to innovative solutions to design problems. Includes industry and
product news. (0191-345x)

0399   RESTAURANT HOSPITALITY   (US)
Penton IPC, 1111 Chester Ave., Cleveland, OH
44114. Ed. Stephen Michaelides. Tel. (216) 696-
7000. M; $40; 1919; circ. 101,000. *Annual Issues*: Jan.—Product Reference File; Feb.—
Kitchen Design Awards; May—Interior Design
Awards; June—Annual 500; Aug.—Top 100
Chains. *Notes*: adv., dwgs., photos (B&W,
color).

Emphasis is on general operation of foodservice establishments but includes regular columns on design. (0147-9989) *

0400   RESTAURANTS AND   (US)
         INSTITUTIONS
Cahners Publishing Co., 475 Park Ave. South,
New York, NY 10016. 270 St. Paul St., Denver,
CO 80206. Ed. Jane Y. Wallace. Tel. (212) 686-
0555. Bi-w; $65 (free to qualified subscribers);
1937; circ. 127,000. *Notes*: adv., bk. rev., photos (B&W, color).

Feature articles, reports, and case studies on
design, construction, and management of food-

service establishments including restaurants, hotels, clubs, school dining halls, fast-food chains, and large institutions. (0273-5520) *

Retail

0401   ARCHITEKTUR UND   (SZ)
       LADENBAU
(Formerly: *Ladenbau*)
Forster-Verlag AG, Alte Landstr. 43, CH-8700, Kuesnacht-Zurich, Switzerland. Ed. Esther Bollman. Tel. 01/9108022. Telex 825729. Bi-m; Fr.50; 1964; circ. 4,000. *Indexed*: Avery. *Notes*: adv., bibl., bk. rev., calendars, dwgs., photos (B&W, color).
A European journal for modern shop windows and store displays. Examines aspects of design and installation including lighting and signage. Of interest to interior designers as well as storeowners. Text in German.

0402   DISCOUNT MERCHANDISER   (US)
MacFadden Publications, 2 Park Ave., 16th fl., New York, NY 10016. Ed. Nathaniel Schwartz. (212) 889-3446. M; $25; 1961. *Indexed*: P.A.I.S. *Notes*: photos (B&W, color). *Micro*: UMI.
Regular features include display, interior design, and store construction. (0012-3579) +

0403   NATIONAL MALL MONITOR   (US)
2535 Landmark Dr., Ste. 201, Clearwater, FL 33519. Ed. Lydon Kuhns. Tel. (813) 796-8870. Bi-m; $45; 1971; circ. 24,745. *Annual Issues*: Jan./Feb.—Top U.S. Developers; March/April —Centers of Excellence (Architectural Competitions); May/June—Convention Issue; Sept./ Oct.—Dealmaking Issue; Nov./Dec.—Expanding Markets. *Notes*: adv., photos (B&W, color).
A key publication for getting current information on shopping centers in the U.S. Topics include planning, design, construction, leasing, financing, management, and promotion. Extensive coverage is given to specific projects and developers. (0194-5017) *

0404   RETAIL TECHNOLOGY   (US)
(Formerly: *Chain Store Age Executive*)
Lebhar-Friedman, Inc., 425 Park Ave., New York, NY 10022. Tel. (212) 371-9400. M; 1924. *Indexed*: ABI/Inform.
Key aspects of planning and operating stores and shopping centers are discussed. Of primary importance to owners, store planners, and operators, but architects would also find it useful for identifying major builders and becoming aware of the needs and problems in retail facility design and construction. +

0405   SHOPPING CENTER WORLD   (US)
Communication Channels, Inc., 6255 Barfield Rd., Atlanta, GA 30328. Ed. Constance Brittain. Tel. (404) 256-9800. M; $39; 1972; circ. 28,665. *Annual Issues*: Jan.—Biennial Shopping Center Census; May—Salary Surveys; Aug.— Product Directory; Oct.—Finance Directory; Dec.—Chain Store Expansion Plans.
In-depth coverage of the shopping center industry. Issues include current information on regional markets, exterior and interior design, leasing, management, and maintenance. An important resource for identifying new and innovative projects. Readership includes developers, builders, center managers, promoters, chainstore executives, architects, interior designers, and realtors. (0049-0393)

0406   STORE PLANNING SERVICE   (US)
Retail Reporting Bureau, 101 Fifth Ave., New York, NY 10003. Tel. (212) 255-9595. M; 1941. (0039-1859) +

0407   STORES   (US)
National Retail Merchants Assn., 100 W. 31st St., New York, NY 10001. Tel. (212) 244-8780. M; 1918.
The emphasis is on marketing; however, there are frequent articles on visual merchandising and store design. The directories of top stores, which include their expansion plans, are useful to investors, builders, and architects. (0039-1867) +

0408   VISUAL MERCHANDISING   (US)
       AND STORE DESIGN
S.T. Publications, 407 Gilbert Ave., Cincinnati, OH 45202. Ed. P.K. Anderson. Tel. (513) 421-2050. Telex 382040. M; $32; 1894; circ. 45,000. *Annual Issues*: Feb.—Buyer's Guide; April, June, Dec.—Trade Show Issues. *Notes*: adv., bk. rev., calendars, dwgs., photos (B&W, color). *Micro*: UMI.
Covers all aspects of visual merchandising and store design including seasonal displays, graphics, store planning, and lighting. International store designs and displays are featured. Readers include store interior planners, designers, store owners and executives, independent lighting designers, and specifiers. (0745-4295) *

Cultural

0409   AUDITORIUM NEWS   (US)
International Assn. of Auditorium Managers, 500 N. Michigan Ave., Suite 1400, Chicago, IL 60611. Ed. Robert A. Bassi. M; $10; 1962. +

0410   AVISO   (US)
American Assn. of Museums, 1055 Thomas Jefferson St., NW, Washington, DC 20007. Ed. Migs Grove. M; $24; 1968.
   Newsletter. +

0411   MARQUEE   (US)
Theatre Historical Society, 6510 41 Ave., Hyattsville, MD 20782. Fred Beall, P.O. Box 767, San Francisco, CA 94101. Ed. Dr. Robert Headley, Jr. Tel. (301) 927-5480. Q; $17; 1969; circ. 900. *Annual Issues*: Special Theater Issues. *Notes*: adv., bibl., bk. rev., dwgs., photos (B&W, color).
   The luxurious architecture of old theaters and movie palaces is the focus of this society journal. The buildings are discussed in a historical, cultural, and artistic context. Includes notes on preservation, archival resources, and exhibits. (0025-3928)

0412   MUSEUM   (US)
UNESCO, 7-9 Place de Fontenoy, 75700 Paris, France. UNIPUB, Box 1222, Ann Arbor, MI 48106. Ed. Anne Erdos. M; $37; 1948; circ. 2,400. *Indexed*: A.P.I., Art Ind. *Notes*: photos (B&W, color).
   An international journal covering all aspects of museography, including facility and exhibition design. Articles discuss special problems of lighting, audio-visual facilities, circulation, security, and access for the disabled. Written for the museum professional, it is also of great interest to anyone involved in the design process. Text in English and French. (0027-3996) *

0413   MUSEUM NEWS   (US)
American Assn. of Museums, 1055 Thomas Jefferson St., N.W., Washington, DC 20007. Ed. Ellen Cochran Hicks. Tel. (202) 338-5300. Bi-m; $24; 1924; circ. 8,000. *Indexed*: Art Ind., Aug. issue. *Annual Issues*: June—Meeting Issue. *Notes*: adv., bk. rev., dwgs., photos (B&W, color).
   The major journal for museum professionals. Articles discuss administration, financing, equipment security, and architecture. Provides philosophical debate and practical advice. (0027-4089)

0414   MUSEUMS JOURNAL   (UK)
Museums Assn., 34 Bloomsbury Way, London WC1A 2SF, England. Q; £20; 1901. *Indexed*: A.P.I., Art Ind. (0027-416x) +

0415   SCENA   (GE)
Institut fuer Technologie Kultureller Einrichtungen, Clara Zetkin Str. 1205, DDR-108 Berlin, E. Germany. Q; 1962. (0036-5726) +

0416   THEATRE DESIGN AND   (US)
          TECHNOLOGY
U.S. Inst. for Theatre Technology, Inc., 330 W. 42nd St., Ste. 1702, New York, NY 10036. Eds. Arnold Aronson, Kate Davy. Tel. (212) 563-5551. Q; $24; 1965; circ. 3,200. *Indexed*: A.P.I. *Notes*: adv., bibl., bk. rev., dwgs., photos (B&W, color). *Micro*: UMI.
   Articles on the construction of theaters, new technical developments, stage design, lighting, and sound administration. Includes a section of article citations from foreign journals on theater design. (0040-5477)

Governmental

1188   COMMERCE BUSINESS
          DAILY

0417   CORRECTIONS MAGAZINE   (US)
Criminal Justice Publications, Inc., 567 Sixth St., No. 11, Brooklyn, NY 11215. Ed. David Anderson. Bi-m; 1974. *Indexed*: CJPI. *Notes*: adv., bk. rev., illus. (0095-4594) +

0418   CORRECTIONS TODAY   (US)
   (Formerly: *American Journal of Corrections*)
American Correctional Association, 4321 Hartwick Rd., Ste. L208, College Park, MD 20740. Ed. Julie N. Tucker. Tel. (301) 699-7600. Bi-m; $25; 1939. *Indexed*: P.A.I.S., CJPI. *Notes*: adv., photos (B&W). *Micro*: MIM, UMI.
   Presents detailed coverage of the corrections field, including facility design. (0190-2563) +

0252   DESIGN ACTION

Health Care

1189   CONSTRUCTION REPORT ON
          HOSPITALS

0112   FACILITIES PLANNING
          NEWS

0954   FROM THE STATE
          CAPITALS: CONSTRUCTION
          —INSTITUTIONAL

0419   HEALTH CARE   (CN)
Southam Communications, Ltd., 1450 Don Mills Rd., Don Mills, Ontario M3B 2X7, Can-

ada. Tel. (416) 445-6641. Ed. Heather Howie. M; $33; 1959; circ. 13,400. *Indexed*: Hosp. Lit. Ind. *Annual Issues*: May—Buyer's Guide. *Notes*: adv., bk. rev., photos (B&W, color). *Micro*: UMI. +

Although primarily a magazine for hospital administrators, architects will find it useful as a buying guide for equipment and a source of information on new technology and systems used in health-care facilities. (0226-5788)

0420   HEALTH CARE SYSTEMS   (US)
(Formerly: *Health Care Product News*)
Gralla Publications, 1515 Broadway, New York, NY 10036. 1501 Broadway, Room 930, New York, NY 10036. Ed. Anthony Rutigliano. Tel. (212) 869-1300. M; $36; 1980. *Annual Issues*: Jan.—Directory of Products and Services. *Notes*: adv., bk. rev., calendars, dwgs., photos (B&W, color).

A review of products, technology, and services in the health-care field. Regular features on aspects of planning and design of health-care facilities. (0745-1717)

0421   HOSPITAL DEVELOPMENT   (UK)
(Formerly: *Hospital Building and Engineering*)
23-29 Emerald St., London WC1N 3QJ, England. Ed. Roy Owen. Tel. (01) 404-5531. Telex 21746 ITPLN6. 9/yr.; £16; 1968; circ. 8,794. *Indexed*: A.P.I., Excerp. Med. *Notes*: adv., photos (B&W).

Provides specialized information on planning, construction, modernization, maintenance, and energy conservation in hospitals. Focus is primarily on the United Kingdom but sometimes offers international coverage. Regular columns deal with products, communication, security, and energy management. Special features cover interior design, floor coverings, waste disposal, etc. Primarily for architects, engineers, hospital consultants, and hospital administrators. (0300-5720)

0422   HOSPITAL TECHNOLOGY   (US)
         SERIES
American Hospital Assn., 840 N. Lake Shore Dr., Chicago, IL 60611. Ed. Susan Frankel. Tel. (312) 280-6084. M; $150 (members); $187 (nonmembers); circ. 1,250. *Indexed*: Hosp. Lit. Ind.

Subscription includes: 1) *Guideline Report* (8/yr.)—focuses on a single technology, offering facility planning and construction criteria and comparisons of various manufacturers' equipment features; 2) *Technology Scanner* (M)—se-

lects articles from major medical and technical journals that relate to hospital operations, technology-based planning, patient-care delivery, and other technology-related questions; 3) *Executive Briefing* (M)—includes concise highlights from *Technology Scanner*. Serves hospital administrators and anyone else involved with design, construction, and procurement. (0735-4681)

0423   HOSPITAL TOPICS   (US)
P.O. Box 5976, Sarasota, FL 34277. Tel. (813) 371-0188. Ed. Gordon M. Marshall. 6/yr.; circ. 92,000. *Indexed*: Excerp. Med. *Notes*: photos (B&W, color). *Micro*: UMI.

New products and systems in health-care facilities are covered. Major articles cover the planning and design of facilities as well as of specific medical departments. Primarily for administrators but also of interest to architects who specialize in health-care facility design. (0018-5868) +

0424   HOSPITAL WEEK   (US)
American Hospital Assn., 211 E. Chicago Ave., Ste. 700, Chicago, IL 60611. Ed. Lynn Kahn. Tel. (312) 951-1100. W; $20; 1964; circ. 55,000.

A four-page newsletter primarily of interest to hospital administrators; however, the news briefs on funding and planning for new facilities would be of interest to architects and consultants who specialize in hospitals. (0149-6352)

0425   HOSPITALS   (US)
American Hospital Publishing, Inc., 211 E. Chicago Ave., Ste. 700, Chicago, IL 60611. Ed. Frank Sabatino. Tel. (312) 951-1100. Bi-w; $35; 1936; circ. 86,000. *Indexed*: A.P.I., Hosp. Lit. Ind., Ind. Med. *Annual Issues*: Feb. 16—Design and Construction Issue. *Notes*: adv., bk. rev., calendars, dwgs., photos (B&W, color).

A major publication that covers the hospital industry. The emphasis is on administration, but regular features and news briefs appear on design, new construction, and technology issues that have an impact on new construction or renovation. (0018-5973)

0426   MODERN HEALTHCARE   (US)
Crain Communications, Inc., 740 N. Rush St., Chicago, IL 60601. Ed. Donald E.L. Johnson. Tel. (312) 649-5342. 16/yr.; $50; 1974; circ. 71,902. *Indexed*: Hosp. Lit. Ind., Ind. Med., Predicasts. *Annual Issues*: March—Construction/Architects Survey. *Notes*: adv., bk. rev., photos (B&W, color). *Micro*: UMI.

Presents general coverage of the health-care industry. Regular features appear on design, construction, and new products of interest to health-care facility planners and designers. (0160-7480)

1193 PROJECT REPORTS

0427 WORLD HOSPITALS   (UK)
International Hospital Federation, 126 Albert St., London NW1 7NX, England. (U.S. sub.) Fairview Park, Elmsford, NY 10523. Ed. M. Leslie Paine. Tel. (01) 267-5176. Q; £21; 1964; circ. 2,000. *Indexed*: Excerp. Med. *Notes*: adv., bibl., bk. rev., calendars, dwgs., photos (B&W, color). *Micro*: UMI.

Articles discuss planning and design of health-care facilities all over the world but primarily in underdeveloped countries. There are general articles on planning and administration of health services worldwide. Text in English; summaries in French and English. (0512-3135) *

Educational

0428 AMERICAN SCHOOL &   (US)
UNIVERSITY
North American Publishing Co., 401 North Broad St., Philadelphia, PA 19108. Ed. Rita Robison. Tel. (215) 574-9600. M; $25; 1928. *Indexed*: Educ. Ind. *Notes*: adv., bk. rev., photos (B&W, color). *Annual Issues*: April—Construction Report; May—Planning Directory & Buyers Guide; Nov.—Portfolio of Educ. Arch. *Micro*: UMI.

Covers planning, design, construction, and management of schools, colleges, and universities. Through the use of case studies, topics such as energy conservation, barrier-free design, renovation, and adaptation/reuse are discussed. (0003-0945) +

0429 C.E.F.P. JOURNAL   (US)
Council of Educational Facility Planners, 29 W. Woodruff Ave., Room 329, Columbus, OH 43210. Ed. Dwayne Gardner. Tel. (614) 422-1521. Bi-m; $15; 1968; circ. 1,200. *Indexed*: ERIC. *Annual Issues*: Nov./Dec.—Profiles of Educational Facilities. *Notes*: adv., bk. rev., dwgs., photos (B&W, color).

Written in a straightforward readable style, this journal covers all aspects of planning, financing, designing, and building educational facilities at all levels. Very useful to school and college administrators, facility managers, architects, engineers, and contractors involved with

this type of construction. The profile issue is particularly interesting to architects. (0007-8220)

0430 C.O.N.E.S.C.A.L.   (MX)
Centro Regional de Construcciones Escolares para America Latina y la Region del Caribe, Apartado Postal 4-518, Mexico 10 D.F., Mexico. Irreg.; $16; 1965; circ. 1,500. *Indexed*: A.P.I., Avery. *Notes*: bibl., bk. rev., dwgs., photos (B&W).

Presents detailed programming information, guidelines, and descriptions of the design and construction of all types of educational facilities including libraries. The projects described are primarily Latin American. Text in Spanish; summaries in English. (0007-8794)

0954 FROM THE STATE
CAPITALS: CONSTRUCTION
—INSTITUTIONAL

0431 LIBRARY JOURNAL   (US)
Bowker Pub. Co., 205 E. 42nd St., New York, NY 10017. P.O. Box 1427, Riverton, NJ 08077. Ed. John Berry III. Tel. (212) 916-1600. 20/yr.; $59; 1876. *Indexed*: Educ. Ind., Lib. Lit., Mag. Ind., P.A.I.S. *Annual Issues*: Dec.—Library Design and Construction. *Micro*: UMI.

A major publication for librarians, it is also a valuable source for library consultants involved with the planning, design, and construction of facilities. In addition to the announcements of new publications and management features, there is regular coverage of new products, equipment, and systems. Helps a designer understand the needs of librarians and their clientele. (0363-0277)

0432 SCHOOL PRODUCT NEWS   (US)
Penton/IPC, Inc., 1111 Chester Ave., Cleveland, OH 44114. P.O. Box 95759, Cleveland, OH 44101. Ed. Roger Morton. Tel. (216) 696-1700. M; $40 (free to school officials); 1962; circ. 63,500. *Notes*: adv., bk. rev., dwgs., photos (B&W, color). *Micro*: UMI.

Although the emphasis is primarily on supplies, furnishings, and equipment, there occasionally are articles on design, construction techniques, and energy efficiency. Of interest to school officials, educational facility planners, and architects who design schools. (0036-6749)

0433 SCHUL UND   (AU)
SPORTSTATTENBAU
Brueder Hollink, Gallgasse 40a, A-1130 Vienna, Austria. Q; 1965. (0036-7095) +

Industrial

1173   AREA DEVELOPMENT

1174   BUSINESS FACILITIES

1130   ENGINEER'S DIGEST

0112   FACILITIES PLANNING
       NEWS

0434   FARM BUILDING EXPRESS   (UK)
Atcost Ltd., The Pantiles, Turnbridge Wells,
Kent, England. Q; free; 1963. *Indexed*: A.P.I.
(0014-7850) +

0435   FARM BUILDING NEWS   (US)
260 Regency Court, Waukesha, WI 53186. Ed.
Frank Lessiter. Tel. (414) 782-0604. 8/yr.;
$11.95; 1967; circ. 23,049. *Annual Issues*: April
—New Products; Sept.—Farm Construction;
Oct.—Buyer's Guide. *Notes*: adv., bk. rev.,
dwgs., photos (B&W, color).
   Aimed at the rural contractor, this publication
presents features and advice on the construction
of farm buildings, installation of livestock feed-
ing and handling systems, construction and installation of grain storage and handling systems,
and other similar buildings. (0014-7869) *

0436   HIGH TECH FACILITIES   (US)
Business Facilities Publishing Co., Inc., Box
8720, Red Bank, NJ 07701. Tel. (201) 842-0433.
Ed. Eric Peterson. Q; $10; 1983; circ. 10,000. +

0960   INDUSTRIAL
       CONSTRUCTION

0437   MATERIAL HANDLING   (US)
       ENGINEERING
122 E. 42nd St., New York, NY 10017. Penton/
IPC, 1111 Chester Ave., Cleveland, OH 44114.
Ed. Bernard Knill. Tel. (212) 867-9191. M; $35;
1945; circ. 110,000. *Indexed*: App. Sci. Tech.
Ind., B.P.I., Eng. Ind. *Annual Issues*: Dec.—
Handbook & Directory. *Notes*: adv., photos
(B&W, color).
   Technology, management, and application of
materials-handling systems are examined. Em-
phasis on the most current automated systems.
(0025-5262)

0438   PLANT ENGINEERING   (US)
Technical Publishing Co., 1301 S. Grove Ave.,
P.O. Box 1030, Burlington, IL 60010. Ed. Leo
Spector. Tel. (312) 381-1840. Telex 394-3733.

Bi-w; $50(US); $55(CN); $120(abroad); 1947;
circ. 105,500. *Indexed*: App. Sci. Tech. Ind.,
Chem. Abst., Compendex, Eng. Ind. *Annual Issues*: Plant Engineering Directory and Specifications Catalog (varies). *Notes*: adv., bk. rev.,
calendars, photos (B&W, color). *Micro*: UMI.
   Covers design, construction, operation, and
maintenance of industrial facilities. Articles discuss new products and techniques in problem
areas such as materials handling and energy
management. Designed to fill the needs of the
plant engineer, although architects are among
the subscribers. (0032-082X) *

0439   PLANT SERVICES   (US)
Putnam Publ. Co., 301 E. Erie St., Chicago, IL
60611. Tel. (312) 644-2020. M; 1980.
   Presents mainly case studies on plant operations, but includes articles on design, construction, and maintenance. (0199-8013) +

Recreational

0440   PARKS AND RECREATION   (US)
National Recreation and Parks Assn., 3101 Park
Center Dr., Alexandria, VA 22302. Ed. Elizabeth Johnston. M; $15; 1965; circ. 11,900. *In-
dexed*: Avery. *Notes*: adv., photos (B&W,
color). *Micro*: UMI.
   Helpful in planning and designing facilities although not design oriented. (0031-2215)

0441   PISCINES   (FR)
Editions Christian Ledoux, 155 Ave. de Paris,
94807 Villejuif, France. Tel. (1) 677-35-87.
Telex 270 105 F TXFRA. Q; F. 84; 1967; circ.
20,000. *Notes*: adv., dwgs., photos (B&W,
color).
   Covers the design of swimming pools, spas,
saunas, and tennis courts. Text in French.
(0032-0285) *

0433   SCHUL UND
       SPORTSTATTENBAU

0442   SCHWIMMBAD UND SAUNA   (GW)
Fachschriften Verlag GmbH, Hoehenstr. 17,
Postfach 1329, 7012 Fellbach, W. Germany.
Bi-m; 1969. +

0443   SPORT-BOEDER-   (GW)
       FREIZEITBAUTEN
Krammer Verlag, Hermannstr. 3, 4000 Duessel-
dorf, W. Germany. Bi-m; 1961. *Indexed*: A.P.I.,
Eng. Ind. (0344-6492) +

0444   SWIMMING POOL   (UK)
Clarke & Hunter, Ltd., 61 London Rd., Staines, Middlesex TW18 4BN, England. Bi-m; 1960. *Indexed*: A.P.I. +

0445   SWIMMING POOL AGE &   (US)
        SPA MERCHANDISER
Communication Channels, 6255 Barfield Rd., Atlanta, GA 30328. Tel. (404) 256-9800. M; 1926. *Micro*: UMI.

All aspects of the swimming pool and spa industry are covered, with an emphasis on products and installation. (0279-134x) +

Religious

0446   CATHEDRAL AGE   (US)
Washington Cathedral, Mt. St. Alban, Washington, DC 20016. Ed. Nancy S. Montgomery. Tel. (202) 537-6247. Q; $10; 1925; circ. 20,000. *Notes*: adv., bk. rev., dwgs., photos (B&W, color). *Micro*: UMI.

Covers cathedral art and architecture as well as other church-related topics. (0008-7874) *

0447   FAITH AND FORM   (US)
Interfaith Forum on Religion, Art and Architecture, 1777 Church St., N.W., Washington, DC 20036. Ed. Betty H. Meyer. Tel. (202) 387-8333. S-a; $10; 1967; circ. 38,000. *Indexed*: Avery. *Annual Issues*: Spring/Summer—Design Awards.

Articles focus on the design and preservation of religious buildings and sites, aimed at architects and building committees. Includes an artisan directory that is helpful in locating consultants and artists for acoustics, lighting, liturgical furnishings, and stained-glass design. (0014-7001)

0448   KUNST UND KIRCHE   (AU)
Dr. Gunter Rombold, Harrachstrasse 7, A-4020 Linz, Austria. OO. Landesverlag GmbH, Zeitschriftenverwaltung, Landstrasse 41, A-4020 Linz, Austria. Ed. Prof. Gunter Rombold. Tel. 0732/271205. Q; S.10; 1971; circ. 5,000. *Indexed*: A.P.I., Avery. *Notes*: adv., bk. rev., dwgs., photos (B&W, color).

Examines religious art and architecture worldwide in detail. Covers current and historical work. Text in German; summaries in English. (0023-5431)

0449   DAS MUNSTER   (GW)
Leinhaldenweg 19, 7800 Freiburg, W. Germany. Verlag Schnell Steiner, Munich, W. Germany. Eds. Sigrid Hofstaetter, Gunther Wolf. Tel.

(0761) 551463. Q; 1947. *Indexed*: A.P.I., Avery. *Notes*: adv., bk. rev., dwgs., photos (B&W, color).

A well-illustrated, high-quality journal on ecclesiastical art and architecture. Most of the work is German, with extensive historical coverage. Articles cover cathedrals, anonymous rural chapels, stained glass, and sculpture and give attention to topics of restoration, history, and aesthetics. Anyone interested in German art and architecture or involved with ecclesiastical design should consider this journal for their collection. Text in German; one-page summaries in English and French. (0027-299X)

0450   TEMPLAR   (UK)
Institute of Geomantic Research, 142 Pheasant Rise, Bar Hill, Cambridge CB3 85D, England. Q; 1982. (0264-1011) +

0451   YOUR CHURCH   (US)
Religious Publ. Co., 198 Allendale Rd., King of Prussia, PA 19406. Tel. (215) 265-9400. Bi-m; 1955. (0049-8394) +

Airports

0452   AIRPORT FORUM   (GW)
Box 1208, 8110 Murnau, W. Germany. Bauverlag GmbH, P.O. Box 1460, 6200 Wiesbaden, W. Germany. Ed. Gottfried Hilscher. Tel. 08841/2255. Bi-m; DM. 147; 1970; circ. 4,255. *Indexed*: A.P.I., Feb. issue. *Notes*: adv., bibl., bk. rev., calendars, dwgs., photos (B&W, color).

An international journal on airport design, construction, and operation. Gives special attention to design and layout. Of interest to airport managers, architects, engineers, suppliers, manufacturers, and planning authorities. Text in English; summaries in French, German, and Spanish. (0002-2802)

0453   AIRPORT FORUM NEWS   (GW)
P.O. Box 27, 7255 Rutesheim, W. Germany. P.O. Box 1460, 6200 Wiesbaden, W. Germany. Ed. Manfred Momberger. Tel. 07152-151640. Bi-w; DM. 420; 1972; circ. 300.

Provides current international news on airport planning, construction, and operation. Emphasis is on business aspects. (0174-3279) *

0454   AIRPORT SERVICES   (US)
        MANAGEMENT
Lakewood Publications, Inc., 50 S. Ninth St., Minneapolis, MN 55403. Ed. Sher Jasperse. Tel. (612) 333-0471. M; 1960; circ. 20,000. *Indexed*: Biannually. *Annual Issues*: Oct.—Direc-

tory of Airport Suppliers (includes consultants). *Notes*: adv., calendars, dwgs., photos (B&W, color).

A management publication edited for aviation officials, airport managers, and airline executives. Articles deal with new equipment and approaches to planning and management of airports, with an emphasis on increasing profits and efficiency. Architects and contractors involved with airport design and construction will find the articles on operations and equipment very useful. (0002-2829)

0455   AIRPORTS INTERNATIONAL   (UK)
Quadrant House, The Quadrant, Sutton, Surrey SM2 5AS, England. Oakfield House, Perrymount Rd., Haywards Heath, W. Sussex RH16 3DH, England. Ed. Richard Whitaker. Tel. (01) 661-3099. Telex 892084 BISPRSG. Bi-m; free to airport executives; 1968; circ. 10,000. *Annual Issues*: World Airport Developments Supplement. *Notes*: adv., bibl., bk. rev., calendars, dwgs., photos (B&W, color). *Micro*: UMI.

Presents reports on new and expanded airports, airport equipment, and operations. Of greater interest to airport managers than architects but still useful because of the reports on new projects. Scope is international. (0261-6513)

0456   FROM THE STATE   (US)
       CAPITALS: AIRPORT
       CONSTRUCTION AND
       FINANCING
State Capitals, Wakeman/Walworth, Inc., Box 1939, New Haven, CT 06509. Ed. Linn Bayne. Tel. (203) 562-8518. M; $75; 1946.

This newsletter presents highlights of airport legislation from state and local capitals throughout the U.S. Coverage includes renovation, expansion, financing, taxation, land acquisition, equipment purchases, ground transportation, and parking. Because it spots trends at the formative stage, it is useful for planning purposes and job leads. (0734-1636) *

Barrier-Free Design: Elderly and Handicapped

0457   DESIGN FOR SPECIAL   (UK)
       NEEDS
Centre on Environment for the Handicapped, 126 Albert St., London NW1 7NF, England. Ed. Sarah Langton-Lockton. Tel. (01) 482-2247. 3/yr.; £8.50; 1973. *Indexed*: A.P.I., Avery. *Notes*: adv., bk. rev., dwgs., photos (B&W).

The only detailed serial publication devoted exclusively to the problems of accommodating the handicapped. It presents seminar reports, building type studies, reviews, case studies, and design guidelines. Topics included are access and transportation, equipment, day-care facilities, education, life safety, housing, and recreation. New developments in other countries are reported, but the emphasis is on British cases. (0309-3042)

0458   JOURNAL OF HOUSING FOR   (US)
       THE ELDERLY
National Policy Center on Housing and Living Arrangements for Older Americans, Univ. of Michigan, 2000 Bonisteel Blvd., Ann Arbor, MI 48109. Haworth Press, Inc., 28 E. 22nd St., New York, NY 10010. Ed. Leon Pastalan. Tel. (313) 763-1275. Q; $35 (indiv.); $65 (inst.); 1983. *Indexed*: A.P.I. *Notes*: bibl., bk. rev., dwgs., photos (B&W).

A new journal devoted to presenting international research on housing for the aged. It is intended to serve the needs of architects, planners, and housing officials who are involved with residential environments for the elderly. Articles cover architectural, psychological, demographic, and economic aspects. (0276-3893)

0459   NATIONAL CENTER FOR A   (US)
       BARRIER-FREE
       ENVIRONMENT REPORT
National Center for a Barrier-Free Environment, 1140 Connecticut Ave., NW, Ste. 10006, Washington, DC 20036. Tel. (202) 466-6896. Bi-m; 1975. (0270-935x) +

Public Works

0460   APWA REPORTER   (US)
American Public Works Assn., 1313 E. 60th St., Chicago, IL 60637. Ed. Rodney Fleming. Tel. (312) 667-2200. M; free with membership; 1955; circ. 23,000. *Notes*: adv., bk. rev., calendars, dwgs., photos (B&W, color).

Industry news, new products, and technology related to municipal, state, and federal public works projects are presented. The primary readership includes public works engineers and public administrators. (0092-4873) *

0461   AMERICAN CITY AND   (US)
       COUNTY
Communication Channels, 6255 Barfield Rd., Atlanta, GA 30328. Ed. Ken Anderberg. Tel. (404) 256-9800. M; $49; 1909; circ. 50,000. *Indexed*: Eng. Ind., R.G. *Notes*: adv., bk. rev., calendars, dwgs., photos (B&W, color). *Micro*: BLH, UMI.

Case studies describe all phases of public works, including design, construction, and maintenance. Topics covered include waste disposal, lighting, wastewater treatment, highway construction, and grounds maintenance. Also covers office automation. Includes municipal cost indexes. Of interest primarily to local city government officials and engineers. (0149-337X)

1146   BAUTECHNIK AUSGABE A

1059   CONCRETE PIPE NEWS

0934   CONSTRUCTION DIGEST

0951   ENGINEERING-NEWS
       RECORD

0462   HIGHWAY AND HEAVY   (US)
       CONSTRUCTION
(Formerly: *Roads and Streets*)
Technical Publishing Co., 1301 S. Grove Rd., Barrington, IL 60010. Ed. David Williams. Tel. (312) 381-1840. M; $35; 1892; circ. 72,000. *Indexed*: App. Sci. Tech. Ind., Compendex, Eng. Ind. *Notes*: adv., bk. rev., calendars, dwgs., photos (B&W, color). *Micro*: BLH, UMI.
   Covers construction and construction management as related to highways and public works projects. (0362-0506) *

0463   MUNICIPAL ENGINEER   (UK)
Institution of Municipal Engineers, 25 Eccleston Sq., London SW1 V1NX, England. M; 1873. *Indexed*: A.P.I., Chem. Abstr., Eng. Ind. +

0464   NATIONAL DEVELOPMENT   (US)
Intercontinental Publications, Inc., 15 Ketchum St., P.O. Box 5017, Westport, CT 06881. Tel. (203) 226-7463. 9/yr.; free; 1954.
   Planning, engineering, and construction of public works projects in developing countries are covered. Topics include highways, electrical power, and water distribution systems (0360-7941) +

0465   PUBLIC WORKS   (US)
Public Works Journal Corp., 200 S. Broad St., P.O. Box 688, Ridgewood, NJ 07451. Ed. Edward Rodie. Tel. (201) 445-5800. M; $30; 1896; circ. 46,000. *Indexed*: App.Sci. Tech. Ind., Chem. Abst., Compendex, Eng. Ind. *Notes*: adv., bk. rev., photos (B&W, color). *Micro*: UMI.

A magazine on the design, operation, and maintenance of public works projects on a city, county, or regional level. Includes articles on highway construction, waste-treatment plants, and new equipment. (0033-3840)

0466   SURVEYOR/PUBLIC WORKS   (UK)
       WEEKLY
IPC Building and Contract Journals, Ltd., Surrey House, 1 Throwley Way, Sutton, Surrey SM1 4QQ, England. Ed. Peter Acton. Tel. (01) 643-8040. Telex 892084 BISPRS G SPP. W; £40; 1892; circ. 6,000. *Indexed*: A.P.I., Eng. Ind. *Annual Issues*: April—Municipal Vehicles; June—Public Works Programme; Sept.—Municipal Innovation Awards. *Micro*: UMI.
   The leading British technical weekly, covering all aspects of municipal engineering in local government including building, transportation, traffic, waste management, and public works. (0039-6303) *

0467   TRAVAUX   (FR)
Science et Industrie, 6 Av. Pierre Premier de Serbie, 75116 Paris, France. Ed. Christine Coville. 11/yr.; F.600; 1933; circ. 5,000. *Indexed*: Eng. Ind. *Notes*: adv., bibl., bk. rev., dwgs., photos (B&W, color).
   An engineering journal concerned with the design and construction of public works, roads, bridges, etc. Discusses new techniques, new projects, and new possibilities for building materials. (0041-1906) *

Parking

0468   PARKING   (US)
National Parking Assn., 1112 16th St., NW, Ste. 2000, Washington, DC 20036. Ed. George V. Dragotta. Tel. (202) 296-4336. Q; $20; 1952; circ. 6,500. *Indexed*: P.A.I.S. *Notes*: adv., bk. rev., dwgs., photos (B&W, color).
   The main magazine covering design, construction, and operation of parking structures and lots. Includes reviews of new products and systems. Useful to architects and engineers as well as to parking facility operators. (0031-2193)

0469   PARKING WORLD   (US)
National Parking Assn., 1112 16th St., N.W., Ste. 2000, Washington, DC 20036. Ed. Thomas Kobus. Tel. (202) 296-4336. 10/yr.; $20 with subscription to *Parking*; 1972; circ. 1,700. *

Historic Preservation and Architectural History

In addition to the following titles, most preservation-related agencies in the public and private sectors publish newsletters. A few samples are included.

0004   AA FILES: ANNALS OF THE
        ARCHITECTURAL
        ASSOCIATION SCHOOL OF
        ARCHITECTURE

0470   A P T BULLETIN   (CN)
Association for Preservation Technology, Box 2487, Station D, Ottawa, Ont. K1P 5W6, Canada. Q; $35; 1969; circ. 2,000. *Indexed*: A.P.I., Amer: H&L, Avery. *Notes*: bibl., bk. rev., photos (B&W, color).
   A scholarly journal that presents technical research on preservation technology. Articles analyze projects and focus on problems and solutions. For the preservation specialist. (0044-9466)

0196   ABACUS

0471   ACORN   (CN)
Architectural Conservancy of Ontario, 86 Augusta St., Port Hope, Ont., Canada. Ed. Marion Garland. Tel. (416) 598-3051. 3/yr.; with membership; 1976; circ. 1,500. *Indexed*: Avery. *Notes*: bk. rev., dwgs., photos (B&W).
   A membership publication on architectural preservation in Ontario. (0704-0083) *

0472   ARCHITECTURA   (GW)
Deutscher Kunstverlag, Vohburger Strasse 1, 8000 Munich 1, W. Germany. S-a; DM. 76. *In-dexed*: A.P.I., Art Ind., Avery, R.I.L.A. *Notes*: dwgs., photos (B&W). *Micro*: UMI.
   Though useful to preservationists, this scholarly journal primarily presents current research in architectural history. Articles are in German, English, or French. (0044-863X)

0473   ARCHITECTURAL HISTORY   (UK)
Society of Architectural Historians of Great Britain, c/o John Newman, Courtauld Inst. of Art, 20 Portman Square, London W1H OBE, England. Jeremy Blake, The Hyde, Handcross, West Sussex, England. Ed. John A. Newman. Tel. (01) 935-9292. A; $12; 1958; circ. 1,100. *Indexed*: A.P.I., Art Ind., Avery, R.I.L.A. *Notes*: dwgs., photos (B&W).
   Useful to preservationists, historians, landscape architects, and architects, this journal presents the results of significant original research in the history of British architecture. (0066-622X)

0474   ARCHITECTURAL   (UK)
        PRESERVATION AND NEW
        DESIGN IN CONSERVATION
Architectural Preservation, 112 City Rd., London EC1, England. Ed. Robert McCallion. Tel. (01) 985-1115. Q; £13; $35; 1982. *Indexed*: A.P.I., Avery. *Notes*: bk. rev., dwgs., photos (B&W).
   Presents various restoration projects in the United Kingdom with an emphasis on contextual design. The preservation of buildings by historic restoration or adaptive reuse is discussed as well as the preservation of historic city centers. Economic and energy considerations are given attention in each project descrip-

tion. General news on legislation or events related to preservation are included. An interesting source for the professional involved in historic preservation. (0262-219x)

0197   ARCHIVES
       D'ARCHITECTURE
       MODERNE

0475   ART DECO SOCIETY NEWS   (US)
Art Deco Society of New York, 667 Madison Ave., Ste. 208, New York, NY 10021. Ed. Glenn Loney. Tel. (212) 758-9447. Q; $20 (free with membership); 1981; circ. 1,000. *Notes*: adv., bk. rev., calendars, dwgs., photos (B&W).

A newsletter containing articles, exhibition reviews, and news briefs on Art Deco architecture and design. Emphasis is on New York work, including highlights of lectures and auctions. News from sister chapters is reported. (0743-3522)

0246   AVENUE MAGAZINE

0410   AVISO

0476   BROWNSTONER   (US)
Brownstone Revival Committee, 200 Madison Ave., New York, NY 10016. Ed. H. Dickson McKenna. Tel. (212) 561-2154. 5/yr.; $25 with membership; 1969. *Indexed*: Avery. *Notes*: adv., bk. rev., calendars.

A twelve-page newsletter devoted to issues of interest to owners of brownstones. Topics include restoration techniques and homeownership problems as well as real estate and workshop notes. Articles are contributed by architects, historians, real-estate brokers, and owners. The issues examined contained an informative series on building materials.

0477   C O P A R NEWSLETTER   (US)
Library of Congress, Prints and Photographs Division, Washington, DC 20540. Tel. (202) 287-6399. Q; donation; 1981.

This four-page newsletter is the official publication that reports news of the Library of Congress' Cooperative Preservation of Architectural Records. It includes important announcements about the location of historic American architectural drawings, notes on drawing preservation techniques, queries about lost drawings, and announcements about architectural exhibits and books. It is of interest to

architectural historians, preservationists, librarians, and archivists.

0478   CHARLES RENNIE   (UK)
       MACKINTOSH SOCIETY
       NEWSLETTER
Charles Rennie Mackintosh Society, Queen's Cross, 870 Garscube Rd., Glasgow G20, Scotland. Ed. Colin B. Kirkwood. Tel. (041) 946-6600. Q; with membership; 1973. *Indexed*: Avery. *Notes*: bk. rev., dwgs., photos (B&W).

An eight-page newsletter of a society devoted to fostering interest in and conserving the buildings and artifacts designed by Mackintosh and his associates. In addition to interesting book reviews and society news, each issue focuses on a Mackintosh building or piece of furniture that may be lost or threatened. (0141-599x)

0479   COMMUNIQUE   (CN)
Assn. for Preservation Technology, Box 2487, Station D, Ottawa, Ontario K1P 5W6, Canada. Bi-m; 1972.

A newsletter that lists research work in progress and notes forthcoming seminars and conferences of interest to its members. Text in English and occasionally in French. (0319-4558) +

0480   CONSERVATION NEWS   (UK)
Museum of London, Attn: Suzanne Keene, London Wall, London EC1, England. United Kingdom Inst. for Conservation of Historic and Artistic Works, c/o Conservation Dept., Tate Gallery, Millbank, London SW1P 4RG, England. 3/yr.; free with membership; 1975; circ. 700.

Newsletter that discusses new methods and techniques of conservation and serves as a forum for discussing conservation issues.*

0791   CONSERVE
       NEIGHBORHOODS

0100   COVJEK I PROSTOR

0481   DEUTSCHE KUNST UND   (GW)
       DENKMALPFLEGE
Institut fur Denkmalpflege, Scharnhorststr. 1, 3000 Hannover 1, W. Germany. Deutscher Kunstverlag GmbH, Vohburger Str. 1, 8000 Munich 1, W. Germany. Ed. H.H. Moeller. S-a; DM. 32; 1944; circ. 1,800. *Notes*: bibl., bk. rev., dwgs., photos (B&W).

Official journal for the preservation of historical and artistic monuments in FRG. Deals with historical, technical, and legislative matters. (0012-0375) *

0482   DISCOVERY   (US)
Assn. for the Preservation of Virginia Antiquities, 2705 Park Ave., Richmond, VA 23220. Ed. Catherine Briechinridge. Tel. (804) 359-0239. A; free with membership; 1969; circ. 6,000. *Notes*: dwgs., photos (B&W, color). *Micro*: UMI.
   Included with the society's annual report is a sampling of articles on preservation topics, primarily of local interest. (0300-7316)

0483   FRANK LLOYD WRIGHT   (US)
         NEWSLETTER
Frank Lloyd Wright Assn., Box 2100, Oak Park, IL 60303. Ed. Thomas Heinz. Tel. (312) 383-1310. Q; $36; 1978; circ. 4,000. *Indexed*: A.P.I., Avery. *Notes*: adv., bibl., bk. rev., calendars, dwgs., photos (B&W).
   Provides a forum for exchanging biographical and architectural information on Frank Lloyd Wright. Cites new research on the architect and offers critical analyses of his work. (0160-7375) *

0484   FRIENDS OF TERRA COTTA   (US)
         NEWSLETTER
P.O. Box 421393, Main Post Office, San Francisco, CA 94142. Ed. Waverly B. Lowell. Tel. (415) 556-7741. Q; $5 (with membership); 1981. *Indexed*: Avery. *Notes*: adv., bibl., bk. rev., dwgs., photos (B&W).
   The primary goal of this association newsletter is "to raise the awareness of the general public and particularly architects, engineers, and owners of terra cotta-clad buildings, to the value and problems associated with the preservation of terra cotta." Articles, contributed by members, discuss preservation projects in process, buildings threatened by destruction, and technical procedures in restoration. Includes notes on useful publications and workshops.

0485   HEADQUARTERS   (US)
         HELIOGRAM
Council on America's Military Past, P.O. Box 1151, Ft. Meyer, VA 22211. Ed. Herbert Hart. Tel. (202) 479-2258. M; $25 (indiv.); $35 (inst.); 1966; circ. 1,500. *Notes*: adv., bk. rev., dwgs., photos (B&W).
   An association newspaper that provides information on preservation programs and legislation involving military installations.

0486   HERITAGE OUTLOOK   (UK)
   (Formerly: *Civic Trust News*)
Civic Trust, 17 Carlton House Terrace, London SW1 5AW, England. Ed. Angela Carvill. Tel. (01) 930-0914. Bi-m; £12; 1974; circ. 3,500. *Indexed*: A.P.I., Avery, Nov./Dec. issue. *Notes*: adv., bk. rev., dwgs., photos (B&W).
   An association publication that examines issues throughout the United Kingdom related to historic preservation, urban revitalization, adaptive reuse, planning, and legislation. Reports on citizens groups nationwide. (0261-1988)

0487   HISTORIC HOUSES   (UK)
Historic Houses Association, P.O. Box 21, 71 Leys Avenue, Letchworth Herts, England. Q; 1981. *Indexed*: A.P.I. +

0488   HISTORIC PRESERVATION   (US)
National Trust for Historic Preservation, 1785 Massachusetts Ave., N.W., Washington, DC 20036. Ed. Thomas J. Colin. Tel. (202) 673-4000. Bi-m; with membership; 1949; circ. 175,000. *Indexed*: A.P.I., Art Ind., Avery. *Notes*: adv., bk. rev., calendars, photos (B&W, color). *Micro*: UMI.
   The magazine most responsible for heightening the public's awareness of preservation in the U.S. Articles are short and illustrated with features on people, sites, public issues related to historic preservation, and adaptive reuse in the U.S. A directory of homes and museums open for tours is included in each issue. Readers include preservationists, developers, architects, and owners and buyers of historic properties, as well as the interested general public. (018-2419)

0489   HISTORIC SEATTLE   (US)
         NEWSLETTER
Historic Seattle Preservation & Development Authority, Attn: Cindy Hughs, 215 Second Ave. S., Seattle, WA 98104. Ed. Ann Alexander. Q; $1; 1976. +

0371   HOME AGAIN

0490   I A: JOURNAL OF THE   (US)
         SOCIETY FOR INDUSTRIAL
         ARCHAEOLOGY
National Museum of History and Technology, Ste. 5020, Smithsonian Inst., Washington, DC 20560. Ed. David Starbuck. Tel. (202) 357-2058. A. *Indexed*: Avery. *Notes*: dwgs., photos (B&W).
   Articles about surviving industrial sites, structures, and equipment that combine the insights of field work and historical research. Also covers conservation, adaptive reuse, museology, instructional techniques, and methodology. The purpose of the journal is to advance industrial archaeology as a discipline. (0160-1040)

0491   I.C.O.M.O.S. JOURNAL   (FR)
International Council on Monuments and Sites, Hotel Saint-Aignan, 75 Rue du Temple, 75003 Paris, France. Tel. 277-35-76. 1985. *Indexed*: A.P.I.
A scholarly journal on the conservation of heritage. Contains technical and theoretical articles on conservation and restoration in addition to news on the organization's activities. *

0492   INDUSTRIAL   (UK)
       ARCHAEOLOGY
Graphmitre, Ltd., 1 West St., Tavistock, Devon, England. Ed. T.D. Bridge. Q; £22. *Indexed*: Avery. *Notes*: bk. rev., dwgs., photos (B&W).
A technical journal on the history and preservation of industrial buildings in Great Britain.

0493   IRISH GEORGIAN SOCIETY   (UK)
       QUARTERLY BULLETIN
Irish Georgian Society, Leixlip Castle, Leixlip Co. Kildare, Ireland. Ed. Desmond Guinness. Tel. (01) 280-430. A; $15; 1958; circ. 3,500. *Indexed*: A.P.I., Avery. *Notes*: bk. rev., photos (B&W, color). *Micro*: UMI. (0021-1206) *

0494   ITALIA NOSTRA   (IT)
via N. Porpora 22, 00198 Rome, Italy. Tel. (06) 852333. Bi-m; L.30,000; 1957; circ. 20,000. *Notes*: adv., bibl., bk. rev., calendars, dwgs., photos (B&W, color).
A journal on the preservation of Italy's historical monuments and works of art. Text in Italian. (0021-2822) *

0495   JOURNAL OF CANADIAN   (CN)
       ART HISTORY
Concordia University, V A Bldg. 432, 1395 Dorchester Blvd. W., Montreal, Quebec H3G 2MS, Canada. Eds. Donald Andrus, Sandra Paikowsky. Tel. (514) 879-5819. S-a; Can.$14; 1972; circ. 1,000. *Indexed*: A.P.I., Art Bib., Art Ind., C.P.I., R.I.L.A. *Notes*: adv., bibl., bk. rev., calendars, dwgs., photos (B&W). *Micro*: MML.
Covers topics in Canadian art, architecture, and the decorative arts. Text in French and English. (0315-4297) *

0496   LANDMARKS OBSERVER   (US)
Portland Landmarks, Inc., 165 State St., Portland, ME 04101. Ed. William H. Johnston. Tel. (207) 772-1585. Bi-m; $20 (with membership); 1973; circ. 6,000. *Indexed*: Avery. *Notes*: adv., bk. rev., calendars, dwgs., photos (B&W).

A newspaper with features on historic preservation in general and news on preservation work in Portland.

0497   M & L/MONUMENTEN EN   (BE)
       LANDSCHAPPEN
Belliardstraat 14-18, 1040 Brussels, Belgium. Ed. H. Stynen. Tel. (02) 513-9920. Bi-m; Fr.840; 1982. *Indexed*: Avery. *Notes*: adv., bk. rev., dwgs., photos (B&W, color).
A handsome journal on the history and preservation of monuments and gardens throughout Belgium. Text in Flemish; summaries in English. (0770-4984)

0411   MARQUEE

0498   MONUMENTS HISTORIQUES   (FR)
Caisse Nationale de Monuments Historiques et des Sites, 62 rue Saint-Antoine, 75004 Paris, France. Ed. Veronique Hartmann. Tel. 274-22-22. Bi-m; F.230; 1936; circ. 12,000. *Indexed*: A.P.I., Avery, Jan. issue. *Notes*: adv., bibl., bk. rev., dwgs., photos (B&W, color).
A substantial review of the architectural history and preservation of French monuments. Beautifully illustrated. Text in French. (0242-830x)

0499   MONUMENTUM   (UK)
D. Linstrum, Univ. of York, Inst. of Advanced Architectural Studies, King's Manor, York YO1 2EP, England. Butterworth Scientific Ltd., Journals Division, Box 63, Westbury House, Bury St., Guilford, Surrey GU2 5BH, England. Ed. Derek Linstrum. Q; $40; 1957. *Indexed*: A.P.I., Avery. *Notes*: bibl., bk. rev., photos (B&W).
A scholarly journal that features articles on endangered sites, new techniques and materials of conservation, and assessments of key historic buildings. Text in English; summaries in French and Spanish. (0027-0776)

0449   DAS MUNSTER

0500   NATIONAL TRUST   (UK)
36 Queen Anne's Gate, London SW1H 9AS, England. Ed. Robin Wright. Tel. (01) 222-9251. *Indexed*: A.P.I., Avery. *Notes*: adv., dwgs., photos (B&W, color).
Similar in content to the American *Historic Preservation* except that the emphasis is on profiles of historic properties rather than on techniques and legislative issues. Includes Trust news.

0501   NETHERLANDS   (NE)
       RIJKSDIENST VOOR DE
       MONUMENTENZORG—
       JAARVERSLAG
Rijksdienst voor de Monumentenzorg, Broeder-
plein 41, Zeist, Netherlands. A; 1974. +

0502   NEWSJOURNAL (SCA)   (US)
Society for Commercial Archaeology, 1829 S.
Pasfield, Springfield, IL 62704. National Museum of American History, Room 5010, Washington, DC 20560. Eds. Keith Sculle, Michael
Jackson. Irreg.; $20; 1978; circ. 175. *Notes*:
adv., bibl., bk. rev., dwgs., photos (B&W).
    An association newsletter devoted to an un-
derstanding of the commercial past through
its artifact remains. It focuses on the documentation, interpretation, and preservation of
American automobile roadside structures and
landscapes. (0735-1399) *

0503   OESTERREICHISCHE   (AU)
       ZEITSCHRIFT FUR KUNST
       UND DENKMALPFLEGE
Verlag Anton Schroll und Co., Spengasse 39,
A-1051 Vienna, Austria. Ed. Ernst Bacher.
5/yr.; S.220; 1856; circ. 150. *Indexed*: A.P.I.,
Avery. *Notes*: adv., bk. rev., dwgs., photos
(B&W).
    Covers the preservation of art and architec-
ture in Austria. Text in German. (0029-9626)

0504   OLD HOUSE JOURNAL   (US)
R.A. Labine, 69A Seventh Ave., Brooklyn, NY
11217. Ed. Patricia Moore. Tel. (718) 636-4514.
10/yr.; $18; 1973; circ. 72,000. *Indexed*: A.P.I.,
Avery, Dec. issue. *Notes*: adv., calendars,
dwgs., photos (B&W).
    A well-illustrated and informative newsletter
that presents preservation and restoration techniques for pre-1939 houses. Contains technical
and how-to articles and case histories on renovation and maintenance. Laymen frequently
contribute ideas based on their own experiences. Good coverage of products and historical
architectural styles. Essential for anyone who
owns and restores old houses. (0094-0178)

0505   OLD MILL NEWS   (US)
Society for the Preservation of Old Mills, 604
Ensley Dr., Rt. 29, Knoxville, TN 37920. Ber-
nard Webb, 4841 Mill Brook Dr., Dunwoody,
GA 30338. Ed. Michael La Forest. Tel. (615)
577-7757. Q; $8; 1972; circ. 1,300. *Indexed*:
Avery. *Notes*: adv., bibl., dwgs., photos
(B&W).

This publication helps to promote interest in
the preservation of old mills by reporting on
preservation projects, techniques, and new uses
for these historic structures. In addition to
chapter news, it includes announcements of
seminars, studies, awards, properties and machinery for sale, and additions to the National
Register of Historic Places.

0506   OLD-TIME NEW ENGLAND   (US)
Society for the Preservation of New England
Antiquities, Harrison Gray Otis House, 141
Cambridge St., Boston, MA 02114. Irreg. *In-
dexed*: Art Ind., Avery. *Micro*: UMI. +

0507   PALLADIO   (IT)
DeLuca Editore, Via S. Anna 11, 00186 Rome,
Italy. Q; 1951. *Indexed*: A.P.I., Art Ind. (0031-
0379) +

0508   PERSPECTIVE   (US)
Gregory P. Warden, Dept. of Art History,
S.M.U., Dallas, TX 75275. SAH/TX, P.O. Box
12392, Capitol Station, Austin, TX 78711. Ed.
Gregory P. Warden. S-a; $15. *Indexed*: A.P.I.,
Avery. *Notes*: dwgs., photos (B&W).
    Devoted to the history and preservation of
architecture in Texas.

0509   PRAIRIE SCHOOL REVIEW   (US)
Prairie School Press, c/o Prairie Avenue Book-
shop, 711 S. Dearborn, Chicago, IL 60605. Q;
1964. *Indexed*: Art Ind., Avery. +

0510   PRESERVATION ACTION   (US)
       ALERT
1700 Connecticut Ave., N.W., Ste. 400-A,
Washington, DC 20009. Ed. Nellie Longsworth.
Tel. (202) 659-0915. Q; $25 with membership;
1976; circ. 1,200.
    A newsletter that covers federal legislation
and regulations concerning national policy on
historic preservation. *

0511   PRESERVATION BRIEFS   (US)
Technical Preservation Service, Nat. Park Service, U.S. Dept. of Interior, Washington, DC
20240. Ed. Lee H. Nelson. Tel. (202) 343-1100.
Irreg.; 1975; circ. 600,000. *Indexed*: Avery.
Notes: bibl., dwgs., photos (B&W).
    A newsletter aimed at building owners and
architects to assist them in evaluating and re-
solving commmon preservation and repair problems. Technical approaches are recommended
for the proper rehabilitation of historic build-

ings. Topics include roofing, painting, cleaning masonry, and repairing windows.

0512   PRESERVATION LAW   (US)
REPORTER
National Trust for Historic Preservation, 1785 Massachusetts Ave., N.W., Washington, DC 20036. Ed. Harrison Wetherill. Tel. (202) 673-4033. Bi-m; $155; 1982; circ. 400. *Notes*: bk. rev.

A looseleaf-format legal service that covers real estate, rehabilitation, financing, tax laws, easements, zoning, and litigation.

0513   PRESERVATION NEWS   (US)
Natl. Trust for Historic Preservation, 1785 Massachusetts Ave., N.W., Washington, DC 20036. Ed. Michael Leccese. Tel. (202) 673-4000. M; with membership; 1957; circ. 168,000. *Indexed*: Avery. *Annual Issues*: Oct.—Historic Preservation Education. *Notes*: adv., bk. rev., calendars, photos (B&W). *Micro*: UMI.

A newspaper with short articles on preservation activities and legislation in the U.S. The "Cross Section" column reports on projects in six regions: West, Plains, South, Midwest, Mid-Atlantic, and Northeast. Includes announcements of tours, special services, and historic properties that are for sale. References to important resources such as special collections and repositories occasionally appear. (0032-7735)

0514   PRESERVATION   (US)
PERSPECTIVE
Preservation New Jersey, Inc., RD 6, Box 864, Mapleton Rd., Princeton, NJ 08540. Ed. Diane Jones Sliney. Tel. (609) 452-0446. Bi-m; $15(US only); 1980; circ. 3,000. *Notes*: adv., bk. rev., calendars, dwgs., photos (B&W).

Historic preservation in New Jersey. (0392-4599) *

0515   PRESERVATION PROGRESS   (US)
Preservation Society of Charleston, Box 521, Charleston, SC 29402. Ed. J. Michael McLaughlin. Tel. (803) 722-4630. Q; 1956. (0478-1392) +

0516   QUADERNI DELL'ISTITUTO   (IT)
DI STORIA
DELL'ARCHITETTURA
Centro di Studi per la Storia dell'Architettura, Casa de Crescenzi, via dell Teatro di Marcello 54, Rome 0186, Italy. Multigrafica Editrice,

viale dei Quattro Ventri 52/A, 00152 Rome, Italy. A; 1953. *Indexed*: A.P.I., R.I.L.A. +

0517   RECUPERARE-EDILIZIA   (IT)
DESIGN IMPIANTI
P.E.G. Spa-Propoganda Editoriale Grafica, via Fratelli Bressan 2, 20126 Milan M1, Italy. Ed. Valerio di Battista. Tel. (02) 25-79-841. Telex 323088 PEGMOS I. Bi-m; L.50,000; 1982; circ. 10,800. *Indexed*: Nov./Dec. issue. *Notes*: adv., bibl., bk. rev., calendars, dwgs., photos (B&W, color).

A specialized periodical on urban and building rehabilitation from a technical, practical, and cultural viewpoint. Themes range from adaptive reuse, installation problems, and contextual considerations to rehabilitation of entire historic districts. Includes interviews with architects such as Portoghesi who discuss philosophical approaches to preservation. Scope is international. Well illustrated. Text in Italian; abstracts in English, French, and German. (0392-4599)

0518   RESTORICA   (SA)
Simon van der Stel Foundation, Box 1743, Pretoria 0001, South Africa. Ed. Mrs. Elize Labuschagne. Tel. (012) 268-651. S-a; R.4; 1960; circ. 7,200. *Notes*: adv., bibl., bk. rev., dwgs., photos (B&W, color).

Journal of architectural history and preservation for South Africa. Text in English and Afrikaans. *

0519   SCOTTISH GEORGIAN   (UK)
SOCIETY BULLETIN
5B Forres St., Edinburgh EH3 6BJ, Scotland. Tel. (031) 225-9724. A; 1973. *Indexed*: A.P.I., Avery. *Notes*: adv., photos (B&W).

Included with this annual society report is a review of the previous year's preservation activities in Scotland and a feature article of historical interest.

0520   SITES ET MONUMENTS   (FR)
Societe pour la Protection des Paysages et de l'Esthetique de la France, 39, Av. de la Motte-Picquet, 75007 Paris, France. Ed. P. Joste. Tel. 705-37-71. Q; F.80. *Indexed*: Avery. *Notes*: dwgs., photos (B&W, color).

A society publication that gives extensive coverage of the preservation of France's monuments and sites. Properties are discussed in detail. Includes list of properties newly designated as landmarks. Text in French. (0489-0280)

0835 SMALL TOWN

0521 SOCIETY FOR INDUSTRIAL   (US)
      ARCHAEOLOGY
      NEWSLETTER
Room 5020, National Museum of History and
Technology, Smithsonian Institution, Washington, DC 20560. Ed. Carol Miller. Tel. (202) 357-
1300. Bi-m; 1972. *Indexed*: Avery. (0160-1067) +

0173 SOCIETY FOR THE STUDY
      OF ARCHITECTURE IN
      CANADA. BULLETIN

0522 SOCIETY OF ANTIQUITIES   (UK)
      OF SCOTLAND.
      PROCEEDINGS
National Museum of Antiquities of Scotland,
Queen St., Edinburgh EH2, Scotland. Ed. Ian
A.G. Shephard. A; 1851. *Indexed*: Avery. (0081-
1564) +

0523 SOCIETY OF   (US)
      ARCHITECTURAL
      HISTORIANS. JOURNAL
Society of Architectural Historians, 1700b Walnut St., Philadelphia, PA 19103. Ed. Elizabeth
McDougall. Tel. (215) 735-0224. Q; 1940. *Indexed*: A.P.I., Art Ind., Avery, R.I.L.A. *Micro*:
UMI.
   A scholarly journal that contains critical reviews of preservation-related publications.
Readership includes members, historians, museums, universities, and preservation organizations. (0037-9808) +

0524 SOCIETY OF   (US)
      ARCHITECTURAL
      HISTORIANS. NEWSLETTER
Society of Architectural Historians, 1700 Walnut St., Ste. 716, Philadelphia, PA 19103. Ed.
Geraldine Fowle. Tel. (215) 735-0224. Bi-m;
1957. *Indexed*: A.P.I., Art Ind.
   Of interest to professional and nonprofes-
sional preservationists. It regularly features a
listing of new regional, state, and local architectural guidebooks and studies. Includes announcements of academic opportunities in
architectural history. (0049-1195) +

0525 SOCIETY OF   (UK)
      ARCHITECTURAL
      HISTORIANS OF GREAT
      BRITAIN. NEWSLETTER
Open University of East Anglian Region, 12
Hills Rd., Cambridge CB2 1PF, England. Jer-

emy Blake, The Hyde, Handcross, W. Sussex
RH17 6EZ, England. Ed. Dr. Colin Cun-
ningham. Tel. 0223-64721. S-a; with membership only; 1969; circ. 1,100. *Notes*: bibl., bk.
rev., calendars.
   Reports on society events, membership activities; reviews books on architectural history. *

0526 STORIA ARCHITETTURA   (IT)
Universita di Roma, Multigrafica Editrice, viale
dei Quattro Venti 52/A, 00152 Rome, Italy. Tel.
(06) 5891496. S-a; L.30,000; 1982. *Indexed*:
Avery, R.I.L.A. *Notes*: bibl., bk. rev., calendars, dwgs., photos (B&W).
   A review of the history and restoration of Italian architecture.

0527 TECHNOLOGY AND   (US)
      CONSERVATION
Technology Organization, Inc., 1 Emerson
Place, Boston, MA 02114. Ed. Susan Schur.
Tel. (617) 227-8581. Q; $12 (free to qualified sub-
scribers); 1975; circ. 14,500. *Indexed*: A.P.I.,
Art Ind., Avery. *Annual Issues*: Winter—Buyer's Guide. *Notes*: adv., bibl., bk. rev., calendars, dwgs., photos (B&W, color).
   In-depth technical articles on the preservation, analysis, and documentation of architecture, art, and antiquities. Includes brief reports
on products and new applications of materials
and equipment. It is primarily of interest to the
professional. Back issues are available from the
publisher and are listed in every issue. (0146-
1214)

0528 UMENI/ARTS   (CS)
Academia Publishing House of the Czechoslo-
vak Academy of Sciences, Hastalska 6, 116 92
Prague 1, Czechoslovakia. Kubon and Sagner,
P.O. Box 3401 08, D-8000, Munich 34, W. Germany. Ed. Josef Krasa. Bi-m; DM.240; 1952;
circ. 14,000. *Indexed*: Avery. *Notes*: bibl.,
dwgs., photos (B&W).
   A historical review of the architecture and art
of Czechoslovakia. Text in Czech; summaries in
English, French, and German. (0049-5123)

0529 UNSERE   (SZ)
      KUNSTDENKMALER
Gesellschaft fur Schweizerische Kunstge-
schichte, Sekretariat, Pavillonweg 2, 3012 Bern,
Switzerland. Ed. Bd. Tel. (031) 234281. Q; 1949.
Indexed: A.P.I., Avery. *Notes*: adv., bibl., bk.
rev., dwgs., photos (B&W).
   A scholarly journal devoted to the study and

preservation of historic art and architecture in Switzerland. Articles relate many of the topics to contemporary context. Text in German, French, and Italian. (0566-263x)

0530 URBAN CONSERVATION (US) REPORT
Preservation Reports, Inc., 1620 I St., N.W., Washington, DC 20006. Tel. (202) 466-4234. Bi-w; $105; 1977. *Indexed*: Avery.

National newsletter on rehabilitation, reinvestment, and neighborhood preservation. Consists primarily of notes on legislation and conferences. (0731-4205)

0531 URBES NOSTRAE (NE)
Huis de Pinto, Sint Antoniesbrestraat 69, 1011 HB Amsterdam, Netherlands. Tel. 020-277706. Q; 1980. *Indexed*: Avery.

On the restoration of historic European cities. +

0532 VERNACULAR (UK) ARCHITECTURE
Vernacular Architecture Group, N.W. Alcock, 18 Portland Place, Leamington Spa, Warwickshire, England. (U.S. sub.) Box 638, Williamsburg, VA 23185. Ed. Mrs. Pauline Fenley. A; 1970. *Indexed*: A.P.I., Avery. *Notes*: bk. rev., dwgs., photos (B&W).

A journal of international research in the study of vernacular architecture worldwide. Presents papers on aspects of design, reconstruction, materials, preservation techniques, typology, and sociocultural factors of such buildings as English cottages, Greek village houses, barns, and slave quarters. (0305-5477)

0533 VERNACULAR (US) ARCHITECTURE NEWSLETTER
Vernacular Architecture Forum, c/o Orlando Ridout V, 47 Fleet St., Annapolis, MD 21401. Ed. Dell Upton. Q; $9 (with membership); 1980. *Notes*: bibl., bk. rev.

Announces news of the organization, which was founded to encourage the study and preservation of all aspects of vernacular architecture and landscapes through interdisciplinary and multidisciplinary methods. The book reviews and bibliographies are very useful. Includes an exchange of news on current research.

0534 VICTORIAN (US)
Victorian Society in America, 219 S. Sixth St., Philadelphia, PA 19106. Tel. (215) 627-4252. M; 1967. *Indexed*: Avery. +

0636 VICTORIAN HOMES

0535 VICTORIAN SOCIETY (UK) ANNUAL
Victorian Society, 1 Priory Gardens, Bedford Park, London W4 1TT, England. Ed. Ian Sutton. A; 1958. *Indexed*: A.P.I. (0083-6079) +

0536 VIELLES MAISONS (FR) FRANCAISES
Association Reconnue d'Utilite Publique, 93 rue de l'Universite, 75007 Paris 7, France. Ed. Bouffard Gascale. Tel. 551-07-02. 5/yr.; F.25; 1961; circ. 22,000. *Notes*: adv., bibl., bk. rev., dwgs., photos (B&W).

Preservation and design of French estates. Text in French. (0049-6316) *

0192 WONEN-TABK

5

Interior Design

General and Professional

0537 ABC DECOR   (FR)
Centre de Presse d'Information et de Promotion. 8 Rue St. Marc, 75002 Paris, France. J. G. Malgras. 10/yr.; 1964. (0044-5614) +

0538 A.D.   (IT)
Giorgio Mondadori Associati S.p.A., Centro Direzionale, Palazzo Canova, 20090 Milan 2, Segrate, Italy. M; 1981. *Micro*: UMI. +

0005 AIT/ARCHITEKTUR INNEN
         ARCHITEKTUR
         TECHNISCHER AUSBAU

0539 ABITARE   (IT)
Editrice Segesta S.p.A., Corso Monforte 15, 20122 Milan, Italy. Tel. (02) 704251. Telex ABIT-1,3 15302. 10/yr.; $65; 1960; circ. 120,000. *Indexed*: Art Ind., Avery, Jan./Feb. issue. *Notes*: adv., bibl., bk. rev., calendars, dwgs., photos (B&W, color).

Focus is on the contemporary Italian interior and product design for home and city living. The supplements offer a collection of carefully selected furniture. Text in Italian and English. (0001-3218)

0540 L'AMBIENTE CUCINA   (IT)
Propoganda Editoriale Grafica S.p.A., via Fratelli Bressan 2, 20126 Milan, Italy. Ed. Grazia Gamberoni. Tel. (02) 257-9841. Telex 323088 PEGMOS I. Bi-m; $30; 1977; circ. 27,000. *Notes*: adv., bk. rev., calendars, dwgs., photos (B&W, color).

Fine designs of residential kitchens worldwide are presented in this richly illustrated publication. Interesting articles examine design problems in detail. Also includes detailed product descriptions and informative historical notes. Text in English, German, and Italian. (0392-5730)

0541 ARCHITECTURAL DIGEST   (US)
Knapp Communications Corp., 5900 Wilshire Blvd., Los Angeles, CA 90036. Box 2415, Boulder, CO 80322. Ed. Paige Rense. Tel. (213) 937-4740. 10/yr.; $39.95; 1920; circ. 465,000. *Indexed*: Arch. Ind., Art Ind., Avery, Mag. Ind., R.G. *Notes*: adv., bk. rev., calendars, photos (B&W, color).

From California ranches to Manhattan lofts, this glossy magazine covers residential architecture, landscaping, and art collections of the rich and often famous. The style is not as fresh as that of recent competitors, but this is still a popular choice for professional and general readers. (0003-8520)

0542 ARCHITECTURE   (FR)
         INTERIEURE CREE
Societe d'Edition et de Presse, 106 Boulevard Malesherbes, 75017 Paris, France. Ed. Joelle Letessier. Tel. 766-04-60. Bi-m; F. 359; 1980; circ. 20,000. *Indexed*: A.P.I., Avery, Jan. issue. *Notes*: adv., bk. rev., calendars, dwgs., photos (B&W, color).

Notable interior architecture projects from all over the world are presented in detail. Various building types are covered. The emphasis is on the work of Europeans, but American and Japanese designers are included. Text in French.

0543   AREA   (IT)
Kata Redazione, via Lucano 3, Milan 20135, Italy. S.I.E.S. via Chiossetto 18, Milan, Italy. Ed. Alberto Maria Prina. Tel. 5459044. Bi-m; L.36,000. *Indexed*: Avery. *Notes*: adv., bk. rev., dwgs., photos (B&W, color).

With its lavish illustrations of some of the most magnificent residences in the world, this publication is certainly recommended to anyone with a love of beauty. The many photographs focus on rich interior details. The text is light but informative. In addition to the feature articles on homes, it includes profiles of designers and recommendations for selecting and caring for high-quality furniture and works of art. Text in Italian and English.

0544   ARREDO ITALIA   (IT)
Piazza Garibaldi, 35100 Padua, Italy. Ed. C. Veronese. Q. +

0545   BAGNO E ACCESSORI   (IT)
Faenza Editrice S.p.A., via Firenze 276, 48018 Faenza, Italy. Ed. Prof. Goffredo Gaeta. Tel. 0546/43120. Telex ITIREF 550410. M; L.80,000; 1976. *Notes*: adv., bk. rev., calendars, dwgs., photos (B&W, color).

A review of bathroom design and fittings from the simplest to the most exotic. Emphasis is on products rather than space planning. Well illustrated. Text in French and English. (0392-2723)

0546   BAGNO OGGI E DOMANI   (IT)
Propoganda Editoriale Grafica S.p.a., via Fratelli Bressan 2, 20126 Milan, Italy. Ed. Grazia Gamberoni. Tel. (02) 2579841. Telex 323088 PEGMOS I. Bi-m; $35; 1924; circ. 34,700. *Notes*: adv., bk. rev., dwgs., photos (B&W, color).

This graphically outstanding magazine is devoted exclusively to the design of bathrooms by international designers. The abundant color photographs, renderings, and plans richly illustrate the layouts and products of residential and public bathrooms. Emphasis is on functionalism, aesthetics, and the representation of the bathroom as a status symbol—a current international trend. Designers are profiled in each issue. Features examine ideas and problems in detail. Should be included in every interior designer's library but is also of great interest to consumers. Text in Italian, English, French, and German. (0392-2715)

0547   BATH & DOMESTICS   (US)
(Formerly: *Bath Products & Domestics Buyer*)

William Dogan Publications, 74 S.E. Fourth Ave., Delray Beach, FL 33444. Ed. Stephen Flanagan. (305) 272-1223. Q; $6; 1969. +

0548   BETRIEB UND   (GW)
**   AUSREUSTUNG**
Bertelsmann Fachzeitschriften GmbH, Kreuzstr 14-16, Postfach 200421, 8000 Munich 2, W. Germany. Ed. H.G. Reuthes. 7/yr.; 1952. +

0549   BRICOLAGE   (FR)
(Formerly: *Bricolage Maison Practique*)
S.E.B.A.M., 42 rue de Louvre, Paris, France. Ed. J. P. Renan. M; 1966. +

0550   CANADIAN INTERIORS   (CN)
MacLean-Hunter Ltd., 481 University Ave., Toronto, Ont. M5W 1A7, Canada. Ed. Dean Shalden. Tel. (416) 596-5881. 8/yr.; $24; 1964; circ. 7,870. *Indexed*: Avery. *Notes*: adv., calendars, dwgs., photos (B&W, color). *Micro*: UMI.

Covers interior design activities in Canada. Of interest to interior designers, architects, specifiers, buyers, contractors, and manufacturers. (0008-3887)+

0674   CASA CLASSICA

0551   CASA E DECORACAO   (BL)
Editora Vecchi. Rua do Resende 144, Rio de Janeiro, Brazil. M. +

0552   CASA E JARDIM   (BL)
Rua Felistelo Freire 671, Sao Paulo, Brazil. M. +

0553   CASA STILE   (IT)
(Formerly: *Stile Casa*)
Agenzia Gestione Periodici. Via M. Gioia 66, 20125 Milan, Italy. Ed. G. Barbieri. Bi-m; $20; 1962. +

0554   CASA VOGUE   (IT)
Edizioni Conde Nast S.p.A., Piazza Castello 27, 20121 Milan, Italy. Ed. Isa Vercelloni. Tel. (02) 8561. (U.S. Tel. 212-628-3434). 11/yr.; $69; 1969; circ. 65,000. *Notes*: adv., photos (B&W, color).

Presents up-to-date trends in furniture, interior architecture, and home products design. Includes attractive designs from Italy and abroad and interiors of modern and traditional homes. (0008-7173)

0555   CHERI MODA   (IT)
Via Burlamacchi 11, 20135 Milan, Italy. +

0556 CLUB MAISON   (FR)
Editions Conde Nast S.A., 4 Place du Palais Bourbon, 75341 Paris Cedex 9m, France. Ed. Jacques Lamboi. Q; 1978. +

0557 CONFORT   (AG)
Instituto de Publicaciones y Estadisticas S.A., Olavarria 1181, 20 Piso, Buenos Aires, Argentina. M; 1968. *Notes*: bk. rev., dwgs. (0010-5708) +

0766 CONNAISSANCE DES ARTS

0767 CONNOISSEUR

0558 CONSEILS SOLS ET MURS   (FR)
S.M.C., 32 rue de Faubourg Poissoniere, 75001 Paris, France. Ed. Jehan Minfir. M; F.105; 1976. *Notes*: adv., bk. rev. (0395-2673) +

0559 CONTRACT MAGAZINE   (US)
Gralla Publications, 1515 Broadway, New York, NY 10036. Ed. Len Corlin. Tel. (212) 869-1300. M; $14; 1958; circ. 28,000. *Annual Issues*: Jan. —Annual Directory and Buyer's Guide; May— NEOCON. *Notes*: adv., photos (B&W, color). *Micro*: UMI.
A major U.S. publication in the contract design field read primarily by interior designers, architects, specifiers, buyers, suppliers, and manufacturers. (0010-7832)

0365 COUNTRY LIFE

0560 COUNTRY LIVING   (US)
Hearst Magazines, 224 W. 57th Street, New York, NY 10019. Ed. Rachel Newman. Tel. (212) 262-5656. M; 1978. *Notes*: adv. (0274-4791) +

0561 CUCINA + BAGNO & LUCI   (IT)
Viale Selvio 21, 20159 Milan, Italy. Ed. Giuseppe Vallardi. Tel. (02) 68-86-723. A; $15.
A guide to purchasing accessories and lighting systems for kitchens and bathrooms. *

0562 D.L.W. NACHRICHTEN   (GW)
DLW Aktiengesellschaft, Postfach 140, 7120 Bietigheim, Bissingen, W. Germany. Ed. Gerhard Schwab. 2/yr.; free; 1927; circ. 35,000. *Notes*: bk. rev., photos.
Text in English, French, and German. +

0563 DECOR A COEUR   (FR)
Soldecor 51, Avenue Aristide-Briand, 94110 Arcueil, France. Ed. Andre Altman. Q; F.5; 1973. (0705-0585) +

0564 DECORATION CHEZ-SOI   (CN)
Publications Chez-Soi, Ltee., 100 Dresden St., Mount Royal, Quebec H3P 2B6, Canada. Ed. Danielle Denis-Cheron. Tel. (514) 735-6361. 11/yr.; Can.$l5; 1977. *Notes*: adv., photos. (0705-1093) +

0565 DECORATION   (FR)
       INTERNATIONAL
Hachett-Rusconi Associes S.A.R.L., 90 rue de Flandre, Paris, France. Ed. Giuseppe Marzulli. 10/yr., F. 350. *Notes*: adv., photos (B&W, color).
A high-quality design magazine that depicts luxurious interiors and gardens of France. Includes interviews with architects and features on furniture design and the decorative arts. Text in French.

0566 DECORS   (BE)
Av. des Mimosas 33, 1150 Brussels, Belgium. Ed. Suzanne Matthys. Tel. (02) 733-89-19. Q; Fr. 700; 1965; circ. 25,000. *Notes*: adv., photos (B&W, color).
Luxurious home interiors and gardens. Emphasis on European homes. Text in French.

0102 DESIGN AND ART IN
       GREECE

0679 DESIGN FROM
       SCANDINAVIA

0567 DESIGN INTERNATIONAL: (GW)
       ISSUE A
Kaufering 57, 5330 Koenigswaller, W. Germany. Bi-m; 1976. *Notes:* adv., bk. rev.
Text in German and English. +

0568 DESIGNER   (US)
HDC Publications, 114 E. 32nd St., New York, NY 10016. Ed. Muriel R. Chess. Tel. (212) 689-4611. M; $30; 1959; circ. 23,000. *Notes*: adv., dwgs., photos (B&W, color).
Primarily for interior designers, architects, contractors, specifiers, and manufacturers. Aspects of the contract interiors industry are covered through short text and many photographs. Emphasis is on presenting new products. (0011-9431)

0569 DESIGNER'S JOURNAL   (UK)
Architectural Press, Ltd., 9 Queen Anne's Gate, London SW1 H9BY, England. Ed. Lance Knobel. Tel. (01) 222-4333. Telex 8953505. Bi-m; £22; 1983; circ. 24,000. *Notes*: adv., bk. rev., dwgs., photos (B&W, color).

An authoritative interior design magazine that analyzes office and retail design as well as the latest innovations in furniture and lighting. (0264-8148) *

0570 DESIGNER'S WEST   (US)
Arts Alliance Corp., 8770 Beverly Blvd., Los Angeles, CA 90048. P.O. Box 48968, Los Angeles, CA 90048-9168. Ed. Carol Sovcek King. Tel. (213) 657-8231. M; $30; 1953; circ. 19,394. *Annual Issues*: March—Resource Directory. *Notes*: adv., bk. rev., calendars, dwgs., photos (B&W, color).
A review of west-coast interior design covering public, corporate, and residential spaces. In addition to the extensive project coverage, there is general industry news. (0192-1487)

0571 DOMUS   (IT)
Editoriale Domus, via Grandi 5/7, 20089 Rozzano, Italy. Ed. Gianni Mazzocchi. Tel. (02) 824721. Telex 313589 EDIDOM -I. M; $72; 1928; circ. 57,000. *Indexed*: A.P.I., Art Ind., Avery, May issue. *Notes*: adv., bk. rev., calendars, dwgs., photos (B&W, color).
A world-renowned international review of architecture and interior and industrial design. Emphasis is on avant-garde industrial, furniture, and product design by Italian designers. Text in Italian and English. (0012-5377)

0572 EIGEN HUIS EN INTERIEUR   (NE)
ID Tijdschriften B.V., Watteaustraat 29, 1007 JB Amsterdam, Netherlands. Europalaan 93, 3526 KP Utrecht, Netherlands. Ed. E. Alderese Baes. Tel. 020-733666. M; fl. 102; 1967; circ. 60,000. *Notes*: adv., bk. rev., dwgs., photos (B&W, color).
A high-quality residential interior design publication with many photographs, floor plans, and detailed descriptions of the fabrics, colors, furniture, and artwork included with each project. Aimed at the high-income homeowner. Text in Dutch. (0165-3083)

0347 FACILITIES DESIGN AND
      MANAGEMENT

0573 FLORIDA DESIGNERS   (US)
      QUARTERLY
Miami Design Village, 4510 N.E. 2nd Ave., Miami, FL 33137. Ed. Gloria Blake. Bi-m; $23; 1977. *Notes*: adv., bk. rev., photos (B&W, color) +

0574 FORM   (GW)
Verlag Form GmbH, Ernsthoefer Str. 12, 6104 Seeheim 3, W. Germany. Q; DM.54; 1957. *Micro*: UMI. (0015-7678) +

0575 FORM   (SW)
Swedish Society of Industrial Design, Box 7404, S-10391, Stockholm, Sweden. Ed. Monica Boman. Tel. 08-635920. 8/yr.; $65; 1905; circ. 6,000. *Notes*: adv., bibl., bk. rev., calendars, dwgs., photos (B&W, color).
A review of the best Swedish design. Articles cover interior, furniture, and industrial design in detail. The issue examined presented "The Bath" in detail from public swimming pools to home bathrooms. (0015-766x)

0576 GLOBAL INTERIOR   (JA)
A.D.A. Edita Tokyo Co., Ltd., 3-12-14 Sendagaya, Shibuya-ku, Tokyo, Japan. Irreg.; $20. *Indexed*: Avery. *Notes*: dwgs., photos (B&W, color).
Beautifully photographed interiors from all over the world. Each issue is devoted to the work of one designer. Text in Japanese; English titles.

0119 GRAN BAZAAR

0487 HISTORIC HOUSES

0577 HUSMODERN   (SW)
Aahlen Och, Aakerlunds Foerlags Ab, Torsgata 2, 105 44 Stockholm, Sweden. Box 3263, S-103 65, Stockholm, Sweden. Ed. Lisa Winnerlid. W; Kr. 320; 1917; circ. 147,500. (0018-8026) +

0578 INTERIOR DESIGN   (UK)
Westbourne Journals, Ltd., Audit House, Field End Rd., Eastcote, Ruislip, Middlesex HA4 9XE, England. Ed. Katherine Tickle. Tel. (01) 868-4499. Telex 926726. M; £30; 1957; circ. 9,642. *Indexed*: A.P.I. *Notes*: adv., bk. rev., dwgs., photos (B&W, color).
Contains informative features on visual environments in hotels, offices, banks, theaters, schools, hospitals, and other public and commercial buildings. Primarily of interest to specifying interior architects, interior designers, and furniture designers and suppliers. (0020-5494) *

0579 INTERIOR DESIGN   (US)
Cahners Publishing Co., 475 Park Ave. South, New York, NY 10016. P.O. Box 1970, Marion, OH 43305. Ed. Stanley Abercrombie. Tel. (212) 686-0555. M; $35.95; 1932; circ. 43,716. *Indexed*: Arch. Ind., Art Ind., Avery. *Annual Is-*

sues: Jan.—Interior Design Giants; May—NEOCON Preview; Sept.—Designer's Saturday; Dec.—Directory and Buyer's Guide. *Notes*: adv., bk. rev., calendars, dwgs., photos (B&W, color). *Micro*: UMI.

Outstanding examples of commercial and residential interiors in the U.S. are presented in each issue. Product news, trends, business issues, and association news are well covered. This is one of the major U.S. periodicals for interior designers, architects, and manufacturers. (0020-5508)

0580 INTERIORS   (US)
Billboard Publications, Inc., 1515 Broadway, New York, NY 10036. P.O. Box 2154, Radnor, PA 19089. Ed. Beverly Russell. Tel. (212) 764-7522. M; $23; 1888; circ. 29,646. *Indexed*: A.P.I., Arch. Ind., Art Ind., Avery. *Annual Issues*: Jan.—Awards Issue; March—NEOCON Preview; Aug.—Seating Directory. *Notes*: adv., bk. rev., calendars, dwgs., photos (B&W, color). *Micro*: BLH, UMI.

A major periodical for the contract design profession. Emphasis is on new products and trends. (0164-8470)

0581 INTERNI   (IT)
(Formerly: *Arredamento Interni*)
Electa Periodici S.r.l., via Trentacoste 7, 20134 Milan, Italy. Agenzia Italiana di Esportazione, via Gadames 89, 20151 Milan, Italy. Ed. Dorothea Balluff. Tel. (02) 236931. Telex 313123. M; $65; 1954; circ. 85,000. *Notes*: adv., photos (B&W, color).

High-quality review of interior and product design. Text in Italian.

0582 KITCHEN AND BATH   (US)
         BUSINESS
Gralla Publications, Inc., 1515 Broadway, New York, NY 10036. Ed. Patrick J. Galvin. Tel. (212) 869-1300. M; $18; 1955; circ. 31,500. *Annual Issues*: Feb.—Annual Directory and Products Guide. *Notes*: adv., photos (B&W, color).

Installation techniques and new products for kitchens and baths are covered. International coverage of stock and custom products. Of interest to manufacturers, distributors, contractors, and interior designers. (0730-2487)

0583 KITCHEN & BATH   (US)
         CONCEPTS
Qualified Remodeler, 8 S. Michigan Ave., Chicago, IL 60603. Ed. Craig Shutt. Tel. (312) 263-4291. Bi-m; $25; 1985. *Notes*: adv., dwgs., photos (B&W, color).

Aimed at interior designers and kitchen and bath dealers. Well illustrated with informative text.

0584 KITCHENS & BATHROOMS   (UK)
AGB Westbourne Journals, Ltd., Audit House, Field End Rd., Eastcote, Ruislip, Middlesex HA4 9XE, England. Ed. Philip Sandoz. Tel. (01) 868-4499. Telex 926726. M; £18; 1975; circ. 6,745. *Notes*: adv., dwgs., photos (B&W, color).

A product-oriented trade journal that serves kitchen and bathroom specialists, manufacturers, retailers, builders, architects, and interior designers. *

0585 KUECHEN FORUM   (GW)
A.W. Gentner Verlag, Forststr. 131, Postfach 688, D-7000 Stuttgart 1, W. Germany. Ed. Manfred Haselbach. Tel. (0711) 638356. Telex 722 244 awgend. Bi-m; DM. 54; 1969; circ. 15,500. *Notes*: adv., dwgs., photos (B&W, color).

Trade review on home kitchen furnishings including furniture, appliances, and plumbing installations. Text in German. (0342-7626)

0586 KULTUR IM HEIM   (GE)
Verlag die Wirtschaft, Am Friedrichschain 22, 1055 Berlin, E. Germany. Ed. Monika Grams. Tel. 4387420. Telex 114566 wirtsdd. Bi-m; 1957. *Notes*: adv., bk. rev., dwgs., photos (B&W, color).

A design magazine on the interiors of socialist housing in urban and rural communities. Covers furniture arranging, industrial design, gardening, and crafts. Text in German; table of contents in German, English, and Russian. (0323-4967) *

0129 DIE KUNST

0587 LAKASKULTURA   (HU)
Lapkiado Vallalat, Lenin korut 9-11, 1073 Budapest 7, Hungary. Kultura, Box 149, H-1389, Budapest, Hungary. Ed. Maria Pataki. Q; 1966; circ. 130,000. *Notes*: adv. (0047-391x) +

0131 LATENT IMAGES

0133 LIVING ARCHITECTURE

0588 M D   (GW)
(Formerly: *Mobel Interior Design*)
Konradin-Verlag Robert Kohlhammer GmbH, Ernst Mey Strasse 8, D-7022, Leinfelden-Echterdingen, W. Germany. Ed. Gisela Schultz. Tel. (0711) 7908287. Telex 7255-421. M;

DM. 136.60; 1954; circ. 13,406. *Indexed*: A.P.I. *Notes*: adv., bk. rev., dwgs., photos (B&W, color). *Micro*: UMI.

An international journal on furnishings and interior design that addresses problems of current and future living conditions. Covers commercial and residential buildings and furnishings. Also reviews prototypes, fairs, and exhibitions. Readership includes architects, interior designers, and furniture manufacturers. (0343-0642) *

0589   MAISON FRANCAISE   (FR)
Publications Vie et Loisirs, 22 rue Saint Augustin, 75083 Paris Cedex 02, France. Ed. Claude Berthod. Tel. 266-9293. Telex PVL643097 F. M; F.345; 1946; circ. 100,000. *Notes*: adv., bk. rev., photos (color).

Presents lavish interiors of some of the most beautiful homes in the world. Extensive coverage of new furniture, lighting, and home accessories. Text in French; summaries in English. (0025-0953)

0590   MAISONS ET DECORS   (FR)
          MEDITERRANEE
Compagnie Regionale de Publications Specialisees, Section Mediterranee, 2 Rond Point des Minimes, 13100 Aix en Provence, France. Ed. Masclaux Pierre. Tel. (42) 272953. Bi-m; F.140; 1974. *Notes*: adv., dwgs., photos (B&W, color).

Residential architecture and interior design from the south of France. Text in French. (0180-4561) *

0591   DIE MODERNE KUECHE   (GW)
Die Planung Verlagsgesellschaft mbH, Holzhofallee 25-31, 6100 Darmstadt, W. Germany. Ed. Horst Bach. Tel. (06151) 314104. Telex 0419363 echo d. Bi-m; DM.40; 1951; circ. 7,000. *Notes*: adv., bk. rev., dwgs., photos (B&W, color).

Covers all aspects of the design of kitchens and bathrooms. Text in German. (0026-864x) *

0592   MODERNES WOHNEN/   (SZ)
          HABITATION MODERNE
Verlag H.G. Franke, 8126 Zumikon, Switzerland. Q; Fr. 20; 1958. (0026-8712) +

0593   MOEBEL UND WOHNRAUM   (GE)
VEB Fachbuchverlag, Karl-Heine Str. 16, DDR 7031, Leipzig, E. Germany. 8/yr.; DM.14.40; 1947. *Notes*: adv., bibl., bk. rev., photos (B&W).

Modern and traditional furnishings for the home. Text in German; summaries in English and Russian. (0026-8844)

0594   MUOTO   (FI)
Finnish Assn. of Designers Ornamo, Rakennuskirja oy Bldg. Book Ltd., Loennrotinkatu 20B, 00120 Helsinki 12, Finland. Ed. Heikki Hyytiaenen. Q; 1980. (0358-3521) +

0595   MY ROOM/WATASHI-NO-   (JA)
          HEYA
Fujin Seikatsu Sha, 19-5, 2 chome, Yushima, Bunkyo-ku, Tokyo, Japan. Ed. Keiko Hirasawa. Bi-m; 1972. +

0596   NYE BONYTT/DESIGN FOR   (NO)
          LIVING
Forlaget Bonytt AS, Bygdoey Alle 9, Oslo 2, Norway. Ed. Tore Gilgane. 10/yr.; 1941. (0029-6783) +

0597   RUSTICA   (FR)
Dargaud Editeur, 12 rue Blaise Pascal, 92200 Neuilly-sur-Seine, France. W; 1928. +

0598   SCHOENER WOHNEN   (GW)
Gruner und Jahr GmbH und Co., Warburg Str. 50, Postfach 3?2040, 2000 Hamburg 36, W. Germany. Ed. J. Kremerskothen. M; DM.48; 1960. *Micro*: UMI. +

0599   SKOENNE HJEM   (DK)
Fogtdals A-S, Noerre Farimagsgade 49, 1364 Copenhagen K., Denmark. Ed. Allan Strauss. Q. +

0388   UNIQUE HOMES

0600   VIDA DOMESTICA   (BL)
Carlos Goncalves Fidalgo, Rua Riachuelo 414, Rio de Janeiro GB, Brazil. M. +

0536   VIELLES MAISONS
          FRANCAISES

0601   WORLD OF INTERIORS   (UK)
          (Formerly: *Interiors*)
Pharos Publications, Ltd., 228-230 Fulham Rd., London SW10 9BR, England. Quadrant Subscr. Services, Ltd., Stuart House, Perrymount Rd., Haywards Heath, W. Sussex RH16 3DH, England. Ed. Min Hogg. Tel. (01) 351-5177. 11/yr.; £55; 1981; circ. 52,666. *Indexed*: Avery. *Notes*: adv., bk. rev., dwgs., photos (B&W, color).

This award-winning publication covers high-quality residential interior design and the fine arts. Articles are well written and richly illustrated. Features cover antiques, gardens, and traditional as well as unusual interiors. (0264-083x)

0780 ZYGOS

Home Decorating

0539 ABITARE

0602 ART ET DECORATION   (FR)
Editions Charles Massin et Cie, 2 rue de
l'Echelle, 75001 Paris, France. Agence Archat,
34 Blvd. Haussman, 75009 Paris, France. Ed.
Claude Gay. Tel. 260-30-05. Telex 240-918
Trace. 7/yr.; F.180; 1897. *Indexed*: Art Ind.
   Focus is on traditional residential interiors.
Text in French; summaries in English. (0004-
3168) *

0603 AUSTRALIAN HOME   (AT)
          BEAUTIFUL
Herald & Weekly Times, Ltd., 44-74 Flinders
St., Melbourne, Victoria 3000, Australia. M;
1926. +

0604 AUSTRALIAN HOUSE AND   (AT)
          GARDEN
168 Castlereagh St., Sydney, NSW 2000, Australia. Box 5252 GPO, Sydney, NSW 2001,
Australia. Ed. Beryl Clark Marchi. Tel. (02) 268-
0666. Telex AA20614. M; Aus.$41; 1948; circ.
100,000. *Annual Issues*: June—Outstanding
Houses Yearbook. *Notes*: adv., bk. rev., photos
(B&W, color).
   Home decorating, gardening, tableware, and
entertaining. (0004-931x) *

0605 AVOTAKKA   (FI)
   (Formerly: *Kaunis Koti*)
A. Lehdet Oy, Hitsaajankatu 10, 00810 Helsinki
81, Finland. Hitsaajan Katu 7, 00810 Helsinki,
Finland. Ed. Leena Nokela. Tel. (90) 782-311.
Telex 124732. M; Fmk. 198; 1967; circ. 80,137.
Indexed: Dec. issue. *Annual Issues*: Oct.—
Home Decorating Extra. *Notes*: adv., dwgs.,
photos (B&W, color).
   A consumer-type home decorating magazine.
Text in Finnish. (0355-2950) *

0606 BETTER HOMES AND   (US)
          GARDENS
Meredith Corp., 17th and Locust St., Des
Moines, IA 50336. Robert Austin, P.O. Box
4536, Des Moines, IA 50336. Ed. David Jordan.
Tel. (515) 284-2336. M; $12.97 (US); $22.97
(abroad); 1922; circ. 8,000,000. *Indexed*: R.G.
Annual Issues: March—100's of Ideas; July—
You Can Do It. *Notes*: adv., dwgs., photos
(B&W, color). *Micro*: BLH, UMI.
   A consumer magazine that offers ideas and

well-illustrated articles on home building designs, gardening, housewares, and furnishings.
Emphasis is on the home as the focal point for
the family. (0006-0151)

0607 BO BEDRE   (DK)
Palle Fogtdals A-S, Noerre Farimagsgade 49,
1364 Copenhagen K, Denmark. Ed. Kare Olof-
sen. Tel. (01) 12-66-12. Telex 15712 Fogtdl DK.
M; 1961; circ. 125,000. *Notes*: adv., dwgs., photos (B&W, color).
   A general-interest magazine on the home that
includes articles on floor layouts, kitchen planning, decorating, gardening, and furniture design. Text in Danish.

0608 BO BRA   (SW)
   (Formerly: *Allt i Hemmet*)
Specialtidningsfoerlaget AB, Drottninggatan
101, S-11360 Stockholm, Sweden. S-72185 Vas-
teras, Sweden. Ed. Caj Anderson. 10/yr.; Kr.
148.50; 1983; circ. 120,000. *Notes*: adv., photos
(B&W, color).
   Home decorating magazine with ideas for
storage, gardening, collecting, and basic home
repairs. (0002-6182)

0609 CASA CLAUDIA   (BL)
R. Geraldo Flausino Gomes, 61-5 Andar, 04575
Sao Paulo SP, Brazil. Divisao de Marketing Di-
reto, Editora Abril S.A., Caixa Postal 11830,
0100 Sao Paulo SP, Brazil. Ed. Olga Krell. Tel.
(011) 545-8145. Telex 01123227 EDAB-BR. M;
$20; 1975; circ. 120,000. *Annual Issues*: Feb.—
Architecture; March—Apartments; May—
Newlyweds. *Notes*: adv., dwgs., photos (B&W,
color).
   Brazil's major home decorating magazine
with features on home furnishings, gardening,
cooking, and space planning. Text in Portuguese.

0610 CASA E GIARDINO   (IT)
Via Marinetti 3, 20127 Milan, Italy. Ed. Paolo
Arione. Tel. (02) 2849042. M; L.85,000; 1966.
Notes: adv., bibl., bk. rev., calendars, dwgs.,
photos (B&W, color).
   Covers furnishings and gardens. (0004-1939)

0611 CASAVIVA   (IT)
Arnoldo Mondadori Editore, Casella Postale
1772, 20090 Segrate Milan, Italy. Ed. Arnoldo
Mondadori. Tel. (02) 75421. Telex 320457
Mondmi I. M; $70; 1973; circ. 208,667. *Annual*

69

Issues: Sept.—International Furniture Exhibition of Milan.

A fine home decorating magazine that focuses on the best in Italian furniture design. Text in Italian.

0612 DECORMAG   (CN)
Publication Decormag, 11440 Albert-Hudon, Montreal Nord, Que. H1G 3J6, Canada. Ed. Nicole Charest. Tel. (514) 325-0724. 11/yr.; $35.50; 1972; circ. 60,000. *Annual Issues*: August—"Poeles a Bois, Chemineer." *Notes*: adv., bibl., bk. rev., calendars, photos (B&W, color).

Text in French. *

0613 DEMEURES ET CHATEAUX   (FR)
21 rue Cassette, 75006 Paris, France. Ed. Jean-Michel Reillier. Tel. (1) 222-0376. 5/yr.; $40; 1978; circ. 27,000. *Notes*: adv., bibl., dwgs., photos (B&W, color).

This publication is a "must" for anyone in the market for a palace or country home in France and a sheer pleasure for anyone who enjoys looking at luxurious homes, gardens, and fine art. Half of each issue is devoted to exclusive properties for sale. Each advertisement includes a color photo and description. The other half of the issue includes brief articles and many illustrations of beautiful homes, gardens, antiques, sculptures, and art in general. (0291-1191)

0614 DOMOV   (CS)
Artia, Spalena 51, 11302 Prague 1, Czechoslovakia. Tel. 2944-41-3. Bi-m; $40; 1960; circ. 52,600.

Text in Czech; summaries in English, French, German, and Russian. (0012-5369) *

0770 EARLY AMERICAN LIFE

0694 HEIMTEX

0615 HOME   (US)
  (Formerly: *Hudson Home*)
Knapp Communications, 140 E. 45th St., New York, NY 10017. 5600 Wilshire Blvd., Los Angeles, CA 90036. Ed. Olivia Buehl. Tel. (212) 682-4040. M; $15; 1953; circ. 600,000. *Indexed*: Dec. issue. *Notes*: adv., bk. rev., dwgs., photos (B&W, color).

A consumer magazine on building, remodeling, and decorating homes. Includes house plans, product information, and articles on landscaping and do-it-yourself construction. (0278-2839) *

0616 HOME/ITALIA   (IT)
Viale Monza 128, 20127 Milan, Italy. 11/yr.; $50.

Lavishly illustrated. Text in Italian. +

0617 HOTEL DOMANI   (IT)
Via Bianconi 10, 20139 Milan, Italy. $65. +

0618 HOUSE AND GARDEN   (UK)
Conde Nast Publications, Ltd., Vogue House, Hanover Sq., London W1R OAD, England. Ed. Robert Harling. Tel. (01) 499-9080. M; $52.50; 1947; circ. 127,500. *Indexed*: A.P.I., Avery. *Notes*: adv., bk. rev., dwgs., photos (B&W, color).

A high-quality magazine of residential interior design and gardening. (0043-5759) *

0619 HOUSE AND GARDEN   (US)
Conde Nast Publications, 350 Madison Ave., New York, NY 10017. Box 5202, Boulder, CO 80322. Ed. Louis Oliver Gropp. Tel. (212) 880-8800. M; $24; 1901; circ. 1,111,000. *Indexed*: R.G. *Notes*: adv., bk. rev., photos (B&W, color). *Micro*: BLH, UMI.

Lavishly descriptive coverage of spectacular home interiors and gardens all over the world. Elegantly presented. Includes articles on art collecting and travel. (0018-6406)

0620 HOUSE AND HOME   (JA)
Gakken Co., Ltd., 40-54 chome, Kamiikedai, Ohta-ku, Tokyo 145, Japan. Ed. Takanari Taguchi. Bi-m; Yen 5880; 1981. +

0621 HOUSE BEAUTIFUL   (US)
Hearst Magazines, 1700 Broadway, New York, NY 10019. Ed. Wallace Guenther. Tel. (212) 903-5101. M; $13.97; 1896; circ. 850,000. *Indexed*: Avery, Mag. Ind., R.G. *Notes*: adv., bk. rev., photos (B&W, color). *Micro*: BLH, UMI.

Consumer magazine on home decorating. Includes plans and product reviews as well as monthly columns on kitchen design, entertaining, and gardening. (0018-6422)

**0622 HOUSE BEAUTIFUL'S HOME   (US)
          DECORATING**
1700 Broadway, 28th fl., New York, NY 10019. Ed. Gordon Firth. Tel. (212) 903-5051. Q; $2.95 (newsstand only); 1962; circ. 300,000. *Notes*: adv., bk. rev., dwgs., photos (B&W, color).

Provides coverage of home furnishings for the consumer. Articles present information on accessories, color selection, furniture arrangement and styles, window treatments, and room planning for apartments, townhouses, and single-family homes.

0374   HOUSE BEAUTIFUL'S HOME
       REMODELING

0623   HOUSE BEAUTIFUL'S   (US)
       KITCHENS/BATHS
1700 Broadway, 28th fl., New York, NY 10019. Ed. Gordon Firth. Tel. (212) 903-5051. S-a; $2.95 (newsstand only); 1980; circ. 200,000. *Notes*: adv., bk. rev., dwgs., photos (B&W, color).

Aimed at families planning to remodel their existing kitchens and baths or build new ones. Presents designs and uses for cabinets, appliances, fixtures, and flooring. Practical articles offer advice on storage. Product information serves a wide range of tastes and budgets.

0624   I.D.E.A.S.   (US)
D O D I Publishing, Box 343392, Coral Gables, FL 33114-3392. Ed. Sam Hirsch. Tel. (305) 662-8924. Q; $14; 1977; circ. 16,000. *Notes:* adv., bk. rev., photos (color).

Articles on interior design, antiques, architecture, environment, and home decorating. Special emphasis is on the Sun Belt region. (0161-1895) *

0625   IDEAL HOME   (UK)
I.P.C. Magazine, Ltd., 28th Fl., King's Reach Tower, Stamford St., London SE1 9LSX, England. M; $31.90; 1939. (0019-1361) +

0626   JOURNAL DE LA MAISON   (FR)
Route de Versailles, 78560 Le Port Marly, France. Ed. Jean Yves Bonhommet. M; 1968. +

0627   MAISON ET JARDIN   (FR)
Conde Nast, S.A., 4 Place du Palais Bourbon, 75341 Paris Cedex 07, France. Ed. Jacques Lamboi. 10/yr.; 1940. (0025-0945) +

0628   MAISON MAGAZINE   (FR)
Editions Conde Nast, S.A., 4 Place du Palais Bourbon, 75341 Paris Cedex 07, France. Ed. Jacques Lamboi. Bi-m; 1978. +

0629   METROPOLITAN HOME   (US)
Meredith Corp., 1716 Locust St., Des Moines, IA 50336. Ed. Dorothy Kalins. Tel. (515) 284-2401. M; $15; 1969; circ. 700,000. *Annual Issues*: Jan.—Home of the Year Winner. *Notes*: adv., photos (B&W, color). *Micro*: UMI.

A popular home design magazine with articles on decorating, home furnishings, real estate, collecting, and home entertaining. Emphasis on personal style. (0273-2858)

0630   MIA CASA   (IT)
Alberto Peruzzo, via Tito Speri 8, 20154 Milan, Italy. 10/yr.; 1968. +

0631   MODERNE HEIM   (AU)
Oskar Riedel, Schottenring 28, A-1010 Vienna, Austria. A; 1950. +

0632   NASH DOM   (BU)
Hemus, 6 Roussky Blvd., 1000 Sofia, Bulgaria. Bi-m; $33. *Notes*: adv., photos (color).

Well-illustrated magazine on contemporary house interiors. Aimed at the general public. Text in Russian and English. (0204-501x)

0633   1001 HOME IDEAS   (US)
Family Media, Inc., 3 Park Ave., New York, NY 10016. P.O. Box 4000, Bergenfield, NJ 07621. Ed. Anne Anderson. Tel. (212) 340-9250. M; $18; 1946; circ. 1,500,000. *Notes*: adv., bk. rev., dwgs., photos (B&W, color).

Home decorating magazine for middle-income families. Includes articles on gardening, remodeling, and food. (0278-0844) *

0634   SOUTHERN ACCENTS   (US)
WRC Smith Publishing Co., 1760 Peachtree Rd., NW., Atlanta, GA 30357. Ed. Lisa Newsom. Tel. (404) 874-4462. Bi-m; $18; 1977; circ. 200,000. *Indexed*: Avery. *Notes*: adv., photos (color).

A glossy publication that focuses on the design of fine Southern homes and gardens. (0149-516x) *

0635   TORONTO LIFE DESIGN   (CN)
       AND DECOR GUIDE
Key Publishers, Ltd., 59 Front St. E., Toronto, Ont. M5E 1B3, Canada. Ed. Marq de Villiers. S-a; 1978. +

0636   VICTORIAN HOMES   (US)
550 7th St., Brooklyn, NY 11215. 6007 Renovator's Old Mill, Millers Falls, MA 01349. Ed. Carolyn Flaherty. Tel. (718) 499-5789. Q; $12; 1982; circ. 70,000. *Indexed*: Avery. *Notes*: adv., bk. rev., dwgs., photos (B&W, color).

An inspiration to owners and admirers of American Victorian styles and homes. Each issue focuses on the decorative arts and lifestyles of the period 1840–1920. Articles provide information on all aspects of the architecture and interior design of the homes of this era and how they can be made compatible with today's lifestyles. Regular departments cover decorating, furniture, textiles, restoration, collecting, fashion, food, gardening, and entertainment in the Victorian mode. Well illustrated and informative. (0744-415x)

0637   VOGUE LIVING   (AT)
Bernard Leser Publications Pty., Ltd., 49 Clarence St., Sydney 2000, Australia. Ed. June McCallum. Tel. 290-6566. Telex VOXYD AA72201. 10/yr.; Aus.$42; 1971; circ. 53,800. *Notes*: adv., bk. rev., photos (B&W, color).
   Consumer-type interior design magazine. (0042-8035) *

0638   VOTRE MAISON   (FR)
Editions du Croissant, 6 Ave. Delcasse, 75008 Paris, France. (U.S. sub.) European Publishers, 11-03 46th Ave., Long Island City, NY 11101. Tel. 359-2372. Telex 640478. Bi-m; newsstand only; 1947; circ. 550,000. *Notes*: adv., bk. rev., photos (B&W, color).
   A consumer-oriented publication on furniture and furnishings for the home. Text in French; summaries in German, Italian, Japanese, Portuguese, and Spanish. (0042-8973)

0639   ZUHAUSE: WOHNUNG,   (GW)
       HAUS UND GARTEN
Jahreszeiten Verlag GmbH, Possmoorweg 1, 2000 Hamburg 39, W. Germany. M; 1967. +

Woodworking/Furniture Design and Production

0640   ARREDORAMA   (IT)
Industria del Mobile S.r.l., via Giambologna 21, 20136 Milan, Italy. Ed. Renzo Cervini. M; L.75,000; 1969; circ. 18,000. *Notes*: adv.
   General publication on furniture design. Text in Italian. (0004-2854) *

0641   BEDDING   (US)
National Assn. of Bedding Manufacturers, 1235 Jefferson Davis Highway, no. 601, Arlington, VA 22202. Ed. Tamar Abrams. Tel. (703) 979-3550. M; $30; 1917; circ. 2,500. *Notes*: adv., bk. rev., calendars, dwgs., photos (B&W).
   Primarily for bedding manufacturers and suppliers. Covers product and marketing information on beds as well as industry news. (0005-7568) *

0642   D.D.S.: DEUTSCHE   (GW)
       SCHREINER UND TISCHLER
   (Formerly: *Der Deutsche Schreiner*)
Der Deutsche Schreiner Verlags, GmbH, Neckar Str. 121, Postfach 209, D-7000 Stuttgart 1, W. Germany. Ed. Ulrich Mueller. Tel. (0711) 26310. Telex 722503. M; DM.104.40; 1900; circ. 17,200. *Notes*: adv., bk. rev., calendars, dwgs., photos (B&W, color).
   A trade journal aimed at woodworkers. Articles cover design and technical issues. Details on equipment, furniture design, and techniques in woodworking and wood handicraft industries. Text in German. (0341-8839)

0750   DESIGN

0643   DESIGN SOLUTIONS   (US)
Jeffrey H. Berman & Assoc., 2025 I St., N.W., Ste. 621, Washington, DC 20006. Architectural Woodwork Inst., 2310 S. Walter Reed Dr., Arlington, VA 22206. Ed. William Mambert. Tel. (202) 775-0892. Q; $18; 1981; circ. 31,500. *Notes*: adv., dwgs., photos (color).
   Features outstanding examples of interior woodwork in residential and nonresidential projects. Includes interviews with designers and, occasionally, technical notes. Primarily photographs. (0277-3538)

0644   FINE WOODWORKING   (US)
Taunton Press, P.O. Box 355, Newtown, CT 06470. Ed. John Kelsey. Tel. (203) 426-8171. Bi-m; $14; 1975; circ. 200,000. *Indexed*: Art Ind. *Notes*: adv., bk. rev., dwgs., photos (B&W, color).
   Covers all aspects of wood craftsmanship. Each article is well illustrated with views of projects and plans. Detailed information on techniques, equipment, and types of woods. (0361-3453).

0645   FIRA BULLETIN   (UK)
Furniture Industry Research Assn., Maxwell Rd., Stevenage Herts SG1 2EW, England. Ed. A.D. Spillard. Tel. 0438-313433. Telex 827653 FIRA G. Q; £44; 1956; circ. 700. *Notes*: adv., bk. rev., dwgs., photos (B&W, color).
   Technical aspects of the furniture industry—design, manufacturing, and marketing. (0014-5904) *

0646   FORESTA   (RM)
Chamber of Commerce and Industry of the Socialist Republic of Rumania, Bd. N. Balcescu

Nr. 22, Bucharest, Rumania. ILEXIM, Str. 13 Decembrie Nr. 3, P.O. Box 136-137, Bucharest, Rumania. Q; $22; 1969. (0015-7503) +

0647 FURNITURE DESIGN & (US) MANUFACTURING

Delta Communications, Inc., 400 N. Michigan Ave., Ste. 1216, Chicago, IL 60611. Ed. Carol Carman. Tel. (312) 222-2000. Telex 210012 UR. M; $25; 1959; circ. 30,000. *Annual Issues*: June —Source of Supply Directory. *Notes*: adv., photos (B&W, color). *Micro*: UMI.

Each issue includes articles on the design and production of wood, metal, plastic, and upholstered furniture and cabinets, with features on fasteners, new technology, and design trends. Includes industry activities and trends from Europe. Of interest to manufacturers, designers, and purchasing agents. (0016-304x)

0648 FURNITURE (UK) MANUFACTURER

Magnum Publications, Ltd., 110-112 Station Rd. E., Oxted Surrey RH8 OQA, England. M; £16; 1935. (0306-0519) +

0649 FURNITURE (US) MANUFACTURING MANAGEMENT

(Formerly: *Furniture Methods and Materials*) Associations Management, 3116 Forest Hill Rd., Box 38629, Germantown, TN 38138. Ed. Bill Wellborn. Tel. (901) 853-7470. M; $20 (free to qualified subscribers); 1954; circ. 21,500. *Annual Issues*: May—Directory and Buyers Guide; Nov.—Product Review. *Notes*: adv., bk. rev., calendars, dwgs., photos (B&W, color).

Covers machinery, production methods, and developments in the wood and pressed-wood furniture industries. Articles deal with in-plant case studies, machinery profiles, and interviews with industry leaders. (0192-799x) *

0650 FURNITURE PRODUCTION (US)

Production Publishing Co., 2916 Sidco Dr., Nashville, TN 37204. Ed. J.H. Whaley, Jr. Tel. (615) 255-7667. M; (U.S. only); 1952; circ. 17,500. *Annual Issues*: July—Red Book Directory of Product Literature; Dec.—Blue Book Directory of Supply Sources. *Notes*: adv., bk. rev., calendars, dwgs., photos (B&W, color). *Micro*: UMI.

Covers furniture and woodworking production in general. (0532-8942) *

0651 FURNITURE PRODUCTION & (CN) DESIGN

(Formerly: *Canadian Wood Products*) Sentinel Business Publications, 6420 Victoria Ave., Unit 8, Montreal, Que. H3W 2S7, Canada. Ed. Keith Frederick. Tel. (514) 731-3523. Bi-m; $20; 1900; circ. 6,224. *Notes*: adv., bk. rev., dwgs., photos (B&W, color).

Covers all aspects of furniture design and production with emphasis on production. (0703-9514) *

0652 FURNITURE WOOD DIGEST (US)

Johnson Hill Press, Inc., 1233 Janesville Ave., Ft. Atkinson, WI 53538. Ed. Richard Rea. Tel. (414) 563-6388. M; $35 (free to qualified subscribers); 1970; circ. 33,500. *Annual Issues*: Jan. —Buyer's Guide Showcase. *Notes*: adv., photos (B&W, color).

A tabloid offering product news of interest to furniture/woodworking manufacturers.

0653 HOLZ IM HANDWERK: THE (AU) AUSTRIAN FURNITURE JOURNAL

Zeitschriftenverlag, Anton Frankgasse 17, A-1181 Vienna, Austria. Ed. Dr. Hildegard Braig. Tel. 0222/34. Telex 115586 iholz a. M; S.340; 1959; circ. 6,000. *Notes*: adv., dwgs., photos (B&W, color).

Presents new woodworking methods and equipment and furniture designs of experts as well as students. Covers the Austrian woodworking market in general. Readership includes all types of woodworkers, interior designers, suppliers, and manufacturers. Text in German. (0018-3776)

0654 HOLZ UND (GW) KUNSTOFFVERARBEITUNG

DRW Verlag Weinbrenner, KG Fasanenweg 18, 7022 Leinfelden-Echterdingen, W. Germany. M; 1966. (0721-2585) +

0655 INDUSTRIA DEL LEGNO E (IT) DEL MOBILE

Societa Edizioni Techniche Arredamento, Corso Magenta 96, 20123 Milan, Italy. Ed. Tito Armellini. M; L.50,000; 1949. *Indexed*: Chem. Abstr. *Notes*: adv., dwgs.

Covers the manufacturing of wood furniture. (0019-7521) +

0656 INDUSTRIA DEL MOBILE (IT)

Industria del Mobile S.r.l., 21 via Giambologna, 20136 Milan, Italy. Ed. Alfio Ferrara. Tel. (02)

8394-780. M; L.90,000; 1959; circ. 6,000. *Notes*: adv., dwgs.

News of the woodworking industry in Italy. Text in Italian. (0019-753x) *

0657   INDUSTRIAL SUR BOIS   (SZ)
Federation Romande des Maitres Menuisiers, Ebenistes Charpentiers, Fabricants de Marbles et Parqueteurs, Ave. Jomini 8, C.P. 66, CH-1000 Lausanne 9, Switzerland. M; Fr. 18; 1923. +

0658   SCHWEIZERISCHE   (SZ)
       SCHREINERZEITUNG
Verband Schweizerischer Schreinermeister und Moevelfabrikanten, Schmelzbergstr. 56, 8044 Zurich, Switzerland. Tel. (01) 473540. Telex 816 207VSSM CH. W; Fr.85; 1890; circ. 10,000. *Notes*: adv., bk. rev., dwgs., photos (B&W).

Detailed coverage of the woodworking industry, including production engineering, interior decoration, woodworking machines; wood drying, workshop equipment; courses and exhibitions. Text in German; summaries in Italian. (0036-7753) *

0659   TRAEETS ARBEJDS GIVERE   (DK)
       (Formerly: *Snedker-og-Toemrermestrene*)
Slotsgade 5A, 5000 Odense C, Denmark. Ed. Knud Meister. Tel. (09) 125777. 8/yr.; Kr.48; circ. 2,000. *Notes*: adv., dwgs.

Danish furniture design and production. *

0660   UPHOLSTERING TODAY   (US)
       (Formerly: *Upholstery Industry*)
Communications Today, Ltd., P.O. Box 2754, High Point, NC 27261. Ed. Patricia Joyce Earnhardt. Tel. (919) 889-0113. M; $15; 1889; circ. 15,000. *Indexed*: P.A.I.S. *Annual Issues*: April —Directory of Industry Resources. *Notes*: adv., bk. rev., calendars, dwgs., photos (B&W, color).

Covers all aspects of the upholstered seating industry that are of primary interest to manufacturing management. (0744-138x) *

0661   WOOD & WOOD PRODUCTS   (US)
Vance Publishing Corp., 400 Knightsbridge Parkway, Lincolnshire, IL 60069. Ed. Harry Urban. M; $18; 1896; circ. 32,000. *Indexed*: Compendex, Eng. Ind. *Annual Issues*: March— Annual Buying Guide. *Notes*: adv., dwgs., photos (B&W, color). *Micro*: UMI.

Covers the design, manufacture, and marketing of furniture, cabinets, and other wood products. Extensive product reviews. Includes

articles on the industry overseas. Emphasis is on production. (0043-7662)

0662   WOOD FINISHING   (US)
       QUARTERLY
Dakota County Area Vocational Technical Inst., Wood Finishing Trade Program, 1300 145th St., E., Rosemont, MN 55068. Ed. Dan McGraw. Tel. (612) 423-8362. Q; free; 1981; circ. 20,000. *Notes*: adv., bibl., bk. rev., calendars, dwgs., photos (B&W).

A newsletter edited for woodworkers and wood finishers. Provides current industry news. *

1019   WORKBENCH

Furniture and Interior Furnishings

0539   ABITARE

0663   AMBIENTARE   (IT)
Editoriale Galfa S.r.l., Viale Monza 57, 20125 Milan, Italy. Ed. Franco Battaglini. Tel. 2841418. M; L.50,000; 1981.

Interior furnishings. Text in Italian. *

0543   AREA

0664   ARMSTRONG LOGIC   (US)
       (Formerly: *Linoleum Logic*)
Armstrong World Industries, Inc., Box 3001, Lancaster, PA 17604. Ed. Joseph DiSanto. Tel. (717) 397-0611. 10/yr.; free to qualified subscribers; 1915; circ. 80,000. *Notes*: photos (B&W).

Primarily a sales magazine for dealers of resilient floors. Installation case histories may be helpful to contractors. May also be of interest to individuals responsible for product selection. (0044-8974) *

0665   ARREDO BIANCHERIA CASA   (IT)
       (Formerly: *Arredo Tessile*)
Nuove Tecniche ed., via San Siro 27, 20100 Milan, Italy. Agenzia Italiana di Esportazione, via Gadames 89, 20151 Milan, Italy. Tel. 482213. Telex 315367 AIEMI-I. Q; $36; 1977; circ. 17,000.

Features fabrics and floorcoverings for the home. Text in English, Italian, French, and German. (0392-6192) *

0666   ARTICOLI CASALINGHI   (IT)
Pubbliemme S.r.l., via Caracciolo 77, 20155 Milan, Italy. Ed. Massimo Martini. M; 1958; L.40,000. (0004-3672) +

**0667   BAU UND   (GW)
        MOEBELSCHREINER**
Konradin-Verlag Robert Kohlhammer GmbH, Postfach 100 252, 7022 Leinfelden-Echterdingen, W. Germany. Ed. Peter Nagel. M; 1946. (0005-6464) +

0668   BLINDS AND SHUTTERS   (UK)
        (Formerly: *Blindmaker*)
British Blind & Shutter Assn., Wheatland Journals Ltd., Penn House, Penn Place, Rickmansworth, Herts. WD3 1SN, England. Q; $21.80; 1952. (0305-733x) +

**0669   BRITISH CARPET   (UK)
        MANUFACTURERS
        ASSOCIATION—INDEX OF
        QUALITY NAMES**
British Carpet Manufacturers Association, Aykroyd House, Hoo Road, Kidderminster, Worcs. DY10 1NB, England. 3/yr.; £21 for 3 yrs.; 1958. +

**0670   CABINET MAKER AND   (UK)
        RETAIL FURNISHER**
Benn Publications, Ltd., Sovereign Way, Tonbridge, Kent TN9 1RW, England. Ed. G.T. White. Tel. 0732-364422. Telex 95132. W; £59; 1880; circ. 9,000. *Annual Issues*: Feb., May, Sept.—Designing Interiors. *Notes*: adv., bk. rev., dwgs., photos (B&W, color).
The emphasis is on the manufacturing, distribution, and sale of interior furnishings, including furniture, textiles, carpets, lighting, and accessories. The articles on new products and the introduction of new companies and designers make this a useful source for interior designers. (0007-9278)

**0671   CARPET AND   (UK)
        FLOORCOVERINGS REVIEW**
        (Formerly: *Carpet Review Weekly*)
Benn Publications, Ltd., Sovereign Way, Tonbridge, Kent TN9 1RW, England. Ed. Mrs. Joy Lawrence. Tel. 0732-364422. Telex 95132. Bi-w; £42; 1982; circ. 4,647. *Notes*: adv., bk. rev., dwgs., photos (B&W, color).
The leading British floorcoverings publication. Covers all aspects of the industry including the latest designs, retail trends, and manufacturing developments. Emphasis is on sales, techniques, and product reviews rather than design. The floorcoverings described are primarily commercial. (0263-4236)

**0672   CARPET AND RUG   (US)
        INDUSTRY**
Rodman Publications, Inc., Box 555, 26 Lake St., Ramsey, NJ 07446. Ed. Frank O'Neill. Tel. (201) 825-2552. M; $24; 1973; circ. 4,500. *Annual Issues*: March—Carpet Expo.; June—Profile of Twenty-five Manufacturers; Sept.—Machinery Buyer's Guide. *Notes*: adv., calendars, dwgs., photos (B&W, color).
Presents the latest trends and developments in the carpet industry. Features appear on tufting, dyeing, new equipment, and economic forecasts. Extensive coverage of mills. Recent articles on computer usage. (0192-4486)

0673   CARPETS AND TEXTILES   (UK)
(U.S. sub.) Joseph Edelman, International Subscription House, P.O. Box 655, Oakland Gardens, NY 13364. $40. +

0674   CASA CLASSICA   (IT)
Via Luigi Barzini 20; Villagio dei Giornalisti, 20125 Milan, Italy. Ed. Falvio Maestrini. Tel. (02) 6072161. Telex 334353/NAFOR RIMA. 10/yr.; L.55,000; 1975; circ. 39,000. *Notes*: adv., bk. rev., calendars, dwgs., photos (B&W, color).
Covers classic Italian furniture design. Text in Italian and English. *

**0675   CERAMICA PER L'EDILIZIA   (IT)
        INTERNATIONAL**
Faenza Editrice S.p.A., via Firenze 276, 48018 Faenza RA, Italy. Ed. Goffredo Gaeta. Tel. 0546/43120. Telex ITIREF 550410. Q; L.40,000; 1972. *Notes*: adv., bibl., bk. rev., calendars, dwgs., photos (B&W, color).
A trade publication that richly illustrates the residential and commercial uses of ceramic tile in buildings. Covers tile designs on floors, walls, and swimming pools. Text in Italian; summaries in English. (0392-4890)

0676   COMPETITIVEDGE   (US)
        (Formerly: *NHFA Reports*)
National Home Furnishings Association, 405 Merchandise Mart Plaza, Chicago, Illinois 60654. Ed. Peggy Heaton. Tel. (312) 836-0077. M; $6; 1927. *Notes*: adv., dwgs. (0149-2276) +

0559   CONTRACT MAGAZINE

0677   DECOR   (US)
Commerce Publishing Co., 408 Olive St., St. Louis, MO 63102. Ed. William Cotner. M; $10; 1880. (0011-7358) +

0678   DECORATION-   (BE)
       AMEUBLEMENT/
       WONINGINRICHTING
Belgium Publishing Co., 193 Avenue Brugman,
1180 Brussels, Belgium. Ed. P.F. de Neef. 6/yr.;
Fr.350; 1948.
   Text in Dutch and French. (0011-7420) +

0565   DECORATION
       INTERNATIONAL

0679   DESIGN FROM   (DK)
       SCANDINAVIA
World Pictures ApS, Martinsvej 8, 1926 Copenhagen, Denmark. (U.S. Sub.) World Pictures,
P.O. Box 305, Racine, WI 53401. Ed. Kirsten
Bjerregaard. Tel. (01) 37-00-44. A; $15; 1967;
circ. 50,000. Indexed: Avery. Notes: adv.,
dwgs., photos (B&W, color).
   Well-illustrated guide that features Scandinavian furniture, textiles, lighting, applied art, and
artistic handicraft. Text thoroughly discusses
products, designers, manufacturers, and applications. Intended for architects, furniture buyers, interior designers, and the general public.
The back of each issue contains a detailed index
of manufacturers. Text in English, French, German, and Swedish. (0011-9369) *

0568   DESIGNER

0570   DESIGNER'S WEST

0680   DIGEST FOR HOME   (US)
       FURNISHERS
   (Formerly: Furniture Digest)
Minnesota 300, 6700 Penn Ave., Minneapolis,
MN 55423. Ed. Richard English. Q; $3.50 per
issue. +

0681   EQUIPMENT DES   (FR)
       COMMERCES-ENSEIGNES-
       ECLAIRAGE
Editions Meteore, 42 rue du Louvre, 75001
Paris, France. Ed. Jacqueline Obermayer. Bi-m;
F.104. +

0682   EUROMUEBLE   (SP)
Editorial Office, German Perez Carrasco 63,
Madrid 27, Spain. Ed. Ch. G. Robba. M; $45;
1965. +

0683   FARVE/TAPET   (DK)
Danmarks Tapet og Farvehandler, Forening,
Jernbanegade 9, 4700 Naestved, Denmark. Ed.
Maren Braun. M; 1934. +

0644   FINE WOODWORKING

0645   FIRA BULLETIN

0684   FLOOR COVERING NEWS   (CN)
Maclean-Hunter Ltd., 777 Bay St., Toronto,
Ont. M5W 1A7, Canada. Ed. Helen Bahen. Tel.
(416) 596-5940. 10/yr.; $46; 1977; circ. 6,501.
Notes: adv., dwgs., photos (B&W, color).
   A tabloid covering the Canadian floorcoverings industry. The brief articles are aimed primarily at manufacturers, distributors, and
retailers. (0319-616x)

0685   FLOOR COVERING WEEKLY   (US)
Hearst Business Media Corp., F.C.W. Division,
919 Third Ave., New York, NY 10022. Ed. Albert Wahnon. Tel. (212) 759-8050. W; $20; 1952;
circ. 21,500. Notes: adv., bk. rev., calendars,
dwgs., photos (B&W, color).
   Industry tabloid aimed primarily at floorcovering retailers, contract dealers, and distributors. Articles on new products, personnel,
business activities, and merchandising methods.
(0015-3761) *

0686   FLOORING   (US)
Harcourt Brace Jovanovich, 545 Fifth Ave.,
New York, NY 10017. 120 W. 2nd St., Duluth,
MN 55802. Ed. Dan Alarmo. Tel. (212) 503-
2926. M; $18; 1932; circ. 22,000. Annual Issues:
Nov.—Directory and Buying Guide. Notes:
adv., photos (B&W, color).
   Covers the merchandising, installation, and
display of carpets, ceramic tiles, and wood
flooring. Primarily of interest to contractors and
retailers, but also to architects and interior designers. (0162-881x) *

0575   FORM

0687   FURNISHING: THE   (AT)
       AUSTRALIAN FURNISHING
       TRADE JOURNAL
Furnishing Media Pty., Ltd., P.O. Box 52,
Hawksburn, Victoria 3142, Australia. Ed. Mau-
reen Horne. Tel. (03) 511485. Telex VANFUR
AA134956. M; Aus.$32; 1948; circ. 4,129. An-
nual Issues: Jan.—Directory. Notes: adv.,
dwgs., photos (B&W, color).
   Directed to the retail furnishing trade. *

0688   FURNISHING FLOORS   (AT)
Furnishing Media Pty., Ltd., P.O. Box 52,
Hawksburn, Victoria 3142, Australia. Ed. Mau-

reen Horne. Tel. (03) 511485. Telex VANFUR AA 134956. Bi-m; Aus.$22; circ. 4,194. *Annual Issues*: Jan.—Directory. *Notes*: adv., dwgs., photos (B&W, color).

All aspects of the floorcovering industry. *

0771 FURNITURE HISTORY

0689 FURNITURE/TODAY (US)
Communications Today, Ltd., Box 2754, High Point, NC 27261. Ed. Bill Peterson. Tel. (919) 889-0113. W; $29.95; 1976; circ. 20,000. *Notes*: adv., bk. rev., calendars, dwgs., photos (B&W, color). *Micro*: BLH.

A business newspaper of the furniture industry that is edited for retail executives in furniture and department stores. Features cover retailing, manufacturing, merchandising, and marketing of residential furniture, lighting, and accessories. (0194-360x) *

0690 FURNITURE WORLD (US)
(Formerly: *Furniture South*)
Towse Publishing Co., 127 E. 31st St., New York, NY 10016. Ed. Russell A. Bienenstock. Tel. (212) 686-3910. 13/yr.; $8; 1870; circ. 18,796. *Notes*: adv., calendars, photos (B&W, color).

For furniture retailers. Presents successful merchandising and marketing ideas as well as in-depth sales training features. *

0691 GOLV TILL TAK (SW)
Foerlags AB Golv Till Tak, Box 5306, S-102 46, Stockholm, Sweden. Ed. Catharina Clinton. 8/yr.; 1972. (0345-3979) +

0692 HALI (UK)
193a Shirland Rd., London W9 2EU, England. (U.S. sub.) P.O. Box 4312, Philadelphia, PA 19118. Ed. Robert Pinner. Tel. (215) 843-3090. Q; $56; 1978; circ. 6,500. *Indexed*: 4th-quarter issue. *Notes*: adv., bk. rev., photos (B&W, color).

Probably the finest international journal of Oriental carpets and textiles in print. Gives comprehensive descriptions of the designs and technical features. Also presents features on collecting and preserving pieces and reports on exhibitions and auctions. Richly illustrated. (0142-0798)

0693 HAUSTEX (GW)
(Formerly: *Aussteuer Bett und Couch*)
Westdeutsche Verlagsanstalt GmbH, Ahmer Str. 190, Postfach 3054, 4900 Herford, W. Ger-

many. Ed. H. Russ. M; DM. 92.40; 1950; circ. 4,800. *Notes*: adv., photos (B&W, color).

International trade journal on home furnishings specializing in bedding, textiles, and accessories. Text in German. *

0694 HEIMTEX (GW)
Westdeutsche Verlagsanstalt GmbH, Ahmer Str. 190, Postfach 3054, 4900 Herford, W. Germany. Ed. H. Russ. Tel. 05221-775-0. Telex 934-717. M; DM. 108; 1949; circ. 10,500. *Notes*: adv., photos (B&W, color).

International trade journal of home furnishings specializing in floor- and wallcoverings. Text in German. (0017-9876) *

0695 HOME FASHION TEXTILES (US)
Fairchild Publications, Inc., 7 E. 12th St., New York, NY 10003. Ed. Christiane Michaels. Tel. (212) 741-4000. 10/yr.; 1979. (0195-654x) +

0696 HOME FURNISHING (UK)
INTERNATIONAL
Textile Trade Publications, Ltd., Knightway House, 20 Soho Square, London W1V 6DT, England. (U.S. sub.) Joseph Adelman, International Subscription House, P.O. Box 655, Oakland Gardens, NY 11364. Ed. Gerald Saunders. S-a; 1981. +

0697 HUSET VAART (NO)
A-S Informa Reklame, Akersgt 64, Oslo 1, Norway. Ed. Jan Landmark. 3/yr.; 1958.

Consumer-oriented information on home and garden products and equipment. (0018-7976) +

0752 INDUSTRIAL DESIGN

0698 INSTALLATION & (US)
CLEANING SPECIALIST
Specialist Publications, Inc., 17835 Ventura Blvd., Ste. 312, Encina, CA 91316. Ed. Howard Olansky. M; 1963. +

0699 INTERIOR (NE)
International Textiles Publishing Co., Overschiestraat 170, 1062 XK, Amsterdam, Netherlands. Ed. B.C.J. Groenevelt. 3/yr.; 1960. *Micro*: UMI. (0020-8922) +

0700 INTERIOR (SW)
Sweden Furniture Manufacturers Assn., Box 140 12, S-104 40 Stockholm 14, Sweden. S-a; 1971. (0047-049x) +

0578   INTERIOR DESIGN

0579   INTERIOR DESIGN

0701   INTERIOR TEXTILES   (US)
(Formerly: *Curtain, Drapery and Bedspread Magazine*)
Columbia Communications, Inc., 370 Lexington Ave., New York, NY 10164. Ed. Maddalena Vitroil. Tel. (212) 532-9290. M; $12; 1925; circ. 16,000. *Annual Issues*: March—Industry Directory & Buyer's Guide. *Notes*: adv., photos (B&W, color).
Aimed at the needs of retailers of textiles, including curtains, draperies, bedspreads, window coverings, and decorative fabrics. Articles on marketing, merchandising, and fashion information. *

0580   INTERIORS

0588   M D

0702   MADE IN EUROPE: (GW)
       FURNITURE AND
       INTERIORS
Made in Europe Marketing Org., Unterlindau 21-29, 6000 Frankfurt 1, W. Germany. (U.S. sub.) Made in Europe, 150 Green St., Brooklyn, NY 11222. Ed. H.E. Reisner. Bi-m; 1978. *Micro*: UMI. (0171-6042) +

0589   MAISON FRANCAISE

0703   MARKET   (FR)
Editions Presse Professionelle, 131 Bd. Sebastopol, 75002 Paris, France. M; 1969. (0025-3537) +

0704   MARKETPLACE   (US)
Marketplace Publications, Box 58421, Dallas, TX 75258. Ed. Nancy Miller. Tel. (214) 747-4274. Bi-m; 1961. (0025-357x) +

0705   MEUBEL   (NE)
Drukkern-Uitgeverij Lakerveld B.V., Postbus 61023, Newtonstraat 441, NL-2506 AA The Hague, Netherlands. Ed. Martin V.D. Drift. Telex 31683 laker vl. W; fl.270; 1919; circ. 6,550.
Covers furniture and home textiles. Text in Dutch. (0165-4543) *

0706   MOBILA   (RM)
Centrul de Documentare Tehnica, Pentru Economia Forestiera, Soseava Pipera Nr. 46, Bucharest, Romania. Ed. Claudiu Lazarescu. S-a; 1964. (0026-7104) +

0707   IL MOBILE   (IT)
Via Carducci 32, 20123 Milan, Italy. Ed. Aldo Blanc. Tel. 808785. Telex 315658 RIBED-I. Bi-w; L.40,000; 1957; circ. 15,500. *Special Issues*: June & Dec. *Notes*: adv., dwgs., photos (B&W).
A newspaper that reports news of the furniture and furnishings industry, including manufacturing and trade. Exhibition announcements appear with features on new designs. Twice a year subscribers also receive a full-color periodical that gives an outstanding overview of the international interior furnishings market and examines the market in a particular country in depth. In addition to features on new furnishings, articles appear on interior design problems and famous designers. The purpose of this publication is to stimulate contact between manufacturers and retailers. Text in Italian. (6026-7112)

0349   MOBILI PER UFFICIO

0708   MOBILIA   (DK)
Mobilia Press A-S, Staget 12, 3070 Snekkersten, Denmark. Ed. Per Mollerup. 8/yr.; 1955. *Indexed*: Art Ind. (0026-7228) +

0709   MODERN FLOOR   (US)
       COVERINGS
Charleson Pub. Co., 124 E. 40th St., New York, NY 10016. Ed. Michael Karol. Tel. (212) 953-0274. M; 1928.
A tabloid on the latest techniques and trends in the production, installation, and retailing of floor products. +

0753   MODO

0710   MOEBEL-KULTUR   (GW)
Ferdinand Holzmann Verlag, P.O. Box 601049, 2000 Hamburg 60, W. Germany. M; 1949. (0047-7796) +

0711   MOEBELHANDLEREN   (NO)
Moebelhandlerenes Landsforbund, Drammensvn. 30, 0255 0510 2, Norway. Ed. Jon Gangdal. Tel. (02) 441994. 10/yr.; Kr.150; 1929; circ. 2,800. *Notes*: adv., dwgs., photos (B&W, color).
For furniture retailers and manufacturers. Text in Norwegian. (0333-354x) *

0712   MOEBELMARKT   (GW)
Verlag Matthias Ritthammer GmbH & Co., KG, Burgschmiet Str. 25, Postfach 3850, 8500 Nuernberg 1, W. Germany. Ed. M. Rithammer.

Tel. 0911-37374. Telex 0622839. M; DM.84; 1960; circ. 12,200. *Notes*: adv., bk. rev., dwgs., photos (B&W, color).

Trade publication for the German furniture and home furnishings industries. *

0713   MOEBLER OCH MILJOE   (SW)
Sveriges Moebelhandlares Centralfoerbund, National Swedish Assn. of Retail Furnishers, Kungsgatan 19, S-105 61 Stockholm, Sweden. Ed. Annika Danielson. 10/yr.; 1921. (0345-7737) +

0714   EL MUEBLE   (SP)
Editorial Quiris S.A., Consell de Cent, 131 Barcelona 15, Spain. Ed. Josep Boloix Traveria. M; 1961. (0027-2930) +

0715   MUEMLEKVEDELEM   (HU)
Hirlapkiado Vallalat, Blaha Lujza ter 3, 1085 Budapest, Hungary. Kultura, P.O.B. 149, 1389 Budapest, Hungary. Q; 1956. +

0716   NEW ENGLAND   (US)
        FURNITURE NEWS
110 Railroad Ave., Box 219, S. Hamilton, MA 01982. Bi-m; 1933. +

0717   NOUVEL OFFICIEL DE   (FR)
        L'AMEUBLEMENT
Editions G.M. Perrin, 108 Ave. Ledru-Rollin, 75011 Paris, France. M; 1950. +

0718   OESTERREICHISCHE   (AU)
        FUSSBODENZEITUNG
Verlag Piletzky, Nikolsdorfer Gasse 7, A-1050 Vienna, Austria. Ed. Heinrich Piletzky. Bi-m; 1965. (0029-9081) +

0719   OFFICIEL DES TEXTILES/   (FR)
        AMEUBLEMENT
P.C.M., 17 Faubourg Montmartre, 75009 Paris, France. S-a. +

0720   ORIENTAL RUG   (US)
Oriental Rug Importers Association of America, 267 Fifth Ave., Rm. 302, New York, NY 10016. Ed. Archie Cherkezian. Tel. (212) 685-1761. Q; $8.50; 1928. *Notes*: adv., bk. rev., photos (B&W).

Of primary interest to rug dealers as a source for exchanging information on exhibits, trade fairs, new publications, members, and industry news. (0030-5332)

0721   OTTAGONO   (IT)
Co. P. IN.A., via Melzi d'Eril 26, 20154 Milan, Italy. Ed. Sergio Mazza. Tel. 4696021. Q; $32; 1966; circ. 20,000. *Indexed*: A.P.I., Avery. *Notes*: adv., dwgs., photos (B&W, color).

A spirited review of furniture and industrial design from all over the world but primarily from Italy. Includes some technical details of construction and some historical background. An extensive directory tells where items can be purchased anywhere in the world. Text in Italian; summaries in English. (0391-7487)

0722   PFM (PROFESSIONAL   (US)
        FURNITURE MERCHANT)
Vista Publications, 180 Allen Rd., N.E., Atlanta, GA 30328. Ed. Gail Walker. Tel. (404) 252-8831. M; $30; 1969; circ. 20,000. *Notes*: adv., photos.

Furniture publication for the retail dealer. (0030-7963) *

0723   PACIFIC MARKETER   (US)
Northwest Furniture Retailers' Assn., 121 Boren Ave., N., Seattle, WA 98109. Ed. Lucy Hazelton. Tel. (206) 622-4515. Bi-m; $6; 1926; circ. 4,000. *Notes*: adv., calendars, dwgs., photos (B&W, color).

A home furnishings magazine aimed at retailers in the Northwestern U.S. (0048-2633)

0724   RAUM UND TEXTIL   (GW)
Konradin-Verlag Robert Kohlhammer GmbH, 7022 Leinfelden-Echterdingen, W. Germany. M; 1948. +

0725   REVUE DE   (FR)
        L'AMEUBLEMENT
Editions du Tigre, 23 rue Joubert, 75009 Paris, France. Ed. Francois Prevot. Tel. 874-5250. Telex 641769 F. 10/yr.; F.410; 1911; circ. 11,306. *Notes*: adv., dwgs., photos (B&W).

A trade magazine that covers all aspects of the furniture and home furnishings industries, including kitchen equipment, lighting, floorcoverings, and textiles. Emphasis is on traditional furnishings. Text in French. (0242-8903)

0726   SADELMAGER-OG-   (DK)
        TAPETSERER TIDENDE
Saddlers and Upholsterers Guild, Fortunstraede 5, 1065 Copenhagen, Denmark. Ed. Frithiof Larsen. M; 1899. (0036-228x) +

0727   SEDIA E IL MOBILE   (IT)
Edizioni Palutan Grafica, Medi Technical Advertising, Via d'Alviano 18, 20146 Milan, Italy. M; 1957. (0037-0711) +

0728   SOL ET MURS MAGAZINE   (FR)
S.E.P. Editions, 194-196 rue Marcadet, 75018 Paris, France. Ed. Marie S. Aubiroux. Tel. (1) 2550033. Telex 172579 +. Q; F.66; 1976; circ. 4,000. *Notes*: adv., photos (B&W, color).

A trade publication of the floor- and wallcovering industries. Primarily of interest to manufacturers, dealers, and some designers. Text in French. (0339-1507)

0729   SVENSK   (SW)
          TAPETSERARETIDNING
Sveriges Tapetseraremaestare, Centralfoerening, Box 22064, 104 22 Stockholm, Sweden. M; 1923. +

0730   TZ/TAPENZEITUNG   (GW)
Verlagsanstalt Alexander Koch GmbH, Postfach 3081, 7000 Stuttgart 1, W. Germany. Ed. Werner Rosskopf. Tel. (0711) 7989-1. Telex 7-255609 drw. Bi-w; DM. 105; 1888; circ. 6,000. *Annual Issues*: Jan., May, Oct.—Wallpaper Journal Inserts. *Notes*: adv., bk. rev., photos (B&W, color).

A trade publication aimed at the floorcovering and wallpaper manufacturer, dealer, and import/export trader. Articles deal with the industry in general and help to identify design trends and forecast sales. Wallpaper samples are included with some issues. Text in German; summaries in English. (0720-6593)

0731   TABLE ET CADEAU   (FR)
Editions G.M. Perrin, 108 Ave. Ledru-Rollin, 75011 Paris, France. M; 1961. (0039-8780) +

0732   TAIWAN FURNITURE   (CH)
China Economic News Service, 561 Chung-Hsiao East Rd., Sec. 4, Taipei, 105 Taiwan, Republic of China. Ed. Brian Yu. Tel. 765-2445/9. Telex 27710 CENSPC. Bi-m; $35; 1979; circ. 5,000. *Annual Issues*: April—Top Taiwan Furniture; April, Sept.—Lighting; June—Buyer's Guide. *Notes*: adv., photos (B&W, color).

Trade publication on furniture made in Taiwan and available for export. *

0733   TAPISSIER DECORATEUR/   (BE)
          WONINGSTOFFEERDER
Federation Nationale Belge des Tapissiers, Garnisseurs et Decorateurs d'Interieur, Ave. Hansen-Soulie 98, 1040 Brussels, Belgium. Ed. J. Delit. M; 1924. (0039-9582) +

0734   TECHSCAN   (US)
Contract Technologies, Inc., P.O. Box S-3211, Carmel, CA 93921. M; $125.

In newsletter format, this publication presents new concepts and technologies of interest to the contract furnishings industry. The information presented is obtained from scanning electronic databases for major issues and trends, such as computer-aided design and ergonomics. +

0735   TERRAZZO TOPICS   (US)
National Terrazzo & Mosaic Assn., Inc., 3166 Des Plaines Ave., Ste. 15, Des Plaines, IL 60018. 10/yr.; 1970. (0040-3806) +

0736   TEXTILES SUISSES—   (SZ)
          INTERIEUR
Schweizerische Zentrale fuer Handelsfoerderung, Swiss Office for the Development of Trade, P.O. Box 720, CH-1001 Lausanne, Switzerland. Ed. Peter Pfister. Tel. (021) 23-18-24. Telex 25 425 OSEC CH. S-a; Fr. 30; 1920; circ. 11,000. *Indexed*: Jan. & Aug. issues. *Notes*: adv., dwgs., photos (B&W, color).

Covers home furnishing fabrics including curtains, carpets, bed linens, and upholstery. Text in English, French, German, and Italian. (0082-3708) *

0737   TILE AND DECORATIVE   (US)
          SURFACES
Tile & Decorative Surfaces Publishing Inc., 17901 Ventura Blvd., Ste. D, Encino, CA 91316. Ed. Jerry Fisher. Tel. (818) 344-4200. Telex 181545. 10/yr.; $25; 1955; circ. 14,500. *Annual Issues*: Dec.—Annual Directory & Purchasing Guide. *Notes*: adv., dwgs., photos (B&W, color).

A trade magazine giving broad technical and business coverage to the industry of tile, terrazzo, and marble. Extensive coverage of international trade fairs and conventions. Oriented toward new products and tools but also discusses legislation and litigation and presents technical tips. Primarily of interest to manufacturers, distributors, and contractors but also to architects and interior designers. (0192-9550) *

0738   TILE NEWS   (US)
Italian Tile Center, 499 Park Ave., New York, NY 10022. Ed. Maria Wiesen. Tel. (212) 980-8866. Q; free; 1980; circ. 20,000. *Notes*: photos (B&W, color).

Informative newsletter on new tile designs from Italy. Includes interviews with interior designers, announcements of seminars, exhibits, and reference materials. Of interest to architects and interior designers.

0739   TRE OG MOEBLER   (NO)
John A. Antonsen A-S, Postboks 78, Sentrum, Oslo 1, Norway. Ed. John A. Antonsen. Tel. 02/673290. 10/yr.; Kr.200; 1969; circ. 4,300. *Notes*: adv., photos (B&W).

A trade publication that reaches the woodworking and furniture industries, architects, and interior designers. *

0740   VARIATOR   (NE)
Bath en Doodehelfver N.V., Prinsengracht 730-736, Amsterdam, Netherlands. M; 1946. (0042-272x) +

0741   W.P.W. DECOR   (UK)
82 W. Valley Rd., Hemel Hempstead, Herts., England. Wallpaper Paint and Wallcoverings Retailers Assn., Box 44, Walsall, W. Midlands, WS3 1TD, England. Ed. Christina Gregory. Tel. 0442-52006. M; £27; 1955; circ. 8,000. *Annual Issues*: April—Co-ordinates; May—New Ranges; June—Wall Fashion. *Notes*: adv., bk. rev., photos (B&W, color).

This publication is intended for the retailer; however, the varieties of paints and wallcoverings featured from various worldwide trade exhibitions make it useful to interior designers as well.

0742   THE WALL PAPER   (US)
Tapis Publishing Co., 1 N.E. 39th St., Ft. Lauderdale, FL 33334. Ed. Janet Verdeguer. Tel. (305) 563-9844. M; $18; 1980; circ. 14,000. *Notes*: adv., bk. rev., dwgs., photos (B&W, color).

Covers all aspects of wallcoverings. (0273-6837) *

0743   WALLCOVERINGS   (US)
Publishing Dynamics, Inc., 15 Bank St., Ste. 101, Stamford, CT 06901. Ed. Peter Hisey. Tel. (203) 357-0028. M; $12; 1919; circ. 9,000. *Annual Issues*: Fall—Directory. *Notes*: adv., calendars, dwgs., photos (B&W, color).

Aimed at wallcovering dealers and manufacturers, this industry publication contains regular features on new products, selling techniques, display, new technology, and design. *

Lighting

0561   CUCINA + BAGNO & LUCI

**0744   HOME LIGHTING &   (US)
        ACCESSORIES**
Ebel-Doctorow Publications, Inc., 1115 Clifton Ave., Clifton, NJ 07013. Ed. Peter Wulff. Tel. (201) 779-1600. M; $20; 1923; circ. 7,200. *Annual Issues*: March, Oct.—Directory of Suppliers. *Notes*: adv., bk. rev., dwgs., photos (B&W, color).

Contains retail case histories and articles on new products. (0162-9077) *

**0745   INTERNATIONAL LIGHTING   (NE)
        REVIEW**
Foundation Prometheus, Box 721, 5600 AS Eindhoven, Netherlands. Ed. J.F. Caminada. Tel. 31-40-75-52-52. Telex 35000 PHTC NL. Q; fl.57; 1949; circ. 20,000. *Indexed*: A.P.I. *Notes*: adv., bibl., bk. rev., calendars, dwgs., photos (B&W, color).

Reports extensively on international developments and trends in lighting, on current problems encountered in lighting design and technology, and on outstanding international projects. Editions are available in English, French, German, and Spanish. (0020-7853) *

**0746   LIGHTING DESIGN +   (US)
        APPLICATION**
Illuminating Engineering Society of North America, 345 E. 47th St., New York, NY 10017. Ed. Wanda Jankowski. Tel. (212) 705-7926. M; $35; 1906; circ. 15,000. *Indexed*: App. Sci. Tech. Ind., Compendex, Eng. Ind. *Notes*: adv., bk. rev., dwgs., photos (B&W, color). *Micro*: UMI.

Features articles on current design and engineering aspects of lighting, written for interior designers, architects, engineers, contractors, and manufacturers. Topics such as energy, street lighting, theater lighting, and office lighting are generally covered. Each issue includes opinions of experts, news of the industry, and columns on new products and jobs. (0360-6325)

**0747   LIGHTING SUPPLY &   (US)
        DESIGN**
Klas Publishing Co., Box 66, Boonton, NJ 07005. Ed. Frank Klas, Jr. M; 1972. +

0748   LUMIERE ACTUALITE   (FR)
Editions du Tigre, 23 rue Joubert, 75009 Paris, France. M; 1979. +

0749   LUMINAIRES ET   (FR)
           ECLAIRAGE
Publication Larrey, 73 bis Avenue de Wagram,
75017 Paris, France. Q. +

0408   VISUAL MERCHANDISING
           AND STORE DESIGN

Industrial Design Products

0750   DESIGN   (UK)
Design Council, 28 Haymarket, London SW1
Y4SU, England. Ed. J. Thackara. Tel. (01) 839-
8000. Telex 8812963. M; $96; 1949; circ. 17,000.
Indexed: A.P.I., Art Ind., Avery. *Notes*: adv.,
bk. rev., photos (B&W, color). *Micro*: UMI.
   Top-quality journal that provides high-quality
illustrations of the best in furniture and product
design worldwide. Features examine issues
such as quality and business aspects of design,
but the emphasis is on presenting current design
developments through photographs. (0011-9245)

0571   DOMUS

0751   ERGONOMICS   (UK)
Taylor & Francis, Ltd., Rankine Rd., Basing-
stoke, Hants. RG24 OPR, England. M; 1957;
$259. *Indexed*: App. Mech. Rev., Chem. Abstr.,
Eng. Ind., Psychol. Abstr. *Micro*: MIM.
   Covers human factors in work, machine con-
trol, and equipment design. (0014-0139) +

0575   FORM

0752   INDUSTRIAL DESIGN   (US)
330 W. 42nd St., New York, NY 10036. Ed.
George Finley. Tel. (212) 695-4955. Bi-m; $30;
1954; circ. 12,000. *Indexed*: Art Ind. *Annual Issues*:   July/Aug.—Annual   Design   Review.
Notes: adv., bk. rev., calendars, dwgs., photos
(B&W, color). *Micro*: BLH, UMI.
   The best American periodical providing overall coverage of industrial design. Every issue
presents development histories, portfolios of interesting new designs, and in-depth features on
special themes. Articles are well illustrated with
color photographs and drawings. There is regular coverage of furnishings, exhibition design,
ergonomics, signage, equipment, and consumer
product design. Interior as well as industrial designers will find this a major source of contemporary design ideas. (0192-3021)

0753   MODO   (IT)
Ricerche Design Editrice S.r.l., via Roma 21,
20094 Corsico, Milan, Italy. Ed. Cesare Se-
condi. Tel. (02) 4491149. M; $52; 1977; circ.
35,000. *Indexed*: A.P.I., Avery. *Notes*: adv.,
bk. rev., dwgs., photos (B&W, color).
   Covers all aspects of design with emphasis on
industrial design. Includes product reviews.
Text in Italian; summaries in English.

0721   OTTAGONO

6

Fine Arts, Decorative Arts, and Antiques

0754 AFRICAN ARTS (US)
University of California, Los Angeles, African Studies Center, 405 Hilgard Ave., Los Angeles, CA 90024. Ed. John Povey. Tel. (213) 825-1218. Q; $20; 1967; circ. 6,000. *Indexed*: Art Ind., Avery, July issue. *Notes*: adv., bibl., bk. rev., calendars, dwgs., photos (B&W, color).

Comprehensive coverage of the arts of Africa. (0001-9933) *

0755 ANTIQUES (US)
Brant Publications, Inc., 551 Fifth Ave., New York, NY 10176. Ed. Wendell Garrett. Tel. (212) 922-1818. M; $38; 1922; circ. 82,000. *Indexed*: Art Ind., Mag. Ind., R.G., R.I.L.A. *Notes*: adv., photos (B&W, color). *Micro*: UMI.

Contains well-illustrated articles on the fine arts, architecture, decorative arts, and connoisseurship. Of interest to interior designers as a historical reference and source for locating antiques. (0161-9284)

0756 APOLLO (UK)
22 Davies St., London W1Y 1LH, England. (U.S. Sub.) P.O. Box 47, N. Hollywood, CA 91603-0047. Ed. Denys Sutton. Tel. (01) 629-3061. M; $88; 1925. *Indexed*: A.P.I., Art Ind., Avery, R.I.L.A. *Notes*: adv., bk. rev., dwgs., photos (B&W, color). *Micro*: UMI.

An international magazine devoted exclusively to fine art and antiques. Tastefully produced, with articles covering all periods and continents. A major source for museums, collectors, and dealers. (0003-6536)

0757 ARCHITECTURAL (US)
ANTIQUES AND ARTIFACTS ADVERTISER
459 Rockland Rd., P.O. Box 31, Merion, PA 19066. 1979. *Indexed*: Avery. +

0543 AREA

0758 ART AND ANTIQUES (US)
(Formerly: *American Art and Antiques*)
89 Fifth Ave., New York, NY 10003. P.O. Box 20600, Bergenfield, NJ 07621. Ed. Wick Al..... Tel. (212) 206-7050. M; $36; 1978. *Indexed*: Avery, R.I.L.A. *Notes*: adv., bk. rev., photos (B&W, color). *Micro*: UMI.

This newly revised publication is elegantly designed and features a rich diversity of coverage in the fine and decorative arts fields. The text and illustrations are of high quality. Recommended for both professional and general readers. (0195-8208)

0759 ART IN AMERICA (US)
Brant Publications, 850 Third Ave., New York, NY 10022. 542 Pacific Ave., Marion, OH 43302. Ed. Nancy Marmer. Tel. (212) 715-2600. M; $34.95; 1913; circ. 50,000. *Indexed*: Amer: H&L, Art Ind., Hist. Abst., R.G., R.I.L.A. *Annual Issues*: August—Guide to Galleries, Museums, Artists. *Notes*: adv., bk. rev., photos (B&W, color). *Micro*: BLH, UMI.

A major art publication that covers art exhibitions and trends. Includes articles on historical as well as contemporary art. Usually includes a major story on an architectural topic. A good source for selecting corporate or public art. (0004-3214)

0760   ARTFORUM   (US)
205 Mulberry St., New York, NY 10012. P.O.
Box 980, Farmingdale, NY 11737. Ed. Ingrid
Sischy. Tel. (212) 925-4000. M; $36; 1962; circ.
22,000. *Indexed*: Art Bib., Art Ind., R.I.L.A.
Notes: adv., bk. rev., photos (B&W, color).
   An influential art journal devoted to modern
art worldwide. Includes reviews of international
shows. Articles are written by qualified critics.
(0004-3532)

0761   ART NEWS   (US)
5 W. 37th St., New York, NY 10018. P.O. Box
969, Farmingdale, NY 11737. Ed. Milton Es-
terow. Tel. (212) 398-1690. M; $25.95; 1902;
circ. 75,000. *Indexed*: Art Ind., R.G., R.I.L.A.
Notes: adv., bk. rev., photos (B&W, color).
Micro: BLH, UMI.
   A major art magazine covering all types of art
in the U.S. and abroad. Includes articles that
are historical or deal with controversial issues.
Architecture is frequently featured. (0004-3273)

0072   ARTS AND ARCHITECTURE

0762   ARTS AND THE ISLAMIC   (UK)
          WORLD
Islamic Arts Foundation, 5A Bathurst St., Lon-
don W2 2SD, England. Q; 1982. *Indexed*:
Avery. +

0763   ARTS MAGAZINE   (FR)
   (Formerly: *Galeria Jardin des Arts*)
106 rue de Richelieu, 75022 Paris, France. Ed.
Andre Parinaud. W; F. 240; 1971. +

0764   BURLINGTON MAGAZINE   (UK)
International Thomsons Ltd., 10-16 Elm St.,
London WC1X OBP, England. 23-29 Emerald
St., London WC1, England. Ed. Neil Mac-
Gregor. Tel. (01) 278-2345. Telex 21746. M;
$200; 1903. *Indexed*: A.P.I., Art Ind., Avery,
Br. Hum. Ind. *Notes*: adv., bibl., bk. rev., cal-
endars, dwgs., photos (B&W, color).
   One of the leading international journals of
fine and applied arts. (0007-6287) *

0765   CIMAISE: ART ET   (FR)
          ARCHITECTURE ACTUELS
J.R. Arnaud, 8 rue Recamier, 75007 Paris,
France. Ed. J.R. Arnaud. Tel. 544-04-82. Bi-m;
$70; 1953; circ. 5,000. *Notes*: adv., bibl., bk.
rev., calendars, dwgs., photos (B&W, color).
   An international review of contemporary art
and architecture. Most of each issue is devoted
to art, but a regular department covers architec-

tural projects and exhibitions. Text in French
and English. (0009-6830)

0766   CONNAISSANCE DES ARTS   (FR)
Societe Francaise de Promotion Artistique, 25
rue de Ponthieu, 75008 Paris, France. (U.S.
Sub.) Eastern News Distributors, Inc., 111
Eighth Ave., New York, NY 10011. Ed. Philip
Jodido. Tel. 359-62-000. M; $65; 1952; circ.
45,000. *Indexed*: A.P.I., Art Ind., Avery,
R.I.L.A. *Notes*: adv., bk. rev., dwgs., photos
(B&W, color). *Micro*: UMI.
   A highly acclaimed international magazine of
the fine arts that often includes architecture and
interior design. Lavish photographs accompany
in-depth text that covers historical and contemporary art. English and French editions are
available. (0293-9274)

0767   CONNOISSEUR   (US)
Hearst Corp., 959 Eighth Ave., New York, NY
10019. P.O. Box 10120, Des Moines, IA 50347.
Ed. Thomas Hoving. Tel. (212) 262-5700. M;
$19.95; 1901; circ. 65,000. *Indexed*: A.P.I., Art
Ind., Avery, R.I.L.A. *Notes*: adv., bk. rev.,
dwgs., photos (B&W, color). *Micro*: UMI.
   A high-quality international magazine of the
fine arts that often includes articles on architecture and interior design as well. (0010-6275).

0768   CORPORATE ART NEWS   (US)
5 W. 37th St., New York, NY 10018. Ed. Karin
Lipson. Tel. (212) 398-1690. Bi-m; $95; 1984.
   A professional update in newsletter format on
the corporate market for paintings, drawings,
sculpture, photography, architecture, graphics,
textiles, folk art, primitive art, and antiques. Includes articles on where corporate collectors
shop for art and how their tastes affect the market. Profiles on art consultants, buyers, and sell-
ers. Section on recent acquisitions by
corporations, exhibits funded by corporations,
and recent commissions. Subscribers include art
dealers, consultants, curators, museums, collectors, architects, and interior designers.

0103   DESIGN QUARTERLY

0769   DU   (SZ)
Conzett und Huber AG, Baslerstr. 30, Postfach
8048, Zurich, Switzerland. (U.S. Sub.) Museum
Books, Inc., 6 W. 37th St., New York, NY
10018. Ed. Wolfhart Draeger. Tel. (01) 492-2500.
Telex 822371. M; Fr. 105; 1941; circ. 19,000.
Indexed: Avery. *Notes*: adv., bk. rev., photos
(B&W, color).
   An outstanding European review of contem-
porary art. Thematic issues occasionally cover

industrial design and historic periods as well. Each issue focuses on one theme and contains diverse material unified by an intelligently written text. Text in German; detailed summaries in English. (0012-6837)

0109   DUTCH ART AND
       ARCHITECTURE TODAY

0770   EARLY AMERICAN LIFE   (US)
Historical Times, Inc., Box 8200, Harrisburg, PA 17105. Box 1620, Mt. Morris, IL 61054. Ed. Frances Carnahan. Tel. (717) 657-9555. Bi-m; $15; 1970; circ. 323,989. *Notes*: adv., bk. rev., calendars, dwgs., photos (B&W, color). *Micro*: UMI.

An informative, entertaining publication that presents ideas on re-creating the lifestyle of early America. Articles cover period home decorating, traditional crafts and projects, regional recipes, antique collecting, and travel to historic sites. (0012-8155)

0771   FURNITURE HISTORY   (UK)
Furniture History Society, Victoria and Albert Museum, Dept. of Furniture and Woodwork, London SW7 2RL, England. Ed. James Lomax. Tel. (01) 741-1461. A; $22; 1965; circ. 1,300. *Indexed*: Art Ind., R.I.L.A., cum. every 5 years. *Notes*: adv., bibl., bk. rev., calendars, dwgs., photos (B&W).

The society's major publication. Each volume is handsomely printed and illustrated with a substantial number of articles on all aspects of the history of English furniture. Occasionally includes articles on furniture from other European countries. (0016-3058) *

0487   HISTORIC HOUSES

0772   KULTUR/ART ET CULTURE   (AU)
Pointengasse 22, A-1170 Vienna, Austria. Ed. Dr. Alfred Weikert. M; 1968. (0023-5113) +

0773   KUNSTHANDWERK IN   (GW)
       EUROPA
Ludwig Schultheiss Verlag, Heilwigstr. 64, 2000 Hamburg 20, W. Germany. Q; 1978. +

0774   MARG: A MAGAZINE OF   (II)
       THE ARTS
Marg Publications, Army & Navy Bldg., 148 Mahatma Gandhi Rd., Fort, Bombay 400 023, India. Ed. Dr. Saryu V. Doshi. Tel. 242520. Q; $32; 1947; circ. 7,000. *Indexed*: A.P.I., Art Ind.

Notes: adv., bibl., bk. rev., dwgs., photos (B&W, color).

A beautifully illustrated journal that presents the splendor of Indian art, architecture, and culture to a scholarly and general audience. Contributions come from eminent scholars worldwide. (0025-2913)

0775   L'OEIL   (SZ)
La Nouvelle Sedo S.A., 39 Avenue de la Gare, CH-1003 Lausanne, Switzerland. Ed. Georges Bernier. Tel. (021) 225011. Telex 24495 irlch. 10/yr.; Fr. 176; 1955; circ. 40,000. *Indexed*: Art Ind., Avery, R.I.L.A., Dec. issue. *Notes*: adv., bk. rev., dwgs., photos (B&W, color).

Focus is on fine art, antiques, and historic interiors. Beautifully illustrated, with text by art historians, museum directors, and other scholars. Text in French. (0029-862x)

0776   ORIENTAL ART   (UK)
89 Thurleigh Rd., Richmond, Surrey TW9 3PG, England. The Secretary, Oriental Art Magazine, Ltd., 12 Ennerdale Rd., Richmond, Surrey TW1 3PG, England. Ed. Dr. John Sweetman. Q; $28; 1955. *Indexed*: Art Ind., Avery, Winter issue. *Notes*: adv., bibl., bk. rev., dwgs., photos (B&W, color).

Fine-art magazine devoted to all forms of Oriental art. (0030-5278) *

0777   PORTFOLIO MAGAZINE   (US)
Portfolio Assoc., 271 Madison Ave., New York, NY 10016. Box 2714, Boulder, CO 80322. Ed. Edwin Grosvenor. Tel. (212) 686-2112. M; 1979. *Indexed*: Avery. *Micro*: UMI. (0163-092x) +

0171   SINTEZA

0778   STUDIO INTERNATIONAL   (UK)
Tower House, Southampton St., London SC 2E 7LS, England. Ed. Michael Spens. Tel (01) 379-6005. Telex 266854. Q; £20; 1893; circ. 5,300. *Indexed*: A.P.I., Art Ind., Avery. *Notes*: adv., bk. rev., photos (B&W, color). *Micro*: MIM.

This is the oldest English-language art magazine and still holds an influential position as a leading journal dealing with contemporary art and design. International circulation, primarily to libraries. (0039-4114) *

0779   WINTERTHUR PORTFOLIO   (US)
Winterthur, DE 19735. University of Chicago Press, Box 37005, Chicago, IL 60637. Ed. Ian M.G. Quimby. Q; $25; 1979; circ. 1,800. *Indexed*: A.P.I., Amer: H&L, Art Ind., Avery,

R.I.L.A., Winter issue. *Notes*: adv., bibl., bk. rev., dwgs., photos (B&W, color). *Micro*: UMI.

A scholarly journal that presents interdisciplinary research by academics and museum scholars on historical aspects of the built environment. Emphasis is on the study of the decorative arts, which are placed in a cultural context. All articles are juried. (0084-0416)

0780 ZYGOS   (GR)
33 Iofontos St., Athens 516A, Greece. Ed. Ion F. Frantzeskakis. Tel. (01) 723-4677. Telex 221926 ABC GR. A; Dr. 1,200; 1982; circ. 7,000.

Indexed: Avery. *Notes*: adv., bk. rev., dwgs., photos (B&W, color).

A beautifully illustrated review of Hellenic fine, decorative, and applied arts. A regular section covers residential interior design and architecture. Covers current and historical work. Articles are written by experts on the works or periods described. Biographical notes on the artists appear at the end of each issue. This outstanding contribution to art publishing should draw world attention to a group of artists who have been little known outside their country but deserve recognition. (0252-8150)

Planning, Environmental Design, Housing, and Transportation Planning

0003   A PLUS

0781   AU   (IT)
IN-ASA (Nat. Inst. for Urban Furnishings and Environmental Structures), via dell'Acqua Traversa 255, 00135 Rome, Italy. Ed. Renato Cecilia. Tel. 06/3273990. Bi-m.
    While dealing with a number of different planning topics, each issue also has a monographic section that provides a closer look at the enhancement of Italian cities in terms of administration and environment. +

0009   A.U.C.A. (ARQUITECTURA,
          URBANISMO,
          CONSTRUCCION Y ARTE)

0782   AKTUELLES BAUEN   (SZ)
Vogt-Schild AG, Dornacherstrasse 39, 4501 Solothurn, Switzerland. Ed. Dietrich Garbrecht. Tel. 065-247247. Fr. 72; 1982. Indexed: A.P.I., Avery. Notes: adv., photos (B&W, color).
    Current housing, planning, and architectural projects are presented. Text in German.

0461   AMERICAN CITY AND
          COUNTY

0013   ARCH PLUS

0015   DE ARCHITECT

0053   ARCHITEKTURA A
          URBANIZMUS/
          ARCHITECTURE UND
          URBANISM

0059   ARHITEKTURA

0783   AUFBAU   (AU)
Jugend und Volk Verlagsgesellschaft, Jenullgasse 4, 1140 Vienna, Austria. Ed. Dr. Helmut Krebs. Tel. (0222) 827480. Telex 133832. M; S. 590; 1946. Indexed: A.P.I., Avery. Notes: adv., bk. rev., dwgs., photos (B&W, color).
    A journal of planning and public projects for Vienna. Presents the activities of the Viennese planning authorities. Projects are thoroughly described and detailed by plans and models through all stages of construction. Text in German; summaries in English and French. (0004-7805)

0784   AUSTRALIAN PLANNER   (AT)
          (Formerly: Royal Australian Planning Institute Journal)
c/o Dr. Stephen Hamnett, Head of Planning, Sait, N. Terrace, Adelaide 2000, Australia. G.P.O. Box 263, Canberra City, Act 2601, Australia. Ed. Dr. Stephen Hamnett. Tel. 08-2280297. Q; $30; 1965; circ. 3,200. Indexed: A.P.I., P.A.I.S. Special Issues: Biennial Congress issues. Notes: adv., bibl., bk. rev., calendars, dwgs., photos (B&W, color).
    A professional planning journal for Australia. (0729-3682) *

0077   BAUMEISTER

0079   BAUWELT

0785   BNA'S HOUSING AND   (US)
          DEVELOPMENT REPORTER
Bureau of National Affairs, 2300 M St., N.W., Washington, DC 20037. Ed. Barry Jacobs. Tel. (202) 955-9610. W; $556; 1973.

Covers housing, community and economic development, and real-estate finance in the U.S. (0091-5939) *

0786 BYPLAN   (DK)
Pederskrams Gade 2B, DK-1054 Copenhagen, Denmark. Arkitektens Forlag, 43 Nyhavn DK 1051, Copenhagen, Denmark. Ed. Arne Gaardmand. Tel. (01) 13-7281. Telex GIRO 9 003134. Bi-m; Kr. 255; 1948; circ. 2,400. *Indexed*: Every 5 years. *Notes*: adv., bk. rev., dwgs., photos (B&W). *Micro*: UMI.
Journal on town, regional, and national planning for Denmark. Text in Danish. (0007-7658)

0787 C.I.P. FORUM   (CN)
Canadian Inst. of Planners, RR3 Belfast, Prince Edward Island COA 1AO, Canada. 30-46 Elgin St., Ste. 30, Ottawa, Ont. K1P 5K6, Canada. Ed. John Curry. Tel. (902) 659-2888. Bi-m; 1956; circ. 3,500. *Notes*: adv., bibl., bk. rev., dwgs., photos (B&W).
News on urban and regional planning. *

**0788 CAMBRIDGE URBAN AND   (UK)
       ARCHITECTURAL STUDIES**
Cambridge University Press, Box 110, Cambridge CB2 3RL, England. (U.S. Sub.) 32 E. 57th St., New York, NY 10022. Leslie Martin. Irreg.; 1972. +

**1150 CANADIAN JOURNAL OF
       CIVIL ENGINEERING**

0090 CARRE BLEU

0096 CITTA E CAMPAGNA

0789 CITTA E SOCIETA   (IT)
Piazza S. Ambrogio 15, 20123 Milan, Italy. Ed. Vittorino Colombo. Bi-m; 1966. *Indexed*: A.P.I. *Notes*: adv., bibl., bk. rev., dwgs. (0009-7640) +

**0790 COMPARATIVE URBAN   (US)
       RESEARCH**
Marie Mount Hall, Univ. of Maryland, College Park, MD 20742. Ed. William J. Hanna. Q; $8 (indiv.); $13 (inst.); 1972; circ. 1,200. *Indexed*: Avery. *Notes*: adv., bibl., bk. rev. *Micro*: MIM, UMI.
Scholarly journal that presents original papers on human ecology, urban anthropology, and sociology. Of particular interest to scholars involved with the comparative study of urban areas worldwide. (0090-3892)

**0791 CONSERVE   (US)
       NEIGHBORHOODS**
National Trust for Historic Preservation, 1785 Massachusetts Ave., N.W., Washington, DC 20036. Tel. (202) 673-4047. 10/yr.; $15; 1977; circ. 5,500. *Indexed*: Avery. *Annual Issues*: two "How-to" Guides *Notes*: adv., bibl., bk. rev., calendars, dwgs., photos (B&W).
A newsletter for citizen groups involved in building and neighborhood rehabilitation. Includes notes on funding and legislation. (0732-1708)

0100 COVJEK I PROSTOR

**0792 DOWNTOWN IDEA   (US)
       EXCHANGE**
Downtown Research and Development Center, 270 Madison Ave., Ste. 1505, New York, NY 10016. Ed. Lawrence C. Alexander. Tel. (212) 889-5666. Bi-w; $85; 1954.
A newsletter dedicated to downtown revitalization. Short articles report on downtown problems and solutions in various cities throughout the country. Subscribers are also alerted to research, publications, and conferences sponsored by the center. (0012-5822)

0111 EDILIZIA POPOLARE

0793 EKISTICS   (GR)
Athens Center of Ekistics, Box 3471, Athens 102 10, Greece. 24 Strat. Syndesmou St., Athens 10673, Greece. Ed. P. Psomopoulos. Tel. 3623216. Telex 215227. Bi-m; $48; 1955; circ. 3,000. *Indexed*: A.P.I., Avery, Ekist. Ind., P.A.I.S., S.S.C.I. *Notes*: adv., bibl., dwgs., photos (B&W). *Micro*: UMI.
This scholarly journal, founded by Constantine Doxiades, examines all aspects of human settlements from local to global/international. Articles discuss the natural environment, individuals, social groups, and all types of construction from economic, social, political, administrative, cultural, and technological points of view. (0013-2942) *

0794 ENVIRONMENT   (US)
Heldref Publications, 4000 Albemarle St., Ste. 302, Washington, DC 20016. Ed. Jane Scully. Tel. (202) 362-6445. 10/yr.; $20 (indiv.); $30 (inst.); 1958; circ. 10,961. *Indexed*: Mag. Ind., Poll. Abstr., R.G., S.S.C.I. *Notes*: adv., bk. rev., calendars, dwgs., photos (B&W). *Micro*: UMI.
A highly respected journal that focuses on en-

vironmental problems created by modern technology, in the areas of energy, pollution, transportation, and land use. (0013-9157)

0213 ENVIRONMENT AND
BEHAVIOR

0795 ENVIRONMENT AND (UK)
PLANNING
Pion Ltd., 207 Brondesbury Park, London NW2 5JN, England. Eds. Dr. Lionel March and M. Batty. Tel. (01) 459-0066. Q; $90; 1974; circ. 600. *Indexed*: Avery, last issue of alt. volumes. *Notes*: adv., bibl., bk. rev., dwgs., photos (B&W).

An international journal providing comprehensive accounts of current research in design science and configurational studies. The papers selected for publication reflect systematic, innovative approaches to design and emphasize processes, techniques, theories, and philosophies. Some of the topics included are: applications of scientific theory and problem-solving methods to the planning process; structural approaches to qualitative plan-making and urban morphology; impact of microcomputing and computer graphics on all areas of planning and design. Primarily for planning and architectural research specialists. (0265-8135)

0796 ESPACE (FR)
Confederation Nationale pour l'Amenagement Rural, 129 bd. Saint Germain, 75006 Paris, France. Ed. Jacques Fournol. M; F.90; 1969. *Indexed*: A.P.I. +

0113 AL-FAISAL ARCHITECTURE
AND PLANNING JOURNAL

0797 HABITAT (CN)
Canada Mortgage and Housing Corp., News and Information Division, Montreal Rd., Ottawa, Ont. K1A OP7, Canada. Ed. Cecylia Podoski. Tel. (613) 748-2000. Q; free in Canada; 1958; circ. 11,000. *Indexed*: A.P.I., Avery, C.P.I. *Notes*: adv., bk. rev., dwgs., photos (B&W, color).

A government agency publication that presents issues on housing, planning, and urban affairs. Topics such as energy conservation and low-income housing, financing, and building design are discussed in a social and economic context. Of interest primarily to government officials, planners, and architects in Canada. Text in English and French. (0017-6370)

0798 HABITAT INTERNATIONAL (UK)
Pergamon Press, Headington Hill Hall, Oxford OX3 OBW, England. (U.S. sub.) Fairview Park, Elmsford, NY 10523. Bi-m; 1976. *Micro*: UMI.

International journal on all aspects of human settlements, both urban and rural. (0197-3975) +

0799 HABITAT NEWS (KE)
(Formerly: *Human Settlements*)
United Nations Centre for Human Settlements, Kenyatta International Conference Centre, P.O. Box 30030, Nairobi, Kenya. UNCHS New York Office, United Nations, NY 10017. Ed. Ellen Kitonga. Tel. 332383. Telex 22996. 3/yr.; free; 1970. *Indexed*: A.P.I., Avery. *Notes*: bk. rev., calendars, photos (B&W).

The official newsletter of UNCHS. Theme papers, policy guidelines, project updates from Third World countries, and news from UN agencies are published. The goal is to present information on and recommendations for the amelioration of the world's problems of sheltering the poor and homeless. Primarily for government officials and planners involved with Third World development and human settlements. (0251-7205)

0800 HABITATION (FR)
Editions Franck, 13 rue du Sentier, Paris 2e, France. M; 1952. *Indexed*: A.P.I. (0017-6400) +

0486 HERITAGE OUTLOOK

0121 HINTERLAND

0371 HOME AGAIN

0801 HOUSING (UK)
Institute of Housing, 12 Upper Belgrave St., London SW1X 8BA, England. Ed. Bill Randall. Tel. (01) 245-9933-7. M; £29; 1931; circ. 6,000. *Notes*: adv., bk. rev., dwgs., photos (B&W).

Discusses planning, design, and legal and financial aspects of housing. Emphasis is on British housing projects, but international projects are sometimes examined. Attention is given to technical problems such as window installations or barrier-free design. Includes news on housing officials and notes on seminars.

0802 HOUSING AND SOCIETY (US)
(Formerly: *Housing Educators Journal*)
Dr. Earl Morris, 169 LeBaron Hall, Iowa State University, Ames, IA 50011. American Assn. of Housing Educators, Justin Hall, Kansas State

University, Manhattan, KS 66506. Tel. (515) 294-8845. 3/yr.; $40; 1974. *Notes*: bibl., bk. rev., dwgs., photos (B&W).

A research journal on housing. Emphasis is sociological and economic, but papers are published on housing-related topics by psychologists, engineers, foresters, energy conservationists, etc. Special issues have appeared on housing for the elderly and real-estate finance. *

0803 HOUSING REVIEW (UK)
Housing Centre Trust, 33 Alfred Place, London WC1E 7JU, England. Ed. Mrs. B. Bernstein. Tel. (01) 637-4202. Bi-m; $30; 1951; circ. 2,500. *Indexed*: A.P.I., Avery, Nov./Dec. issue. *Notes*: adv., bk. rev., dwgs., photos (B&W). *Micro*: UMI.

A forum for the exchange of information on housing, both public and private. Economic, legal, social, and design aspects are reviewed. Extensive coverage of seminars and conferences. (0018-6651)

0804 I.F.H.P. NEWSSHEET (NE)
International Federation for Housing and Planning, Wassenaarseweg 43, 2596 CG The Hague, Netherlands. Ed. Jon Leons. Tel. (070) 244557. Telex 31578 Inter NLI99. 7/yr.; $34; 1977; circ. 1,200. *Indexed*: Avery. *Annual Issues*: Conference Issue.

Presents news of the International Federation for Housing and Planning. Text in English, French, and German. *

0805 INTERNATIONAL JOURNAL (UK) OF URBAN AND REGIONAL RESEARCH
Edward Arnold Publishers, Ltd., 41 Bedford Sq., London WC1B 3DQ, England. (U.S. Sub.) Cambridge University Press, 32 E. 57th St., New York, NY 10022. Ed. Michael Harloe. Q; $44 (indiv.); $67 (inst.); 1976; circ. 1,100. *Indexed*: Avery. *Notes*: adv., bk. rev., dwgs., photos (B&W).

Presents current international research in urban and regional development with an emphasis on interdisciplinary aspects. Primary concern is with the "study of conflicting interests in development, demonstrating the social basis of different approaches to planning and state intervention." Four sections include: major articles and symposia, urban praxis (current developments in urban policy and protest), argument, book reviews. Text in English; summaries in French, German, and Spanish. (0309-1317) *

0806 INTERSECTIONS (US)
Rensselaer Polytechnic Inst., Center for Urban and Environmental Studies, Troy, NY 12181. Ed. Bob Huneau. Tel. (518) 270-6000. A; $3; 1973; circ. 2,000. *Indexed*: Avery. *Notes*: bk. rev.

Journal of urban and environmental studies. Articles cover several disciplines related to the field and are written by professors, practicing professionals, and students. (0095-6945)

0214 JOURNAL OF ARCHITECTURAL AND PLANNING RESEARCH

0215 JOURNAL OF ENVIRONMENTAL PSYCHOLOGY

0807 JOURNAL OF HOUSING (US)
National Assn. of Housing and Redevelopment Officials, 2600 Virginia Ave., NW, Washington, DC 20037. Ed. Terence Cooper. Tel. (202) 333-2020. Bi-m; $24; 1944; circ. 13,500. *Indexed*: Avery, P.A.I.S., S.S.C.I.

Agency publication that focuses on housing issues. Topics include legislation, research, financing, rehabilitation, and low-income housing programs. Reports on city and state activities. (0272-7374)

0458 JOURNAL OF HOUSING FOR THE ELDERLY

0808 JOURNAL OF PLANNING (UK) AND ENVIRONMENT LAW
Sweet & Maxwell Stevens Journal, 11 New Fetter Lane, London EC4P, 4EE England. (U.S. & Canada Sub.) Carswell Co., Ltd., 233 Midland Ave., Agincourt, Ont., Canada. Ed. Harold J. Brown. Telex 263398 ABPLDNG. M; £37; 1948; circ. 4,500. *Indexed*: A.P.I., P.A.I.S., cum. each issue. *Notes*: adv., bk. rev.

A journal that documents current developments in planning and environmental law in the United Kingdom. In addition to feature articles, each issue carries parliamentary news, notes on cases, news of court decisions, and statutes. (0307-4870)

0809 JOURNAL OF THE (US) AMERICAN PLANNING ASSOCIATION
(Formerly: *Journal of the American Institute of Planners*)
Center for Urban & Regional Studies, Hickerson House 067A, University of North Carolina,

Chapel Hill, NC 27514. American Planning Assn., Subscription Dept., 1313 E. 60th St., Chicago, IL 60637. Eds. Edward Kaiser, Raymond Burby. Tel. (919) 962-3074. Q; $20 (members); $30 (nonmembers); 1935; circ. 11,000. *Indexed*: A.P.I., Art Ind., Avery, P.A.I.S. *Notes*: adv., bibl., bk. rev., calendars, dwgs., photos (B&W, color). *Micro*: UMI.

Professional journal primarily for planners but also of interest to urban designers, developers, architects, and public officials. Presents ideas and research on planning and urban affairs and reports on their implications for practice and public policy. (0194-4363) *

0810   JOURNAL OF URBAN   (US)
HISTORY

Univ. of Alabama in Birmingham, School of Social & Behavioral Sciences, University Station, Birmingham, AL 35294. Sage Publications, 275 S. Beverly Dr., Beverly Hills, CA 90212. Ed. Blaine Brownell. Tel. (205) 934-5643. Q; $50; 1974. *Indexed*: Amer: H&L, Avery, Hist. Abst. *Notes*: adv., bk. rev., photos (B&W).

Scholarly journal that presents varied approaches to the history of cities and urban societies in all periods of history and throughout the world. Material is analytical and interpretive, with special attention given to new insights. Articles compare urban societies over space and/or time. (0096-1442) *

0811   KUNNALLISTEKNIIKKA/   (FI)
KOMMUNALTEKNIK

Suomen Kunnallisteknillinen Yhdistys r.y., Box 51, 00131 Helsinki 13, Finland. Bi-m; 1946. (0023-5385) +

0130   KWARTALNIK
ARCHITEKTURY I
URBANISTYKI

0812   LAND DEVELOPMENT   (UK)
STUDIES

E & FN Spon Ltd., 11 New Fetter Lane, London EC4P 4EE, England. Associated Book Publishers, Ltd., Subscriptions Dept., North Way, Andover, Hampshire SP10 5BE, England. Ed. Dr. Ashley Dabson. Tel. 0245-351119. Telex 263398. 3/yr.; $72; 1984. *Indexed*: Every third issue. *Notes*: adv., bibl., bk. rev., dwgs., photos (B&W).

A new international research journal on land development. Papers cover all aspects of development in many countries. Topics include financial and environmental issues as well as the relation of land development to public policy

and private enterprise. It is of interest primarily to planning officials, consultants, and researchers but also to developers, especially those who invest widely overseas. (0264-0821)

0813   LAND USE DIGEST   (US)
Urban Land Inst., 1090 Vermont Ave., N.W., Washington, DC 20005. Ed. Libby Howland. Tel. (202) 289-8500. M; 1968. (0023-768x) +

0814   LAND USE LAW AND   (US)
ZONING DIGEST

(Formerly: *Zoning Digest*)
American Planning Assn., 1776 Massachusetts Ave., NW, Washington, DC 20036. 1313 E. 60th St., Chicago, IL 60637. Ed. Rodney Cobb. M; $160; 1948; circ. 1,200. *Indexed*: Avery. *Micro*: UMI.

Abstracts federal and state decisions and recently adopted legislation related to zoning, housing, energy, real property taxation, and environmental regulations. Also reports on current developments in land-use planning and related areas. Short articles by lawyers analyze significant cases. Useful to attorneys, planners, developers, officials, and concerned citizens. (0094-7598)

0865   LANDSCAPE

0815   LIVABILITY   (US)
Partners for Livable Places, 1429 21st St., NW, Washington, DC 20036. Ed. Elizabeth Dahlstein. Tel. (202) 887-5990. A; free (U.S.); 1978; circ. 10,000. *Notes:* bk. rev., photos (B&W).

A newsletter "dedicated to the transfer of innovative ideas on the enhancement of the built and natural environments." Primarily it documents the activities of the organization, which promotes this goal.

0816   LIVABILITY DIGEST   (US)
Partners for Livable Places, 1429 21st St., NW, Washington, DC 20036. Publishing Center for Cultural Resources, 625 Broadway, New York, NY 10012. Ed. Elizabeth Dahlstein. Tel. (202) 887-5990. Irreg.; $5 ea.; 1981; circ. 2,000. *Notes*: photos (B&W).

A thematic anthology of extracts from recent articles and reports on economic development, urban and architectural design, and civic leadership. (0278-9485)

0817   LONDON JOURNAL   (UK)
c/o Dept. of Geography, Queen Mary College, London E1, England. Ed. John M. Hall. S-a;

$25, *Indexed:* A P I Avery *Notes:* blk. *cov.,* dwgs., photos (B&W).

A multidisciplinary journal that presents research papers on all aspects of London metropolitan society including the built and natural environment, the fine and performing arts, and general commentaries. Of interest to planners, historians, geographers, social scientists, government officials, and architects. Readership includes generalists with an interest in London. (0305-8034)

0818   MACADAM (FR)
9 rue Turbigo, 75001 Paris, France. Ed. Francois Chaslin. Bi-m; 1977. *Indexed:* A.P.I. +

0819   MASS TRANSIT (US)
337 National Press Bldg., Washington, DC 20045. Ed. Nanette Wiese. Tel. (202) 638-0330. M; 1974. *Indexed:* Avery. *Micro:* UMI.

Presents all aspects of mass transit, including planning, financing, designing, constructing, and operating large facilities and systems in urban areas. International news is also covered. (0364-3484) +

0820   NATIONAL ASSOCIATION (US)
FOR OLMSTEAD PARKS
NATIONAL NEWSLETTER
Nat. Assn. for Olmstead Parks, 175 Fifth Ave., Flatiron Bldg., New York, NY 10010. Ed. Alexander Allport. Q; 1980. +

0821   NATION'S CITIES WEEKLY (US)
National League of Cities, 1301 Pennsylvania Ave., NW, Washington, DC 20004. Ed. Raymond Dick. Tel. (202) 626-3040. W; 1963. *Indexed:* P.A.I.S., S.S.C.I. *Micro:* BLH, UMI.

Problems in city and town planning are studied. Topics such as urban revitalization and financing are discussed, with an emphasis on legislative and administrative issues. +

0146   NUOVA CITTA

0504   OLD HOUSE JOURNAL

0822   OPEN HOUSE (NE)
INTERNATIONAL
N. Wilkinson, University of Newcastle-Upon-Tyne, Dept. of Architecture, Newcastle-Upon-Tyne NE1 7RU, England. Stichting Architecten Research, Postbus 429, 5600 AKJ, Eindhoven, Netherlands. Ed. N. Wilkinson. Tel. (0632) 328511. Q; $25; 1982. *Indexed:* Avery.

A research journal concerned with the dynamics of the built environment, particularly housing and human settlements in the Third World. Emphasizes the involvement of the users in decision-making processes and construction. *

0823   OUT OF JERUSALEM (IS)
Jerusalem Committee, 20a Radak St., 92 186 Jerusalem, Israel. Ed. Tom Sawicki. Tel. (02) 662-554. Q. *Indexed:* Avery. *Notes:* photos (B&W).

Aesthetic and cultural themes concerning Jerusalem are the focus of this magazine. Articles cover planning, preservation, history, and the arts of this ancient city. The publishing committee is an international advisory council of distinguished architects, planners, historians, philosophers, theologians, artists, and writers. (0333-6271)

0149   PARAMETRO

0824   PARIS PROJECT (FR)
Atelier Parisien d'Urbanisme, 17 Blvd. Morland, 75004 Paris, France. Ed. P.Y. Ligen. S-a; 1969. +

0825   PLACE: THE MAGAZINE OF (US)
LIVABILITY
Partners for Livable Places, 1429 21st St., N.W., Washington, DC 20036. Ed. Duke Johns. Tel. (202) 887-5990. 11/yr.; $24 (US only); 1981; circ. 2,000. *Notes:* adv., bk. rev., photos (B&W).

Presents news and commentary on community affairs, urban design, natural resource management, and economic development. Reports on activities of the organization. (0278-274x)

0826   PLACES (US)
Center for Environmental Design, 373 Wurster Hall, University of California, Berkeley, CA 94720. M.I.T. Press Journals, 28 Carlton St., Cambridge, MA 02142. Eds. Donlyn Lyndon, William Porter. Tel. (415) 642-1495. Q; $20 (indiv.); $40 (inst.); 1983; circ. 1,800. *Notes:* adv., bk. rev., dwgs., photos (B&W, color). *Micro:* UMI.

A journal that explores the total human environment. Articles cover projects, theories, history, and contemporary problems. The editorial goal is "transmitting a lively sense of a place's unique and universal qualities." The well-illustrated articles are contributed by experts from the fields of urban planning, architecture, environmental science, and geography. Provides coverage of parks, schools, neighborhoods, city squares, private gardens, exotic habitats, historical structures, and geological formations. (0731-0455)

0154 PLAN: MAANDBLAD VOOR
       ONTWERP ON OMGEVING

0827 PLAN CANADA   (CN)
Canadian Inst. of Planners, 30-46 Elgin St., Ste. 30, Ottawa, Ont. K1P 5K6, Canada. RR3 Belfast, Prince Edward Island COA 1AO, Canada. Ed. John Curry. Tel. (902) 659-2888. Q; Can.$15 (indiv.); Can.$25 (inst.); 1959; circ. 3,500. *Indexed*: A.P.I. *Notes*: adv., bibl., bk. rev., calendars, dwgs., photos (B&W).
Journal of urban and regional planning for Canada. Text in English and French. (0032-0544) *

0828 PLANNER   (UK)
      (Formerly: *Royal Town Planning Inst. Journal*)
Royal Town Planning Institute, 26 Portland Place, London W1N 4BE, England. Ed. Anthony Fyson. Tel. (01) 930-8903. M; £20; 1914; circ. 14,200. *Indexed*: A.P.I. *Notes*: adv., bibl., bk. rev., calendars, dwgs., photos (B&W).
Contains news, features, and technical articles on British town and county planning. (0309-1384) *

0829 PLANNING   (US)
American Planning Assn., 1313 E. 60th St., Chicago, IL 60637. Ed. Sylvia Lewis. Tel. (312) 955-9100. M; $29; 1972; circ. 24,000. *Indexed*: Avery, Mgt. Contents, P.A.I.S. *Notes*: adv., bibl., bk. rev., calendars, dwgs., photos (B&W, color). *Micro*: BLH, UMI.
The major U.S. periodical devoted to city planning. Through the use of case studies, news reports, critiques, and abstracts, major trends are studied and particular locales and planning efforts are examined. Articles cover issues in urban design, environment, neighborhood development, housing, and downtown revitalization. Regular columns contain timely information on planning practice, legal cases, and new legislation. (0001-2610)

0830 PLANNING AND BUILDING   (SA)
      DEVELOPMENTS
Avonwold Publishing Co. (Pty.) Ltd., Box 52068, Saxonwald 2132, South Africa. Ed. Carol Knoll. Tel. (011) 7881610. Bi-m; R.21.50; 1973; circ. 3,000. *Indexed*: A.P.I. *Notes*: adv., bibl., dwgs., photos (B&W, color).
Articles cover housing, planning, civil engineering, and building services in South Africa. *

0831 PLANNING OUTLOOK   (UK)
School of Town and Country Planning, University of Newcastle-Upon-Tyne, Newcastle-Upon-Tyne NE1 7RU, England. Ed. Patrick Whitehead. Tel. 0632-328511, ext. 2806. S-a; $24; 1948; circ. 500. *Indexed*: A.P.I., B.T.I. *Notes*: adv., bibl., bk. rev., dwgs., photos (B&W).
Devoted to new developments in planning, landscape architecture, environmental studies, housing, and Third World development. Consists of research papers contributed by academics and practitioners from the western world. The international readership includes planners, geographers, landscape architects, and environmentalists. (0032-0714)

0158 PROA

0832 PROGRESSIVE PLANNING   (UK)
Pergamon Press, Headington Hill Hall, Oxford OX3 OBW, England. Bi-m; 1973. +

0517 RECUPERARE-EDILIZIA
       DESIGN IMPIANTI

0833 REGIONAL STUDIES   (UK)
Cambridge University Press, Edinburgh Bldg., Shaftesbury Rd., Cambridge CB2 2RU, England. (U.S. sub.) 32 E. 57th St., New York, NY 10022. Bi-m; 1966. *Indexed*: A.P.I., Avery. *Micro*: MIM, UMI. (0034-3404) +

0834 S.P.A. JOURNAL   (II)
      (Formerly: *Urban and Rural Planning Thought*)
School of Planning and Architecture, Indraprastha Estate, New Delhi 110002, India. Ed. Prof. B. Misra. Tel. 273015. Q; $20; 1958; circ. 250. *Notes*: bk. rev., dwgs., photos (B&W).
Covers topics in the areas of architecture, city planning, transport planning, landscape, housing, urban design, and building science. *

0835 SMALL TOWN   (US)
Small Town Inst., Box 517, 3rd Ave. & Poplar Street, Ellensburg, WA 98926. Ed. Kenneth Munsell. Tel. (509) 925-1830. Bi-m; $30 (indiv.); $35 (inst.); 1969; circ. 1,200. *Notes*: bk. rev., dwgs., photos (B&W).
Publishes case studies of small communities that have developed innovative programs to solve their problems and to improve the quality of life of their residents. Topics include town management and economic development, planning, and historic preservation. (0196-1683) *

0206   SPAZIO E SOCIETA/SPACE AND SOCIETY

0178   STADT

0836   STORIA DELLA CITTA   (IT)
Edizioni Kappa, Piazza Borghese 6, 00186 Rome, Italy. Ed. Enrico Guidoni. Tel. (06) 6790356. Q; $50. *Notes*: bibl., dwgs., photos (B&W).

Prepared under the auspices of Rome University, this international journal presents the history of town planning and problems concerning territorial management. Text in Italian.

**0837   STRUTTURE AMBIENTALI/   (IT)
ENVIRONMENTAL STRUCTURES**
Pio Manzu International Research Centre, via Budro 35-47040 Verucchio (FO), Italy. Ed. Gerardo Dasi. Tel. (541) 668139. Telex 550432 cirsa I. Bi-m; free to contributors to Centre; 1970; circ. 3,500. *Notes*: adv., dwgs., photos (B&W).

Covers environment, energy, development, architecture, urbanistics, and ecology. *

0180   T.A.

**0838   THIRD WORLD PLANNING   (UK)
REVIEW**
Dept. of Civic Design, Univ. of Liverpool, P.O. Box 147, Liverpool L69 3BX, England. Liverpool University Press, Box 147, Liverpool L69 3BX, England. Ed. Prof. Gerald Dix. Tel. 051-709-6022, ext. 2534. Telex 627095. Q; $43; 1979. *Indexed*: A.P.I., Avery, Nov. issue. *Notes*: adv., bk. rev., dwgs., photos (B&W). *Micro*: UMI.

A distinguished journal with academic and professional readership from nearly seventy countries. The papers cover all aspects of urban and regional planning in the Third World, including housing, resource and transport planning, and the social and economic issues involved with urbanization and industrialization. Also of interest to the informed general public. (0142-7849)

0387   TOSHI-JUTAKU

**0839   TOWN AND COUNTRY   (UK)
PLANNING**
Town and Country Planning Assn., 17 Carlton House Terrace, London SW1Y 5AS, England. Ed. Jim Dumsday. Tel. (01) 930-8903. 11/yr.; $77; 1899; circ. 3,000. *Indexed*: A.P.I., Art Ind.,

B.T.I., P.A.I.S., S.S.C.I. *Notes*: adv., bk. rev., dwgs., photos (B&W).

Short but informative articles discuss timely issues in the field of urban and rural planning in Great Britain. Incisive commentaries challenge the reader. Includes news and reports on new projects, trends, products, innovative techniques, and legislation. Aimed at the British planner but also of interest to anyone concerned with the environment. (0040-9960)

0840   TOWN PLANNING REVIEW   (UK)
Dept. of Civic Design, Univ. of Liverpool, P.O. Box 147, Liverpool L69 3BX, England. Liverpool University Press, Box 147, Liverpool L69 3BX, England. Ed. David Massey. Tel. 051-709-6022, ext. 2534. Telex 627095. Q; £29; 1910; circ. 2,000. *Indexed*: A.P.I., Art Ind., Avery, B.T.I., P.A.I.S., S.S.C.I., Oct. issue. *Notes*: adv., bibl., bk. rev., dwgs., photos (B&W).

One of the most important planning journals in the world, with extensive academic and professional readership in over sixty countries throughout the world. Covers all aspects of urban and regional planning, rural planning, transportation, landscape design, housing, and new towns. Papers discuss issues under current debate and are followed by comments from colleagues. An author/subject index of major articles from planning journals worldwide is provided in each issue. (0041-0020) *

0841   TRANSPORTATION   (NE)
Elsevier Science Publishers, P.O. Box 211, 1000 AE Amsterdam, Netherlands. (U.S. Sub.) Elsevier Science Pub. Co., 52 Vanderbilt Ave., New York, NY 10017. Ed. Martin & Voorhees Assoc. Q. *Indexed*: Avery. *Notes*: adv., bk. rev., dwgs., photos (B&W).

International research journal that presents papers on transportation analysis, design, and planning that utilize an interdisciplinary approach. Attention is given to the interaction between transportation activities and the social, economic, and environmental aspects of urban life. (0049-4488)

**0842   TRANSPORTATION   (US)
QUARTERLY**
(Formerly: *Traffic Quarterly*)
Eno Foundation for Transportation, Box 2055, Westport, CT 06880-0055. Ed. Wilbur Smith. Tel. (203) 227-4852. Q; free; 1947; circ. 5,000. *Indexed*: App. Sci. Tech. Ind., Avery, Eng. Ind., S.S.C.I.

This journal serves as a forum to encourage the dissemination of ideas, opinions, and facts relating to the field of transportation. Covers planning, design, operation, and regulation activities. (0278-9434)

0843 UNDERGROUND SPACE (US)
Pergamon Press, Journals Div., Maxwell House, Fairview Park, Elmsford, NY 10523. Ed. Charles Fairhurst. Tel. (914) 592-7700. Bi-m; 1977. *Indexed*: Eng. Ind., Excerp. Med., Sci. Abstr. (0362-0565) +

0844 URBAN AFFAIRS QUARTERLY (US)
Center for Urban Affairs & Policy Research, Northwestern Univ., 2040 Sheridan Rd., Evanston, IL 60201. Sage Publications, Inc., 275 S. Beverly Blvd., Beverly Hills, CA 90212. Ed. Albert Hunter. Tel. (312) 492-5536. Q; $25 (indiv.); $60 (inst.); 1965. *Indexed*: Amer: H&L, Avery, Ekist. Ind., P.A.I.S., S.S.C.I. *Notes*: bk. rev., dwgs. *Micro*: UMI.
The oldest professional journal of international urban research, this quarterly provides a forum for those involved in making or implementing public policy to exchange ideas and concerns with individuals engaged in urban research. Features "Research Notes" in the areas of sociology, political science, education, economics, planning, history, anthropology, and psychology. (0042-0816) *

0845 URBAN DESIGN INTERNATIONAL (US)
(Formerly: *Urban Design*)
Social Science Div., S.U.N.Y. Purchase, Purchase, NY 10577. Inst. for Urban Design, Main P.O. Box 105, Purchase, NY 10577. Ed. Ann Ferebee. Tel. (914) 253-9341. Q; $65; 1979. *Indexed*: A.P.I., Art Ind., Avery. *Annual Issues*: Fall—Membership Directory. *Notes*: dwgs., photos (B&W).
Covers a wide range of urban design issues from the U.S. and abroad, focusing on specific projects. Articles are written in depth and include historical background, problems, and solutions. Makes extensive use of maps, drawings, and renderings. (0731-6259)

0846 URBAN INNOVATION ABROAD (US)
Council for International Urban Liaison, 1120 G St., N.W., Ste. 300, Washington, DC 20005. Ed. George Wynne. Tel. (202) 626-4624. M; $48; 1977; circ. 9,000. *Indexed*: Semiannually. *Notes*: bk. rev. *Micro*: UMI.
A newsletter on new urban trends from abroad. Subscription includes the quarterly

newsletter *Urban Transportation Abroad* and *Learning From Abroad* reports. Of interest to officials in local, state, or federal government and to planners involved with innovative management, service, and quality-of-life improvements throughout the world. Subscribers have access to the council's computerized contact and resource files. (0163-6499)

0847 URBAN LAND (US)
Urban Land Inst., 1090 Vermont Ave., N.W., Washington, DC 20005. Ed. Eric Smart. Tel. (202) 289-8500. M; $58; 1941; circ. 7,000. *Indexed*: A.P.I., Avery, P.A.I.S. *Notes*: adv., bk. rev., dwgs., photos (B&W, color). *Micro*: UMI.
Presents in-depth feature articles on major issues in the planning field. Brief articles discuss new developments in the U.S. The "Solution File" offers case histories. Regulatory trends are also discussed. Readership includes planners, developers, real-estate professionals, architects, engineers, and bankers. (0042-0891)

0848 URBAN LAW AND POLICY (NE)
P.O. Box 1991, 1000 B2 Amsterdam, Netherlands. North-Holland Pub. Co., Box 211, 1000 AE Amsterdam, Netherlands. Ed. Patrick McAuslan. 5/yr.; $81.50; 1978. *Indexed*: Avery, Leg. Per. *Notes*: adv., bk. rev., dwgs.
A legal journal that includes papers on the roles of law and urbanization and their impact on each other. Aimed at lawyers, public administrators, and urban sociologists. (0165-0068) *

0849 URBAN STUDIES (UK)
Adam Smith Bldg., Glasgow University, Glasgow G12 9RT, Scotland. Longman Group, Ltd., Fourth Ave., Harlow, Essex CM19 5AA, England. Eds. W.J. Money, G.A. Wood, W.F. Lever. Tel. 041-339-8855. Bi-m; $64; 1964; circ. 1,650. *Indexed*: A.P.I., Avery, S.S.C.I., Nov. issue. *Notes*: adv., bibl., bk. rev., dwgs., photos (B&W).
Provides an international forum for articles on urban and regional planning and urban and regional problems. Covers social and economic issues and other disciplines within the field. (0042-0980) *

0850 URBANISM PAST AND PRESENT (US)
University of Wisconsin, College of Letters and Sciences, Box 413, Milwaukee, WI 53201. Ed. Bruce Fetter. Tel. (414) 963-5207. S-a; $8 (indiv.); $15 (inst.); 1979; circ. 2,000. *Indexed*: A.P.I., Amer: H&L, Avery, ERIC. *Notes*: adv., bibl., dwgs., photos (B&W). *Micro*: UMI.

An interdisciplinary journal that deals with research on urbanization. Articles appear on urban history, geography, urban policy, sociology, and planning. Emphasis is on the process of urbanization and on the development and functioning of urban institutions. Each issue contains an extensive bibliography of recent international urban studies publications. (0160-2780)

0851   URBANISME   (FR)
Societe des Editions Regirex France, 62 rue Ampere, 75017 Paris, France. Ed. Robert Koenig. Bi-m; 1932. *Indexed*: A.P.I., Avery. *Micro*: UMI. (0042-1014) +

0852   URBANISTICA   (IT)
Istituto Nazionale di Urbanistica, via Massena 71, 10128 Turin, Italy. Q; 1949. *Indexed*: Art Ind., Avery. (0042-1022) +

0853   URBIS   (US)
Catholic University, Dept. of Architecture & Planning, Washington, DC 20064. 1983. +

0854   VOLUNTARY HOUSING   (UK)
National Federation of Housing Associations, 175 Gray's Inn Rd., London WC1X 8UP, England. M; 1935. *Indexed*: A.P.I. +

0855   WATERFRONT WORLD   (US)
Waterfront Center, 1536 44th St., N.W., Washington, DC 20007. Eds. Ann Breen, Richard Rigby. Tel. (202) 337-0356. Bi-m; $24 (indiv.); $48 (inst.); 1982; circ. 600. *Annual Issues*: May/June—Waterfront Festivals; Nov./Dec.—Waterfront Design. *Notes*: bk. rev., calendars dwgs., photos (B&W).

A newsletter for developers, architects, planners, city officials, and citizens interested in the development of waterfront properties throughout the U.S. Current and proposed projects are featured. Opinions from qualified individuals and organizations involved in urban waterfront enhancement are published in each issue. Correspondents are located throughout the U.S. Provides leads to current information. (0733-0677)

0192   WONEN-TABK

**0195   Z.E.D./ZIMBABWE
         ENVIRONMENT AND
         DESIGN**

8

Landscape Design and Gardening

Professional

0856 AGORA (US)
Landscape Architecture Foundation, 1733 Connecticut Ave., N.W., Washington, DC 20009. Ed. Sharon Barndollar. Tel. (202) 223-6229. Q; 1980; circ. 25,000. *Notes*: bk. rev., dwgs., photos (B&W).

Brief articles present research activities affecting landscape architecture and its allied professions. As the title suggests, it is published as a marketplace of ideas and a meetingplace for landscape architects and kindred spirits.

0857 ANTHOS (SZ)
International Federation of Landscape Architects, Graf und Neuhaus AG, P.O. Box 121, CH-8044 Zurich, Switzerland. Ed. H. Mathys. Tel. 031-543233. Q; Fr.56; 1962; circ. 5,000. *Indexed*: A.P.I., Avery. *Notes*: adv., bibl., bk. rev., dwgs., photos (B&W).

Covers all aspects of landscape architecture and planning with focus on Switzerland but applications worldwide. Text in German, French, and English. (0003-5424)

0365 COUNTRY LIFE

0858 GARDEN DESIGN (US)
American Society of Landscape Architects, 1733 Connecticut Ave., N.W., Washington, DC 20009. Ed. Susan Frey. Tel. (202) 466-7730. Q; $16; 1982; circ. 18,000. *Notes*: adv., bk. rev., dwgs., photos (B&W, color).

A handsomely illustrated publication that covers residential landscape design from all over the world, from urban penthouses to es-

tates. Articles carefully describe the types of plants and trees found in the gardens discussed. Each issue includes a "Plant Page" that cites sources of plants described. The "Gardens in Plan" section consists of pen-and-ink-rendered plans of the gardens featured. (0733-4923)

0859 GARDEN HISTORY (UK)
Garden History Society, 361 Milkwood Rd., Herne Hill, London SE2 40HA, England. Ed. Brent Elliott. Q; 1972. *Indexed*: A.P.I., Avery, R.I.L.A. *Notes*: bk. rev., dwgs., photos (B&W).

Contains society news and scholarly papers on the history of landscape design and the landscape's relation to architecture, art, literature, philosophy, and society. Includes articles on plant propagation and taxonomy as well as grounds-planning and maintenance. (0307-1243)

0860 GARTEN + LANDSCHAFT (GW)
Verlag Georg D.W. Callwey, Streitfeldstr. 35, 8000 Munich 80, W. Germany. M; DM. 99.60; 1890; circ. 5,700. Tel. (089) 989892. Telex 5216752 calv. *Indexed*: Avery. *Notes*: adv., bk. rev., dwgs., photos (B&W).

Review of international landscape planning and architecture. Text in German and English. (0016-4720)

0861 GROUNDS MAINTENANCE (US)
Intertec Publishing Co., P.O. Box 12901, Overland Park, KS 66212-0930. Ed. Kathy Copley. (913) 888-4664. M; $24; 1966; circ. 42,000. *Indexed*: Dec. issue. *Notes*: adv., bk. rev., dwgs., photos (B&W, color). *Micro*: UMI.

Provides technical information on landscape design, construction, and maintenance. Reviews on new equipment, supplies, and plant selection are prepared for the primary interest of landscape contractors and grounds managers of recreational, commercial, and industrial properties. Also of interest to landscape designers. Special attention is given to golf courses. (0017-4688) *

0862   JOURNAL OF GARDEN   (NE)
       HISTORY
Prof. Hunt, Sir Thomas Brown Inst., Rijksuniversiteit te Leiden, Postbus 9515 RA Leiden, Netherlands. (U.S. Sub.) Publications Expediters, Inc., 200 Meacham Ave., Elmont, NY 11003. Ed. John Dixon Hunt. Q; $43 (indiv.); $86 (inst.); 1981. *Indexed*: A.P.I., Art Ind., Avery, R.I.L.A. *Notes*: adv., bibl., bk. rev., dwgs., photos (B&W).
A scholarly journal of international scope. Approaches garden history from a multidisciplinary point of view. (0144-5170)

0863   LAND: LANDSCAPE   (US)
       ARCHITECTURAL NEWS
       DIGEST
American Society of Landscape Architecture, 1733 Connecticut Ave., N.W., Washington, DC 20009. Ed. Richard Lippman. Tel. (202) 466-7730. 11/yr.; $19; 1972; circ. 8,000. *Notes*: bk. rev., calendars, photos (B&W).
Newsletter with notes on landscape architecture in the U.S. (0023-7544) *

0864   LAND DESIGN   (CN)
Canadian Society of Landscape Architecture, P.O. Box 3304, Station C, Ottawa, Ont., Canada. 3/5 yr. +

0865   LANDSCAPE   (US)
P.O. Box 7107, Berkeley, CA 94707. Ed. Bonnie Lloyd. Tel. (415) 549-3233. 3/yr.; $22; 1951; circ. 2,000. *Indexed*: A.P.I., Amer: H&L, Art Ind., Avery, Ekist. Ind., Environ. Ind. *Notes*: bibl., bk. rev., dwgs., photos (B&W). *Micro*: UMI.
The aim of this unusual and thoughtful publication is to encourage new ways of looking at the common elements of the urban landscape. Articles focus on such ordinary places as backyards, fences, alleys, and gas stations—how they are combined in complex relationships and how we interact with them. The articles are written by designers, freelance writers/photographers, and social scientists. Of interest to anyone interested in the built environment. (0023-8023)

0866   THE LANDSCAPE   (NZ)
New Zealand Inst. of Landscape Architects, P.O. Box 10-022, Terrace, Wellington, New Zealand. Q. *Indexed*: Avery. *Notes*: adv., dwgs., photos (B&W).
Explores issues on landscape design and the environment of New Zealand. Also contains articles on professional practice and landscape education of interest to the New Zealand architect. (0110-1439)

0867   LANDSCAPE & TURF   (US)
       INDUSTRY
Brantwood Publications, Drawer 23389, Tampa International Airport, FL 33623. Tel. (414) 786-2900. 7/yr.; 1955. *Micro*: UMI. +

0868   LANDSCAPE   (US)
       ARCHITECTURE
American Society of Landscape Architects, 1733 Connecticut Ave., N.W., Washington, DC 20009. Ed. Susan R. Frey. Tel. (202) 466-7730. Bi-m; $42; 1910; circ. 17,000. *Indexed*: A.P.I., Arch. Ind., Art Ind., Avery, Jan./Feb. issue. *Annual Issues*: Sept.—ASLA Design Competition Awards. *Notes*: adv., bk. rev., dwgs., photos (B&W, color).
An international magazine of regional and land planning, landscape design, construction, and management. Readers include ASLA members, landscape architects, architects, planners, urban designers, public officials, conservationists, related contractors, and suppliers. (0023-8031)

0869   LANDSCAPE AUSTRALIA   (AT)
Landscape Publications, 17 Carlyle Cres., Mont Albert, Vic. 3127, Australia. Ed. Ralph Neale. Tel. (03) 890-5764. Q; Aus.$39; 1979; circ. 3,000. *Indexed*: A.P.I., Avery. *Notes*: adv., bibl., bk. rev., calendars, dwgs., photos (B&W, color).
Official journal of the Australian Institute of Landscape Architects. Australia's only journal of landscape design covering a variety of topics from overseas as well as within Australia. Includes technical and general articles about Australian trees and shrubs, landscape histories, etc. (0310-9011)

0870   LANDSCAPE CONTRACTOR   (US)
Better Business Communicators, 4 AE Wilson St., Batavia, IL 60510. Ed. Bonnie Sylvester Zaruba. Tel. (312) 879-0353. M; 1965. (0194-7257) +

0871   LANDSCAPE DESIGN   (UK)
Landscape Inst., 12 Carlton House Terrace, London SW1, England. Ed. Ken Fieldhouse. Tel. (01) 839-3855. Bi-m; £12; 1971; circ. 5,000. *Indexed*: A.P.I., Avery. *Notes*: adv., bibl., bk. rev., calendars, dwgs., photos (B&W, color).

An international journal of landscape design and management. Includes articles on landscape education, office computer applications, environmental legislation, and resource management. An index of practices and an office profile appear in each issue. (0020-2908)

0872   LANDSCAPE HISTORY   (UK)
Society for Landscape History, 39 Eldon Terrace, Leeds Rd., Wakefield, W. Yorkshire, WF1 3JW, England. J. Wood, Honorary Secretary, c/o Sites & Monuments Record, Archaeology Unit, Architects Dept., County Hall, Beverly, N. Humberside HU179 BA England. Ed. Dr. Margaret L. Faull. Tel. 379690. A; £11; 1979; circ. 360. *Indexed*: A.P.I., Avery. *Notes*: adv., bk. rev., dwgs., photos (B&W).

An interdisciplinary journal of landscape studies. Articles discuss the architecture, history, and archaeology of the British landscape. (0143-3768)

0873   LANDSCAPE JOURNAL   (US)
Council of Education in Landscape Architecture, University of Wisconsin Press, Journal Div., 114 N. Murray St., Madison, WI 53715. Eds. Arnold Alanen, Darrel Morrison. Tel. (608) 263-3956. S-a; $12 (indiv.); $30 (inst.); 1981; circ. 1,500. *Notes*: adv., bk. rev., dwgs., photos (B&W). *Micro*: UMI.

An international journal of academic research and technical information on the landscape. Subject areas include: visual quality assessment, human behavior and the environment, historic and cultural preservation, landscape history, planting design, landscape restoration, and energy considerations. Large format and well illustrated. Recommended for practitioners, academicians, and students of landscape architecture. (0277-2426) *

0874   LANDSCAPE PLANNING   (NE)
Elsevier Scientific Publishing Co., Box 330, 1000 AE Amsterdam, Netherlands. Ed. A.E. Weddle. Q; $80; 1974. *Indexed*: A.P.I., Avery. *Notes*: adv., bibl., bk. rev., dwgs., photos (B&W).

An international journal on landscape ecology, reclamation, and conservation, outdoor recreation, and land-use management. Deals with conceptual, philosophical, and scientific approaches to land use. Studies the problems of urban expansion in land that has not been urbanized. (0304-3924) *

0875   LANDSCAPE RESEARCH   (UK)
Landscape Research Group, Dept. of Landscape Architecture, Univ. of Sheffield, Sheffield S10 2TN, England. Mrs. Carys Swanwick, Dale Cottage, The Dale, Eyam Nr., Sheffield S30 1QU, England. Ed. Ian Brotherton. Tel. 0742-78555. 3/yr.; £10.50; 1976; circ. 500. *Indexed*: Avery. *Notes*: bk. rev., dwgs., photos (B&W).

A scholarly journal that contains research papers on historical aspects or contemporary problems in landscape design. International in scope with an emphasis on interdisciplinary collaboration. (0142-6397)

0876   LANDSCHAFT UND STADT   (GW)
Verlag Eugen Ulmer, Wollgrasweg 41, Postfach 700561, 7000 Stuttgart 70, W. Germany. Ed. U. Schleuter. Q; 1969. (0023-8058) +

0877   LANDSKAB   (DK)
Melvillevej 16, DK-2900 Hellerup, Denmark. Arkitektens Forlag, 43 Nyhavn, DK-1051, Copenhagen, Denmark. Ed. Annemarie Lund. Tel. (01) 136200. Telex GIRO 9-00-31-34. 8/yr.; Kr.285; 1923; circ. 1,250. *Indexed*: A.P.I., Avery. *Notes*: adv., bibl., bk. rev., dwgs., photos (B&W). *Micro*: UMI.

Journal of garden and landscape planning. Text in Danish; summaries and captions in English. (0023-8066)

0131   LATENT IMAGES

0878   PARK MAINTENANCE   (US)
Madison Publ. Co., P.O. Box 1936, Appleton, WI 54913. Ed. Tom Luba. Tel. (414) 733-2301. M; 1948. *Annual Issues*: March—Swimming Pools; April—Athletic Facilities; Oct.—Buyer's Guide.

Focuses on parks, school campuses, golf courses, and other large-scale properties. (0031-2134) +

0879   SOUTHERN LANDSCAPE   (US)
             AND TURF
Brantwood Publications, P.O. Drawer 23389, Tampa International Airport, FL 33623. Ed. R.W. Morey. Tel. (813) 796-3877. Bi-m. *Micro*: UMI. +

0880   TUTTOVILLE   (IT)
Gruppo Editoriale Electa, S.p.A., via Goldoni 1, 20129 Milan, Italy. Bi-m; 1967.

More technical than *Ville Giardini*, this journal covers technical problems and solutions relating to single-family dwellings and garden landscapes. The scope is international. (0041-445x) +

0389 VILLE—GIARDINI

0881 WESTERN LANDSCAPING   (US)
Hester Communications, Inc., Box 19531, Irvine, CA 92713. Ed. Jack Schember. Tel. (714) 250-8060. M; $12.50; 1961; circ. 17,000. *Annual Issues*: Dec.—Buyer's Guide. *Notes*: adv., calendars, dwgs., photos (B&W, color).
A professional journal for landscape designers, landscape contractors, and maintenance contractors in the western U.S. (0043-3861) *

Consumer

0882 AMI DES JARDINS ET DE LA   (FR)
      MAISON
Ami des Jardins, S.A., 35 rue du Tonkin, 69100 Villeurbanne, France. M; F.75; 1930. *Notes*:

adv., bk. rev., photos (B&W, color). (0041-8095) +

0604 AUSTRALIAN HOUSE AND
      GARDEN

0606 BETTER HOMES AND
      GARDENS

0609 CASA E GIARDINO

0552 CASA E JARDIM

0618 HOUSE AND GARDEN

0619 HOUSE AND GARDEN

0627 MAISON ET JARDIN

0634 SOUTHERN ACCENTS

0639 ZUHAUSE: WOHNUNG,
      HAUS UND GARTEN

Building and Construction

General and Professional

1104   A E CONCEPTS IN WOOD
       DESIGN

0883   AFRICAN CONSTRUCTION   (UK)
       (Formerly: *West African Construction*)
Surrey House, 1 Throwley Way, Sutton, Surrey
SM1 4QQ, England. Ed. Roger Sargent. Tel.
(01) 643-8040. Telex 892084BISPRSG (SRB). Q;
$65; 1978; circ. 6,439. *Indexed*: A.P.I. *Notes*:
adv., photos (B&W).
   Offers comprehensive coverage of construction in black Africa, including roads, dams,
bridges, hospitals, factories, and industrial
buildings. Circulation is strictly limited to individuals in the industry, primarily contractors,
engineers, architects, and specifiers. Detailed,
illustrated articles discuss design and construction methods, equipment, and materials, emphasizing new technology. The editorial goal is the
establishment of common standards and codes
of practice in African construction. International correspondents report news on budgets
and loans, new projects, business opportunities,
and the establishment of new companies in the
region. (0142-596x) *

0245   ALABAMA BUILDER

0884   ALLGEMEINE BAUZEITUNG (GW)
Patzer Verlag GmbH und Co. KG, Alter Flug-
hafen 15, 3000 Hannover 1, W. Germany. W;
DM.88.40; 1930. *Notes*: adv., bk. rev., dwgs.
(0002-5801) +

0885   AMERICAN PROFESSIONAL   (US)
       CONSTRUCTION
Dept. of Bldg. Construction, Texas A & M University, College Station, TX 77843. American
Inst. of Constructors, Box 22622, Cleveland,
OH 44122. Ed. Albert Pedulla. Tel. (216) 663-
0365. S-a; free to members; circ. 3,000. *Notes*:
dwgs., photos (B&W).
   An association journal that presents original
papers on technical, management, and education topics of interest to builders.

0886   AMERICAN ROOFER AND   (US)
       BUILDER IMPROVEMENT
       CONTRACTOR
Shelter Communications, Inc., Box 279, Boli-
nas, CA 94924. Ed. J.C. Gudas. Tel. (312) 852-
1848. M; $12; 1911; circ. 30,000. *Notes*: adv.,
bk. rev., dwgs., photos (B&W, color). *Micro*:
UMI.
   Primarily for contractors, this publication is
devoted to roofing, siding, insulating, and
waterproofing. (0003-0880) *

0887   APARTMENT & BUILDING   (CN)
BKN Publications, 4580 Victoria Dr., Vancou-
ver, BC V5N 4N8, Canada. Ed. Noel Marples.
Tel. (604) 873-4781. Bi-m; 1971. *Notes*: adv. +

0033   ARCHITECTURE &
       BUILDING INDUSTRY

0888   ARCHITECTURAL AND   (UK)
       BUILDING INFORMATION
       SELECTOR
B&M Publications (London) Ltd., Box 13,
Hereford House, Bridle Path, Croydon, Surrey

CR 4NL, England. Ed. B. Owen. Tel. (01) 680-4200. S-a; £15; 1971; circ. 40,000. *Notes*: adv., photos (B&W).

Primarily product information. *

0889   ARCHITECTURAL   (JA)
     ENGINEERING/SEKOH
Shokokusha Publishing Co., Ltd., 25 Sakamachi, Shinjuku Tokyo, Japan. Ed. Kiyoshi Kamahara. M; 1966. *Notes*: adv. +

0359   ARCHITECTURAL SERVICES
     BOOK OF HOUSE PLANS

0029   ARCHITECTURAL
     TECHNOLOGY

0890   ASIA PACIFIC CONTRACTOR   (HK)
Thomson Press, Hong Kong, Ltd., Tai Sang Commercial Bldg., 19th Fl., 24-34 Hennessy Rd., Hong Kong. Ed. Suvesh Shavma. M; 1980. +

0074   ASIAN ARCHITECTURE &
     BUILDER

0891   ASIAN BUILDING AND   (UK)
     CONSTRUCTION
(Formerly: *Far East Architect and Builder*)
IPC Asian Publishing Co., Surrey House, 1 Throwley Way, Sutton, Surrey SM1 4QQ, England. Ed. Nicola Carr. Tel. (01) 643-8040. Telex 892084 BISPRSG (SRB). M; $35; 1980; circ. 14,000. *Notes*: adv., bk. rev., calendars, dwgs., photos (B&W, color).

Covers current building and engineering activity in Southeast Asia and international products/technology available in the area. Readership includes contractors, consultants, and architects working in Asia. (0264-8164) *

0892   AUSTRALIAN BUILDER   (AT)
Australian Builder Publishing Co. Pty., Ltd., 332-334 Albert St., E. Melbourne 3002, Australia. Ed. Kevin Randall. Tel. (03) 4194555. M; Aus.$40; 1949; circ. 4,000. *Notes*: adv., bk. rev., dwgs., photos (B&W, color).

Trade publication of the Australian construction industry. (0004-878x)

0893   AUTOMATION IN HOUSING   (US)
     AND MANUFACTURED
     HOME DEALER
Don O. Carlson, P.O. Box 120, Carpinteria, CA 93013. Tel. (805) 684-7659. M; $30 (free to qual-

ified subscribers); 1964; circ. 25,400. *Indexed*: Dec. issue. *Annual Issues*: Jan.—Buyers Guide. *Notes*: adv., bk. rev., calendars, dwgs., photos (B&W, color). *Micro*: UMI.

This national magazine covers all aspects of manufactured housing. Categories include: large-volume production builders; modular home manufacturers; mobile home manufacturers; panelized home producers; component manufacturers; and dealers in mobile/modular/panelized homes. Features contain details on both marketing and manufacturing techniques. (0362-0395) *

0894   B.R.E. DIGEST   (UK)
Building Research Establishment, Garston, Watford WD2 7JR, England. Tel. (0923) 674040. Telex 923220. M; £12. *Indexed*: A.P.I.

Newsletter that reviews all aspects of building technology.

0895   B.R.E. INFORMATION   (UK)
     PAPERS
Building Research Establishment, Garston, Watford WD2 7JR, England. Tel (0923) 674040. Telex 923220. Bi-w; £18. *Indexed*: A.P.I.

Newsletter that reports the latest building research results and how to apply them.

0896   B.R.E. NEWS   (UK)
Building Research Establishment, Garston, Watford WD2 7JR, England. Tel. (0923) 674040. Telex 923220. 1967. *Indexed*: Avery.

Published in three newsletter editions, each catering to a distinct field of interest: construction research (Bi-m), timber research (3/yr.), fire research (3/yr.).

0897   BATIMENT   (CN)
1001 de Maisoneuve West, Ste. 1000, Montreal, Quebec H3A 3E1, Canada. Ed. Marc Castro. Tel. (514) 845-5141. Bi-m; $48; 1926; circ. 4,250. *Notes*: adv., bk. rev., calendars, dwgs., photos (B&W, color).

A sister publication to *Canadian Building,* it serves the building industry in French Canada. Text in French. *

0898   BATIMENT-BATIR   (FR)
Revue Technique de la Federation Nationale du Batiment et des Organismes, Professionels Techniques, 6 rue Paul Valery, 75009 Paris, France. Editions Eyrolles 61 Bd. St. Germain, 75240 Paris Cedex 5, France. M; 1950. +

0899   BATIMENT   (UK)
       INTERNATIONAL/BUILDING
       RESEARCH
108 Kent House Rd., Beckenham, Kent BR3
1JY, England. International Council for Building Research, Studies and Documentation,
Centre Scientifique et Technique du Batiment, 4
Av. du Recteur Poincare, 75782 Paris Cedex 16,
France. Ed. L.W. Madden. Tel. (01) 778-6968.
Bi-m; $45; 1972. *Indexed*: A.P.I., Avery, Com-
pendex, Eng. Ind., Jan./Feb. issue. *Notes*:
bibl., dwgs., photos (B&W).
   Research journal that contains papers by
member institutes of C.I.B. on structural integ-
rity, behavior, and durability of materials, fire-
safe design, performance analysis, energy conservation, etc. Text in English and French.
(0182-3329) *

0900   BAU & HOLZ   (SZ)
Schweizerische Bau und Holzarbeiter Verband,
Strassburgstr. 5, P.O. Box 8021, CH-8004 Zu-
rich, Switzerland. W. *Notes*: adv. +

0901   BAUEN   (GW)
Fachseniften Verlag GmbH, Hoehnstr. 17, Post-
fach 1329, 7012 Fellbach, W. Germany. Ed. O.
Strebel. Q; DM.30; 1975. *Notes*: dwgs. +

0902   BAUMASCHINE UND   (GW)
       BAUTECHNIK
Bauverlag GmbH, P.O. Box 1460, 6200 Wiesbaden, W. Germany. Ed. M.A. Schmitt. M;
1954; circ. 7,000. *Indexed*: Compendex, Eng.
Ind. *Notes*: adv., bk. rev., dwgs., photos
(B&W).
   Detailed reviews and performance studies of
construction equipment. Text in German; summaries in English, French, and Italian. (0005-
6693)

1145   BAUPLANUNG-BAUTECHNIK

0903   BAUSPAR-JOURNAL   (GW)
Deutsche Bausparkasse AG, Heinrichstr. 2,
6100 Darmstadt, W. Germany. Ed. E. Nierich.
Q; with membership; 1979. (0174-3058) +

0079   BAUWELT

1044   BETON I ZHELEZOBETON

1045   BETONWERK UND
       FERTIGTEIL TECHNIK
       BAUINGENIEUR

0904   BETTER BUILDINGS   (US)
12 W. 37th St., New York, NY 10018. Ed. Robert Burns. Tel. (212) 563-6460. Bi-m; $30; 1982;
circ. 12,000. *Notes*: adv., photos (B&W).
   Although it is subtitled "the operations magazine for Metro New York owners and managers," it is of interest to anyone involved in the
maintenance and rehabilitation of commercial
buildings. It presents case histories, features on
techniques, and reports on legislation, New
York area projects, and new products. (0744-
530x)

0905   BODEN, WAND, DECKE   (GW)
Lobrecht Verlag Max Rauscher KG, Postfach
1454, 8939 Bad Woerishofen, W. Germany. Ed.
Max Rauscher. M; DM.108; 1954. *Notes*: adv.,
bk. rev., dwgs. (0006-5463) +

0906   BOUW   (NE)
Stichting Bouw, Box 299, 3000 AG Rotterdam,
Netherlands. Ed. J.C. Rutten. Tel. (010) 11-61-
81. Telex 22530. Bi-w; 1946; circ. 7,200. *In-
dexed*: A.P.I., Avery, Feb. and Aug. issues.
Notes: adv., bk. rev., calendars, dwgs., photos
(B&W, color).
   A review of building in the Netherlands. Cov-
ers housing, environmental and physical plan-
ning, architecture, and building techniques.
Text in Dutch. *

0360   BUILDER

0907   BUILDER & CONTRACTOR   (US)
Associated Builders & Contractors, Inc., 729
15th St., NW, Washington, DC 20005. Ed. Victoria Tanner. Tel. (202) 637-8800. M; $12; 1952;
circ. 21,000. *Annual Issues*: Jan.—Annual Report; Sept.—Convention Issue; Oct.—Directory. *Notes*: adv., bk. rev., photos (B&W).
   Edited for Open Shop contractors. Features
national and regional construction news, articles
on government activities, construction management, finance, labor, insurance, job safety, design, equipment, and products. (0273-7965) *

0908   BUILDER ARCHITECT   (US)
Sunshine Media, Inc., 7720 N. 17th Place, P.O.
Box 9400, Phoenix, AZ 85068. Ed. Linda Kil-
bourne. Tel. (602) 943-3575. M; $12; 1938; circ.
3,000. *Notes*: adv., calendars, dwgs., photos
(B&W, color).
   A trade publication for builders, architects,
developers, and the light construction industry.
Each month the cover story focuses on a leading

U.9. builder. Regional issues are published. (0193-7472)

0083   BUILDING

0909   BUILDING AND   (US)
       ENVIRONMENT
(Formerly: *Building Science*)
Pergamon Press, Maxwell House, Fairview Park, Elmsford, NY 10523. Ed. C.B. Wilson. Tel. (914) 592-7700. Q; $135; 1965; circ. 1,000. *Indexed*: A.P.I., Compendex, Eng. Ind. *Micro*: MIM, UMI.

The aim of this journal is to publish original papers on important topics in building and architectural research. Presents articles describing and assessing applications in building design and construction. (0360-1323)

0910   BUILDING & REALTY   (US)
       RECORD
105 Chestnut St., Philadelphia, PA 19106. Ed. James Smart. Tel. (215) 629-1611. M; 1953.

For builders, realtors, and design professionals in the Philadelphia area. +

0084   BUILDING DESIGN

0911   BUILDING FAILURE BRIEFS   (US)
Raymond di Pasquale & Assoc., 121 W. State St., P.O. Box 848, Ithaca, NY 14850. Tel. (607) 272-8585. M; $48; 1983.

A newsletter of forensic architecture and engineering. Includes references to building failure cases published in other sources.

0247   BUILDING INDUSTRY
       DIGEST OF HAWAII

0912   BUILDING INDUSTRY   (US)
       TECHNOLOGY ABSTRACT
       NEWSLETTER
National Technical Information Service, 5285 Port Royal Rd., Springfield, VA 22161. Ed. Linda Lagarde. Tel. (703) 487-4929. W; $65. *Indexed*: last issue in January.

A newsletter containing summaries of federally sponsored research reports on architectural design and environmental engineering; construction management and techniques; structural analyses; building standards and codes; construction materials, components, and equipment; building equipment, furnishings, and maintenance. (0163-1500)

0913   BUILDING   (UK)
       REFURBISHMENT &
       MAINTENANCE
Morgan-Grampian Construction Press, Ltd., 30 Calderwood St., London SE18 6QH, England. Ed. Nick Jones. Bi-m. (0141-0784) +

0914   BUILDING RENOVATION   (CN)
MacLean-Hunter, 777 Bay St., Toronto M5W 1A7, Canada. Ed. John Fennell. Tel. (416) 596-5760. Telex 06219547. Bi-m; $39; 1984; circ. 14,985. *Notes*: adv., bk. rev., calendars, dwgs., photos (B&W, color).

This new glossy tabloid presents news and case histories of commercial and residential renovations. *

0915   BUILDING RESEARCH   (CN)
       NEWS
Div. of Bldg. Research, National Research Council of Canada, Ottawa K1A OR6, Canada. Ed. J.F. Gallagher. Tel. (613) 993-2463. 3/yr.; free; 1960; circ. 8,000. *Notes*: bk. rev., dwgs., photos (B&W).

Contains short reports on the council's research projects as well as staff news, book notes, and information on building research carried out in other organizations in Canada. Text in English and French. (0007-361x) *

0916   BUILDING RESEARCH   (CN)
       NOTES
Div. of Bldg. Research, National Research Council of Canada, Ottawa K1A OR6, Canada. Tel. (613) 993-2463. Irreg.; free. *Notes*: dwgs., photos (B&W).

Short reports designed for immediate publication of research results. Suitable for a specialized audience. Text in English and occasionally in French. *

0917   BUILDING SERVICES   (UK)
Builder House, 1-3 Pemberton Row, Red Lion Court, Fleet St., London EC4P 4HL, England. Ed. Stephen Ashley. Tel. (01) 353-2300. Telex 25212 BUILDA G. Q; free to qualified subscribers; 1978; circ. 17,500. *Indexed*: A.P.I., B.T.I., Compendex, Eng. Ind. *Annual Issues*: Spring—Air Conditioning; Summer—Heating; Autumn—Specialist Electrical. *Notes*: adv., bk. rev., dwgs., photos (B&W, color).

A high-quality technical publication that presents concise, in-depth articles on all mechanical and electrical systems. Discussions range from new construction and renovation to building maintenance. Energy is a major topic. General industry news and new research is reported regularly. Extensive use of drawings and illustrations. The "Opus Design Files" give detailed specifications on new equipment and systems. Readership includes building managers, architects, contractors, specifiers, and mechanical and electrical engineers. (0142-3630)

0918 BUILDING SUPPLY AND (US) HOME CENTER
Cahners Publishing Co.. 475 Park Ave. South, New York, NY 10016. Ed. Patricia Coleman. Tel. (212) 686-0555. M; 1917. +

0919 BUILDING TECHNOLOGY (UK) AND MANAGEMENT
Chartered Inst. of Building, Englemere, Kings Ride, Ascot, Berkshire SL5 8BJ, England. Ed. Kenneth J. Lane. Tel. 0990-23355. M; £26.50; 1963; circ. 28,000. *Indexed*: A.P.I., Compendex, Eng. Ind. *Notes*: adv., bk. rev., photos (B&W, color).
Technical articles relating to the building industry in the United Kingdom, with occasional overseas columns. (0007-3709)

0920 BUILDING TRADES (UK) JOURNAL
(Formerly: *Illustrated Carpenter and Builder*) Northwood Publications, Ltd., Elm House, 10-16 Elm St., London WC 1X OBP, England. Ed. Peter Jones. Tel. (01) 278-2345. Telex 21746 ITPLNG. W; £37; 1878; circ. 23,500. *Indexed*: A.P.I. *Notes*: adv., bk. rev., calendars, dwgs., photos (B&W, color).
Contains technical information and news of the building industry. Analyzes materials and processes. *

0921 BUILDINGS (US)
Stamats Communications, Inc., 427 Sixth St. S.E., Cedar Rapids, IA 52406. Ed. Craig Henrich. Tel. (319) 364-6167. M; $35; 1906; circ. 33,000. *Indexed*: Dec. issue. *Annual Issues*: Jan. —Office Space Survey; March—Interiors; May —Neocon Preview and Directory of Associations; June—Modernization; Sept.—Building Census; Oct.—Roofing. *Notes*: adv., bk. rev., calendars, dwgs., photos (B&W, color).
Issues relating to the design, construction, maintenance, and management of commercial buildings are discussed in depth. Attention is given to such issues as life safety, energy management, space planning, security, and leasing. Includes occasional developer profiles. (0007-3725)

0922 BYGGMAESTAREN (SW)
Byggfoerlaget, Narvavaegen 19, 114 60 Stockholm, Sweden. Ed. Olle Vanare. M; Kr. 136; 1922. *Indexed*: A.P.I. *Notes*: adv., bk. rev., dwgs. (0007-7550) +

0923 C.E.E. (US)
Sutton Publ. Co., Inc., 707 Westchester Ave., White Plains, NY 10604. Ed. Milton O'Neal. 13/yr.; free to qualified subscribers; $40 to others; 1949; circ. 98,000. *Annual Issues*: Sept.— Product Reference Issue; Nov.—Office Systems; Dec.—Health Care. *Notes*: adv., photos (B&W, color). *Micro*: UMI.
A publication serving people in the electrical construction field whose responsibilities include specifying, buying, installation, and maintenance of all types of commercial, residential, and industrial electrical equipment and wiring materials, including all types of electrical heating and lighting. Each issue focuses on a special theme in addition to presenting new products. (0192-1274)

0924 CAHIERS DU CENTRE (FR) SCIENTIFIQUE ET TECHNIQUE DU BATIMENT
Centre Scientifique et Technique du Batiment, 4 Av. du Recteur Poincare, 75782 Paris Cedex 16, France. Ed. R. Mayer. Tel. 524-43-02. Telex PAR 610 710F. 10/yr.; F.980; 1948; circ. 6,000. *Indexed*: Every 3 years. *Notes*: adv., bk. rev., dwgs.
Research papers on technical aspects of building. Text in French; summaries in French, English, and Spanish. (0008-9850) *

0248 CALIFORNIA BUILDER

0925 CANADIAN BUILDING (CN)
MacLean-Hunter, 777 Bay St., Toronto, Ontario M5W 1A7, Canada. Ed. John Fennell. Tel. (416) 596-5760. Telex 06219547. 9/yr.; $50; 1950; circ. 18,600. *Notes*: adv., bk. rev., calendars, dwgs., photos (B&W, color).
Residential and nonresidential projects in all stages of completion are described. Topics include renovation, industry trends, building types, and life safety. (0008-3070) *

0926 CANADIAN BUILDING (CN) ABSTRACTS
Div. of Bldg. Research, National Research Council of Canada, Ottawa K1A OR6, Canada. Ed. Anne Marie Dorais. Tel. (613) 993-2463. A; free; 1960; circ. 750.

Abstracts of building technology articles and reports published in Canada or published in foreign periodicals by Canadian authors. Articles are selected for their value to building practitioners. Text in French and English. (0008-3089) *

0927 CANADIAN BUILDING (CN) DIGEST
Div. of Bldg. Research, National Research Council of Canada, Ottawa K1A OR6, Canada. Ed. Anne Marie Dorais. Tel. (613) 993-2463. Irreg.; free; 1960; circ. 18,500. *Indexed*: A.P.I., Chem. Abstr. *Notes*: dwgs., photos (B&W).
Four-page treatises on building problems, concepts, techniques, and materials. Subscribers include architects, engineers, and universities. English and French editions available. (0008-3097) *

1150 CANADIAN JOURNAL OF CIVIL ENGINEERING

0928 CARPENTER (US)
United Brotherhood of Carpenters and Joiners of America, 101 Constitution Ave. N.W., Washington, DC 20001. Ed. John S. Rogers. Tel. (202) 546-6206. M; $10; 1881; circ. 630,000. *Notes*: adv., dwgs., photos (B&W).
A forty-page monthly magazine of industry news and information for members of the United Brotherhood. (0008-6843) *

0929 CHARTERED QUANTITY (UK) SURVEYOR
Builder House, 1-3 Pemberton Row, Fleet St., London ECAP 4H2, England. Ed. Andrew Wilson. Tel. (01) 353-2300. Telex 25212 BUILDA G. M; £23; 1979; circ. 29,000. *Indexed*: A.P.I., Aug. issue. *Notes*: adv., bibl., bk. rev., calendars, dwgs., photos (B&W, color).
Features and reports on construction projects and details on writing specifications. (0142-5196) *

0364 COLONIAL HOMES

0930 COMMERCIAL (US) RENOVATION
(Formerly: *Commercial Remodeling*)
David Sauer, 8 S. Michigan Ave., Chicago, IL 60603. c/o Orlock Co., Ste. 900, Union Carbide Bldg., 230 N. Michigan Ave., Chicago, IL 60601. Ed. Craig Shutt. Tel. (312) 263-4291. Bi-m; $30 (US only); 1979; circ. 42,000. *Notes*: adv., calendars, dwgs., photos (B&W, color).

Contractors, architects, interior designers, building owners, and managers read this magazine for news on commercial remodeling and building rehabilitation. Case studies on problems in remodeling are presented in before/after format. Also contains product reviews and technical reports (0163-8440) *

0251 CONNECTICUT CONSTRUCTION

0931 CONSTRUCTION (US)
Construction Publishing Co., 7297 Robert Lee Highway, Falls Church, VA 22201. Ed. Jack C. Lewis. Bi-w; $26; 1933. *Indexed*: Compendex, Eng. Ind. *Notes*: adv., dwgs. (0010-6704) +

0932 CONSTRUCTION CANADA (CN)
Construction Specifications Canada, One St. Clair Ave., W., Suite 1206, Toronto, Ontario M4V 1K6, Canada. Ed. Clifford Fowke. Tel. (416) 922-3159. Bi-m; 1959. *Notes*: adv., photos (B&W, color). +

0933 CONSTRUCTION (US) CONTRACTING
(Formerly: *Construction Methods & Equipment*)
Bobit Publishing Co., 2500 Artesia Blvd., Redondo Beach, CA 90278. Subscription Dept., Box 509, Hightstown, NJ 08520. Ed. Jeffrey Abugel. M; $10; 1919. *Indexed*: App. Sci. Tech. Ind. *Micro*: UMI. (0270-1588) +

0934 CONSTRUCTION DIGEST (US)
7355 Woodland Dr., P.O. Box 603, Indianapolis, IN 46206. Ed. Arthur Graham. Tel. (317) 297-5500. Bi-w; $50; 1928; circ. 14,000. *Annual Issues*: Jan.—Construction Forecast; March—Buyer's Guide; Nov.—Construction Trucks. *Notes*: adv., photos (B&W, color).
Serves the construction and public works industries in Illinois, Indiana, Kentucky, Ohio, and eastern Missouri. Editorial content features bids and awards information, photos of construction projects, industry trends, and new products. (0010-6739) *

0935 CONSTRUCTION (US) DIMENSIONS
Assn. of the Wall & Ceiling Industries, 25 K Street, NE, Washington, DC 20002. Ed. Gerald Wykoff. Tel. (202) 783-2924. M. *Notes*: adv., bk. rev., photos (B&W, color). +

0097   CONSTRUCTION MODERNE

0936   CONSTRUCTION   (US)
       NEWSLETTER
National Safety Council, 444 N. Michigan Ave.,
Chicago, IL 60611. Tel. (312) 527-4800. Bi-m. +

0937   CONSTRUCTION PRODUCT   (US)
       NEWS
Johnson Hill Press, Inc., 1233 Janesville Ave.,
Ft. Atkinson, WI 53538. Ed. Dave Thompson.
Tel. (414) 563-6388. Bi-m; 1979. +

0938   CONSTRUCTION REPORTS: (US)
       HOUSING STARTS
Bureau of the Census, Washington, DC, Super-
intendent of Documents, U.S. Government
Printing Office, Washington, DC 20402. Ed.
David Fondelier. Tel. (301) 763-5731. M; $21;
1959; circ. 500.
Statistics on new single and multifamily housing units started under private and public own-
ership. Gives value and number of units of new
construction that were put in place. Includes
type of structure, purpose of construction (sale,
rent), backlog of unused permits, shipments of
mobile homes, and selected characteristics of
apartment buildings.

0939   CONSTRUCTION REVIEW   (US)
U.S. Dept. of Commerce, Washington, DC
20230. Supt. of Documents, U.S. Government
Printing Office, Washington, DC 20402. Tel.
(202) 377-4356. Bi-m; $19; 1955; circ. 3,000. In-
dexed: B.P.I., Compendex, Eng. Ind., P.A.I.S.
Micro: MIM, UMI.
Updates on U.S. building permits, contract
awards, construction in place, housing costs,
prices, interest rates, and more. Each issue examines some important aspects of the construction industry such as forecasts or energy
conservation. (0010-6917)

1111   CONSTRUCTION SPECIFIER

0940   CONSTRUCTIONAL REVIEW   (AT)
Concrete Publishing Co. Pty., Ltd., 25-27 Berry
St., N. Sydney, NSW 2060, Australia. Ed.
Diane Kell. Tel. (02) 923-1244. Telex 75575. Q;
Aus.$31.50; 1927; circ. 5,500. Indexed: Com-
pendex, Eng. Ind. Notes: adv., bk. rev., dwgs.,
photos (B&W, color).
A major publication of the Australian building
construction industry. Emphasis is on concrete
construction. (0010-695x) *

0941   CONSTRUCTOR   (US)
Associated General Contractors of America,
1957 E St., NW, Washington, DC 20006. Ed.
Diane B. Snow. Tel. (202) 393-2040. Telex
7108229406. M; $10; 1919; circ. 40,000. Annual
Issues: July—AGC's Who's Who in the World
of Construction, AGC Membership Directory
and Buyers Guide; Dec.—Computer Software
Inventory. Notes: adv., bk. rev., dwgs., photos
(B&W, color). Micro: UMI.
Reports on industry trends, management,
new techniques and products, and legislation.
(0162-6191) *

0942   CONTRACTOR   (US)
Morgan-Grampian Pub. Co., 1050 Common-
wealth Ave., Boston, MA 02215. Ed. Seth Shepard. Tel. (413) 449-2550. Bi-w; $18; 1954.
Notes: adv., bk. rev., photos (B&W, color).
(0010-7891) +

0943   CONTRACTOR ENGINEER   (US)
P.O. Box 9400, 7720 N. 17th Place, Phoenix, AZ
85068. M; 1938. +

0944   CONTRACTOR'S GUIDE   (US)
Century Communications, Inc., 5520-G Touhy
Ave., Skokie, IL 60077. P.O. Box 1088, Skokie,
IL 60076. Ed. Michael Beightol. Tel. (312) 676-
4060. M; $25; 1968; circ. 32,000. Notes: adv.,
calendars, photos (B&W, color).
A magazine that offers practical management
ideas to contractors and others in allied fields on
roofing, insulation, siding, and windows. Of primary interest to contractors but manufacturers,
suppliers, building owners, architects, and specifying engineers may also find it useful. (0273-
5954) *

0945   COSTRUIRE LATERIZI   (IT)
Associazione Nazionale Industriali dei Laterizi,
via Cavour 71, 00184 Rome, Italy. Bi-m; 1959.
Notes: bk. rev., dwgs., photos (color). (0010-
9649) +

0946   COSTRUTTORI ITALIANI   (IT)
       NEL MONDO
Edilstampa, via Guattani 20, 00161 Rome, Italy.
Ed. Dr. Luciano Melini. Tel. 8488263. Telex
613439. M; L.50,000; 1954; circ. 3,000. Notes:
adv., bk. rev., dwgs., photos (B&W).
Official publication of the Italian contractors
association. Text in Italian. *

0947   DAILY PACIFIC BUILDER   (US)
McGraw-Hill Information Systems, 2450 17th
St., San Francisco, CA. Tel. (415) 864-8600. D;
1890. +

**0366   DISTINGUISHED HOME
PLANS & PRODUCTS**

0948   EARTH SHELTER LIVING   (US)
Webco Publishing, Inc., 110 S. Greeley, Still-
water, MN 55082. Ed. William Baker. Tel. (612)
430-1113. Bi-m; $18; 1979. *Indexed*: A.P.I.,
Avery. *Notes*: adv., bk. rev., dwgs., photos
(B&W).
Devoted to the design and construction of
earth sheltered buildings. Emphasis is on residential construction. Thoroughly examines all
aspects of building underground. Products and
mechanical systems are given extensive coverage. Includes feature articles on landscaping.
Maps frequently update the locations of earth
shelters located in the U.S. (0744-1932)

**0949   ELECTRICAL   (US)
CONSTRUCTION AND
MAINTENANCE**
McGraw-Hill Publishing Co., 1221 Ave. of the
Americas, New York, NY 10020. Ed. Joseph
McPartland. Tel. (212) 512-2847. M; $18; 1901;
circ. 77,000. *Indexed*: App. Sci. Tech. Ind.,
Compendex, Eng. Ind. *Notes*: adv., bibl., bk.
rev., calendars, dwgs., photos (B&W, color).
Covers design and construction of electrical
systems, analysis of materials, estimating, and
specifications. Intended for contractors, engineers, architects, and inspectors who design, install, or maintain industrial, commercial, or
residential electrical systems. (0013-4260)

0950   ELEVATOR WORLD   (US)
354 Morgan Ave., P.O. Box 6506, Loop Branch,
Mobile, AL 36606. Ed. W.C. Sturgeon. Tel.
(205) 479-4514. Telex 782-722 ELE World. M;
$37; 1953; circ. 5,300. *Notes*: adv., bibl., bk.
rev., calendars, dwgs., photos (B&W, color).
Serves industries that transport through com-
pactly engineered systems on cables or rails.
(0013-6158) *

**0951   ENGINEERING-NEWS   (US)
RECORD**
McGraw-Hill Publishing Co., 1221 Ave. of the
Americas, New York, NY 10020. Ed. Arthur J.
Fox, Jr. Tel. (212) 512-2000. W; $33; 1874; circ.
104,000. *Indexed*: App. Sci. Tech. Ind., B.P.I.,
Compendex, Eng. Ind.. Mgt. Contents, semi-
annually. *Annual Issues*: Jan.—Forecast; Feb.

—Construction's Man of the Year; March,
June, Sept., Dec.—Quarterly Cost Reports;
April—400 Top Contractors in the U.S.; May—
Top 500 Design Firms; July—Top International
Contractors, Design Firms; August—Top Specialty Contractors. *Notes*: adv., bibl., bk. rev.,
calendars, dwgs., photos (B&W, color). *Micro*:
UMI.
A major publication that focuses on trends
and events in construction and engineering
worldwide. The emphasis is on large-scale construction and public works projects. Feature articles cover topics such as foreign markets and
computers while regular columns deal with issues of labor and legislation. The "Pulse Section" reports new projects in the U.S. and
abroad and is a good source for alerting architects, contractors, and suppliers to new business. (0013-807x)

**0952   F UND I—BAU   (GW)
(FERTIGTEILBAU UND
INDUSTRIALISIERTES
BAUEN)**
Element-Verlag GmbH, Zeppelinstr. 3, 7050
Waiblingen, W. Germany. Ed. H. Schmid. Q;
DM.22.50; 1966. (0340-2967) +

0953   FIBRECEMENT REVIEW   (SZ)
(Formerly: *International Asbestos Cement
Review*)
Verlag Karl Kraemer & Co., Spiegelgasse 14,
CH-8001 Zurich, Switzerland. Ed. Florian
Adler. Tel. (058) 231271. Telex 875919ETUS.
S-a; Fr.24; 1956; 40,000. *Indexed*: A.P.I. *Notes*:
dwgs., photos (B&W, color).
Demonstrates uses of fibrecement in all parts
of a variety of building types. Brief articles but
well illustrated. Scope is international. Text in
English, French, Spanish, and German. (0379-
8615)

0367   FINE HOMEBUILDING

0253   FLORIDA BUILDER

**0254   FLORIDA CONSTRUCTION
INDUSTRY**

0115   FRAMES/PORTE & FINESTRE

**0954   FROM THE STATE   (US)
CAPITALS: CONSTRUCTION
—INSTITUTIONAL**
Wakeman-Walworth, Inc., Box 1939, New
Haven, CT 06509. M; $75; 1946.
Reports on state and local legislation action

regarding the construction or renovation of correctional facilities, hospitals, universities, sports arenas, and civic auditoriums. (0741-3491) *

0955   IL GIORNALE DELLA   (IT)
       PREFABBRICAZIONE
       ITALIANA
Viale Papiniano 50, 20123 Milan, Italy. Bi-w. +

0956   GUIDELINES ERRORS AND   (US)
       OMISSIONS BULLETIN
Box 456, Orinda, CA 94563. Bi-m; $60; 1984.
   Detailed reports that cover building and materials failure. Looseleaf format.

0957   GULF CONSTRUCTION AND   (BA)
       SAUDI ARABIA REVIEW
Al Hilal Publishing and Marketing Group, P.O. Box 224, Manama, Bahrain. Ed. John Rowles. Tel. 262504. Telex 8981 HILAL BN. M; $75; 1980; circ. 11,250. Notes: adv., bibl., bk. rev., calendars, dwgs., photos (B&W, color).
A glossy trade publication with news reports and technical features on construction in the Arabian Gulf States. Building techniques and materials are examined in detail, with attention given to their performance in the region. Exterior and interior products are reviewed. Covers small-scale and large public works projects.

0958   HOME & BUILDING   (NZ)
Associated Group Media, Ltd., Box 28349, Auckland 5 New Zealand. Bi-m; 1936. Indexed: A.P.I. (0018-392x) +

0959   HOME BUILDER NEWS   (US)
Eneguess Publ. Co., 42 Grove St., Peterborough, NH 03458. Tel. (603) 924-3859. M; 1960. (0018-3970) +

0372   HOUSE AND BUNGALOW

0373   HOUSE BEAUTIFUL'S
       BUILDING MANUAL

0375   HOUSE BEAUTIFUL'S
       HOUSES AND PLANS

0376   HOUSE BUILDER AND
       ESTATE DEVELOPER

1063   L'INDUSTRIA ITALIANA
       DEL CEMENTO

0960   INDUSTRIAL   (US)
       CONSTRUCTION
North American Publ. Co., 401 N. Broad St., Philadelphia, PA 19108. M; 1968. +

0961   INFORMES DE LA   (SP)
       CONSTRUCCION
Instituto Eduardo Torrojo de la Construccion y del Cemento, Costillares (Chamartin) Apdo. 19002, Madrid 33, Spain. M; 1948. Indexed: A.P.I., App. Sci. Tech. Ind., B.P.I. (0020-0883) +

0962   INSIDE CONTRACTING   (US)
       (Formerly: Sound Ideas)
Ceilings and Interior Systems Contractors Assn., 1800 Pickwick Ave., Glenview, IL 60025. Ed. Sheila Wertz. Tel. (312) 724-7700. Bi-m; $30; 1957; circ. 6,000. Annual Issues: Dec./Jan.—Buyer's Guide. Notes: adv., bibl., bk. rev., calendars, dwgs., photos (B&W).
   Industry publication that specializes in walls, ceilings, and interior systems in new construction and renovation. Presents case histories, technical information, and product news. Primarily for contractors and manufacturers. (0193-2586) *

0963   INSULATION GUIDE   (US)
Insulation International Corp., 1145 19th St., N.W., Ste. 717, Washington, DC 20036. Box 53132, Temple Heights Station, Washington, DC 20009. Ed. Marylou Humphrey. Tel. (202) 483-2552. 8/yr.; $24; 1983; circ. 15,000. Annual Issues: Midwinter—Directory; Midsummer—Buyer's Guide. Notes: adv., bibl., bk. rev., calendars, dwgs., photos (B&W, color).
   An international magazine of industrial, utility, commercial, and marine insulation. Emphasis is on techniques, procedures, products, standards, evaluations, and management. (0737-2817)

0964   INSULATION OUTLOOK   (US)
National Insulation Contractors Assn., 1025 Vermont Ave., NW., Ste. 410, Washington, DC 20005. Ed. D.M. Lee. Tel. (202) 783-6277. M; $24; 1953; circ. 6,000. Indexed: Dec. issue. Notes: adv., bk. rev., calendars, dwgs., photos (B&W, color).
   Articles focus on energy conservation through the use of the latest technology in industrial and commercial insulation. New projects are featured. Scope is international. *

0965   INTERNATIONAL   (UK)
       CONSTRUCTION
IPC Building and Contract Journals, Ltd., Surrey House, 1 Throwley Way, Sutton Surrey SM1 4QQ, England. Ed. Alan Peterson. Tel. (01) 643-8040. Telex 892084 BISPRS G (SRB).

M; $39; 1962; circ. 31,012. *Indexed*: Compendex, Eng. Ind. *Annual Issues*: March—Tabular Reference Guide to Earthmovers; June—Guide to Roadmaking Machinery; Oct.—Truck Buying Guide. *Notes*: adv., photos (B&W). *Micro*: UMI.

Provides comprehensive coverage of the construction industry worldwide. Features present the latest technological innovations, international trends, and management information. Detailed coverage of new equipment includes tests with reports from end users. Loans, studies, projects, and awards are published to provide business opportunities to the reader. Primary readers are contractors. Circulation is international with a majority of subscribers from Europe. Text in English; summaries in French, German, Italian, and Spanish. (0020-6415) *

0966   JOB/SCOPE   (US)
P.O. Box 208, Bethlehem, CT 06751. Ed. John Carlson. Tel. (203) 266-7224. Bi-m; $12; 1967.

For heating, plumbing, and air-conditioning contractors. (0449-0495) +

**0967   JOURNAL OF   (US)
        CONSTRUCTION
        ENGINEERING AND
        MANAGEMENT**
(Formerly: *Journal of the Construction Division*)
American Society of Civil Engineers, 345 E. 47th St., New York, NY 10017. Ed. Robert Harris. Tel. (212) 644-7505. Q; $42; 1957; circ. 8,500. *Indexed*: Compendex, Eng. Ind. *Notes*: bibl., dwgs., photos (B&W). *Micro*: UMI.

This research journal deserves consideration among architects as well as engineers because of the in-depth analyses given to difficult but common construction or construction management problems. Papers examine building standards, new construction techniques, aspects of contract administration, estimating, etc. The issue examined included timely and informative research papers on computerized specifications. (0733-9364)

**0256   JOURNAL OF DESIGN AND
        CONSTRUCTION**

0968   JOURNEE DU BATIMENT   (FR)
Causee et Cie, 7 rue Dom-Vaissette, Montpellier, France. Ed. Henri Albert. W; 1947. (0022-5630) +

0969   MH/RV BUILDERS NEWS   (US)
Dan Kamrow, P.O. Box 72367, Roselle, IL 60172. Ed. Pat Finn. Tel. (312) 743-4994. Bi-m; $10; 1965; circ. 11,000.

A national tabloid for builders and suppliers of modular and mobile homes. Emphasis is on products. *

**0970   MANUFACTURED HOUSING   (US)
        NEWSLETTER**
Shephard D. Robinson, 410 Grove Ave., Box 1307, Barrington, IL 60010. Bi-w; $60; 1969; circ. 750.

Reports marketing trends and legislative activities that have an impact on the component, panelized, mobile, and modular housing industries. (0197-1816) *

**0971   MANUFACTURED HOUSING   (US)
        REPORTER**
(Formerly: *Mobile Home Reporter*)
Box 786, Kerrville, TX 78028. Ed. Jerre Kneip. Tel. (512) 896-3466. M; $15; 1957; circ. 6,000.

Presents articles related to the manufacture, distribution, installation, and financing of manufactured housing. *

**0972   MASTER BUILDERS'   (UK)
        JOURNAL**
Federation of Master Builders' Trade Press, Ltd., 33 John St., Holborn, London WC1N 2BB, England. Ed. John Hayes. Tel. (01) 242-75893. M; £16; 1956; circ. 20,000. *Indexed*: B.T.I. *Notes*: adv., bk. rev., photos (B&W). *Micro*: UMI.

Provides business, technical, and legislative features for contractors. Of particular interest to members of the British Federation. (0025-4991)

**0973   MEDITERRANEAN   (CY)
        CONSTRUCTION**
P.O. Box 5748, 7th fl., Eagle Star House, Kyr. Matsis, Nicosia, Cyprus. P.O. Box 224, Manama, Bahrain. Ed. Peter Fagan. Tel. (021) 72757. M; $75; 1984; circ. 11,500. *Notes*: adv., bibl., bk. rev., calendars, dwgs., photos (B&W, color).

News and technical coverage of the building and construction industries in the Mediterranean countries. Detailed examinations of materials, products, equipment, and techniques and their performance in the region.

0974   METAL BUILDING REVIEW   (US)
1800 Oakton St., Des Plaines, IL 60018. Circ. Dept., 240 Fend Lane, Hillside, IL 60162. M; $16; 1965; circ. 22,000. *Annual Issues*: Dec.—

Buyer's Guide. *Notes*: adv., bibl., bk. rev., calendars, dwgs., photos (B&W, color). *Micro*: UMI.

Brief articles on the production and construction of metal buildings for commercial, industrial, multistory residential, agricultural, and recreational use. Each issue emphasizes a particular product and includes interviews with executives of construction companies. Primarily for manufacturers and contractors but frequently deals with architect/contractor relationship. (0026-0525)

0975   MIDDLE EAST   (UK)
       CONSTRUCTION
New World Publishers Ltd., Surrey House, 1 Throwley Way, Sutton Surrey, England. Ed. Anthony Davis. Tel. (01) 643-8040. Telex 946564 BISPRS G. M; $130; 1976; circ. 10,400. *Indexed*: A.P.I., Avery, Mid East File. *Notes*: adv., bibl., bk. rev., calendars, dwgs., photos (B&W, color).

A major publication on building design, planning, and construction in the Middle East. Includes interesting features on major issues, news analysis, business statistics, leads and contacts, and a technical file on equipment and products. Circulates to engineers, architects, surveyors, contractors, and senior management personnel engaged in building, civil engineering, and public works. Covers the design, construction, importation, and distribution of plants, equipment, building materials, and components. (0308-0528)

0976   MIDWEST CONTRACTOR   (US)
3170 Mercier, Ste. 202, Kansas City, MO 64141. Ed. Marcia Gruver. Tel. (816) 931-2080. Bi-w; $49; 1901; circ. 8,102. *Annual Issues*: Jan.—Construction Forecast; March—Buyer's Guide. *Notes*: adv., bk. rev., photos (B&W).

Serves the construction and public works industries in Iowa, Kansas, Nebraska, and western/northeastern Missouri. Features bids and awards information; new product reviews; reports on meetings, legislation, and industry news. (0026-3044) *

0381   MULTI-HOUSING NEWS

0977   NATIONAL BUILDER   (UK)
       (Formerly: *The Builder*)
Federated Employers' Press, Ltd., 82 New Cavendish St., London W1M 8AD, England. Ed. David Crawford. M; £20; 1921; circ. 15,000. *Indexed*: A.P.I. *Notes*: adv., bk. rev., calendars, dwgs., photos (B&W, color).

This is the official journal of the Building Employers' Confederation and covers general news of the British construction industry. (0027-8807) *

0259   NEW ENGLAND ARCHITECT
       AND BUILDER
       ILLUSTRATED

0260   NEW ENGLAND
       CONSTRUCTION

0382   NEW SHELTER

0261   NEW YORK CONSTRUCTION
       NEWS

0978   IL NUOVO CORRIERE DEI   (IT)
       COSTRUTTORI
Edilstampa, via Guattani 1, 00161 Rome, Italy. Tel. 8488220. Telex ANCE 613439. W; L.40,000; 1921; circ. 24,000. *Notes*: adv., bk. rev., dwgs., photos (B&W, color).

A journal of economic problems of Italian and European buildings. Text in Italian. *

0383   101 HOME PLANS

0979   OVERSEAS BUILDING   (UK)
       NOTES
Building Research Establishment, Garston, Watford WD2 7JR, England. Ed. W. Kinniburgh. Tel. 0923-67040. Telex 923220. Irreg.; £1 per issue; 1960; circ. 4,500. *Indexed*: A.P.I. *Notes*: dwgs., photos (B&W).

Information on housing and construction in tropical and subtropical countries. Each issue presents technical research on a single topic. Distributed throughout the developing world to a wide range of organizations with a professional interest in building. (0030-7432)

0980   PACIFIC BUILDER AND   (US)
       ENGINEER
Vernon Publications, Inc., 109 W. Mercer St., Seattle, WA 98119. Ed. Douglas Canfield. Tel. (206) 285-2050. Bi-w; $18 (qualified); $44 (others); 1902; circ. 8,900. *Indexed*: Compendex, Eng. Ind. *Annual Issues*: Mid-March—Buyer's Guide; Mid-Oct.—Construction Materials Suppliers Guide.

The authoritative source on the Pacific Northwest construction industry. Edited for management-level personnel in heavy construction or nonresidential building industries. Includes: notice of bid calls, low bidders, contract awards, and unit costs on area projects; cost-cutting construction methods; market analysis; industry news; timber report, legal advice, and management features. (0030-8544) *

0981   PLANS & SPACES   (US)
PPG Industries, Inc., One Gateway Center, Pittsburgh, PA 15??? Q; 197? +

0982   PRACTICAL CIVIL DEFENSE   (UK)
Maidenwell House, Maidenwell Lane, Navenby, Lincolnshire LN5 OED, England. Ed. C. Bruce Sibley. Tel. 0522-810208. Bi-m; $38; 1983. *Indexed*: A.P.I.

This journal is published as a major source of public information on civil defense and has a broad worldwide readership spanning all disciplines, including emergency planning and civil defense. Subscribers include officials, architects, engineers, doctors, strategists, and concerned citizens. Articles cover all aspects of civil defense of interest to the general population, particularly the construction of various types of shelters. Articles describe how to construct one's own shelter, ventilating systems, where to buy shelters, drainage, and heating. Discusses shelter systems worldwide. *

0983   PREFABBRICARE-EDILIZIA   (IT)
**   IN EVOLUZIONE**
A.I.P., Associazione Italiana Prefabbricazione per l'Edilizia, Galleria Passarella 1, 20122 Milan, Italy. +

0984   LA PREFABBRICAZIONE   (IT)
I.T.E.C., via S. dell'Uomo 7, 20129 Milan, Italy. Tel. 74-92-442. M; L.85,000; 1965; circ. 8,000.

A leading publication in Italy on industrialized building. Audience includes architects, builders and manufacturers. Text in Italian; summaries in English. *

0384   PROFESSIONAL BUILDER
**   AND APARTMENT**
**   BUSINESS**

0985   PROFESSIONAL   (US)
**   REMODELING**
Harcourt Brace Jovanovich, Inc., 757 Third Ave., New York, NY 10017. One E. First St., Duluth, MN 55802. Ed. Dan Alaimo. M; 1978. *Micro*: UMI. +

0986   PROGRESSIVE BUILDER   (US)
SolarVision, Inc., Deborah Napior, 7 Church Hill, Harrisville, NH 03450. Tel. (603) 827-3347. Q; 1985.

A magazine on construction techniques that is a supplement to *Solar Age*. +

0987   QUALIFIED REMODELER   (US)
8 S. Michigan Ave., Ste. 1616, Chicago, IL 60603. Ed. Craig Shutt. Tel. (312) 263-4291. M; $30; 1975; circ. 42,000. *Annual Issues*: Sept.—Top 500 U.S. Remodelers; Dec.—Buyers Guide. *Notes*: adv., calendars, dwgs., photos (B&W, color).

Residential remodeling news for contractors and manufacturers. Issues cover new products and applications for installation of windows, roofs, cabinets, security systems, fireplaces, etc. (0098-9207)*

0988   QUEBEC CONSTRUCTION   (CN)
Publication les Affaires, Inc., 465 rue Saint-Jean, Rm. 903, Montreal, Quebec H2Y 3S4, Canada. Ed. Jean Garon. Tel. (514) 842-6491. Telex 055-61971. M; free; 1984; circ. 27,008. *Annual Issues*: Sept.—Quebec's 100 Largest Construction Firms. *Notes*: adv., bibl., calendars, dwgs., photos (B&W, color).

A new tabloid that focuses on Quebec's construction industry. Each issue includes: a profile of a contracting firm; an innovation page that describes a new product or technology that has been developed; an editorial on a noteworthy activity; columns on work safety, the market, legal issues, computer applications, and real estate taxes; a homebuilders section; a report on a major project underway. The publisher also prints a weekly paper by the same name that lists tender notices for the province. Both are in French.

0989   R.S.I./ROOFING, SIDING,   (US)
**   INSULATION**
7500 Old Oak Blvd., Cleveland, OH 44130. Ed. John Karolefski. M; $15; 1945; circ. 18,000. *Notes*: adv., photos (B&W, color). *Micro*: UMI.

Roofing, siding, and insulation news for contractors, architects, and engineers. Articles on solar energy systems and waterproofing are included. (0033-7129)

0990   RAKENNUSTAITO   (FI)
Rakentajain Kustannus Oy, P.O. Box 141, 00101 Helsinki 10, Finland. Ed. Markku Haikala. Bi-w; 1905. (0048-6663) +

0991   RAKENNUSTUOTANTO   (FI)
Suomen Rakennusteollisuusliitto, Federation of the Finnish Building Industry, Unionkatu 14,

00131 Helsinki, Finland. Ed. Simo E. Laine. W; 1966. +

1185   REALTY AND BUILDING

0992   REMODELING   (US)
       CONTRACTOR
(Formerly: *Home Improvement Contractor*)
MacLean Hunter Publishing Corp., 300 W. Adams St., Chicago, IL 60606. Ed. Rob Cuscaden. Tel. (312) 726-2802. M; $20; 1947; circ. 40,000. *Notes*: adv., bk. rev., calendars, dwgs., photos (B&W, color). *Micro*: UMI.

This well-illustrated magazine is edited for the professional remodeling contractor engaged in a variety of exterior and interior projects. Includes product and industry news. Each issue focuses on a different aspect of remodeling, such as kitchens, roofing, or fireplaces. Articles frequently use "before and after" photos to help illustrate the successful techniques discussed. (0146-5996)

0993   RENOVATIONS   (US)
Nolan-Sands Publ., Inc., 10526 Venice Blvd., Culver City, CA 90230. Tel. (213) 202-8600. Bi-m. +

0994   ROOF DESIGN   (US)
7500 Old Oak Blvd., Cleveland, OH 44130. 1 East First St., Duluth, MN 55802. Ed. John Karolefski. Tel. (216) 243-8100. Q; $25; 1983; circ. 25,000. *Notes*: adv., bibl., calendars, dwgs., photos (B&W, color).

New materials, trends, and techniques of roofing are discussed in short, illustrated articles intended for contractors, architects, and specifiers. Commercial, industrial, and residential roofing systems are analyzed by roofing specialists and trade associations. (0747-1092)

0995   ROOFING SPEC   (US)
National Roofing Contractors Assn., 8600 Bryn Mawr Ave., Chicago, IL 60631. Ed. Martin Eastman. Tel. (312) 693-0700. M; $15; 1968; circ. 8,800. *Annual Issues*: July—Member Index. *Notes*: adv., bibl., bk. rev., calendars, dwgs., photos (B&W, color).

Primarily for roofing contractors. Issues contain general news on the industry and information on new products, techniques, publications, codes, and standards. (0199-7742)

0996   SECURITY MANAGEMENT   (US)
       (Formerly: *Industrial Security*)
American Society for Industrial Security, 1655 N. Ft. Meyer Dr., Ste. 1200, Arlington, VA 22209. Ed. Mary Alice Crawford. Tel. (703) 522-5800. M; $27; 1957; circ. 23,000. *Indexed*: CJPI, Mgt. Contents. *Notes*: adv., bibl., bk. rev., calendars, dwgs., photos (B&W, color).

Examines all aspects of protecting organizational assets (people, property, and information) against loss by theft, sabotage, and natural or human-caused disasters. Articles focus on identification of vulnerabilities, protective measures, and management approaches. Includes case studies, opinions, industry news, and product information. The information on hardware, equipment, and consulting services is useful to architects. The articles on computer security are of interest to architectural firms that rely heavily on computer data. (0145-9406)

0385   SELECT HOMES

0386   SMALL HOME PLANS

0997   SOLAR AGE   (US)
SolarVision, Inc., 7 Church Hill, Harrisville, NH 03450. P.O. Box 985, Farmingdale, NY 11737. Ed. William D'Alessandro. Tel. (603) 827-3347. M; $24; 1976; circ. 70,000. *Indexed*: Arch. Ind. *Annual Issues*: July—Agency and Product Directory. *Notes*: adv., bk. rev., dwgs., photos (B&W, color).

This official magazine of the American Solar Energy Society presents information on the design, construction, and installation of commercial and residential solar systems and facilities. Case studies present various uses of solar energy systems in heat storage, insulation, and energy conservation. A good source for identifying new products, patents, and updates on legislation. Recommended for architects, engineers, contractors, research labs, and manufacturers. (0160-8401)

0998   SOLAR ENGINEERING AND   (US)
       CONTRACTING
Business News Publishing Co., P.O. Box 3600, Troy, MI 48007. Ed. Timothy Fausch. Tel. (313) 362-3700. Telex 23-0295. Bi-m; $24; 1976; circ. 16,000. *Indexed*: Nov./Dec. issue. *Annual Issues*: July/Aug.—Buyer's Guide of Energy Manufacturers and Products. *Notes*: adv., bk. rev., calendars, dwgs., photos (B&W, color). *Micro*: BLH, MIM, UMI.

Articles emphasize products, construction trends, regulations, and marketing programs related to solar energy. Readership includes anyone involved in designing, selling, installing, or maintaining solar or other alternative energy systems. (0731-2970)

0999   SOUND AND VIBRATION   (US)
Acoustical Publications, Inc., 27101 E. Oviatt Rd., Box 40416, Bay Village, OH 44140. Ed. Jack Mowry. Tel. (216) 835-0101. M; free to qualified subscribers; 1967; circ. 21,000. *Indexed*: App. Mech. Rev., Compendex, Eng Ind. *Notes*: adv., dwgs., photos (B&W, color). *Micro*: UMI.

Discusses the fields of noise and vibration control, structural analysis, dynamic measurements, dynamic testing, and architectural acoustics. (0038-1810) *

1000   SOUND IDEAS   (US)
Ceilings and Interior Systems Contractors Assn., 1800 Pickwick Ave., Glenview, IL 60025. Ed. Allan Stahl. Tel. (312) 724-7700. M; 1956. (0038-1837) +

1001   SOUTHAM BUILDING GUIDE   (CN)
(Formerly: *Building Guide Magazine*)
280 Yorkland Blvd., Willowdale, Ont. M2J 4Z6, Canada. Ed. David Thompson. Tel. (416) 494-4990. Telex 06-966612. 5/yr.; $29; 1921; circ. 17,000. *Notes*: adv., photos (B&W, color).

A products publication with literature reviews. Published in conjunction with *Daily Commercial News* and the *Journal of Commerce.**

1002   SOUTHEAST ASIA   (SI)
BUILDING MATERIALS AND
EQUIPMENT
150 Cecil St., Wings on Life Bldg., 12th fl., Singapore 0105, Singapore. Ed. Peggy Fong. M; 1974. *Indexed*: A.P.I. +

1141   SPECIFYING ENGINEER

1003   STRUCTURAL SAFETY   (NE)
Elsevier Scientific Publications, P.O. Box 211, 1000 AE Amsterdam, Netherlands. Ed. E.H. Vanmarcke. Q; $78; 1982. *Indexed*: App. Mech. Rev., Compendex, Eng. Ind.

An international journal that presents research on integrated risk assessment for constructed facilities such as buildings, bridges, earth structures, and dams. Aspects of safety considered are loads and environmental influences, soil behavior, material properties, performance criteria, and human error. Publishes case studies and applications. (0167-4730) *

1004   SUN/COAST ARCHITECT   (US)
BUILDER
(Formerly: *Pacific Coast Builder*)
McKellar Publications, 2801 W. 6th St., Ste. 401, Los Angeles, CA 90057. Ed. Thelma Imschweiler. Tel. (213) 384-1261. M; $18; 1982; circ. 43,000. *Notes*: adv., bibl., bk. rev., calendars, dwgs., photos (B&W, color).

A glossy publication with brief articles on current trends in architecture, interior design, and construction in the sun belt area—from Florida and Georgia across to the west coast to Washington. Includes news on the economic climate, marketing concepts, and new products. In addition there are profiles of prominent firms or people in the industry. Covers residential and commercial projects. (0192-1703) *

1005   UNDERLINE   (US)
University of Minnesota, Underground Space Center, 790 Civil and Mineral Engineering Bldg., 500 Pillsbury Dr., S.E., Minneapolis, MN 55455. Ed. Donna Ahrens. Tel. (612) 376-5341. Telex TWX 9105762955. Q; $7; 1979; circ. 1,000. *Notes*: adv., bibl., bk. rev., calendars, dwgs., photos (B&W, color).

Newsletter that reports on the Center's current activities and research on earth sheltered and underground construction. Articles cover construction techniques, legislative topics, cost information, and energy topics. The Center is engaged in disseminating this information to the public in order to optimize the wise use of underground space, both in individual building types and in overall resource planning. (0276-0298)

1006   VYSTAVBA A   (CS)
ARCHITEKTURA
Vyzkumny Ustav Vystavby a Architektury, Letenska 3, 118 00 Prague 1, Czechoslovakia. Vuva 18600, Prague 8, Sokolovska 93, Czechoslovakia. Tel. 539-651-6. Bi-m; Kcs.160; 1954; circ. 1,400. *Indexed*: Avery. *Notes*: adv., bibl., bk. rev., dwgs., photos (B&W).

Technical coverage of building, architecture, environment, and sociology. Text in Czechoslovakian. (0042-9376)

1007   WALKER'S ESTIMATING   (US)
AND CONSTRUCTION
JOURNAL
5030 N. Harlem Ave., Chicago, IL 60656. Ed. Scott Siddens. Tel. (312) 867-7070. Q; $12; 1982; circ. 160,000.

A newspaper that focuses on construction management topics such as estimating, bidding, and job cost-control methods. Features cover computer applications, labor law, construction education, and communications.

1008 WALLS AND CEILINGS (US)
Robert F. Welch, 14006 Ventura Blvd., Sherman Oaks, CA 91423. Ed. Robert Welch. Tel. (818) 789-8733. M; $10; 1938; circ. 11,000. *Indexed*: Jan. issue. *Annual Issues*: Feb.—Economic Forecast; April—Conventions; August—Steel Framing; Nov.—New Products. *Notes*: adv., bk. rev., calendars, dwgs., photos (B&W, color).

New projects featuring unusual wall or ceiling applications are presented for the interest of contractors, architects, and interior designers. Articles cover drywall, acoustics, partitions, steel fireproofing, lathing, and plastering. (0043-0161) *

1009 WEST AFRICAN BUILDER (NR)
       AND ARCHITECT
JMP Services (West Africa) Ltd., P.O. Box 12002, Lagos, Nigeria. Ed. J.B. Lear. Bi-m; 1961. (0043-2970) +

1010 WESTERN BUILDER (US)
Western Builder Publ. Co., 6526 River Parkway, Milwaukee, WI 53213. Ed. John Keyes. Tel. (414) 782-4834. W; 1911. (0043-3535) +

1011 WINDOW INDUSTRIES (UK)
Comprint, Ltd., 177 Hagden Lane, Watford Herts, WD1 8LW, England. Ed. Simon Napper. M; 1975. +

1012 WORLD CONSTRUCTION (US)
Technical Publishing Co., 875 Third Ave., New York, NY 10022. Ed. Ruth Stidger. Tel. (212) 605-9400. M; $46; 1919; circ. 30,500. *Indexed*: Eng. Ind. *Notes*: adv., bk. rev., calendars, dwgs., photos (B&W, color). *Micro*: BLH, UMI.

A journal of construction edited for contractors. Covers automation, products, and techniques. Text in English; summaries in French, German, Spanish, Italian, and Arabic. (0043-8375)

1013 WRAP UP ON LATIN (US)
       AMERICAN
       CONSTRUCTION, HOUSING
       AND REAL ESTATE
Aurora International, Box 668, 6 Wall St., Norwalk, CT 06856. Ed. Andres C. Aquino. Tel. (203) 852-1475. Telex 230199 SWIFT UR AU-

RORA. 11/yr.; $100; 1983. *Indexed*: Dec. issue. *Notes*: bk. rev., calendars.

Arranged by country. Concise information is given on buildings, costs, hotel and office space, housing, investments, land sales, international bids, and trade opportunities for material and machinery. (0741-8566)

Do-It Yourself Construction

1014 CANADIAN WORKSHOP (CN)
Nordais Publications, Ltd., 100 Steelcase Rd. E., Markham, Ont. L3R 1E8, Canada. P.O. Box 8440, Don Mills, Ont. M3C 929, Canada. Ed. Bob Pennycook. Tel. (416) 475-8440. M; $27; 1977; circ. 70,000. *Notes*: adv., bk. rev., dwgs.

A do-it-yourself home magazine on woodworking, renovations, and repairs. (0704-0717) *

1015 DO IT YOURSELF (UK)
Link House Magazines, Link House, Dingwall Ave., Croydon CR9 2TA, England. Ed. Tony Wilkins. M; £4.60; 1957. (0012-4370) +

1016 FAMILY HANDYMAN (US)
Webb Co., 1999 Shepard Rd., St. Paul, MN 55116. 52 Woodhaven Rd., Marion, OH 43302. Ed. Gary Havens. Tel. (612) 690-7534. 10/yr.; $9.95; 1951; circ. 1,300,000. *Notes*: adv., bibl., bk. rev., calendars, dwgs., photos (B&W, color). *Micro*: BLH, UMI.

Articles cover everything pertaining to home maintenance and repairs. Presents step-by-step instructions for do-it-yourself projects. Many illustrations. (0014-7230) *

0369 GARLINGHOUSE HOME
       PLAN GUIDES

1017 THE HOMEOWNER (US)
Family Media, Inc., 3 Park Ave., New York, NY 10016. P.O. Box 2842, Boulder, CO 80322. Ed. James Liston. Tel. (212) 340-9620. 10/yr.; $15; 1974; circ. 650,000. *Notes*: adv., dwgs., photos (B&W, color). *Micro*: UMI.

Covers the full range of home improvement projects in depth, providing readers with step-by-step directions for "doing it themselves." Includes advice on working with professionals. *

0374 HOUSE BEAUTIFUL'S HOME
       REMODELING

0377 LOG HOME &
       ALTERNATIVE HOUSING
       BUILDER

0378   LOG HOME GUIDE FOR
        BUILDERS AND BUYERS

0504   OLD HOUSE JOURNAL

1018   WOODWORKER'S JOURNAL   (US)
Madrigal Publ. Co., Inc., 25 Town View Dr.,
Box 1629, New Milford, CT 06776. Ed. James
McQuillan. Tel. (203) 355-2697. Bi-m; 1977. +

1019   WORKBENCH   (US)
Modern Handcraft, Inc., 4251 Pennsylvania St.,
Kansas City, MO 64111. Ed. Jay Hedden. Tel.
(816) 531-5730. Bi-m; $6; 1946; circ. 860,000. *Indexed*: R.G. *Notes*: adv., bibl., bk. rev., calendars, dwgs., photos (B&W, color). *Micro*: UMI.
    A magazine for the do-it-yourself home-owner. Articles clearly describe how to add rooms and install roofs, windows, shelves, and doors. Woodworking projects range from simple toys to museum furniture reproductions. Includes easy-to-follow instructions. (0043-8057)

Materials, Methods, and Equipment

GENERAL

1020   CONSTRUCTION   (US)
        EQUIPMENT
Cahners Publ. Co., 475 Park Ave. South, New
York, NY 10016. 270 Paul St., Denver, CO.
80206. Ed. Arnold Consdorf. Tel. (212) 686-0555. M; $35; 1949; circ. 90,000. *Notes*: adv., photos (B&W, color).
    Major publication for contractors involved in heavy construction. Covers management, use, and maintenance of heavy equipment. (0192-3978) *

1021   THE CONSULTANT   (US)
Foodservice Consultants Society International,
13227 8th Ave., N.W., Seattle, WA 98177. Ed.
C. Russell Nickel. Tel. (206) 362-7780. Q; $24.
Notes: dwgs., photos (B&W).
    Discusses planning, design, construction, and products of foodservice facilities.

1022   CONTRACTORS'   (US)
        EQUIPMENT GUIDE
P.O. Box 324, Needham Heights, MA 02194.
Ed. John La Camera. Tel. (617) 449-1250. Bi-w;
$30; 1960; circ. 20,000. *Notes*: adv., photos
(B&W, color).
    A newspaper that advertises used equipment and supplies for sale and auction. A companion

publication that reaches Latin America is the
Pan American Trader.

1023   DOORS AND HARDWARE   (US)
Door & Hardware Inst., 7711 Old Springhouse
Rd., McLean, VA 22102-3474. Ed. Richard
Hornaday. Tel. (703) 556-3990. M; $12.50; 1936;
circ. 8,000. *Notes*: adv., photos (B&W, color).
    Covers all aspects of the door and hardware industry including design, installation, manufacture, and distribution. Case studies and general industry news are presented. Of interest to manufacturers, suppliers, contractors, and architects. (0361-5294)

1024   DURABILITY OF BUILDING   (NE)
        MATERIALS
Elsevier Scientific Publishing Co., Box 211,
1000 AE Amsterdam, Netherlands. Ed. P. Sereda. Q; $75.75; 1982. *Indexed*: Chem. Abstr.,
Compendex, Eng. Ind. *Notes*: bk. rev., photos
(B&W).
    Technical journal that reports research on the durability and performance of construction materials, including information on deterioration, design strength, and effects of the environment. Deals with building components such as roofing, walls, cladding, sealants, flooring, coatings, and foundations. (0167-3890) *

1025   EQUIPMENT GUIDE NEWS   (US)
        (Formerly: *Construction Product News*)
Johnson Hill Press, Inc., 1290 Ridder Park Dr.,
San Jose, CA 95131. 1233 Janesville Ave., Ft.
Atkinson, WI 53538. Ed. James Harrah. Tel.
(408) 971-9000. M; free to qualified subscribers;
1966; circ. 58,295. *Notes*: adv., bk. rev., photos
(B&W, color).
    This tabloid gives product news of interest to the construction industry. Features primarily North American products. Circulation is international. (0149-5240)

1026   FASTENER TECHNOLOGY   (US)
        INTERNATIONAL
Huebner Publications, Inc., 6521 Davis Industrial Parkway, Solon, OH 44139. Ed. Frank Akstens. Tel. (216) 248-1125. Telex 980533. Bi-m;
free to qualified subscribers; 1977; circ. 10,000.
Annual Issues: Sept.—Buyer's Guide. *Notes*:
adv., bibl., bk. rev., calendars, dwgs., photos
(B&W, color).
    Presents articles on a full range of topics in the fastener industry, from raw material to machinery to fasteners, distribution, and end-use consideration. (0746-2441) *

1027   FERMETURES   (FR)
       D'AUJOURD'HUI
2 rue Laure Surville, 75015 Paris, France.
8/yr. +

1028   FIRE AND MATERIALS   (UK)
Heyden and Son, Ltd., Spectrum House, Hillview Gardens, London NW4 2JQ, England. Tel.
(01) 203-5171. Telex 28303. Q. *Indexed*: Compendex, Eng. Ind. *Notes*: bibl., dwgs.

   Technical papers on the behavior of all materials in fire in a variety of environments. Studies, hazards, test methods, standards, and
fundamentals are covered. (0308-0501)

1029   FIRE JOURNAL   (US)
National Fire Protection Assn., Batterymarch
Park, Quincy, MA 02269. Ed. Paul E. Teague.
Tel. (617) 770-3000. Bi-m; membership; 1907;
circ. 33,000. *Indexed*: Compendex, Eng. Ind.,
each issue. *Notes*: adv., bk. rev., photos
(B&W). *Micro*: UMI.

   Offers in-depth coverage of association activities and new developments in fire technology.
Discusses codes in detail and analyzes causes
and effects of fires. (0015-2617)

1030   FIRE NEWS   (US)
National Fire Protection Assn., Batterymarch
Park, Quincy, MA 02269. Ed. Paul Sawin. Tel.
(617) 770-3000. 10/yr.; membership; 1916; circ.
33,000. *Notes*: bk. rev., photos (B&W). *Micro*:
UMI.

   A newsletter that reports committee actions
on fire codes and standards. (0015-2625)

1031   FIRE PREVENTION   (UK)
       (Formerly: *F.P.A. Journal*)
Fire Protection Assn., Aldemary House, Queen
St., London EC4N 1TJ, England. Ed. D. Ash-
ford. Bi-m; £12; 1948. *Indexed*: A.P.I. *Micro*:
UMI. (0309-6866) +

1032   FIRE SURVEYOR   (UK)
Victor Green Publications, Ltd., Cavendish
House, 128-134 Cleveland St., London W1P
5DN, England. Ed. J.W. Northey. Tel. (01) 387-
5050. Telex 8811108 1F 5SEC 9. Bi-m; £10.50;
1973; circ. 5,000. *Indexed*: A.P.I. *Notes*: adv.,
bk. rev., dwgs., photos (B&W).

   Covers issues of fire prevention and detec-
tion. *

1033   FIRE TECHNOLOGY   (US)
National Fire Protection Assn., Batterymarch
Park, Quincy, MA 02269. Ed. Gordon Mc-

Kinnon. Tel. (617) 770-3000. Q; $16; 1965; circ.
6,000. *Indexed*: App. Sci. Tech. Ind., Compendex, Eng. Ind. *Notes*: bk. rev., dwgs.

   Technical articles present research on fire
protection and engineering. Includes extensive
references and notes on meetings. (0015-2084)

1034   FOODSERVICE EQUIPMENT   (US)
       SPECIALIST
Cahners Publishing Co., 475 Park Ave. South,
New York, NY 10016. 270 St. Paul St., Denver,
CO 80206. Ed. Robin Ashton. Tel. (212) 686-
0555. M; $35; 1947; circ. 16,500. *Annual Issues*:
Jan.—Annual Forecast and Buyer's Guide;
June—Giants. *Notes*: adv., calendars, dwgs.,
photos (B&W, color).

   This specialty magazine is aimed at those who
manufacture, sell, distribute, and specify foodservice equipment and supplies. Regular features include distributor profiles, kitchen design
case studies, and industry and product news.
(0148-4958) *

1035   FORM & FUNCTION   (US)
U.S. Gypsum Co., 101 S. Wacker Dr., Chicago,
IL 60606. Ed. William Levitt. Tel. (312) 321-
4181. Q; free to qualified subscribers; 1964;
110,000. *Notes*: dwgs., photos (B&W, color).

   An attractive product publication. Features
the various uses of gypsum in construction. A
technical pull-out section is designed for filing.
Of interest to architects, specifications writers,
contractors, and engineers. (0015-7686)

1036   HARDWARE AGE   (US)
Chilton Co., Chilton Way, Radnor, PA 19089.
Ed. Terrence Gallagher. Tel. (215) 964-4270.
Telex 6851035. M; $10; 1855; circ. 71,000. *In-
dexed*: Chem. Abstr. *Annual Issues*: Jan.—
Forecast; Oct.—DIY Selling Guide; Dec.—
Buyer's Guide. *Notes*: adv., bk. rev., calendars,
dwgs., photos (B&W, color). *Micro*: BLH,
UMI.

   Covers the hardware industry with emphasis
on retail and wholesale management, merchandising, market analysis, and new products.
Serves the industry that retails, distributes, and
manufactures hardware, lumber/building materials, and allied lines. (0162-5896) *

1037   INTERNATIONAL FIRE   (UK)
       SECURITY SAFETY NEWS
Victor Green Publications, Ltd., Cavendish
House, 128-134 Cleveland St., London W1P
5DN, England. Q; free; 1975; circ. 70,000.
Notes: adv.

Covers all aspects of fire protection, security, and occupational health.

**1038 JOURNAL OF PROTECTIVE   (US)
        COATINGS AND LININGS**
4400 Fifth Ave., Pittsburgh, PA 15213. Technology Publishing Co., P.O. Box 89, Pittsburgh, PA 15230. Ed. John Keane. Tel. (412) 578-3106. M; $24; 1984. *Notes*: bk. rev., photos (B&W, color).

This technical publication of the Steel Structures Painting Council presents research papers on coatings. Includes articles on techniques, regulations, new products, and association news. Of special interest to specifiers.

1039 LOCKSMITH LEDGER   (US)
Nickerson & Collins Co., 1800 Oakton St., Des Plaines, IL 60018. Ed. William Reed. Tel. (312) 298-6210. M; $28.50; 1939; circ. 20,000. *Indexed*: Jan. issue. *Notes*: adv., dwgs., photos (B&W, color).

Covers the total physical security market. Features describe installation techniques, profile distributors, and present economic/legal issues related to locksmithing. Includes product reviews. Detailed drawings and photographs appear in each article. (0273-625x)

**1040 ORNAMENTAL/   (US)
        MISCELLANEOUS METAL
        FABRICATOR**
National Ornamental & Miscellaneous Metals Assn., 2996 Grandview Ave., N.E., Ste. 109, Atlanta, GA 30305. Tel. (404) 237-5334. Ed. Blanche Blackwell. Bi-m; $50; 1959; circ. 11,000. *Notes*: adv., bk. rev., calendars, dwgs., photos (B&W).

Industry publication for those who design, manufacture, install, and sell ornamental, miscellaneous, and light structural metal products and suppliers of materials, equipment, products, and services. Includes information on doorknobs, handles, gates, etc.

**0658 SCHWEIZERISCHE
        SCHREINERZEITUNG**

SPECIFIC MATERIALS
Concrete and Cement

**1041 AMERICAN CONCRETE   (US)
        INSTITUTE JOURNAL**
American Concrete Inst., P.O. Box 19150, Redford Station, Detroit, MI 48219. Ed. Robert G. Wiedyke. Tel. (313) 532-2600. Telex 810-221-1454. Bi-m; $63; 1929; circ. 17,000. *Indexed*:

App. Sci. Tech. Ind., Compendex, Eng. Ind., March/April issue. *Notes*: photos (B&W). *Micro*: ACI, UMI.

A technical journal reporting concrete technology research by members. Includes abstracts of ACI separate publications, discussions of previously published reports, abstracts of manuscripts in progress, and synopses of articles published in *Concrete International*. (0002-8061)

1042 ARTE Y CEMENTO   (SP)
Zancoeta 9, Bilbao 48013, Spain. Ed. D. Eduardo Gonzalez del Castillo. Tel. (94) 441-07-50. Telex 31013. Q; 1957; circ. 10,500. *Notes*: adv., bibl., bk. rev., calendars, dwgs., photos (B&W, color).

Covers the use of concrete in buildings. Text in Spanish. (0212-8578) *

**1043 BETON HERSTELLUNG UND (GW)
        VERWENDUNG**
P.F. 110-134, 4000 Dusseldorf 11, W. Germany. Ed. Dieter Bausch. Tel. 0211/571068. M; DM.160; 1964. *Indexed*: Compendex, Eng. Ind. *Notes*: adv., bk. rev., dwgs., photos (B&W, color).

Includes some general architecture articles but focuses primarily on concrete construction. (0005-9846)

1044 BETON I ZHELEZOBETON   (UR)
Kalia Evskaja 23A, Moscow 101442 GSP-4, USSR. Victor Kamkin, Inc., 12224 Parklawn Dr., Rockville, MD 20852. Ed. K.V. Mikhailov. Tel. 292-14-34. M; $33.50; 1955; circ. 12. *Indexed*: App. Mech. Rev., Compendex, Eng. Ind. *Notes*: adv., bibl., bk. rev., dwgs., photos (B&W).

Technical journal on concrete construction. Text in Russian; contents page in English, French, and German. (0005-9889)

**1045 BETONWERK UND   (GW)
        FERTIGTEIL TECHNIK
        BAUINGENIEUR**
(Formerly: *Betonstein—Zeitung*)
Bauverlag GmbH, P.O. Box 1460, D-6200 Wiesbaden, W. Germany. Ed. S. Schwarz. Tel. 06121-791-256. Telex 4-186792. M; DM. 234; 1933; circ. 5,300. *Indexed*: Chem. Abstr., Compendex, Eng. Ind.

Trade journal dealing with all aspects of the production and use of precast concrete, the machines used in concrete plants, and the assembly of precast and reinforced concrete members. (0373-4331) *

1046 CEMENT (II)
Manufacturers' Association, Pragati Towers, 13th fl., 26 Rajendra Place, Pusa Rd., New Delhi 110008, India. Ed. P.V. Gunishastri. Q; 1968. *Notes*: bk. rev. (0008-8803) +

1047 CEMENT (NE)
Vereniging Nederlandse Cementindustrie, Sint Teunislaan 1, Postbus 3011, 5203 DA S-Hertogenbosch, Netherlands. M; 1949. *Indexed*: every 5 yrs. (0008-8811) +

1048 CEMENT AND CONCRETE (US)
RESEARCH
Pergamon Press, Maxwell House, Fairview Park, Elmsford, NY 10523. Ed. D.M. Roy. Tel. (914) 592-7700. Bi-m; $160; 1971; circ. 1,500. *Indexed*: App. Mech. Rev., Compendex, Eng. Ind. *Notes*: adv., bk. rev., dwgs., photos (B&W).

Presents papers on cement and concrete research from laboratories throughout the world. The American Concrete Institute is a sponsoring society of this research journal. Text in English, German, French, and Russian. (0008-8846)

1049 CEMENT, CONCRETE AND (US)
AGGREGATES
American Society for Testing Materials, 1916 Race St., Philadelphia, PA 19103. Ed. Prof. Presley Wedding. Tel. (215) 299-5414. S-a; $35; 1979; circ. 800. *Notes*: bibl., bk. rev., dwgs., photos (B&W).

Offers information on new developments in testing and evaluating standardized cement, concrete, and concrete aggregates and admixtures. Includes news of committee activities as well as full-length articles, technical notes, letters, and discussions. Covers new equipment and methods and presents analyses of properties and standards. (0149-6123)

1050 IL CEMENTO (IT)
Associazione Italiana Tecnica Economica del Cemento, via di S. Teresa 23, 00198 Rome, Italy. Ed. Gaetano Bologna. Q; 1903; circ. 2,000. *Indexed*: Oct./Dec. issue. *Notes*: adv., bibl., bk. rev., dwgs., photos (B&W).

A technical publication that presents research on cement. Aimed at an international audience of cement manufacturers, research laboratories, universities, contractors, engineers, and architects. Each issue includes a useful section of article abstracts on perforated cards for filing. Text in Italian and English; summaries in French and German.

1051 CIMENTS, BETON, (FR)
PLATRES, CHAUX
Septima, 14 rue Falguiere, 75015 Paris, France. Ed. D. Lecat. Tel. (1) 273-03-59. Telex 205-916 AGOR. Bi-m; F.525; 1904; circ. 1,550. *Annual Issues*: Buyers Guide. *Notes*: adv., bibl., bk. rev., calendars, dwgs., photos (B&W).

The only French journal dealing with the fabrication and utilization of cement, lime, and plaster. Contains technical research papers. (0397-0006x) *

1052 CONCRETE (UK)
(Formerly: *Concrete and Constructional Engineering*)
Eyre & Spottiswoode Publications, Ltd., 11 Grosvenor Crescent, London SW1X 7EE, England. Ed. R.J. Barfoot. Tel. (01) 245-6767. Telex 8952418 Queens G. M; $60; 1906; circ. 8,818. *Indexed*: A.P.I., Avery, Compendex, Eng. Ind. *Notes*: adv., bibl., bk. rev., calendars, dwgs., photos (B&W, color). *Micro*: UMI.

Covers concrete construction and production, plants, equipment, and other topics of interest to the concrete industry. Aimed at civil engineers, the journal focuses on site features, precast production, block manufacturing processes and techniques, surface finishes, and such aspects as repairs, protection, placing, and special applications. (0010-5317)

1053 CONCRETE (US)
Harcourt Brace Jovanovich, 7500 Old Oak Blvd., Cleveland, OH 44130. Ed. Buren Herod. Tel. (216) 243-8100. M; $12; 1937; circ. 21,000. *Indexed*: Compendex, Eng. Ind. *Micro*: UMI.

Covers important developments in the concrete industries that affect the production and use of ready-mixed concrete, concrete block, and prestressed and precast concrete components. (0279-4705)

1054 CONCRETE ABSTRACTS (US)
American Concrete Inst., Box 19150, 22400 W. Seven Mile Rd., Detroit, MI 48219. Tel. (313) 532-2600. Telex 810-2211454. Bi-m; $110; 1971; circ. 700. *Indexed*: Each issue. *Micro*: ACI.

Summarizes and indexes U.S. and international publications that report developments in concrete technology; over 200 abstracts in each issue. Subjects include design, construction, products, equipment, and performance related to architecture, construction, and structural and civil engineering. Keywords and bibliographic data are included with each abstract. Approximately 250–300 abstracts appear in each issue. Microfiche edition available. (0045-8007)

1055 CONCRETE CONSTRUCTION (US)
Concrete Construction Publications, Inc., 426 S. Westgate, Addison, IL 60101. Ed. Ward Malisch. Tel. (312) 543-0870. M; $12; 1956; circ. 75,000. *Indexed*: Compendex, Eng. Ind. *Annual Issues*: Dec.—Reference Guide. *Notes*: adv., bk. rev., dwgs., photos (B&W, color). *Micro*: UMI.

Techniques of precast and cast-in-place concrete construction are covered. Pages of worthwhile articles are subject coded and perforated for quick filing. Of interest to contractors, architects, engineers, and manufacturers of concrete products. (0010-5333)

**1056 CONCRETE CONSTRUCTION (II)
        AND ARCHITECTURE**
L.K. Pandeya, Block F, 105C, New Alipore, Calcutta 70053, India. M; 1968. (0010-5341) +

**1057 CONCRETE INDUSTRY (US)
        BULLETIN**
Concrete Industry Board, Inc., 95 Madison Ave., New York, NY 10016. 516 Bloomfield Ave., Montclair, NJ 07042. Ed. Tom Hogarty. Tel. (201) 783-2200. Q; free to qualified subscribers; 1961; circ. 1,600. *Notes*: adv., bk. rev., photos (B&W).

Industry news and reports on new construction, primarily in New York City. (0010-535x)

**1058 CONCRETE (US)
        INTERNATIONAL: DESIGN
        AND CONSTRUCTION**
American Concrete Inst., P.O. Box 19150, Detroit, MI 48219. Ed. Robert Wilde. Tel. (313) 532-2600. M; $63; 1979; circ. 17,000. *Indexed*: Compendex, Eng. Ind., Feb. issue. *Annual Issues*: April—Annual ACI Awards; June—Annual Report. *Notes*: adv., bk. rev., dwgs., photos (B&W). *Micro*: ACI.

Contains reports on design construction, products, and materials related to concrete as well as industry news, news of members, and ACI policy changes. Feature articles appear on architectural concrete, projects utilizing concrete techniques, design aids, tests, and management. Emphasis of articles is on practicality and timeliness. (0162-4075)

1059 CONCRETE PIPE NEWS (US)
American Concrete Pipe Assn., 8320 Old Courthouse Rd., Vienna, VA 22180. Ed. John Duffy. Tel. (703) 821-1990. Bi-m; membership; 1949; circ. 14,000. *Notes*: dwgs., photos (B&W).

Covers the installation of concrete pipe. (0045-8015) *

1060 CONCRETE PRODUCTS (US)
MacLean Hunter Publishing Corp., 300 W. Adams St., Chicago, IL 60606. Ed. William J. Blaha. Tel. (312) 726-2802. M; 1903. *Notes*: adv., dwgs. *Micro*: UMI. (0010-5368) +

1061 CONCRETE QUARTERLY (UK)
Cement & Concrete Assn., Wexham Springs, Slough, Bucks SL3 6PL, England. Ed. George Perkin. Tel. (02816) 2727. Telex 848352. Q; £16; 1947. *Indexed*: A.P.I. *Notes*: bk. rev., dwgs. *Micro*: UMI. (0010-5376) +

**1062 INDIAN CONCRETE (II)
        JOURNAL**
Associated Cement Companies, Ltd., Concrete Assn. of India, Cement House, 121 M. Karve Rd., Bombay 400020, India. Ed. T.A.E. D'Sa. M; $24; 1927; circ. 3,800. *Indexed*: Compendex, Eng. Ind. *Notes*: adv., bibl., bk. rev., dwgs., photos (B&W).

Technical papers on concrete engineering. Includes notes on new products and equipment. (0019-4565)

**1063 L'INDUSTRIA ITALIANA (IT)
        DEL CEMENTO**
via S. Teresa 23, 00198 Rome, Italy. Ed. Gaetano Bologna. Tel. 858-505. Telex 611321 AITEC I. M; L.60,000; 1930; circ. 13,500. *Indexed*: Dec. issue. *Notes*: adv., bibl., bk. rev., calendars, dwgs., photos (B&W, color).

A technical review of concrete design and construction projects worldwide. Well illustrated. Text in Italian and English. (0019-7637)

**1064 MAGAZINE OF CONCRETE (UK)
        RESEARCH**
Cement and Concrete Assn., Wexham Springs, Slough SL3 6PL, England. Ed. Edward Brooks. Tel. (02816) 2727. Telex 848352. Q; £28; 1949; circ. 4,500. *Indexed*: B.T.I., Compendex, Eng. Ind. *Notes*: adv., bibl., bk. rev., dwgs., photos (B&W). *Micro*: UMI.

Papers on international concrete research. Includes extensive bibliography in each issue. (0024-9831)

**1065 NEW ZEALAND CONCRETE (NZ)
        CONSTRUCTION**
New Zealand Concrete Research Assn., Private Bag, Porirua, New Zealand. Ed. M.D. Brice. Tel. (04) 328-379. M; N.Z.$46; 1957; circ. 1,350. *Indexed*: Compendex, Eng. Ind., Feb. issue. *Notes*: adv., bibl., bk. rev., calendars, dwgs., photos (B&W).

Current information on concrete design, standards, manufacture, and construction is presented in this practical publication aimed at contractors, architects, engineers, and manufacturers. Articles on new materials, equipment, techniques, and applications are regular features along with other industry news. (0549-0219)

1066 NORDISK BETONG (SW)
Nordiska Betongfoerbundet Fack, 100 44 Stockholm 70, Sweden. Ed. Sten Forsstrom. Tel. (08) 7827473. Bi-m; Kr. 160; 1957; circ. 5,000. *Indexed*: App. Mech. Rev., Chem. Abstr., Compendex, Eng. Ind. *Notes*: adv., bibl., bk. rev., calendars, dwgs., photos (B&W, color).
Covers all aspects of concrete including durability, design, and construction. Text in Swedish, Danish, Norwegian, and English. (0029-1307) *

1067 PCI IDEAS (US)
Prestressed Concrete Inst., 201 N. Wells, Chicago, IL 60606. Ed. Catherine Kielas. Tel. (312) 346-4071. Q; $7; circ. 12,000. *Notes*: adv., dwgs., photos (B&W, color).
A twelve-page, full-color publication that promotes the uses of prestressed and precast concrete in construction. New projects that emphasize the architectural and structural beauty of precast and prestressed concrete are featured.

1068 PIT AND QUARRY (US)
205 W. Wacker Dr., Chicago, IL 60606. 1 E. First St., Duluth, MN 55802. Ed. Buren Herod. Tel. (312) 726-7151. M; $12; 1916; circ. 22,000. *Indexed*: App. Sci. Tech. Ind., Chem. Abstr., Compendex, Eng. Ind. *Annual Issues*: July—Annual Cement Report. *Notes*: photos (B&W, color). *Micro*: UMI.
An industry journal on concrete production and stone quarrying. Includes surveys, forecasts, equipment reviews, and general industry reports. (0032-0293)

1069 WORLD CEMENT (UK)
(Formerly: *World Cement Technology*)
Eyre & Spottiswoode Publications, Ltd., 11 Grosvenor Crescent, London SW1X 7EE, England. Ed. P.V. Maxwell-Cook. Tel. (01) 245-6767. Telex 8952418 Queens G. 10/yr.; $65; 1928; circ. 1,143. *Indexed*: B.T.I., Chem. Abstr., Compendex, Eng. Ind. *Notes*: adv., bibl., calendars, dwgs., photos (B&W, color). *Micro*: UMI.
Covers all aspects of cement production from raw materials stage to final distribution. Scope

is international. Includes news on international projects and contracts. (0263-6050)

1070 ZEMENT-KALK-GIPS (GW)
Bauverlag GmbH, Wittelsbacherstr. 10, Postfach 1460, 6200 Wiesbaden, W. Germany. Ed. Michael Schirmer. Tel. (06121) 139-0. M; DM.395; 1911; circ. 3,000. *Indexed*: App. Mech. Rev., Chem. Abstr., Compendex, Eng. Ind. *Notes*: adv., photos (B&W).
A journal for the cement, lime, and gypsum industries covering research, manufacture, and applications. Text in German; English translations of articles two months prior. (0722-4400)

Glass and Glazing

1071 GLASFORUM (GW)
Verlag Karl Hofmann, Steinwasenstr. 6-8, Postfach 1360, 7060 Schondorf, W. Germany. Bi-m; 1951. *Indexed*: A.P.I. (0017-0852) +

1072 GLASS AGE (UK)
Link House Magazines, Ltd., Link House, Dingwall Ave., Croydon CR9 2TA, England. M; 1958. *Indexed*: B.T.I. *Micro*: UMI. (0017-0992) +

1073 GLASS DIGEST (US)
Ashlee Publishing Co., 310 Madison Ave., New York, NY 10017. G.P.O., Box 1797, New York, NY 10116. Ed. Oscar Glasberg. Tel. (212) 682-7681. Telex 62-480. M; $21; 1922; circ. 9,000. *Annual Issues*: Jan.—Forecast Issue; Dec.—Sealants Issue. *Notes*: adv., bk. rev., photos (B&W). *Micro*: UMI.
Includes design, technical, and management articles on construction glass, stained glass, architectural metal, and allied products. Extensive coverage of products, equipment, and techniques. (0017-1018)

1074 STAINED GLASS (US)
Stained Glass Assn. of America, 1125 Wilmington Ave., St. Louis, MO 03111. Ed. Richard Millard. Q; 1906. *Indexed*: Art Ind., Avery. (0038-9161) +

1075 U.S. GLASS, METAL AND (US)
        GLAZING
U.S. Glass Publications, Inc., 2701 Union Ave. Extension, Ste. 410, Memphis, TN 38112-4479. Ed. Felicia Stott. Tel. (901) 452-6802. Bi-m; $12; 1966; circ. 13,500. *Annual Issues*: Jan./Feb.—Forecast; May/June—Machinery and Equipment Directory; July/August—Sealants and

Glazing Systems; Nov./Dec.—Buyers Guide. *Notes*: adv., bk. rev., dwgs., photos (B&W, color).

A valuable source for information on new products and applications related to glass. Regular columns cover issues on labor, law, management, and stained glass. Primarily edited for the glass/metal dealer, distributor, and manufacturer but articles are also of interest to specifiers and contractors. (0041-7661)

Metals

1076 ACCIAIO   (IT)
Centro Italiano Sviluppo Impeighi Acciaio, Piazza Velasca 8, 20122 Milan, Italy. Tel. 865-840. M; L. 38,000; 1959; circ. 3,500. *Indexed*: Dec. issue. *Notes*: adv., bibl., bk. rev., calendars, dwgs., photos (B&W, color).

Presents the latest technology and current projects using structural steel. International scope. Text in Italian. (0001-4559)

1077 ACIER DANS LE MONDE   (FR)
Office Technique pour l'Utilisation de l'Acier, 5 bis rue Madrid, 75379 Paris, France. Ed. Jacques Mazieres. Tel. 522-83-00. Telex 650392. 3/yr.; free; 1973; circ. 30,000. *Notes*: adv., bibl., bk. rev., calendars, dwgs., photos (B&W, color).

A publication that promotes the various uses of steel, including exterior and interior uses in buildings. Text in French. (0001-4931)

1078 ARCHITECTURAL METALS   (US)
National Assn. of Metal Manufacturers, 221 N. LaSalle, Ste. 2026, Chicago, IL 60601. Ed. James Mruk. Tel. (312) 346-1600. S-a; free; circ. 15,000. *Notes*: adv., bk. rev., dwgs., photos (B&W).

Primarily for architects, this magazine presents design and technical information on metal building products including railings, firedoors, bar gratings, stairs, and flagpoles. Articles are contributed by readers.

1079 BUILDING WITH STEEL   (UK)
Constrado, 12 Addiscombe Rd., Croydon CR9 3JH, England. Ed. M.H. Shepheard. S-a; free in UK; 1969. *Indexed*: A.P.I. (0140-8488) +

1080 COPPER INFORMATION   (SA)
       ARCHITECTURAL SERIES
South African Copper Development Assn., Ltd., Box 61943, Marshalltown, Transvaal 2107, South Africa. Q; free. +

1081 METALS IN CONSTRUCTION   (US)
Iron and Steel Industry Promotion Fund of New York, 211 E. 43rd St., New York, NY 10017. Tel. (212) 697-5553. S-a; 1983. *Notes*: dwgs., photos (B&W, color).

By publishing this glossy magazine, the Fund seeks to foster the greater use of metals in construction. It presents an attractive display of buildings that utilize metal both on the exterior and interior. Articles are well written and detailed.

1082 MODERN STEEL   (US)
       CONSTRUCTION
American Inst. of Steel Construction, Wrigley Bldg., 400 N. Michigan Ave., Chicago, IL 60611. Ed. George Harper. Tel. (312) 670-2400. Q; free to qualified subscribers; 1961. *Indexed*: App. Mech. Rev. *Notes*: adv., dwgs., photos (B&W).

This association magazine presents detailed, illustrated articles on new projects throughout the U.S. that are constructed with steel. Articles are written by professionals in the field. Announcements of important new publications, software, and competitions are included. (0026-8445)

1083 STEEL CONSTRUCTION   (AT)
Australian Inst. of Steel Construction, 110 Alfred St., P.O. Box 434, Milsons Point, NSW 2061, Australia. Ed. G.A. Day. Tel. (Sydney) 929-6666. Q; membership; 1967; circ. 3,200. *Notes*: bibl., dwgs., photos (B&W).

A professional engineering journal devoted to the improvement and advancement of the use of steel in construction. It presents papers on new developments and techniques in steel design and research and the design and construction of new projects. Each issue is based on a single theme and may include many papers by different authors. The scope is primarily Australian. (0049-2205)

Paints and Coatings

1084 AMERICAN PAINT AND   (US)
       COATINGS JOURNAL
(Formerly: *American Paint Journal*)
American Paint Journal Co., 2911 Washington Ave., St. Louis, MO 63103. Ed. Chuck Reitter. Tel. (314) 530-0301. W; $25; 1916; circ. 7,000. *Indexed*: Chem Abstr. *Annual Issues*: Last week of Dec.—Directory of Raw Materials Distribution. *Notes*: adv., bk. rev., calendars, dwgs., photos (B&W, color).

Covers the manufacturing branch of the paints and coatings industry. Contains commentary on conditions affecting the availability and prices of raw materials. (0098-5430)

1085   AMERICAN PAINTING   (US)
        CONTRACTOR
(Formerly: *American Painter and Decorator*)
American Paint Journal Co., 2911 Washington Ave., St. Louis, MO 63103. Ed. Rick Hirsch. Tel. (314) 530-0301. M; $24; 1924; circ. 20,000. *Annual Issues*: Sept.—Tool and Equipment Catalog. *Notes*: adv., bk. rev., calendars, dwgs., photos (B&W).
Covers all aspects of the paint contracting business. Issues include announcements and reviews of new products and equipment. In addition to paint contractors, interior designers and facility managers will find it of interest. (0003-0325) *

1086   DECORATIVE PRODUCTS   (US)
        WORLD
(Formerly: *American Paint and Wallcovering Dealer*)
American Paint Journal Co., 2911 Washington Ave., St. Louis, MO 63103. Ed. Rick Hirsh. Tel. (314) 530-0301. Bi-m; $26; 1980; circ. 31,752. *Annual Issues*: July—Buyers Guide. *Notes*: adv., dwgs., photos (B&W, color).
Covers merchandising of paint, wallcoverings, and decorative products. (0199-4328) *

1087   MODERN PAINT &   (US)
        COATINGS
Communications Channels, Inc., 6255 Barfield Rd., Atlanta, GA 30328. Ed. Barrie Rissman. Tel. (404) 256-9800. M; 1910. *Indexed*: Chem. Abst., Predicasts. *Micro*: UMI. (0098-7786) +

1088   PAINTING & WALLPAPER   (US)
        CONTRACTOR
7223 Lee Highway, Falls Church, VA 22046. Ed. Gerald Wykoff. Tel. (703) 534-1201. M; 1938. (0735-9713) +

Plastics

1089   CANADIAN PLASTICS   (CN)
Southern Communications, Ltd., 1450 Don Mills Rd., Don Mills, Ont. M3B 2X7, Canada. Ed. Judith Nancekiven. Tel. (416) 445-6641. M; Can.$30; 1943. *Indexed*: C.P.I. *Micro*: UMI.
Covers all aspects of the plastics industry in Canada. It is particularly useful to architects,

engineers, and specification writers. (0008-4778) +

1090   MODERN PLASTICS   (US)
McGraw-Hill, 1221 Ave. of the Americas, New York, NY 10020. P.O. Box 430, Hightstown, NJ 08520. Ed. Sidney Gross. Tel. (212) 512-2000. M; $28; 1925; circ. 50,300. *Indexed*: App. Sci. Tech. Ind., Chem. Abstr., Compendex, Eng. Ind. *Annual Issues*: Jan.—Annual Review of Resin Sales; April—Annual Report on Primary Processing Equipment; Sept.—Annual Issue on Chemicals and Additives. *Notes*: adv., photos (B&W, color). *Micro*: UMI.
Covers all aspects of the plastics industry, including research, technology, and design. Contains frequent articles on applications of plastics in building. (0026-8275)

1091   PLASTICS IN BUILDING   (US)
        CONSTRUCTION
Technomic Publishing Co., 851 New Holland Ave., Box 3535, Lancaster, PA 17604. Ed. Richard Dunn. Tel. (717) 291-5609. M; $75; 1976; circ. 200. *Indexed*: Compendex, Eng. Ind. *Notes*: bibl., bk. rev., photos (B&W).
Industry news and technical articles on plastic products and their applications in buildings. (0147-2429) *

Stone, Brick, and Tile

1092   BRICK AND CLAY RECORD   (US)
Cahners Publishing Co., Inc., 475 Park Ave. South, New York, NY 10016. P.O. Box 5624, Denver, CO 80217. Ed. Wayne A. Endicott. Tel. (212) 686-0555. M; $15; 1894; circ. 5,000. *Indexed*: Chem. Abstr., Compendex, Eng. Ind. *Notes*: adv., dwgs., photos (B&W, color).
The main themes in all issues are the manufacturing, marketing, and uses of brick and clay products in construction. Masonry buildings and ceramic applications are occasionally featured. Includes unconventional uses of structural clay products. (0006-9760)

1093   BRICK BULLETIN   (UK)
Ronald Adams Assoc., 10 Elm Close, Hayling Island, Hants PO11 9EF, England. Brick Development Assn., Woodside House, Winkfield Windsor SL4 2DX, England. Ed. Ronald Adams. Tel. 0705-467411. Q; £4; 1947; circ. 35,000. *Indexed*: A.P.I. *Notes*: bibl., bk. rev., dwgs., photos (color).
Presents examples of the use of brick in con-

temporary English building of architectural merit.

**1094 BUILDING STONE   (US)
       MAGAZINE**
Building Stone Inst., 420 Lexington Ave., 28th fl., New York, NY 10170. Ed. Dorothy Kender. Tel. (212) 490-2530. Bi-m; $50; 1977; circ. 12,000. *Notes*: adv, photos (B&W, color).

The various exterior and interior uses and types of stone in construction are covered. Articles feature landscape, residential, and commercial building projects that utilize stone. Industry news and technical notes are included. Of major interest to manufacturers, architects, builders, suppliers, and landscape architects.

1095 CERAMIC INDUSTRY   (US)
Cahners Publishing Co., 475 Park Avenue South, New York, NY 10016. P.O. Box 5624, Denver, CO 80217. Ed. Patricia Janeway. Tel. (212) 686-0555. M; $30; 1923; circ. 7,000. *Indexed*: App. Sci. Tech. Ind., Compendex, Eng. Ind. *Annual Issues*: Jan.—Raw Materials; April —Advanced Ceramics; June—Forecast; Aug. —Giants; Sept.—Data Book; Nov.—Product Showcase; Dec.—International Giants.

The only publication devoted exclusively to the traditional and advanced ceramics fields. Readership consists primarily of plant managers, ceramics engineers, and materials engineers. (0009-0220)

1096 GLAZED EXPRESSIONS   (UK)
Tiles & Architectural Ceramics Society, Ironbridge Gorge Museum, Ironbridge, Telford TF8 7AW, England. 3/yr.; 1981. *Indexed*: A.P.I. (0261-0329) +

1097 INDUSTRIE CERAMIQUE   (FR)
14 rue Falguiere, 75015 Paris, France. Ed. D. Lecat. Tel. (01) 2730359. Telex 205916AGOR. M; F.585; 1947; circ. 2,000. *Annual Issues*: Buyers Guide. *Notes*: adv., bibl., bk. rev., calendars, dwgs., photos (B&W).

Technical journal on the fabrication and utilization of ceramic products, including heavy clays, tile, domestic ware, and technical ceramics. Text in French and English. (0019-9044) *

**1098 JOURNAL OF THE   (US)
       INTERNATIONAL UNION OF
       BRICKLAYERS AND ALLIED
       CRAFTSMEN**
815 15th St., NW, Washington, DC 20005. Ed. Richard Daley. Bi-m; 1897. +

1099 MARMI, GRANITI, PIETRE   (IT)
Via Boccaccio 24, 20123 Milan, Italy. Ed. Ciro Borgonovi. Bi-m; 1959. (0047-603x) +

1100 MASONRY   (US)
Mason Contractors Assn. of America and the Masonry Contractors Assn. of Canada, 17W601 Fourteenth St., Oakbrook Terrace, IL 60181. Ed. Stan Misunas. Tel. (312) 620-6767. 7/yr.; 1961.

Masonry industry news and project articles on various uses of brick, concrete block, stone, granite, and marble in construction. (0025-4681) +

1101 STONE   (US)
Review Publishing Co., 1100 Waterway Blvd., Indianapolis, IN 46202. Ed. David Hall. M; 1888. +

1102 STONE WORLD   (US)
Tradelink Publishing Co., 485 Kinderkamack Rd., Oradell, NJ 07649. Ed. Mike Leach. Tel. (201) 599-0136. M; $28; 1984. *Notes*: adv., photos (B&W, color).

Trade publication aimed at producers and users of granite, marble, limestone, slate, sandstone, onyx, and other natural products. Reports on design, technology, and sources.

1103 TROWEL   (US)
International Union of Bricklayers and Allied Craftsmen, 815 15th St., NW, Washington, DC 20005. Ed. John Joyce. Q; 1982. +

Wood

**1104 A E CONCEPTS IN WOOD   (US)
       DESIGN**
American Wood Preservers Inst., 1651 Old Meadows Rd., Ste. 105, McLean, VA 22102. Ed. Donna Sanders. Bi-m; $7.50; 1975; circ. 60,000. *Indexed*: Avery, Jan./Feb. issue. *Notes*: adv., photos (B&W, color).

Features projects of wood construction. Deals with aesthetics and technical issues. (0099-1716)

**1105 COURRIER DE   (FR)
       L'INDUSTRIEL DU BOIS ET
       DE L'AMEUBLEMENT**
Centre Technique du Bois, 10 Avenue de Saint Mande, 75012 Paris, France. Ed. Pierre Malaval. Tel. (1) 344-06-20. Telex 214-280 F CTBOIS. Q; F.150; 1972; circ. 1,200. *Notes*: bibl., dwgs., photos (B&W).

A publication consisting of technical papers

devoted to wood-related topics, particularly building construction, furniture manufacturing, and preservation. Primarily of interest to engineers. Papers are printed loose in a folder and can be put into research notebooks. Text in French. (0335-5276)

Codes, Standards, and Specifications

**1106   ASTM STANDARDIZATION   (US)
        NEWS**
American Society for Testing and Materials, 1916 Race St., Philadelphia, PA 19103. Tel. (215) 299-5400. Telex 710-670-1037. M; $12.50; 1973; circ. 23,000. *Indexed*: App. Sci. Tech. Ind., Avery, Compendex, Eng. Ind. *Notes*: adv., bk. rev., dwgs., photos (B&W). *Micro*: UMI.

Official publication devoted to testing and standardization of materials, products, systems, and services. Covers news from committees and discussions of new projects. Of interest to specification writers as well as others involved in standards and testing. (0090-1210)

1107   B.S.I. NEWS   (UK)
British Standards Institution, 2 Park St., London W1A 2BS, England. Ed. M. Ladd. M; £8 (nonmembers); 1956. *Indexed*: A.P.I. *Notes*: adv., bibl., illus. (0005-3309) +

**1108   THE BUILDING OFFICIAL   (US)
        AND CODE
        ADMINISTRATOR**
Building Officials and Code Administrators, International, 4051 W. Flossmoor Rd., Country Club Hills, IL 60477. Ed. Clarence Bechtel. Tel. (312) 799-2300. Bi-m; 1967; circ. 4,000. *Indexed*: Compendex, Eng. Ind. *Notes*: adv., bk. rev., calendars, dwgs., photos (B&W).

Presents updates on interpretations and developments in building codes. Covers municipal codes, legislation, construction techniques, and related items. (0007-3547)

1109   BUILDING STANDARDS   (US)
International Conference of Building Officials, 5360 S. Workman Mill Rd., Whittier, CA 90601. Ed. Beverly J. Eicholtz. Tel. (213) 699-0541. Bi-m; $15; 1929; circ. 7,500. *Indexed*: Compendex, Eng. Ind. *Notes*: adv., bibl., bk. rev., calendars, dwgs., photos (B&W).

This official publication of the ICBO publishes revisions and interpretations of the Uniform Building Code, in addition to important articles dealing with technical and administrative topics. Each issue contains a listing of evaluation reports on materials, methods, and types of construction. The scope is international; subscribers include building officials, contractors, architects, and engineers. (0270-1197) *

1110   CODES AND STANDARDS   (US)
Kelly P. Reynolds & Assoc. Inc., 2624 N. Troy St., Chicago, IL 60647. Tel. (312) 486-7142. M; $75; 1980; circ. 1,000.

A digest of recent events in model codes and standards affecting design professionals, code officials, and the industry as a whole. The publishers are fire- and life-safety consultants and plan-review specialists.

1111   CONSTRUCTION SPECIFIER   (US)
601 Madison St., Alexandria, VA 22314. Ed. Jack Reeder. Tel. (703) 684-0300. M; $40; 1950; circ. 11,400. *Indexed*: Avery, Eng. Ind., Dec. issue. *Annual Issues*: Jan.—Membership Directory; Aug.—Catalog Directory. *Notes*: adv., bk. rev., photos (B&W, color).

This official publication of the Construction Specifications Institute presents technical articles on construction practices and technology. Emphasis is on applications rather than design. Of interest to specifiers, engineers, architects, and contractors. (0010-6925)

1112   SOUTHERN BUILDING   (US)
Southern Building Code Pub. Co., Inc., 900 Montclair Rd., Birmingham, AL 35213. Ed. Richard Moore. Tel. (205) 591-1853. Bi-m; $15; 1943; circ. 5,200. *Annual Issues*: June/July—Bluebook of Proposed Standard Code Revisions; Oct./Nov.—Redbook of Code Committee Recommendations. *Notes*: adv., bibl., bk. rev., calendars, dwgs., photos (B&W, color).

Communicates news and technical information relating to building codes, standards, and testing to code administrators, the design professions, and the construction industry. Scope of articles is international but emphasis is on the U.S. Announces revisions to the model code and publishes general industry reports. (0038-3864)

0263   UPDATE

Cost Estimating

**1113   BUILDING ECONOMIST   (AT)
        (Formerly: *Quantity Surveyor*)**
West Publishing Corp. Pty, Ltd., 5 Ashley Gr. Garden, Sydney NSW, Australia. Ed. Stuart Jacobs. Q; Aus.$9; 1962. *Indexed*: A.P.I.; every 3

years. *Notes*: adv., bk. rev., illus. (0007-3431) +

0313   CCAN/CONSTRUCTION
       COMPUTER APPLICATIONS
       NEWSLETTER

0327   CONSTRUCTION
       MANAGEMENT AND
       ECONOMICS

1114   DESIGN COST & DATA   (US)
       (Formerly: *Architectural Design, Cost & Data*)
Quail Ridge Center, Ste. 103, 1200 E. Alosta, Glendora, CA 91740. Ed. Allan Thompson. Tel. (818) 914-2835. 7/yr.; 1958; circ. 20,000. *Indexed*: B.T.I. *Notes*: adv., bk. rev., dwgs., photos (B&W, color). *Micro*: UMI.

Case history approach to building costs. Accumulated data formatted to be saved for future reference. (0739-3946) *

1115   SPON'S ARCHITECTS' AND   (UK)
       BUILDERS' PRICE BOOK
E & FN Spon Ltd., 11 New Fetter Lane, London EC4P 4EE, England. E & FN Spon, North Way, Andover, Hampshire SP10 5BE, England. Ed. Davis, Belfield & Everest. Tel. (01) 583-9855. Telex 263398. A; £20; 1874.

The only detailed source of information on overseas building costs, devoting a large section to European building prices. Includes wage rates and professional services fees. Covers both small building projects and large-scale commercial projects. Updated quarterly. Similar to the U.S.'s annual Dodge and Means cost books. (0303-3046) *

1007   WALKER'S ESTIMATING
       AND CONSTRUCTION
       JOURNAL

Building Services and Systems

1116 ASHRAE JOURNAL (US)
American Society of Heating, Refrigeration and Air Conditioning Engineers, 1791 Tullie Circle NE, Atlanta, GA 30329. Ed. Victor Petchul. Tel. (404) 636-8400. M; $30; 1959; circ. 50,000. *Indexed*: App. Sci. Tech. Ind., Compendex, Eng. Ind. *Notes*: adv., bibl., bk. rev., calendars, dwgs., photos (B&W, color).

A professional journal providing state-of-the-art information on heating, refrigeration, and air conditioning. Read primarily by engineers and mechanical contractors but also by architects and specifiers. (0001-2491)

1117 AIR CONDITIONING, (US)
HEATING AND
REFRIGERATION NEWS
Business News Pub. Co., P.O. Box 2600, Troy, MI 48007. Ed. Gordon Duffy. Tel. (313) 362-3700. Telex 311782. W; $41; 1926; circ. 26,622. *Indexed*: B.P.I., first issue in January. *Annual Issues*: first week in Jan.—Manufacturing Directory; first week in April—Statistical Panorama. *Notes*: adv., bk. rev., dwgs., calendars, photos (B&W).

A tabloid covering new developments in the residential, commercial, and industrial indoor comfort and refrigeration industries. Feature articles focus on research and development and project applications. Primary interests are in system design, installation, energy conservation, health and safety, service, business management, law, labor, and education as they relate to the mechanical systems. (0002-2276)

1118 BUILDING OPERATING (US)
MANAGEMENT
Trade Press Pub. Co., 2100 W. Florist Ave., Box 694, Milwaukee, WI 53201. Ed. Jack Pomrening. Tel. (414) 228-7701. M; 1954; circ. 65,000. *Notes*: adv., bk. rev., photos (B&W, color). *Micro*: UMI.

Building operating management, maintenance, and remodeling of commercial, industrial, institutional, and educational buildings are covered. Each month features a different theme such as life safety, lighting, energy management, or construction. Of interest to building managers, developers, contractors, architects, and engineers. (0007-3490)

1119 BUILDING SERVICES (UK)
ENGINEERING RESEARCH
AND TECHNOLOGY
Chartered Institution of Building Services, Delta House, 222 Balham High Rd., London SW1 9BS, England. Ed. Henry Swinburne. Tel. (01) 675-5211. Q; £38; 1980. *Indexed*: Sci. Abstr., fourth-quarter issue. *Notes*: bk. rev., dwgs., photos (B&W). *Micro*: UMI.

A high-technology quarterly covering energy use and the environment in buildings. Each issue contains technical research papers that discuss heating, ventilation, air conditioning, electrical services, fire protection, elevators, telecommunications, and management. Primarily for mechanical engineers and researchers involved with building systems. (0143-6244) *

0921 BUILDINGS

1120 CONTRACTING BUSINESS   (US)
(Formerly: *Air-conditioning & Refrigeration Business*)
Penton/IPC, Inc., 1111 Chester Ave., Cleveland, OH 44114. Ed. Jeff Forker. Tel. (216) 579-6333. M; 1944. *Micro*: UMI.

Reports on new products and methods of mechanical systems contracting. (0279-4071) +

1121 DOMESTIC ENGINEERING   (US)
Construction Industry Press, 135 Addison Ave., Elmhurst, IL 60123. Ed. Stephen Shafer. Tel. (312) 530-6161. M.

New products, installations methods, and management of mechanical systems are reviewed for plumbing and mechanical contractors. +

**1122 ELECTRIC COMFORT   (US)
      CONDITIONING NEWS**
Electrical Information Publications, Inc., 2132 Fordem Ave., Madison, WI 53704. Ed. Shirley Baumann. Tel. (608) 244-3528. M; $20; 1957. *Notes*: adv., photos (B&W).

A national magazine for the electric heating industry. Includes new technology, materials, and maintenance for residential, commercial, and institutional buildings. Information on HVAC and lighting design and case studies are featured. +

**1123 ELECTRICAL CONSULTANT (US)
      MAGAZINE**
Cleworth Pub. Co., 1 River Rd., Cos Cob, CT 06807. Ed. Robert Morgan. Tel. (203) 661-5000. Bi-m; $12; 1920; circ. 20,000. *Notes*: adv., dwgs., photos (B&W, color). *Micro*: UMI.

Covers electrical design and specification of electrical equipment for commercial, institutional, and industrial projects. Articles focus on new techniques and equipment. (0361-4972) *

1124 ENERGY AND BUILDINGS   (SZ)
Alan Meier, Bldg. 90H, Lawrence Berkeley Laboratory, Univ. of California, Berkeley, CA 94720. Elsevier Science Pub., 52 Vanderbilt Ave., New York, NY 10017. Ed. Alan Meier. Tel. (415) 486-4740. Q; $119; 1977; circ. 490. *Indexed*: A.P.I., App. Mech. Rev., Energy Ind., S.S.C.I. *Notes*: adv., bibl., bk. rev., calendars, dwgs., photos (B&W).

An international journal that presents the results of research activities on topics that can improve energy efficiency in the built environment. Papers discuss thermal properties of building materials, solar energy design, innovative environmental control systems, cost/benefit analyses of new energy-efficient options, and social influences on energy consumption behavior. Aimed at a technical audience. (0378-7788)

1125 ENERGY ENGINEERING   (US)
Fairmont Press, Box 14227, Atlanta, GA 30324. Ed. Richard Koral. Tel. (404) 447-5314. Bi-m; $44; 1904. *Indexed*: App. Sci. Tech. Ind., Eng. Ind. *Notes*: photos. *Micro*: UMI.

A professional publication emphasizing energy management systems and new energy resources for building systems design. Of interest to energy engineers and researchers, plant engineers, and architects. (0199-8595) +

**1126 ENERGY MANAGEMENT   (US)
      TECHNOLOGY**
Walker-Davis Pub., Inc., 2500 Office Center, Willow Grove, PA 19090. Ed. Frank McGill. Tel. (215) 657-3203. 9/yr.; $36; 1977; circ. 47,000. *Notes*: adv., bk. rev., dwgs., photos (B&W, color). *Micro*: BLH.

Technical magazine focusing on new technologies in energy conservation systems in industrial, commercial, and institutional establishments. Primarily for energy managers. *

1127 ENERGY REVIEW   (US)
Environmental Studies Inst. of the International Academy of Santa Barbara, 2060 Alameda Padre Serre, Stes. 105/106, Santa Barbara, CA 93103. Ed. Susan Williams. Tel. (805) 965-5010. Bi-m; $170; 1957; circ. 1,000. *Indexed*: Dec. issue. *Notes*: bk. rev., dwgs.

Contains digests of approximately 1,000 articles, books, and reports on all facets of energy, selected from the technical and general press. (0094-8063) *

1128 ENERGY USER NEWS   (US)
Fairchild Pub., Inc., 7 E. 12th St., New York, NY 10003. Ed. Robert Butler. Tel. (212) 741-4428. W; $49; 1976; circ. 16,000. *Notes*: adv., photos (B&W).

Tabloid of news briefs and in-depth features on energy topics emphasizing conservation and management. Focuses on successes and failures in industry. (0162-9131)

1129 ENGINEERED SYSTEMS   (US)
7314 Hart St., Mentor, OH 04406. Donna Olah, P.O. Box 2600, Troy, MI 48007. Ed. Robert Schwed. Tel. (216) 255-6264. Bi-m; $24; 1985; circ. 37,000. *Notes*: adv., bibl., bk. rev., calendars, dwgs., photos (B&W, color).

Aimed at commercial-industrial-institutional HVAC/R specifiers and buyers. Some of the topics covered are cogeneration, computer applications, HVAC system retrofits, corrosion, construction management, intelligent buildings, alternative energy design, and indoor air quality. Subscribers include consulting engineers, contractors, building owners, and operating personnel.

1130 ENGINEER'S DIGEST   (US)
Walker-Davis Pub., Inc., 2500 Office Center, Willow Grove, PA 19090. Ed. Anita Brazill. Tel. (215) 657-3203. M; 1973; circ. 110,500. *Notes*: adv., bibl., bk. rev., calendars, dwgs., photos (B&W, color). *Micro*: UMI.

Covers new products, new industrial plant design, and industrial plant maintenance. Emphasis is on high-tech and energy topics. Articles are written in a "how-to" style. (0192-1290)

1131 ENVIRONMENT SYSTEMS   (CN)
     AND INDUSTRIES
Wadham Publications, 109 Vanderhoof Ave., Ste. 101, Toronto, Ont. M4G 2J2, Canada. Ed. Kenneth Gould. Tel. (416) 425-9021. M; Can.$8; 1969. (0705-9272) +

1132 G A   (GW)
Karl Kraemer Verlag, Schulze-Delitzsch Str. 15, 7000 Stuttgart 80, W. Germany. Ed. Karl Horst. Tel. (0711) 620893. Bi-m; DM. 30; 1963; circ. 19,000.

Journal on the use of gas in architecture. Text in German. (0016-3406) *

1133 HEATING AND   (UK)
     VENTILATING ENGINEER
Technitrade Journal Ltd., Penn House, Penn Place, Rickmansworth, Hertfordshire WD3 1SN, England. Ed. Norman Shepherd. Tel. (0923) 777000. Telex 888095. M; £33; 1927; circ. 6,000. *Indexed*: A.P.I., B.T.I., Compendex, Eng. Ind. *Notes*: adv., bk. rev., dwgs.

A journal of the environmental sciences. Articles cover systems applications for heating, ventilating, air conditioning, and energy.

1134 HEATING, PIPING AND AIR   (US)
     CONDITIONING
Reinhold Pub. Div., 600 Summer St., Stamford, CT 06904. Penton Plaza, 1111 Chester Ave., Cleveland, OH 44114. Ed. Robert Korte. Tel. (312) 861-0880. M; $35; 1929; circ. 45,000. *Indexed*: App. Sci. Tech. Ind., Compendex, Eng. Ind., June issue. *Annual Issues*: Jan.—Market Forecast; June—Directory Issue; Sept.—Econ-

omies of Energy Management. *Notes*: adv., bk. rev., dwgs., photos (B&W). *Micro*: UMI.

Covers mechanical systems for nonresidential buildings. Case studies on design, installation, modernization, and maintenance are presented primarily for engineers and contractors. (0017-940x)

1135 HEATING, PLUMBING, AIR   (CN)
     CONDITIONING
Southam Pub. Ltd., 1450 Don Mills Rd., Don Mills, Ont. M3B 2X7, Canada. Ed. Ronald Shuker. Tel. (416) 445-6641. M; $41; 1923; circ. 14,600. *Annual Issues*: Aug.—Buyers Guide to Manufacturers and Products. *Notes*: adv., bk. rev., dwgs., photos (B&W, color).

A tabloid for professionals who design, install, and service mechanical systems. Articles appear on new technology and new products. Emphasis is on management topics. (0017-9418) *

1136 INTERNATIONAL JOURNAL   (UK)
     OF AMBIENT ENERGY
17 W. Mead, London SW15 5BH, England. Ambient Press, Ltd., Hornby, Lancaster LA2 81B, England. Ed. A.F.C. Sherratt. Tel. (01) 788-5337. W; $115; 1980. *Indexed*: A.P.I. *Notes*: adv., bk. rev., dwgs., photos (B&W).

A research journal of case studies and original papers on new technology and practical applications of ambient energy. Special attention is given to application of ambient energy in environmental control in buildings. Articles cover solar, wind, tidal, wave, and geothermal energy. (0143-0750) *

1137 IRISH HEATING AND   (IE)
     VENTILATING NEWS
517 Main St., Blackrock Co., Dublin, Ireland. Ed. Patrick Lehane. Tel. 885001. Telex 92258. M; £18; 1961; circ. 2,600. *Notes*: adv., bk. rev., calendars, dwgs., photos (B&W, color).

Provides coverage of the heating, ventilating, air conditioning, refrigeration, plumbing, and environmental control industries in Ireland. Readers are primarily contractors and building officials. *

1138 PASSIVE SOLAR NEWS   (US)
1414 Prince St., Alexandria, VA 22314. Ed. Elena Marcheso. Tel. (703) 683-5003. M; $9.95; 1980. *Notes*: bk. rev., dwgs., photos (B&W).

Covers passive solar energy conservation and construction. *

1139   PLANT MANAGEMENT AND   (CN)
       ENGINEERING

MacLean-Hunter, Ltd., 777 Bay St., Toronto, Ont. M5W 1A7, Canada. Ed. Ron Richardson. Tel. (416) 596-5801. M; $32; 1941; circ. 25,500. *Indexed*: C.P.I. *Notes*: adv., bk. rev., dwgs., photos (B&W, color). *Micro*: UMI.

Canadian case studies present problems and solutions in areas of plant layout, energy management, plant safety, materials handling, and environmental control. (0315-9183) *

1140   REFRIGERATION SERVICE   (US)
       AND CONTRACTING

Nickerson & Collins, Inc., 1800 Oakton St., Des Plaines, IL 60018. Ed. Steve Reed. Tel. (312) 298-6210. M; 1933.

A technical magazine for distributors, engineers, and contractors involved in the refrigeration, air conditioning, and heating industries. Information is given on refrigeration and environmental control systems in commercial, institutional, residential, and industrial facilities. (0034-3145) +

0356   SKYLINES

1141   SPECIFYING ENGINEER   (US)

1350 E. Touhy Ave., P.O. Box 5080, Des Plaines, IL 60018. Cahners Pub. Co., 270 St. Paul St., Denver, CO 80206. Ed. Robert Oliverson. Tel. (312) 635-8800. 13/yr.; $35; 1958; circ. 40,095. *Indexed*: Jan. issue. *Annual Issues*: Sept.—M/E Products Guide. *Notes*: adv., bk. rev., calendars, dwgs., photos (B&W, color).

A major magazine for mechanical/electrical systems design and operation in commercial and institutional buildings. Includes articles on life-safety systems, energy retrofitting, codes and standards, and computer applications. It serves engineers engaged in design, specification, and product selection. Since 1979 it has received many editorial awards. (0164-5242)

1142   WESTERN HVAC NEWS   (US)

Sam Jaffe, 3055 Overland Ave., Los Angeles, CA 90034. Tel. (213) 202-7775. M; 1981. +

Engineering

1143 AMERICAN CERAMIC (US)
SOCIETY BULLETIN
American Ceramic Society, 65 Ceramic Dr., Columbus, OH 43214. Ed. Donald Snyder. Tel. (614) 268-8645. M; $12.50; 1922; circ. 11,421. *Indexed*: Ceram. Abst., Chem. Abst. *Annual Issues*: Jan.—Directory Issue. *Notes*: adv., bibl., bk. rev., dwgs., photos (B&W). *Micro*: UMI.
Articles on applied ceramic research and engineering. (0002-7812) *

1041 AMERICAN CONCRETE
INSTITUTE JOURNAL

0899 BATIMENT
INTERNATIONAL/BUILDING
RESEARCH

1144 BAUINGENIEUR (GW)
Technische Universitat, Braunschweig, Institut fur Stahlbau, Beethovenstrasse 51, D-3300 Braunschweig, W. Germany. Springer-Verlag, Kurfurstendamm 237, D-1000 Berlin, W. Germany. Ed. J. Scheer. M; $97; 1920. *Indexed*: Compendex, Eng. Ind. *Notes*: adv., photos (B&W). *Micro*: MIM.
Structural engineering journal. Text in German. (0005-6650)

1145 BAUPLANUNG-BAUTECHNIK (GE)
V E B Verlag fuer Bauwesen, Franzoesische Str. 13/14, 1086 Berlin, E. Germany. Ed. Hans Wendt. Tel. 20410. Telex 11-22-29 Trave. M; 1947. *Indexed*: Compendex, Eng. Ind. *Notes*: bk. rev., dwgs., photos (B&W).

Technical articles for the building engineer. Includes product reviews. Text in German; table of contents in English and Russian. (0005-6758)

1146 BAUTECHNIK AUSGABE A (GW)
Wilhelm Ernst und Sohn, Hohenzollerndamm 170, 1000 Berlin, W. Germany. Ed. R. von Halasz. Tel. 030/8600030. Telex 184-143 ernst d. M; DM.192; 1923; circ. 8,000. *Indexed*: Compendex, Eng. Ind. *Notes*: adv., bibl., bk. rev., dwgs., photos (B&W).
A technical journal that covers engineering topics of concern to large-scale industrial and public works projects. Includes product reviews. Text in German. (0341-1052)

1044 BETON I ZHELEZOBETON

1147 BETON UND (GW)
STAHLBETONBAU
Huebschstr. 21, D-7500 Karlsruhe 1, W. Germany. Wilhelm Ernst und Sohn, Hohenzollerndamm 190, 1000 Berlin 31, W. Germany. Ed. Dr. Klaus Stiglat. Tel. (0721) 813038. M; DM.180; 1902; circ. 10,600. *Indexed*: App. Mech. Rev., Chem. Abstr., Compendex, Eng. Ind. *Notes*: adv., bibl., bk. rev., calendars, dwgs., photos (B&W).
The oldest German professional journal dedicated to problems of concrete construction. Publishes engineering research reports on the design, calculation, dimensioning, and execution of concrete, reinforced, and prestressed concrete structures. Includes reports on exhibitions, trends, and equipment. Text in German; summaries in German and English. (0005-9900)

1148 C.O.D.I.A.   (DR)
Colegio Dominicano de Ingenieros, Arquitectos y Agrimensores, Calle Fantino Falco, Jose Ortega y Gasset, Apdo. Postal 1514, Santo Domingo, Dominican Republic. Bi-m; 1967. *Indexed*: A.P.I. *Notes*: adv., illus. (0045-7310) +

1149 CANADIAN CONSULTING   (CN)
       ENGINEER
Southern Communications, Ltd., 1450 Don Mills Rd., Don Mills, Ont. M3B 2X7, Canada. Ed. Jack Chisuin. Tel. (416) 445-6641. M; Can.$40; 1959. *Notes*: photos (B&W, color). *Micro*: UMI.
   Professional publication for engineers in architectural practice and in consulting engineering. Articles cover management issues, new design, and association news. (0008-3267) +

1150 CANADIAN JOURNAL OF   (CN)
       CIVIL ENGINEERING
National Research Council of Canada, Ottawa, Ont. K1A OR6, Canada. Ed. R.A. Dorton. Tel. (416) 248-3516. Q; $50; 1974; circ. 5,100. *Indexed*: Compendex, Eng. Ind., S.S.C.I., Dec. issue. *Notes*: bk. rev., dwgs., photos (B&W). *Micro:* UMI.
   Publishes original research papers in structural engineering, hydrotechnical engineering, transportation and urban planning, environmental and sanitary engineering, and construction. Text in French or English. (0315-1468) *

1151 CIVIL ENGINEERING   (UK)
   (Formerly: *Civil Engineering and Public Works Review*)
Morgan-Grampian, Ltd., 30 Calderwood St., Woolwich, London SE18 6QH, England. Ed. Phil Abbott. Tel. (01) 885-7777. M; 1906; circ. 13,000. *Indexed*: B.T.I., Compendex, Eng. Ind. *Notes*: adv., bk. rev., dwgs., photos (B&W).
   Articles cover concrete and steel construction worldwide, with an emphasis on public works. (0305-6473)

1152 CIVIL ENGINEERING ASCE   (US)
American Society of Civil Engineers, 345 E. 47th St., New York, NY 10017. Ed. Virginia Fairweather. Tel. (212) 705-7463. M; $42; 1930; circ. 92,000. *Indexed*: App. Mech. Rev., App. Sci. Tech. Ind., Chem. Abstr., Compendex, Eng. Ind., Dec. issue. *Annual Issues*: July—Civil Engineering Awards; Sept.—Infrastructure. *Notes*: adv., bk. rev., calendars, dwgs., photos (B&W, color). *Micro:* UMI.
   Professional journal covering significant projects and issues of interest to civil engineers.

Topics include geotechnical, environmental, structural, and transportation engineering, water resources, and standards. Features articles on professional practice. (0360-0556)

1052 CONCRETE

1054 CONCRETE ABSTRACTS

1153 CONSTRUCTII   (RM)
Institutul Central de Cercetare Proiectare si Directivare in Constructii. SOS. Pantelimon 266, Of. Postal 24, Bucharest, Rumania. Ed. Ecaterina Stamate. Tel. 274085/176. M. *Indexed*: Compendex, Eng. Ind. *Notes*: bibl., bk. rev., photos (B&W).
   Technical papers on structures, energy, and strength and durability of materials. Text in Rumanian; table of contents in English and Russian.

1154 CONSULTING ENGINEER   (US)
Technical Publishing Co., 1301 S. Grove Ave., P.O. Box 1030, Barrington, IL 60010. Ed. Jane Edmunds. Tel. (312) 381-1840. Telex 910 651 1924. M; $35; 1952; circ. 49,000. *Indexed*: Compendex, Eng. Ind. *Notes*: adv., bk. rev., dwgs., photos (B&W, color). *Micro*: UMI.
   Articles focus on all aspects of the consulting engineering profession including business forecasts, design concepts, and association activities. Monthly departments on taxes, economics, contract documents, computers, marketing, and legal matters. (0010-7107)

0943 CONTRACTOR ENGINEER

1155 ENGINEERING JOURNAL   (CN)
Engineering Inst. of Canada, 2050 Mansfield St., Montreal H3A 1Z2, Canada. Ed. Marta Meana. Tel. (514) 842-8121. Bi-m; Can.$14; 1918; circ. 19,000. *Indexed*: App. Sci. Tech. Ind., Compendex, Eng. Ind. *Notes*: adv., bk. rev., dwgs. *Micro*: UMI.
   Text in English and French. (0013-8010) *

1156 ENGINEERING JOURNAL   (US)
American Inst. of Steel Construction, 400 N. Michigan Ave., Chicago, IL 60611. Ed. George E. Harper. Tel. (312) 670-2400. Q; $8; 1964; circ. 8,000. *Indexed*: Compendex, Eng. Ind., first-quarter issue. *Notes*: dwgs. *Micro*: UMI.
   Technical articles on steel design, research, design and/or construction of new projects, steel fabrication methods, and new products of significance to the user of steel in construction. (0013-8029)

0951   ENGINEERING-NEWS
       RECORD

1157   FOUNDATION FACTS   (US)
Raymond International, Inc., P.O. Box 22718,
Houston, TX 77027. Tel. (713) 623-1446. Irreg.;
1965.
   Case histories of design and installation of
deep foundations and related heavy construction, with an emphasis on piling. +

1158   HERON   (NE)
Technische Hogeschool te Delft, Dept. of Civil
Engineering, Stevin Lab., c/o G.J. Alphen, Box
5048, 2600 GA Delft, Netherlands. Ed. J. Wit-
teveen. Tel. 0031-15-785919. Telex 38070
BITHD. Q; free to qualified subscribers; 1970;
circ. 2,000. Indexed: App. Mech. Rev., Compendex, Eng. Ind. Notes: bibl., dwgs., photos
(B&W).
   Technical research papers on structural and
civil engineering. Deals primarily with concrete.
(0046-7316)

0462   HIGHWAY AND HEAVY
       CONSTRUCTION

0122   INDIAN ARCHITECT

1062   INDIAN CONCRETE
       JOURNAL

1063   L'INDUSTRIA ITALIANA
       DEL CEMENTO

1159   INGEGNERI ARCHITETTI   (IT)
       CONSTRUTTORI
Associazione Ingegneri della Provincia di Bologna, Strada Maggiore 13, Bologna, Italy. M;
1974. +

1160   INSTITUTION OF CIVIL   (UK)
       ENGINEERS: PROCEEDINGS
       —DESIGN AND
       CONSTRUCTION
P.O. Box 101, 26-34 Old St., London EC1P 1JH,
England. Thomas Telford, Ltd., Publications
Div., 1-7 Great George St., Westminster, London SW1P 3AA, England. Ed. Ann Thompson.
Tel. 253-9999. Telex 298105 CIVILS G. 10/yr.;
£94; 1972; circ. 22,250. Indexed: B.T.I., Compendex, Eng. Ind. Notes: bk. rev., dwgs., photos (B&W).
   Journal of the planning and construction of
civil engineering projects. (0307-8353) *

1161   INTERNATIONAL ASSN.   (SP)
       FOR SHELL AND SPATIAL
       STRUCTURES—BULLETIN
I.A.S.S. Secretariat, Alfonso XII, no. 3, Madrid
7, Spain. Q; Fr.60; 1959. Indexed: Compendex,
Eng. Ind. Notes: dwgs., photos (B&W).
   Technical papers on the design, analysis, and
construction techniques of spatial structures in
general and of shell structures in particular.
(0304-3622)

1162   JOURNAL OF BUILDING   (CC)
       STRUCTURES
China Publications Centre, Chegongzhuang Xilu
21, P.O. Box 339, Beijing, China. Bi-m; 1979.
Indexed: Compendex, Eng. Ind.
   Technical papers on structures. Text in
Chinese; table of contents and summaries in En-
glish.

1163   JOURNAL OF STRUCTURAL   (US)
       ENGINEERING
   (Formerly: Amer. Soc. of Civil Eng. Structural Div. Journal)
American Society of Civil Engineers—Stuctural
Division, 345 E. 47th St., New York, NY 10017-
2398. Ed. Donald McDonald. M; $31.50; 1956;
circ. 9,000. Indexed: App. Sci. Tech. Ind., Compendex, Eng. Ind. Notes: dwgs. Micro: UMI.
   Presents technical research papers on structural engineering. Includes discussions of previously published papers and proceedings.
(0733-9445) *

1164   JOURNAL OF STRUCTURAL   (US)
       MECHANICS
Marcel Dekker Journals, 270 Madison Ave.,
New York, NY 10016. Box 11305, Church St.
Station, New York, NY 10049. Ed. E. Haug.
Tel. (212) 696-9000. Q; $195; 1972. Indexed:
App. Mech. Rev., Compendex, Eng. Ind.
S.S.C.I.
   Devoted to structural mechanics. Emphasizes
contemporary research of applications to civil,
automotive, marine, aerospace, machine, and
related structures. (0360-1218)

1165   JOURNAL OF TECHNICAL   (US)
       TOPICS IN CIVIL
       ENGINEERING
American Society of Civil Engineers, 345 E.
47th St., New York, NY 10017. Ed. Paul Keil-
stadt. Tel. (212) 705-7517. Irreg.; $9.50. In-
dexed: Compendex, Eng. Ind.
   Technical research papers on topics in civil
engineering. Includes discussions of previously
published papers or proceedings. (0733-9461)

0131 LATENT IMAGES

1166 NEW CIVIL ENGINEER (UK)
Thomas Telford, Ltd., Publications Div., 26 Old
St., London EC1P 1JH, England. Ed. Hugh
Ferguson. Tel. (01) 259-9999. Telex 298105 CIV-
ILS G. W; £80; 1972; circ. 55,000. *Notes*: adv.,
bk. rev., dwgs., photos (B&W, color).
Construction of civil engineering projects.
(0307-7683) *

1167 NEW ZEALAND (NZ)
ENGINEERING
Engineering Publications Co., Ltd., P.O. Box
12241, Wellington North, New Zealand. Ed.
L.W. Eldowney. Tel. 739444. M; N.Z.$28;
1946; circ. 6,322. *Indexed*: Chem. Abstr., Compendex, Eng. Ind., Feb. issue. *Annual Issues*:
May—Membership Directory; Nov.—Conference Issue; Dec.—Annual Report. *Notes*: adv.,
bibl., bk. rev., calendars, dwgs., photos (B&W,
color).
An association publication with general and
nontechnical professional articles of interest to
engineers. Attention is given to management
and computer topics, problems in working with
architects, environmental concerns, conference
news, and products. (0111-946x)

1168 P.C.I. JOURNAL (US)
(Formerly: *Prestressed Concrete Institute
Journal*)
Prestressed Concrete Inst., 201 N. Wells, Chicago, IL 60606. Ed. George Nasser. Tel. (312)
346-4071. Bi-m; $22; 1956; circ. 6,400. *Indexed*:
Compendex, Eng. Ind., Nov./Dec. issue.
Notes: bibl., bk. rev., dwgs., photos (B&W).
Micro: UMI.
Technical journal covering design and construction of prestressed/precast concrete structures. Includes recommended practices and
standards, project descriptions, reports on new
technical developments, research, and seminars. (0032-793x)

1169 SCHWEIZER INGENIEUR (SZ)
UND ARCHITEKT
Society of Swiss Engineers and Architects, Verlag der Akademischen Technischen Vercine,
Rudigerstrasse 11, Postfach 630, CH8021 Zurich, Switzerland. Ed. Dr. B. Peyer. Tel. (01141)
1/2015536. W; Fr.161; 1883; circ. 6,000. *Indexed*: App. Mech. Rev., Compendex, Eng.
Ind., Excerp. Med. *Notes*: adv., bibl., bk. rev.,
calendars, dwgs., photos (B&W).
The official society journal, covering architecture and civil, mechanical, electrical, and chemical engineering. *

1170 STAVEBNICKY CASOPIS (CS)
Veda Publishing House of the Slovak Academy
of Sciences, Dubravska Cesta, 842-20 Bratislava, Czechoslovakia. Slovart, Gottwaldovo
nam.6, 813 81 Bratislava, Czechoslovakia. Ed.
Jan Balas. M; Kcs. 144; 1953; circ. 1,050. *Indexed*: Compendex, Eng. Ind. *Notes*: bk. rev.,
dwgs., photos (B&W).
Discusses theoretical problems of construction and civil engineering. Articles examine the
technology of building materials, thermal performance, and the lighting of buildings. Text in
Czechoslovakian; table of contents and summaries in English and Russian. (0039-078x) *

1083 STEEL CONSTRUCTION

1171 STRUCTURAL ENGINEER (UK)
Inst. of Structural Engineers, 11 Upper Belgrave St., London SW1X 8BH, England. Ed.
R.J.W. Milne. Tel. (01) 235-4535. M; £60; 1908;
circ. 16,000. Part B: Q; 1978. *Indexed*: A.P.I.,
B.T.I., Eng. Ind. Part A: *Notes*: adv., bk. rev.,
photos (B&W). *Micro*: UMI.
Includes research papers by members, reports on professional development, news briefs
on the latest standards and codes, and information on new projects of interest due to unusual
structural features. (0039-2553)

0467 TRAVAUX

1070 ZEMENT-KALK-GIPS

12

Real Estate Development and Facility Planning

1172 APPRAISAL JOURNAL (US)
American Inst. of Real Estate Appraisers, Nat. Assn. of Realtors, 430 N. Michigan Ave., Chicago, IL 60611-4088. Ed. Charles Olson. Tel. (312) 329-8521. Q; $25; 1932; circ. 15,500. *Indexed*: Oct. issue. *Notes*: bk. rev., dwgs., photos (B&W). *Micro*: UMI.

The most important U.S. journal on real estate appraisal. Includes seven to twelve main articles plus shorter notes and comments and feature columns on finance, law, and computers. Scope is international but focus is primarily on U.S. (0003-7087)

1173 AREA DEVELOPMENT (US)
525 Northern Blvd., Great Neck, NY 11021. Ed. Tom Bergeron. Tel. (516) 829-8995. M; $55; 1965; circ. 35,000. *Annual Issues*: Aug.—Foreign Trends; Oct.—Industrial and Office Parks Directory. *Notes*: adv., bibl., bk. rev., dwgs., photos (B&W, color). *Micro*: UMI.

Covers planning aspects involved in the building and relocation of industrial facilities. Intended for owners, executives, and real estate managers of major corporations. Also of interest to designers, contractors, and consultants in the construction field. Scope is international. Case studies are used to show site-selection experiences and facility planning. Building activities of developers and major corporations are reported. (0004-0908) *

1174 BUSINESS FACILITIES (US)
(Formerly: *American Industrial Properties Report*)
P.O. Box 2060, 121 Monmouth St., Red Bank, NJ 07701. Ed. Eric C. Peterson. Tel. (201) 842-

7433. M; free to qualified subscribers; 1968; circ. 32,000. *Annual Issues*: Feb., May, Aug., Nov.—High-tech Facilities; April—Site Seekers Guide; Aug.—Worldwide Guide. *Notes*: adv., calendars, dwgs., photos (B&W, color).

News, trends, and features cover industrial/commercial real estate, economic development, and facilities design worldwide. Emphasis is on business expansion and relocation, with articles ranging from the site selection process to the design, construction, and operation of the business facility. (0193-7308) *

1175 CHARTERED SURVEYOR (UK)
WEEKLY
(Formerly: *Chartered Surveyor*)
R.I.C.S. Journals, Ltd., Box 87, 1-3 Pemberton Row, London EC4P 4HL, England. Ed. Michael Hanson. Tel. (01) 353-2300. Telex 25212 BUILDA G. W; £41; 1868; circ. 43,444. *Indexed*: A.P.I., Eng. Ind. *Notes*: adv., bk. rev., calendars, dwgs., photos (B&W, color). *Micro*: UMI.

Short features and reports present a wide range of information on British real estate and property development. Covers industrial, commercial, and residential buildings. Discussions focus on market trends, planning law, restoration projects, people, costs, and facility management topics. The official journal of the Royal Institution of Chartered Surveyors. (0264-049x)

0346 CORPORATE DESIGN &
REALTY

0347 FACILITIES DESIGN AND
MANAGEMENT

0112   FACILITIES PLANNING
       NEWS

1176   INDUSTRIAL   (US)
       DEVELOPMENT
Conway Publications, Inc., Peachtree Air Ter-
minal, 1954 Airport Rd., Atlanta, GA 30341.
Tel. (404) 458-6026. Bi-m; 1956. *Indexed*: B.P.I.
Micro: UMI. (0097-3033) +

1177   JOURNAL OF PROPERTY   (US)
       MANAGEMENT
Inst. of Real Estate Management of the National
Assn. of Realtors, 430 N. Michigan Ave., Chicago, IL 60611-4090. Ed. Marilyn Evans. Tel.
(312) 661-1930. Bi-m; $18; 1934; circ. 13,916. *In-
dexed*: P.A.I.S., Jan./Feb. issue. *Notes*: adv.,
bk. rev., calendars, dwgs., photos (B&W,
color).
   Articles on leasing, marketing, maintenance,
finance, and legal aspects of commercial industrial and residential property. Special attention
given to computer applications for management
and maintenance. Primarily for property managers and developers. (0022-3905)

0812   LAND DEVELOPMENT
       STUDIES

0403   NATIONAL MALL MONITOR

1178   NATIONAL REAL ESTATE   (US)
       INVESTOR
Communication Channels, Inc., 6255 Barfield
Rd., Atlanta, GA 30328. Ed. Paula S. Stephens.
Tel. (404) 256-9800. M; $42; 1959; circ. 26,200.
Indexed: ABI/Inform, P.A.I.S. *Annual Issues*:
Jan.—International Market; April—Industrial;
May—Shopping Centers; June—Office Buildings; June—Investor Directory; July—Apartments; Sept.—Institutional; Nov.—Annual
Review; Dec.—Hospitality Review. *Notes*:
adv., bk. rev., calendars, photos (B&W, color).
Micro: UMI.
   Covers news of real estate development, investment, and construction in the U.S. Articles
on new projects, leases, financing, and developers. Includes monthly city reviews. Intended
for developers, realtors, builders, property managers, investment institutions, appraisers,
consultants, architects, contractors, and development authorities. (0027-9994)

1179   PLANTS, SITES AND PARKS   (US)
10240 W. Sample Rd., Coral Springs, FL 33065.
Ed. Kathleen Dempsey. Tel. (305) 753-2660.

Bi-m; $18; 1974; circ. 31,000. *Notes*: adv., pho-
tos (B&W, color). *Micro*: UMI.
   Covers industrial park and office development, facility planning, and site selection for
manufacturing and service industries. Each
issue includes state/area reviews. (0191-2933) *

1180   REAL ESTATE FORUM   (US)
12 W. 37th St., New York, NY 10018. Ed. Harold Kelman. Tel. (212) 563-6460. M; $50; 1946;
circ. 12,000. *Annual Issues*: Feb.—Annual Review; July—Mid-year Office Review. *Notes*:
adv., photos (B&W, color).
   Covers real estate activities and trends in the
U.S. and occasionally abroad. Sometimes includes profiles of a company or project type.
Regional and major-city reviews provide in-
depth analyses of potential markets. An important publication for developers and builders but
useful to architects as well. (0034-0707)

1181   REAL ESTATE   (US)
       NEWSLETTER
LL&IL Publishing, Inc., 1615 Northern Blvd.,
Manhasset, NY 11030. Ed. Ivan Levine. Tel.
(516) 365-3650. W; $84; 1969.
   In-depth analysis of development and leasing
activities in the New York metropolitan area.
Also serves the national market with news on
real estate and pension funds, corporate real estate and executive relocation, and retail chain
site analysis and selection. Very useful to architects, builders, and real estate professionals interested in the New York area. Timely.

1182   REAL ESTATE REVIEW   (US)
P.O. Box 1019, Manhasset, NY 11030. Warren,
Gorham & Lamont, 210 South St., Boston, MA
02111. Ed. Alvin L. Arnold. Tel. (212) 790-1331.
Q; $54; 1971; circ. 16,000. *Indexed*: ABI/Inform,
Mgt. Contents, Winter (odd years). *Notes*: adv.,
bk. rev., photos (B&W). *Micro*: BLH, UMI.
   In-depth feature articles on real estate for
practicing professionals. Reaches an audience
that includes investors, developers, lenders,
brokers, attorneys, and accountants. (0034-
0790)

1183   REAL ESTATE WEEKLY   (US)
235 Park Ave., S., New York, NY 10003. Ed.
Robert S. Pace II. Tel. (212) 677-3131. W; $24;
1955; circ. 7,500. *Notes:* adv., photos (B&W).
   A newspaper that gives current news of the
U.S. real estate market, with an emphasis on

the New York metropolitan area. Each issue includes a profile of a private developer.

1184   REALTY   (US)
Leader Observer, Inc., 80-34 Jamaica Ave., Woodhaven, NY 11421. Ed. Lester Sobel. Tel. (212) 296-2233. Bi-w; $12; 1950; circ. 8,000. *Notes*: adv., photos (B&W).
    A newspaper covering the U.S. real estate market. (0481-9004)

1185   REALTY AND BUILDING   (US)
Realty & Building, Inc., 311 W. Superior St., Chicago, IL 60610. Ed. George Sterns. Tel. (312) 944-1204. W; 1888. (0034-1045) +

0405   SHOPPING CENTER WORLD

1186 SITE SELECTION   (US)
         HANDBOOK
Conway Publications, Inc., Peachtree Air Terminal, 1954 Airport Rd., Atlanta, GA 30341. Ed. Linda Liston. Tel. (404) 458-6026. Q; 1956. *Indexed*: Mgt. Contents. *Micro*: BLH, UMI. (0080-9810) +

0388   UNIQUE HOMES

0530   URBAN CONSERVATION
         REPORT

1013   WRAP UP ON LATIN
         AMERICAN
         CONSTRUCTION, HOUSING
         AND REAL ESTATE

13

Job Leads

**1187 BUILDING PROJECT (US)
PLANNED LIST**
Live Leads Corp., 200 Madison Ave., New York, NY 10016. Tel. (212) 689-7202. Telex 645-215. M; $80/mo. (U.S. list); $40/mo. (regional list).

Reports on large projects in the U.S. in the planning stage, reported early enough to get specified. About 300–350 projects are reported monthly. All are over $1 million and over 50,000 square feet. National or regional subscriptions may be obtained. Arranged by state and type of construction, projects include description, whom to contact, and whether an architect has been selected.

**1188 COMMERCE BUSINESS (US)
DAILY**
U.S. Dept. of Commerce, Room 1304, 433 W. Van Buren St., Chicago, IL 60607. Supt. of Documents, U.S. Government Printing Office, Washington, DC 20402. D; $160; 1950; circ. 39,000.

A daily list of U.S. government procurement invitations, contract awards, subcontracting leads, sales of surplus property, and foreign business opportunities. Section R advertises for architect and engineer services. Section H advertises for consultant services that sometimes require building design/construction expertise. Section Y advertises new construction and major section additions to existing buildings. Section Z announces needs in maintenance, repair, and alteration of real property. Available on-line through Dialog Information Services. (0095-3423)

0934 CONSTRUCTION DIGEST

**1189 CONSTRUCTION REPORT ON (US)
HOSPITALS**
American Hospital Publishing, Dennis K. Fallen, Director of Marketing Research, 211 E. Chicago Ave., Chicago, IL 60611. M; $150.

A lead service for U.S. hospital construction projects. Leads are generated from health planning agencies and newspaper clippings. About 20 percent of the seventy or more projects reported have not yet selected an architect. +

1190 DODGE REPORTS (US)
McGraw-Hill Information Systems, 1221 Ave. of the Americas, Ste. 1900, New York, NY 10020. Tel. (212) 512-3754. D; price varies.

A news service that reports action on new projects at various stages from preplanning to construction. Of interest primarily to contractors and subcontractors but also to financial groups, manufacturers, distributors, real estate investors, and architects. Subscription can be tailored to pinpoint specific building types and regions. Provides full contact information.

**0951 ENGINEERING-NEWS
RECORD**

**0456 FROM THE STATE
CAPITALS: AIRPORT
CONSTRUCTION AND
FINANCING**

**0965 INTERNATIONAL
CONSTRUCTION**

**1191   INTERNATIONAL   (US)
         CONSTRUCTION WEEK**
Engineering News-Record, McGraw-Hill Publications, 1221 Ave. of the Americas, New York, NY 10020. Ed. Charles Pinyan. Tel. (212) 512-2534. Telex 232365. W; $650; 1975; circ. 800. *Indexed*: Semiannually.

A newsletter that announces new projects worldwide, in all stages from planning through construction bids, that require expertise, manpower, or equipment. Brief descriptions of the projects are given. Contacts are listed for further information and for sending proposals and tender documents. Major new developments are announced early enough to take advantage of advance opportunities for winning studies and design contracts. Reporters are located in ninety-two countries. Primarily announces large-scale and public works projects in developing regions. (0149-5585)

**0975   MIDDLE EAST
         CONSTRUCTION**

1192   PROJECT ALERT SYSTEM   (US)
Tecton Media, Inc., 350 Madison Ave., New York, NY 10017. Tel. (800) 223-2170. Bi-w; 1976.

Reports leads, primarily on private projects in the U.S. Sixty-five percent are reported prior to selection of architects. Subscribers are architects, engineers, and contractors. +

1193   PROJECT REPORTS   (US)
         (Formerly: *HSA Reports*)
2256 NW Parkway, Ste. B, Marietta, GA 30067. James & Douglas Publishers, Inc., P.O. Box 7375, Marietta, GA 30065. M; price varies; 1978.

A series of construction project lead services in the areas of medical, educational, and correctional facilities. The projects listed range in budget size from $500,000 to over $80 million and cover construction, renovation, and major equipment purchases. Each project listing, arranged by state, includes exact address, contact person, budget, construction starting date, and note if A/E has not been selected. The publisher promises advance lead time that justifies the cost of the subscription. This series would be useful to contractors, suppliers, and architects who specialize in these types of facilities. *

**1181   REAL ESTATE
         NEWSLETTER**

1183   REAL ESTATE WEEKLY

1194   SALES PROSPECTOR   (US)
751 Main St., P.O. Box 518, Waltham, MA 02254. Tel. (617) 899-1271. M; Single regional editions $98; 1958.

Reports on expansions and relocations of manufacturing firms, distribution centers, and transportation terminals in new or existing buildings. Reports are available for regional or national coverage. Of interest to anyone involved in facility expansion or relocation. In most cases, architects have already been selected by the time of publication; however, it is still a good source for developing a potential client file from the contacts listed. (0036-3456)

1197   SAUDI ECONOMIC SURVEY

**1195   WEEKLY CONSTRUCTION   (US)
         PREVIEW**
National Building News Service, Harrisville, NH 03450. Ed. Carol Arteta. Tel. (603) 827-3358. W; $795; 1965.

Leads on about 300 major building projects in the U.S. and Canada that are valued at over $1 million. Only about 10 percent are published prior to architect selection; therefore, it is of more interest to contractors and suppliers than to architects or engineers. Each listing includes cost and complete contact details. Divided into three sections: new projects-first reports, updates on earlier reports, and bidding information. Covers all building types except highways and bridges.

**1013   WRAP UP ON LATIN
         AMERICAN
         CONSTRUCTION, HOUSING
         AND REAL ESTATE**

14

Doing Business Abroad

0975 MIDDLE EAST
CONSTRUCTION

1196 MIDDLE EAST EXECUTIVE (US)
REPORTS
1101 Vermont Ave., N.W., Ste. 400, Washington, DC 20005. Ed. Joseph Saba. Tel. (202) 289-3900. Telex 440462 MEERU 1. M; $395; 1978; circ. 2,023. *Indexed*: Mid East File, June issue.

A legal and business guide to the Middle East for business executives, attorneys, bankers, accountants, and consultants. Frequent articles on setting up offices, joint ventures, manpower issues, and construction developments. (0271-0498)

1197 SAUDI ECONOMIC SURVEY (SU)
P.O. Box 1989, Jeddah, Saudi Arabia. Ed. Zakaria Ghaith. Tel. 642-8245. W; $370; 1967.

A weekly review of Saudi Arabian economic and business activity. Announces plans for new projects, information on new firms, and regulations for foreign business operations.

1198 SAUDI INTROSPECT (US)
c/o Leland Publishing Co., 81 Canal St., Ste.

800, Boston, MA 02114. Ed. Regina Hersey. Tel. (617) 227-9314. M; $275; 1976.

A twelve-page newsletter on doing business in Saudi Arabia. Issues include articles analyzing politics, announcements of conferences, business leads, profiles of companies, contract awards, and news briefs. Written for the executive who wants to expand or initiate business in the Kingdom. Readers include architects, contractors, suppliers, attorneys, and exporters in nineteen countries.

1199 WORLDWIDE PROJECTS (US)
Intercontinental Publications, Inc., 15 Ketchum St., Westport, CT 06880. Ed. Virginia Fairweather. Tel. (203) 226-7463. Telex 996423. Bi-m; 1967; circ. 14,000. *Annual Issues*: Oct./Nov.—Outlook Issue. *Notes*: adv., photos (B&W).

A publication for the multinational community that engineers, constructs, and finances international projects. Includes articles on doing business abroad, problems of living abroad, project prospects, and joint venture opportunities. Regular features on equipment from all over the world. (0091-4800)

Indexes and Abstracts

A. *Specifically Related to Building Design and Construction*

ARCHITECTURAL INDEX
P.O. Box 1168
Boulder, CO 80306
Annual.

ARCHITECTURAL PERIODICALS INDEX
R.I.B.A. Publications, Ltd.
Finsbury Mission
London CIV 8VB
England
Quarterly with annual cumulations.

ART INDEX
H.W. Wilson Co.
950 University Ave.
Bronx, NY 10452
Quarterly with annual cumulations.
   Online beginning November 1985.

ARTBIBLIOGRAPHIES MODERN
ABC-Clio, Riviera Campus
2040 Alameda Padre Serra
Santa Barbara, CA 93103
Also available through DIALOG.

AVERY INDEX TO ARCHITECTURAL
PERIODICALS
Columbia University, Avery Library.
G.K. Hall Publications
70 Lincoln St.
Boston, MA 02111
1973, 1975, 1979. Currently online through RLIN.

COMPENDEX
Online version of Engineering Index available
   through DIALOG.

ENGINEERING INDEX
Engineering Information, Inc.
345 E. 47th St.
New York, NY 10017

R.I.L.A. (International Repertory of the
   Literature of Art)
J. Paul Getty Trust
c/o Sterling & Francine Art Institute
Williamstown, MA 01267

B. *Additional Indexes and Computer Database
   Services Cited in Text*

AMERICA: HISTORY AND LIFE
Available online through DIALOG.

APPLIED MECHANICS REVIEW
American Society of Mechanical Engineers
345 E. 47th St.
New York, NY 10017

APPLIED SCIENCE AND TECHNOLOGY INDEX
H.W. Wilson Co.
950 University Ave.
Bronx, NY 10452

BRITISH HUMANITIES INDEX
Library Association Publishing, Ltd.
7 Ridgemount St.
London WC1E 7AE
England

BUSINESS PERIODICALS INDEX
H.W. Wilson Co.
950 University Ave.
Bronx, NY 10452
Available online beginning 1985.

CANADIAN PERIODICAL INDEX
Canadian Library Association
151 Sparks St.
Ottawa, Ont. K1P 5E3
Canada

CERAMIC ABSTRACTS
American Ceramic Society, Inc.
65 Ceramic Dr.
Columbus, OH 43214

CHEMICAL ABSTRACTS
Chemical Abstracts Service
Box 3012
Columbus, OH 43210

COMPUTER DATABASE
Available online through DIALOG.

COMPUTER LITERATURE INDEX
Applied Computer Research, Inc.
Box 9280
Phoenix, AZ 85068

CRIMINAL JUSTICE PERIODICAL INDEX
University Microfilms International
300 N. Zeeb Rd.
Ann Arbor, MI 48106

DATA PROCESSING DIGEST
c/o Gisela Wermke
Box 1249
Los Angeles, CA 90078

DIALOG INFORMATION SERVICES, INC.
Marketing Dept.
3460 Hillview Ave.
Palo Alto, CA 94304
Vendor for over 300 computer databases.

EDUCATION INDEX
H.W. Wilson Co.
950 University Ave.
Bronx, NY 10452
Available online beginning 1985.

EKISTIC INDEX
Athens Center of Ekistics
24 Strat. Syndesmou St.
Box 471
Athens 136, Greece

ENERGY INDEX
Available online through DIALOG.

ERIC CLEARINGHOUSE
Available online through DIALOG.

EXCERPTA MEDICA
Box 211
1000 AE, Amsterdam
Netherlands

HISTORICAL ABSTRACTS
ABC-Clio Information Services
2040 Alameda Padre Serra
Box 4397
Santa Barbara, CA 93103

HOSPITAL LITERATURE INDEX
American Hospital Association
840 N. Lake Shore Dr.
Chicago, IL 60611

INDEX MEDICUS
National Library of Medicine
c/o Chief Bibliographic Services Div.
8600 Rockville Pike
Bethesda, MD 20209

INDEX TO LEGAL PERIODICALS
H.W. Wilson Co.
950 University Ave.
Bronx, NY 10452

INSPEC
Available online through DIALOG.

LIBRARY LITERATURE
H.W. Wilson Co.
950 University Ave.
Bronx, NY 10452

MAGAZINE INDEX
Available online through DIALOG.

MANAGEMENT CONTENTS
Available online through DIALOG.

MID-EAST FILE
Available online through DIALOG.

NEWSNET
945 Haverford Rd.
Bryn Mawr, PA 19010
Bibliographic retrieval service.

POLLUTION ABSTRACTS
Available online through DIALOG.

PREDICASTS
Available online through DIALOG.

PSYCHOLOGICAL ABSTRACTS
American Psychological Association
1200 17th St., N.W.
Washington, DC 20036

PUBLIC AFFAIRS INFORMATION SERVICE
11 W. 40th Street
New York, NY 10018
Also available online through DIALOG.

READERS GUIDE TO PERIODICAL
LITERATURE
H.W. Wilson Co.
950 University Ave.
Bronx, NY 10452

SOCIAL SCIENCES CITATION INDEX
Institute for Scientific Information
3501 Market St.
Philadelphia, PA 19104

Alphabetical Index

Geographical Index

Canada

A P T BULLETIN
ARQ ARCHITECTURE/QUEBEC
ACORN
APARTMENT & BUILDING
ARCHITECTS FORUM
ARCHITECTURE CANADA
ARCHITECTURE CONCEPT
BATIMENT
BUILDING RENOVATION
BUILDING RESEARCH NEWS
BUILDING RESEARCH NOTES
C.I.P. FORUM
CANADIAN ARCHITECT
CANADIAN BUILDING
CANADIAN BUILDING ABSTRACTS
CANADIAN BUILDING DIGEST
CANADIAN CONSULTING ENGINEER
CANADIAN HOTEL AND RESTAURANT
CANADIAN INTERIORS
CANADIAN JOURNAL OF CIVIL
     ENGINEERING
CANADIAN OFFICE
CANADIAN PLASTICS
CANADIAN WORKSHOP
COMMUNIQUE
CONSTRUCTION CANADA
CONSTRUCTION LAW LETTER
DECORATION CHEZ-SOI
DECORMAG
DETAIL
ENGINEERING JOURNAL
ENVIRONMENT SYSTEMS AND INDUSTRIES
FIFTH COLUMN
FLOOR COVERING NEWS
FOODSERVICE & HOSPITALITY
FURNITURE PRODUCTION & DESIGN
HABITAT
HEALTH CARE
HEATING, PLUMBING, AIR CONDITIONING
JOURNAL OF CANADIAN ART HISTORY
LAND DESIGN
LOG HOME GUIDE FOR BUILDERS AND
     BUYERS
MONTREAL SOCIETY OF ARCHITECTS
     COMMUNIQUE
NOVA SCOTIA ASSOCIATION OF ARCHITECTS
OFFICE EQUIPMENT AND METHODS
ORDRE DES ARCHITECTES DU QUEBEC.
     BULLETIN
PARACHUTE
PLAN CANADA
PLANT MANAGEMENT AND ENGINEERING
QUEBEC CONSTRUCTION
SECTION A
SELECT HOMES
SOCIETY FOR THE STUDY OF
     ARCHITECTURE IN CANADA. BULLETIN
SOUTHAM BUILDING GUIDE
TORONTO LIFE DESIGN AND DECOR GUIDE
TRACE: A CANADIAN REVIEW OF
     ARCHITECTURE

Chile

A.U.C.A. (ARQUITECTURA, URBANISMO,
     CONSTRUCCION Y ARTE)

China, Mainland

ARCHITECTURAL JOURNAL/JIANZHU
     XUEBAO
JOURNAL OF BUILDING STRUCTURES
WORLD ARCHITECTURE

China, Nationalist

TAIWAN FURNITURE

Colombia

INGENIERIA ARQUITECTURA
     CONSTRUCCION
PROA

Cyprus

MEDITERRANEAN CONSTRUCTION

Czechoslovakia

ARCHITEKTURA A URBANIZMUS/
     ARCHITECTURE UND URBANISM
ARCHITEKTURA CSR
CESKOSLOVENSKY ARCHITEKT
DOMOV
STAVEBNICKY CASOPIS
UMENI/ARTS
VYSTAVBA A ARCHITEKTURA

Denmark

ARCHITECTURE FROM SCANDINAVIA
ARKITEKTEN
ARKITEKTUR DK
BO BEDRE
BYPLAN
DESIGN FROM SCANDINAVIA
FARVE/TAPET
LANDSKAB
LIVING ARCHITECTURE
MOBILIA
SADELMAGER-OG-TAPETSERER TIDENDE
SKOENNE HJEM
TRAEETS ARBEJDS GIVERE

Dominican Republic

C.O.D.I.A.

Finland

ABACUS
ARKKITEHTI/FINNISH ARCHITECTURAL
     REVIEW
ARKKITEHTIUUTISET/ARKITEKTNYTT

DEUTSCHES ARCHITEKTENBLATT
F UND I—BAU (FERTIGTEILBAU UND
    INDUSTRIALISIERTES BAUEN)
FORM
G A
GARTEN + LANDSCHAFT
GLASFORUM
HAUSTEX
HEIMTEX
HOLZ UND KUNSTOFFVERARBEITUNG
KUECHEN FORUM
DIE KUNST
KUNSTHANDWERK IN EUROPA
LANDSCHAFT UND STADT
M D
MADE IN EUROPE: FURNITURE AND
    INTERIORS
DIE MODERNE KUECHE
MOEBEL-KULTUR
MOEBELMARKT
DAS MUNSTER
RAUM UND TEXTIL
SCHOENER WOHNEN
SCHWIMMBAD UND SAUNA
SPORT-BOEDER-FREIZEITBAUTEN
STADT
TZ/TAPENZEITUNG
WERK UND ZEIT
ZEMENT-KALK-GIPS
ZUHAUSE: WOHNUNG, HAUS UND GARTEN

Greece

ARCHITECTURE IN GREECE
DESIGN AND ART IN GREECE
EKISTICS
ZYGOS

Hong Kong

ASIA PACIFIC CONTRACTOR
ASIAN ARCHITECTURE & BUILDER
VISION

Hungary

LAKASKULTURA
MAGYAR EPITOMUVESZET
MUEMLEKVEDELEM
PERIODICA POLYTECHNICA. ARCHITECTURE

India

ARCHITECTS TRADE JOURNAL
ARCHITECTURE & BUILDING INDUSTRY
CEMENT
CONCRETE CONSTRUCTION AND
    ARCHITECTURE
INDIAN ARCHITECT
INDIAN CONCRETE JOURNAL
INDIAN INSTITUTE OF ARCHITECTS
    JOURNAL

MARG: A MAGAZINE OF THE ARTS
S.P.A. JOURNAL

Indonesia

POLA

Ireland

IRISH HEATING AND VENTILATING NEWS
PLAN
R.I.A.I. BULLETIN

Israel

OUT OF JERUSALEM

Italy

A.D.
AU
ABITARE
ACCIAIO
AMBIENTARE
L'AMBIENTE CUCINA
ARCHITETTO
L'ARCHITETTURA—CRONACHE E STORIA
AREA
ARREDO BIANCHERIA CASA
ARREDO ITALIA
ARREDORAMA
ARTICOLI CASALINGHI
BAGNO E ACCESSORI
BAGNO OGGI E DOMANI
CASA CLASSICA
CASA E GIARDINO
CASA STILE
CASA VOGUE
CASABELLA
CASAVIVA
CASE AL MARE
CASE DI CAMPAGNA
CASE DI MONTAGNA
IL CEMENTO
CERAMICA PER L'EDILIZIA INTERNATIONAL
CHERI MODA
CITTA E CAMPAGNA
CITTA E SOCIETA
CONTROSPAZIO/COUNTERSPACE
COSTRUIRE LATERIZI
COSTRUIRE PER ABITARE
COSTRUTTORI ITALIANI NEL MONDO
CUCINA + BAGNO & LUCI
DOMUS
EDILDOMANI
EDILIZIA POPOLARE
EUPALINO
FRAMES/PORTE & FINESTRE
IL GIORNALE DELLA PREFABBRICAZIONE
    ITALIANA
GRAN BAZAAR
HINTERLAND

HOME/ITALIA
HOTEL DOMANI
INDUSTRIA DEL LEGNO E DEL MOBILE
INDUSTRIA DEL MOBILE
INDUSTRIA DELLE COSTRUZIONI
L'INDUSTRIA ITALIANA DEL CEMENTO
INGEGNERI ARCHITETTI CONSTRUTTORI
INTERNI
ITALIA NOSTRA
LOTUS INTERNATIONAL
MARMI, GRANITI, PIETRE
MIA CASA
IL MOBILE
MOBILI PER UFFICIO
MODO
NUOVA CITTA
IL NUOVO CORRIERE DEI COSTRUTTORI
OP CIT
OTTAGONO
PALLADIO
PARAMETRO
POLITECHNICO DI TORINO
PREFABBRICARE-EDILIZIA IN EVOLUZIONE
LA PREFABBRICAZIONE
QUADERNI DELL'ISTITUTO DI STORIA
      DELL'ARCHITETTURA
RASSEGNA: ARCHITETTURA E URBANISTICA
RECUPERARE-EDILIZIA DESIGN IMPIANTI
SEDIA E IL MOBILE
SPAZIO E SOCIETA/SPACE AND SOCIETY
STORIA ARCHITETTURA
STORIA DELLA CITTA
STRUTTURE AMBIENTALI/ENVIRONMENTAL
      STRUCTURES
TUTTOVILLE
UFFICIOSTILE
URBANISTICA
VILLE—GIARDINI

Japan

A & U/ARCHITECTURE AND URBANISM
APPROACH
ARCHITECTURAL ENGINEERING/SEKOH
ARCHITECTURE CULTURE/KENCHIKU
      BUNKA
DETAIL/DITERU
GA (GLOBAL ARCHITECTURE) DETAIL
GA (GLOBAL ARCHITECTURE) DOCUMENT
GA (GLOBAL ARCHITECTURE) HOUSES
GLOBAL ARCHITECTURE
GLOBAL INTERIOR
HOUSE AND HOME
JAPAN ARCHITECT
KENCHIKU TECHO/ARCHITECT
MY ROOM/WATASHI-NO-HEYA
PROCESS: ARCHITECTURE
SPACE DESIGN
TOSHI-JUTAKU
TRANSACTIONS OF THE ARCHITECTURAL
      INSTITUTE OF JAPAN

Kenya

HABITAT NEWS

Korea

SPACE/KONGGAN

Luxembourg

REVUE FORMES NOUVELLES

Malta

ATRIUM

Mexico

C.O.N.E.S.C.A.L.

Netherlands

DE ARCHITECT
BOUW
CEMENT
DURABILITY OF BUILDING MATERIALS
DUTCH ART AND ARCHITECTURE TODAY
EIGEN HUIS EN INTERIEUR
FORUM
HERON
I.F.H.P. NEWSSHEET
INTERIOR
INTERNATIONAL LIGHTING REVIEW
LANDSCAPE PLANNING
MEUBEL
NETHERLANDS RIJKSDIENST VOOR DE
      MONUMENTENZORG—JAARVERSLAG
OPEN HOUSE INTERNATIONAL
PLAN: MAANDBLAD VOOR ONTWERP ON
      OMGEVING
STRUCTURAL SAFETY
TRANSPORTATION
URBAN LAW AND POLICY
URBES NOSTRAE
VARIATOR
WONEN-TABK

New Zealand

HOME & BUILDING
THE LANDSCAPE
NEW ZEALAND ARCHITECT
NEW ZEALAND CONCRETE CONSTRUCTION
NEW ZEALAND ENGINEERING

Nigeria

WEST AFRICAN BUILDER AND ARCHITECT

Norway

ARKITEKTNYTT
BYGGEKUNST
HUSET VAART
MOEBELHANDLEREN
NYE BONYTT/DESIGN FOR LIVING
TRE OG MOEBLER

Philippines

PHILIPPINE ARCHITECTURE & BUILDING
    JOURNAL
PHILIPPINE ARCHITECTURE, ENGINEERING
    & CONSTRUCTION RECORD

Poland

ARCHITEKTURA
KWARTALNIK ARCHITEKTURY I
    URBANISTYKI

Portugal

ARQUITECTURA
BINARIO

Rumania

ARHITECTURA
CONSTRUCTII
FORESTA
MOBILA

Saudi Arabia

ALBENAA
AL-FAISAL ARCHITECTURE AND PLANNING
    JOURNAL
SAUDI ECONOMIC SURVEY

Singapore

MIMAR: ARCHITECTURE IN DEVELOPMENT
S.I.A.J.
SOUTHEAST ASIA BUILDING MATERIALS
    AND EQUIPMENT

South Africa

ARCHITECT & BUILDER
ARCHITECTURE S.A.
COPPER INFORMATION ARCHITECTURAL
    SERIES
PLANNING AND BUILDING DEVELOPMENTS
RESTORICA
SOUTH AFRICAN ARCHITECTURAL RECORD

Spain

ARQUITECTURA
ARQUITECTURAS BIS
ARTE Y CEMENTO

CERCHA
EUROMUEBLE
INFORMES DE LA CONSTRUCCION
INTERNATIONAL ASSN. FOR SHELL AND
    SPATIAL STRUCTURES—BULLETIN
EL MUEBLE
QUADERNS D'ARQUITECTURA I URBANISME
T.A.

Sweden

A.T. ARKITEKTTIDNINGEN
ARKITEKTUR
BO BRA
BYGGMAESTAREN
FORM
GOLV TILL TAK
HUSMODERN
INTERIOR
MOEBLER OCH MILJOE
NORDISK BETONG
SVENSK TAPETSERARETIDNING

Switzerland

AKTUELLES BAUEN
ANTHOS
ARCHITECTURE & BEHAVIOR
    (ARCHITECTURE ET COMPORTEMENT)
ARCHITEKTUR UND LADENBAU
BAU & HOLZ
DU
ENERGY AND BUILDINGS
FIBRECEMENT REVIEW
HABITATION
INDUSTRIAL SUR BOIS
L'OEIL
MODERNES WOHNEN/HABITATION
    MODERNE
PLANEN UND BAUEN
SCHWEIZER INGENIEUR UND ARCHITEKT
SCHWEIZER JOURNAL
SCHWEIZERISCHE SCHREINERZEITUNG
TEXTILES SUISSES—INTERIEUR
UNSERE KUNSTDENKMALER
WERK/ARCHITHESE
WERK, BAUEN UND WOHNEN

USSR

ARKHITEKTURA SSR
BETON I ZHELEZOBETON
LENINGRADSKAYA PANORAMA

United Kingdom

A & S
AA FILES: ANNALS OF THE ARCHITECTURAL
    ASSOCIATION SCHOOL OF
    ARCHITECTURE
ACROSS ARCHITECTURE
AFRICAN CONSTRUCTION
AIRPORTS INTERNATIONAL

APOLLO
ARCHIGRAM
ARCHITECTS' JOURNAL
ARCHITECTURAL AND BUILDING
    INFORMATION SELECTOR
ARCHITECTURAL DESIGN
ARCHITECTURAL HISTORY
ARCHITECTURAL MONOGRAPHS
ARCHITECTURAL PRESERVATION AND NEW
    DESIGN IN CONSERVATION
ARCHITECTURAL REVIEW
ARCHITECTURAL SERVICES BOOK OF HOUSE
    PLANS
ARCHITECTURAL TECHNOLOGY
ARCHITECTURE EAST MIDLANDS
ARCHITECTURE WEST MIDLANDS
ARTS AND THE ISLAMIC WORLD
ARUP JOURNAL
ASIAN BUILDING AND CONSTRUCTION
B.R.E. DIGEST
B.R.E. INFORMATION PAPERS
B.R.E. NEWS
B.S.I. NEWS
BATIMENT INTERNATIONAL/BUILDING
    RESEARCH
BLINDS AND SHUTTERS
BLUEPRINT
BRICK BULLETIN
BRITISH CARPET MANUFACTURERS
    ASSOCIATION—INDEX OF QUALITY
    NAMES
BUILDING
BUILDING DESIGN
BUILDING REFURBISHMENT &
    MAINTENANCE
BUILDING SERVICES
BUILDING SERVICES ENGINEERING
    RESEARCH AND TECHNOLOGY
BUILDING TECHNOLOGY AND
    MANAGEMENT
BUILDING TRADES JOURNAL
BUILDING WITH STEEL
BURLINGTON MAGAZINE
CABINET MAKER AND RETAIL FURNISHER
CAMBRIDGE URBAN AND ARCHITECTURAL
    STUDIES
CARPET AND FLOORCOVERINGS REVIEW
CARPETS AND TEXTILES
CHARLES RENNIE MACKINTOSH SOCIETY
    NEWSLETTER
CHARTERED QUANTITY SURVEYOR
CHARTERED SURVEYOR WEEKLY
CIVIL ENGINEERING
COMPUTER-AIDED DESIGN
CONCRETE
CONCRETE QUARTERLY
CONSERVATION NEWS
CONSTRUCTION MANAGEMENT AND
    ECONOMICS
COUNTRY LIFE
DESIGN
DESIGN FOR SPECIAL NEEDS
DESIGN STUDIES

DESIGNER'S JOURNAL
DO IT YOURSELF
E.A.R./EDINBURGH ARCHITECTURAL
    RESEARCH
ENVIRONMENT AND PLANNING
ERGONOMICS
F.I.R.A. BULLETIN
FARM BUILDING EXPRESS
FIRE AND MATERIALS
FIRE PREVENTION
FIRE SURVEYOR
FURNITURE HISTORY
FURNITURE MANUFACTURER
GARDEN HISTORY
GLASS AGE
GLAZED EXPRESSIONS
HABITAT INTERNATIONAL
HALI
HEATING AND VENTILATING ENGINEER
HERITAGE OUTLOOK
HISTORIC HOUSES
HOME FURNISHING INTERNATIONAL
HOSPITAL DEVELOPMENT
HOUSE AND BUNGALOW
HOUSE AND GARDEN
HOUSE BUILDER AND ESTATE DEVELOPER
HOUSING
HOUSING REVIEW
IDEAL HOME
INDUSTRIAL ARCHAEOLOGY
INSTITUTION OF CIVIL ENGINEERS:
    PROCEEDINGS—DESIGN AND
    CONSTRUCTION
INTERIOR DESIGN
INTERNATIONAL CONSTRUCTION
INTERNATIONAL FIRE SECURITY SAFETY
    NEWS
INTERNATIONAL JOURNAL OF AMBIENT
    ENERGY
INTERNATIONAL JOURNAL OF PROJECT
    MANAGEMENT
INTERNATIONAL JOURNAL OF URBAN AND
    REGIONAL RESEARCH
IRISH GEORGIAN SOCIETY QUARTERLY
    BULLETIN
JOURNAL OF ENVIRONMENTAL
    PSYCHOLOGY
JOURNAL OF GARDEN HISTORY
JOURNAL OF PLANNING AND
    ENVIRONMENT LAW
KITCHENS & BATHROOMS
LAND DEVELOPMENT STUDIES
LANDSCAPE DESIGN
LANDSCAPE HISTORY
LANDSCAPE RESEARCH
LONDON JOURNAL
MAGAZINE OF CONCRETE RESEARCH
MASTER BUILDERS' JOURNAL
MIDDLE EAST CONSTRUCTION
MONUMENTUM
MUNICIPAL ENGINEER
MUSEUMS JOURNAL
NATIONAL BUILDER

NATIONAL TRUST
NATO MAGAZINE
NEW CIVIL ENGINEER
9H
OFFICE EQUIPMENT NEWS
OFFICE SYSTEMS
ORIENTAL ART
OVERSEAS BUILDING NOTES
PLANNER
PLANNING OUTLOOK
PORTICO
PRACTICAL CIVIL DEFENSE
PROGRESSIVE PLANNING
R.I.B.A. JOURNAL
REGIONAL STUDIES
SCOTTISH GEORGIAN SOCIETY BULLETIN
SOCIETY OF ANTIQUITIES OF SCOTLAND.
    PROCEEDINGS
SOCIETY OF ARCHITECTURAL HISTORIANS
    OF GREAT BRITAIN. NEWSLETTER
SPON'S ARCHITECTS' AND BUILDERS' PRICE
    BOOK
STRUCTURAL ENGINEER
STUDIO INTERNATIONAL
SURVEYOR/PUBLIC WORKS WEEKLY
SWIMMING POOL
TEMPLAR
THIRD WORLD PLANNING REVIEW
THIRTIES SOCIETY JOURNAL
TOWN AND COUNTRY PLANNING
TOWN PLANNING REVIEW
TRANSACTIONS
U.I.A.—INTERNATIONAL ARCHITECT
ULSTER ARCHITECT
URBAN STUDIES
VERNACULAR ARCHITECTURE
VICTORIAN SOCIETY ANNUAL
VOLUNTARY HOUSING
W.P.W. DECOR
WINDOW INDUSTRIES
WORLD CEMENT
WORLD HOSPITALS
WORLD OF INTERIORS
YORKSHIRE ARCHITECT

United States

A.B.A. BANKING JOURNAL
ACSA NEWS
A E CONCEPTS IN WOOD DESIGN
A/E LEGAL NEWSLETTER
A/E MARKETING JOURNAL
A/E SYSTEMS REPORT
A-E-C AUTOMATION NEWSLETTER
A.I.A. COLORADO FIELD REPORT
A.I.A. MEMO
A.I.A. REPORTS
APWA REPORTER
ASHRAE JOURNAL
ASN QUARTERLY
ASO NEWS JOURNAL
ASTM STANDARDIZATION NEWS
AFRICAN ARTS

AGORA
AIR CONDITIONING, HEATING AND
    REFRIGERATION NEWS
AIRPORT SERVICES MANAGEMENT
ALABAMA ARCHITECT
ALABAMA BUILDER
AMERICAN CERAMIC SOCIETY BULLETIN
AMERICAN CITY AND COUNTY
AMERICAN CONCRETE INSTITUTE JOURNAL
AMERICAN PAINT AND COATINGS JOURNAL
AMERICAN PAINTING CONTRACTOR
AMERICAN PROFESSIONAL CONSTRUCTION
AMERICAN ROOFER AND BUILDER
    IMPROVEMENT CONTRACTOR
AMERICAN SCHOOL & UNIVERSITY
ANDERSON REPORT NEWSLETTER ON
    COMPUTER GRAPHICS
ANTIQUES
APPRAISAL JOURNAL
ARCHIMAGE
ARCHITECTURAL ANTIQUES AND
    ARTIFACTS ADVERTISER
ARCHITECTURAL DIGEST
ARCHITECTURAL METALS
ARCHITECTURAL PSYCHOLOGY
    NEWSLETTER
ARCHITECTURAL RECORD
ARCHITECTURAL TECHNOLOGY
ARCHITECTURE AND PLANNING
ARCHITECTURE CALIFORNIA
ARCHITECTURE MINNESOTA
ARCHITECTURE NEW JERSEY
ARCHITECTURE: THE A.I.A. JOURNAL
ARCHITECTURES
AREA DEVELOPMENT
ARMSTRONG LOGIC
ART AND ANTIQUES
ART DECO SOCIETY NEWS
ART IN AMERICA
ART NEWS
ARTFORUM
ARTS AND ARCHITECTURE
AUDITORIUM NEWS
AUTOMATION IN HOUSING AND
    MANUFACTURED HOME DEALER
AVENUE MAGAZINE
AVISO
BNA'S HOUSING AND DEVELOPMENT
    REPORTER
BANK SYSTEMS AND EQUIPMENT
BATH & DOMESTICS
BEDDING
BETTER BUILDINGS
BETTER HOMES AND GARDENS
BLUEPRINTS
BRICK AND CLAY RECORD
BROWNSTONER
BUILDER
BUILDER & CONTRACTOR
BUILDER ARCHITECT
BUILDING AND ENVIRONMENT
BUILDING & REALTY RECORD
BUILDING DESIGN & CONSTRUCTION

ENERGY USER NEWS
ENGINEERED SYSTEMS
ENGINEER'S DIGEST
ENGINEERING JOURNAL
ENGINEERING-NEWS RECORD
ENVIRONMENT
ENVIRONMENT AND BEHAVIOR
EQUIPMENT GUIDE NEWS
FACILITIES DESIGN AND MANAGEMENT
FACILITIES PLANNING NEWS
FAITH AND FORM
FAMILY HANDYMAN
FARM BUILDING NEWS
FASTENER TECHNOLOGY INTERNATIONAL
FINE HOMEBUILDING
FINE WOODWORKING
FIRE JOURNAL
FIRE NEWS
FIRE TECHNOLOGY
FLOOR COVERING WEEKLY
FLOORING
FLORIDA ARCHITECT
FLORIDA BUILDER
FLORIDA CONSTRUCTION INDUSTRY
FLORIDA DESIGNERS QUARTERLY
FOODSERVICE EQUIPMENT SPECIALIST
FORM & FUNCTION
FOUNDATION FACTS
FRANK LLOYD WRIGHT NEWSLETTER
FRIENDS OF TERRA COTTA NEWSLETTER
FROM THE STATE CAPITALS: AIRPORT
    CONSTRUCTION AND FINANCING
FROM THE STATE CAPITALS:
    CONSTRUCTION—INSTITUTIONAL
FURNITURE DESIGN & MANUFACTURING
FURNITURE MANUFACTURING
    MANAGEMENT
FURNITURE PRODUCTION
FURNITURE WOOD DIGEST
FURNITURE WORLD
FURNITURE/TODAY
GSD NEWS
GARDEN DESIGN
GARLINGHOUSE HOME PLAN GUIDES
GLASS DIGEST
GREAT LAKES ARCHITECTURE &
    ENGINEERING
GROUNDS MAINTENANCE
GUIDELINES ERRORS AND OMISSIONS
    BULLETIN
GUIDELINES FOR IMPROVING PRACTICE:
    ARCHITECTS AND ENGINEERS
    PROFESSIONAL LIABILITY
GUIDELINES LETTER
HARDWARE AGE
HARVARD ARCHITECTURE REVIEW
HAWAII ARCHITECT
HEADQUARTERS HELIOGRAM
HEALTH CARE SYSTEMS
HEATING, PIPING AND AIR CONDITIONING
HIGH TECH FACILITIES
HIGHWAY AND HEAVY CONSTRUCTION
HISTORIC PRESERVATION

HISTORIC SEATTLE NEWSLETTER
HOME
HOME AGAIN
HOME BUILDER NEWS
HOME FASHION TEXTILES
HOME LIGHTING & ACCESSORIES
THE HOMEOWNER
HOSPITAL TECHNOLOGY SERIES
HOSPITAL TOPICS
HOSPITAL WEEK
HOSPITALS
HOTEL & MOTEL MANAGEMENT
HOTELS & RESTAURANTS INTERNATIONAL
HOUSE AND GARDEN
HOUSE BEAUTIFUL
HOUSE BEAUTIFUL'S BUILDING MANUAL
HOUSE BEAUTIFUL'S HOME DECORATING
HOUSE BEAUTIFUL'S HOME REMODELING
HOUSE BEAUTIFUL'S HOUSES AND PLANS
HOUSE BEAUTIFUL'S KITCHENS/BATHS
HOUSING AND SOCIETY
I A: JOURNAL OF THE SOCIETY FOR
    INDUSTRIAL ARCHAEOLOGY
I.D.E.A.S.
IEEE COMPUTER GRAPHICS AND
    APPLICATIONS
INDUSTRIAL CONSTRUCTION
INDUSTRIAL DESIGN
INDUSTRIAL DEVELOPMENT
INLAND ARCHITECT
INSIDE CONTRACTING
INSTALLATION & CLEANING SPECIALIST
INSULATION GUIDE
INSULATION OUTLOOK
INTERIOR DESIGN
INTERIOR TEXTILES
INTERIORS
INTERNATIONAL CONSTRUCTION WEEK
INTERSECTIONS
IOWA ARCHITECT
ISLAMIC ART AND ARCHITECTURE
JOB/SCOPE
JOURNAL OF ARCHITECTURAL AND
    PLANNING RESEARCH
JOURNAL OF ARCHITECTURAL EDUCATION
JOURNAL OF CONSTRUCTION ENGINEERING
    AND MANAGEMENT
JOURNAL OF DESIGN AND CONSTRUCTION
JOURNAL OF ENVIRONMENTAL EDUCATION
JOURNAL OF HOUSING
JOURNAL OF HOUSING FOR THE ELDERLY
JOURNAL OF PROPERTY MANAGEMENT
JOURNAL OF PROTECTIVE COATINGS AND
    LININGS
JOURNAL OF STRUCTURAL ENGINEERING
JOURNAL OF STRUCTURAL MECHANICS
JOURNAL OF TECHNICAL TOPICS IN CIVIL
    ENGINEERING
JOURNAL OF THE AMERICAN PLANNING
    ASSOCIATION
JOURNAL OF THE INTERNATIONAL UNION
    OF BRICKLAYER AND ALLIED
    CRAFTSMEN

JOURNAL OF URBAN HISTORY
KSA REVIEW
KITCHEN AND BATH BUSINESS
KITCHEN & BATH CONCEPTS
L.A. ARCHITECT
LAND USE DIGEST
LAND: LANDSCAPE ARCHITECTURAL NEWS
    DIGEST
LAND USE LAW AND ZONING DIGEST
LANDMARKS OBSERVER
LANDSCAPE
LANDSCAPE & TURF INDUSTRY
LANDSCAPE ARCHITECTURE
LANDSCAPE CONTRACTOR
LANDSCAPE JOURNAL
LATENT IMAGES
LEGAL BRIEFS
LIBRARY JOURNAL
LIGHTING DESIGN + APPLICATION
LIGHTING SUPPLY & DESIGN
LIVABILITY
LIVABILITY DIGEST
LIVABLE CITY
LOCKSMITH LEDGER
LODGING HOSPITALITY
LOG HOME & ALTERNATIVE HOUSING
    BUILDER
MCA NEWSLETTER
MH/RV BUILDERS NEWS
M S A MONTHLY BULLETIN
MANAGEMENT TECHNOLOGY
MANUFACTURED HOUSING NEWSLETTER
MANUFACTURED HOUSING REPORTER
MARKETPLACE
MARQUEE
MASONRY
MASS
MASS TRANSIT
MATERIAL HANDLING ENGINEERING
METAL BUILDING REVIEW
METALS IN CONSTRUCTION
METROPOLIS
METROPOLITAN HOME
MIDDLE EAST EXECUTIVE REPORTS
MIDWEST CONTRACTOR
MISSISSIPPI ARCHITECT
MISSOURI ARCHITECT
MODERN FLOOR COVERINGS
MODERN HEALTHCARE
MODERN OFFICE TECHNOLOGY
MODERN PAINT & COATINGS
MODERN PLASTICS
MODERN STEEL CONSTRUCTION
MODULUS
MONTANA STATE ARCHITECTURAL REVIEW
MULTI-HOUSING NEWS
MUSEUM
MUSEUM NEWS
NCAIA
NATIONAL ASSOCIATION FOR OLMSTEAD
    PARKS NATIONAL NEWSLETTER
NATIONAL CENTER FOR A BARRIER-FREE
    ENVIRONMENT REPORT

NATIONAL DEVELOPMENT
NATIONAL MALL MONITOR
NATIONAL REAL ESTATE INVESTOR
NATION'S CITIES WEEKLY
NATION'S RESTAURANT NEWS
NEW ENGLAND ARCHITECT AND BUILDER
    ILLUSTRATED
NEW ENGLAND CONSTRUCTION
NEW ENGLAND FURNITURE NEWS
NEW MEXICO ARCHITECTURE
NEW SHELTER
NEW YORK CONSTRUCTION NEWS
NEWS
NEWSJOURNAL (SCA)
NEWSLETTER
NORTH CAROLINA ARCHITECT
NORTH CAROLINA STATE UNIVERSITY: THE
    STUDENT PUBLICATION OF THE SCHOOL
    OF DESIGN
NORTHWEST ARCHITECTURE
NORTHWEST ARCHITECTURE
NOTRE DAME ARCHITECTURE REVIEW
OC/AIA ADVISOR
OCULUS
OFFICE
OFFICE ADMINISTRATION AND
    AUTOMATION
OLD HOUSE JOURNAL
OLD MILL NEWS
OLD-TIME NEW ENGLAND
101 HOME PLANS
1001 HOME IDEAS
ORIENTAL RUG
ORNAMENTAL/MISCELLANEOUS METAL
    FABRICATOR
PCI IDEAS
P.C.I. JOURNAL
PFM (PROFESSIONAL FURNITURE
    MERCHANT)
P S A NEWS
PACIFIC BUILDER AND ENGINEER
PACIFIC MARKETER
PAINTING & WALLPAPER CONTRACTOR
PARK MAINTENANCE
PARKING
PARKING WORLD
PARKS AND RECREATION
PASSIVE SOLAR NEWS
PERSPECTA; YALE ARCHITECTURAL
    JOURNAL
PERSPECTIVE
PIT AND QUARRY
PLACE: THE MAGAZINE OF LIVABILITY
PLACES
PLAN & PRINT
PLANNING
PLANS & SPACES
PLANT ENGINEERING
PLANT SERVICES
PLANTS, SITES AND PARKS
PLASTICS IN BUILDING CONSTRUCTION
PORTFOLIO MAGAZINE
PRAIRIE SCHOOL REVIEW

PRECIS
PRESERVATION ACTION ALERT
PRESERVATION BRIEFS
PRESERVATION LAW REPORTER
PRESERVATION NEWS
PRESERVATION PERSPECTIVE
PRESERVATION PROGRESS
PRINCETON JOURNAL
PROFESSIONAL BUILDER AND APARTMENT
    BUSINESS
PROFESSIONAL MARKETING REPORT
PROFESSIONAL REMODELING
PROFESSIONAL SERVICES MANAGEMENT
    JOURNAL
PROFESSIONAL SERVICES QUARTERLY
THE PROFIT CENTER
PROGRESSIVE ARCHITECTURE
PROGRESSIVE BUILDER
PROJECT ALERT SYSTEM
PROJECT MANAGEMENT QUARTERLY
PROJECT REPORTS
PUBLIC WORKS
QUALIFIED REMODELER
QUAPAW QUARTER CHRONICLE
R.I.A.I.A. NEWSLETTER
R.S.I./ROOFING, SIDING, INSULATION
RE:CAP
REAL ESTATE FORUM
REAL ESTATE NEWSLETTER
REAL ESTATE REVIEW
REAL ESTATE WEEKLY
REALTY
REALTY AND BUILDING
REFLECTIONS
REFRIGERATION SERVICE AND
    CONTRACTING
REMODELING CONTRACTOR
RENOVATIONS
RESOURCE
RESOURCE
RESTAURANT AND HOTEL DESIGN
RESTAURANT HOSPITALITY
RESTAURANTS AND INSTITUTIONS
RETAIL TECHNOLOGY
ROOF DESIGN
ROOFING SPEC
S. KLEIN NEWSLETTER ON COMPUTER
    GRAPHICS
SCAIA NEWSLETTER
SMPS NEWS
SALES PROSPECTOR
SAN FRANCISCO BAY ARCHITECTS REVIEW
SAUDI INTROSPECT
SCHOOL PRODUCT NEWS
SECURITY MANAGEMENT
SEMESTER REVIEW
SEQUENCE
SHOPPING CENTER WORLD
SITE SELECTION HANDBOOK
SITES
SKYLINES
SMALL HOME PLANS

SMALL TOWN
SOCIETY FOR INDUSTRIAL ARCHAEOLOGY
    NEWSLETTER
SOCIETY OF ARCHITECTURAL HISTORIANS.
    JOURNAL
SOCIETY OF ARCHITECTURAL HISTORIANS.
    NEWSLETTER
SOLAR AGE
SOLAR ENGINEERING AND CONTRACTING
SOUND AND VIBRATION
SOUND IDEAS
SOUTHERN ACCENTS
SOUTHERN BUILDING
SOUTHERN LANDSCAPE AND TURF
SPECIFYING ENGINEER
STAINED GLASS
STONE
STONE WORLD
STORE PLANNING SERVICE
STORES
SUN/COAST ARCHITECT BUILDER
SWIMMING POOL AGE & SPA
    MERCHANDISER
TECHNOLOGY AND CONSERVATION
TECHSCAN
TENNESSEE ARCHITECT
TERRAZZO TOPICS
TEXAS ARCHITECT
TEXAS SOCIETY OF ARCHITECTS
    NEWSLETTER
THEATRE DESIGN AND TECHNOLOGY
THRESHOLD
TILE AND DECORATIVE SURFACES
TILE NEWS
TODAY'S OFFICE
TODAY'S S.C.I.P. (SMALL COMPUTERS IN
    PRACTICE)
TRANSPORTATION QUARTERLY
TRIGLYPH
TROWEL
TULANE ARCHITECTURAL VIEW
U.S. GLASS, METAL AND GLAZING
UNDERGROUND SPACE
UNDERLINE
UNIQUE HOMES
UNIVERSITY OF TENNESSEE JOURNAL OF
    ARCHITECTURE
UPDATE
UPHOLSTERING TODAY
URBAN AFFAIRS QUARTERLY
URBAN CONSERVATION REPORT
URBAN DESIGN INTERNATIONAL
URBAN INNNOVATION ABROAD
URBAN LAND
URBANISM PAST AND PRESENT
URBIS
UTAH ARCHITECT
VERNACULAR ARCHITECTURE
    NEWSLETTER
VIA
VICTORIAN
VICTORIAN HOMES

VIRGINIA RECORD
VISUAL MERCHANDISING AND STORE
   DESIGN
WALKER'S ESTIMATING AND
   CONSTRUCTION JOURNAL
THE WALL PAPER
WALLCOVERINGS
WALLS AND CEILINGS
WATERFRONT WORLD
WEEKLY CONSTRUCTION PREVIEW
WESTERN BUILDER
WESTERN HVAC NEWS
WESTERN LANDSCAPING
WINTERTHUR PORTFOLIO
WISCONSIN ARCHITECT
WOMEN IN DESIGN INTERNATIONAL
WOOD & WOOD PRODUCTS
WOOD FINISHING QUARTERLY
WOODWORKER'S JOURNAL

WORKBENCH
WORKSTATION ALERT
WORLD CONSTRUCTION
WORLDWIDE PROJECTS
WRAP UP ON LATIN AMERICAN
   CONSTRUCTION, HOUSING AND REAL
   ESTATE
YOUR CHURCH

Yugoslavia

ARHITEKTURA
COVJEK I PROSTOR
SINTEZA

Zimbabwe

Z.E.D./ZIMBABWE ENVIRONMENT AND
   DESIGN

Subject Index

Numbers in roman refer to primary publications in a given field. Numbers in *italic* refer to publications of secondary importance.

Acoustics, *0999*, *1000*, 1008
Aesthetics. *See* Theory and criticism
Agricultural facilities, *0434*, *0435*
Air conditioning, 0966, *1116*, *1117*, 1142
Airports, *0452*, *0453*, *0454*, *0455*, *0456*
Alabama, *0245*, *0268*, *0276*
Antiques, 0487, *0755*, *0756*, *0757*, *0758*, 0766, 0767, *0770*, *0771*, *0775*, 0777, 0779
Apartments. *See* Residential design
Architectural education, *0216*, *0223*, 0227, 0228
Architectural history. *See* Section 4
Architecture—general. *See* Section 1
Arizona, *0273*, *0295*
Art, 0072, 0103, 0109, 0171, 0543, 0613, 0619, *0754*, *0756*, *0758*, *0759*, *0760*, *0761*, *0762*, *0763*, *0764*, *0765*, *0766*, *0767*, *0768*, *0769*, *0772*, *0773*, *0774*, *0775*, *0776*, *0778*, *0779*, *0780*
Art Deco, *0475*
Auditoriums, 0409

Banks, *0343*, *0344*, 0893, 0948
Barns. *See* Agricultural facilities
Barrier-free design—elderly, 0457, *0458*
Barrier-free design—handicapped, 0457, 0458, *0459*
Bathrooms, *0545*, *0546*, *0547*, 0561, *0582*, *0583*, *0584*, *0591*, *0623*
Beds, 0641, 0693
Brick, *1092*, *1093*, *1098*, *1100*, *1103*
Building. *See* Section 9
Building maintenance, 0356, 0917, 0921, *1118*, *1119*, *1130*, *1139*, 1140, 1142
Building materials, *1024*. *See also specific materials*
Business development. *See* Marketing

California, 0248, *0249*, *0269*
Carpentry, 0657, *0928*, *1014*, *1018*. *See also* Do-it-yourself construction; Woodworking

Carpets, 0559, *0669*, 0670, *0671*, *0672*, *0673*, 0678, 0683, 0686, 0692, *0720*, 0730, 0733. *See also* Floors and floor coverings
Ceilings, 0691, *0905*, *0935*, *1008*
Churches. *See* Religious architecture
Coatings, *1038*, *1084*, *1087*
Codes, 0263, *1106*, *1108*, *1109*, *1110*, *1112*
Colorado, *0264*
Competitions, 0034, *0068*
Computers, *0309*, *0310*, *0311*, *0312*, *0313*, *0314*, *0315*, *0316*, *0317*, *0318*, *0319*, *0320*, *0321*, *0322*, *0323*, *0324*, *0325*, *0326*, 0342
Concrete, 0940, 0953, *1041*, *1042*, *1043*, *1044*, *1045*, *1046*, *1047*, *1048*, *1049*, *1050*, *1051*, *1052*, *1053*, *1054*, *1055*, *1056*, *1057*, *1058*, *1059*, *1060*, *1061*, *1062*, *1063*, *1064*, *1065*, *1066*, *1067*, *1068*, *1069*, *1070*, 1147, 1155, 1158, 1168
Connecticut, 0251, *0272*
Construction. *See* Section 9
Construction management, *0313*, 0327, 0941, 0947
Contracting, *0306*, *0313*, 0941, *0942*, *0943*, *0944*. *See also* Section 9
Copper, *1080*
Correctional facilities, 0417, 0418
Cost estimating, 1007, *1113*, *1114*, *1115*

Detail drawings, *0104*, *0105*, *0106*, *0116*
Displays, 0401, 0408, 0412. *See also* Stores
Do-it-yourself construction, 0369, 0374, 0377, 0378, 0504, *1014*, *1015*, *1016*, *1017*, *1018*, *1019*. *See also* Carpentry
Doing business abroad. *See* Section 14
Doors, 0115, *1023*

Earth shelters, *0377*, *0843*, *0948*, *0982*, *1005*
Elderly housing. *See* Barrier-free design
Electrical systems, 0923, 0949, *1123*
Elevators, *0950*
Energy, 0382, 0794, 0917, 0997, 0998, *1124*, *1125*, *1126*, *1127*, *1128*, 1134, *1136*, *1138*
Engineering. *See* Section 11
Environmental behavior. *See* Psychology